The Journals of George Eliot

The Journals of George Eliot publishes for the first time the entire text of the surviving journals of the great Victorian novelist, and constitutes a new text by her – the closest she came to autobiography. The journals span her life from 1854, when she entered into a common-law union with George Henry Lewes, to her death in 1880, revealing the professional writer George Eliot as well as the remarkable woman Marian Evans. Many aspects of her writing life are illuminated, such as the separation of 'George Eliot' – and the account of her work's public reception – from her 'private' self, at the time she began to write fiction. The journals present a George Eliot of many moods, not only the serious sybilline figure so admired in her later years. The edition's extensive apparatus includes a chronology, introduction, headnotes to each diary, and an annotated index supplying valuable contextual and explanatory information.

MARGARET HARRIS is Professor in English Literature at the University of Sydney. She has edited *The Notebooks of George Meredith* (with Gillian Beer, 1983) and several of Meredith's novels, and has published on various topics in nineteenth- and twentieth-century English and Australian literature.

JUDITH JOHNSTON is Faculty of Arts Teaching and Research Fellow in the Department of English at the University of Western Australia. She is the author of *Anna Jameson: Victorian, Feminist, Woman of Letters* (1997) and of a number of essays and articles on Victorian prose. With Margaret Harris she edited George Eliot's *Middlemarch* for Everyman Paperbacks (1997).

The Journals of George Eliot

Edited by MARGARET HARRIS *and* JUDITH JOHNSTON

CAMBRIDGE
UNIVERSITY PRESS

PUBLISHED BY THE PRESS SYNDICATE OF THE UNIVERSITY OF CAMBRIDGE
The Pitt Building, Trumpington Street, Cambridge, United Kingdom

CAMBRIDGE UNIVERSITY PRESS
The Edinburgh Building, Cambridge CB2 2RU, UK http://www.cup.cam.ac.uk
40 West 20th Street, New York, NY 10011–4211, USA http://www.cup.org
10 Stamford Road, Oakleigh, Melbourne 3166, Australia
Ruiz de Alarcón 13, 28014 Madrid, Spain

First published 1998
Reprinted 1999

Printed in the United Kingdom at the University Press, Cambridge

Typeset in 9pt Lexicon (from *The Enschedé Font Foundry*), in QuarkXPress™ [SE]

A catalogue record for this book is available from the British Library

Library of Congress cataloguing in publication data

Eliot, George, 1819–1880.
The Journals of George Eliot / edited by Margaret Harris and
Judith Johnston.
p. cm.
Includes index.
ISBN 0 521 57412 9 (hardback)
1. Eliot, George, 1819–1880 – Diaries. 2. Women novelists,
English – 19th century – Diaries. I. Harris, Margaret.
II. Johnston, Judith, 1947– . III. Title.
PR4681.A3H37 1998
828′.803–dc21
[B] 98-3679
CIP

ISBN 0 521 57412 9 hardback

Contents

Illustrations

Preface

This edition provides the complete text of George Eliot's surviving journals and diaries, which run from the time of her union with G. H. Lewes in 1854 to her death in 1880. She customarily kept a notebook for daily diary entries, and at times took a different book to record particular journeys, to Germany in 1858 and to Italy in 1864, for example. In addition, she wrote more formal essays, most of them entitled 'Recollections' (usually of travels both within Britain and abroad) in the same journal volumes. The journals were extensively quoted in the three volumes of *George Eliot's Life as related in her letters and journals, arranged and edited by her husband J. W. Cross* (1885), and selections from them included by Gordon S. Haight in his edition of *The George Eliot Letters* (1954–78) and in his biography, *George Eliot* (1968). Certain of the journals, particularly 'Recollections of Ilfracombe' and 'How I came to write Fiction', have been reprinted in collections of George Eliot's nonfiction prose. Only now do the journals appear entire: about one-quarter of the text has not been published previously.

The contents of six manuscript volumes are reproduced here. Five of them are in the Beinecke Rare Book and Manuscript Library, Yale University, while the sixth is in the Henry W. and Albert A. Berg Collection, New York Public Library. This last is George Eliot's 1879 Diary, a brown cloth 'Beeching's Annual Diary for 1879'. She chose its black-bound counterpart as her diary for 1880 (16×9.5 cm., Beinecke George Eliot MS IV 5). The richest of the Beinecke manuscripts is Diary 1854–1861 (21×15 cm., George Eliot MS IV 1), a small exercise book re-covered in oilcloth, now somewhat worn, which (at one end) contains diary entries, and at the other, 'Recollections' of Weimar, Berlin, Ilfracombe, Jersey and the Scilly Isles, and 'How I came to write Fiction' and 'History of *Adam Bede*'. The morocco-bound notebook containing Diary 1861–1877 (15×10 cm., George Eliot MS IV 3) is also worn, as might be expected given the long period over which it was in use. George Eliot thriftily made her travel diaries do double duty: thus the trip to Germany in 1858 appears at one end of MS IV 2 (18×12 cm.) and 'Recollections of Italy. 1860' at the other, while the journeys to Italy in 1864 and to Normandy in 1865 are recorded at opposite ends of MS IV 6 (12×8 cm.).

A typescript transcription with handwritten emendations,

made for Richard Little Purdy, is kept with the manuscript volumes in Beinecke, along with a transcription of the 1879 Diary by R. H. Nims for Gordon S. Haight. Our transcription was made independently of these, though reference has been made to them for purposes of comparison and occasional inspiration.

The preparation of this edition posed several challenges. The first was to confront the question of whether a complete edition of the journals would provide more than a dutiful exercise in scholarship. We were not far into the task of transcription before the question was answered affirmatively, as it became apparent that to read any of the material in the context of companion pieces in George Eliot's diary volumes is very different from reading it in the selections made by Cross and Haight. Here is George Eliot speaking for herself. Our conclusions about the interest and significance of the journals are developed in the Introduction.

The order in which the separate journals were to be presented involved another set of decisions. Initially, we thought of constructing a single chronological sequence, for instance by interpolating 'Recollections of Italy. 1860' with the diary for that year. The realisation of the import of George Eliot's placement of 'How I came to write Fiction', 'History of *Adam Bede*', and the other entries in the section we have called 'The Making of George Eliot' – in brief, that at this stage George Eliot was making an effective separation of her 'public' and 'private' selves in her journal – brought us to the final arrangement, which preserves the integrity of her divisions of her text. The diaries appear in chronological order, followed by a second sequence of the essay-type journals: connections and intertextualities are pointed out in the headnotes.

A major challenge was to determine how traditional an edition this should be. Since the prime justification of this edition is that it makes available more of the writings of George Eliot, we endeavoured to make the journals accessible in every sense by supplying a diplomatic transcription of the manuscripts supported by unobtrusive editorial apparatus.

Our principal concern has been to provide an accurate and readable text with minimal editorial intervention. There are a few words and sentences which have resisted our best efforts to decipher them (notably the first page at each end of Diary 1854–1861, where the oilcloth cover has stuck to the paper in places and obliterated the text): these are noted where they occur.

Some modifications have been made to George Eliot's

manuscript. The ampersand and most other frequently used contractions (e.g. 'wh.', 'art.') have been expanded. In general, obvious errors of spelling (including such matters as errors of case in German) have been silently corrected, though George Eliot's preferred spellings are retained (e.g. she prefers 'staid' to 'stayed', and consistently uses 'surprized' and 'Shakspeare'). Variant forms are generally normalised according to her most frequent usage, but some vagaries are retained (e.g. she alternates between such spellings as 'Charlie' and 'Charley'). Punctuation has been added only where it is necessary to clarify the sense, and removed only where there is evident error, and where she follows the now obsolete practice of inserting a period after numerals in dates, times and the like. Beyond closing inverted commas when George Eliot has omitted to do so, no attempt has been made to regularise the way she indicates titles of books, plays, and so on (which are sometimes italicised, sometimes in inverted commas, sometimes not indicated at all). Similarly her capitalisation and emphases have been retained. Dates have been left in the form in which she wrote them. Occasionally, George Eliot makes a slip in dating her diary entries: correct dates in square brackets follow what she wrote.

The chronology of George Eliot's life provides perspective on the journals. Context and background to each section of the journals are provided in headnotes. Unacknowledged translations in the apparatus in this edition are our own, considerable assistance with German having been provided by Rosemary Ashton. Footnotes have been kept to a minimum, and the weight of annotation carried by the explanatory index which is designed as a glossary as well as a guide to contents. It includes substantive references for example, to people George Eliot met, books she read, and music she heard. George Lewes is omnipresent: the index lists references to his works, but not every mention of him in George Eliot's text. Similarly, after much deliberation, we restricted the index entry for George Eliot to her writings, places of residence, and travels. Principal entries appear under the names of authors or composers, with cross-references from named works. There has been no attempt to index all visual art works by name, though particular artists are indexed (a glance at the Italian journals will indicate the reason for this decision). Not all places mentioned are included, only those where she spent some time or which have particular significance. These entries gloss George Eliot's text: they are not encyclopaedia entries. For the most part, a reader who wants to know who Thomas

Allbutt was, or whether and where George Eliot refers to him, will simply look under 'Allbutt'. Again for the most part, it has been possible to elucidate allusions or quotations in the index: for example, when George Eliot refers to 'Byron's praise' of the Rhine near Coblentz (p. 18), the reader who turns to 'Byron' in the index will find the relevant passage of *Childe Harold's Pilgrimage* identified. But at pp. 42 and 237, the Milton quotations and allusions require a footnote since George Eliot did not name the poet to provide a headword. This procedure has been adopted to ensure the readability of the text, and to facilitate the use of the edition for reference. Inevitably there will be some readers who do not find their questions answered as readily as they might wish: to conscientious editors (who none the less hope to have provided more satisfaction than frustration) this must remain a matter of regret. Haight's edition of *The George Eliot Letters* was indispensible to our project, especially because of the detail in his editorial apparatus which has substantially informed ours.

We are most grateful for the permission to publish manuscript material both of George Eliot and George Henry Lewes granted by Jonathan Ouvry, great-great-grandson of G. H. Lewes, and holder of the George Eliot copyright. In addition, we acknowledge the permission of the Beinecke Rare Book and Manuscript Library, Yale University, and the Henry W. and Albert A. Berg Collection in the Research Libraries of the New York Public Library, to publish manuscript material in their collections. We thank Ralph Franklin, Vincent Giroud, and Marjorie Wynne at Beinecke for their particular courtesies. We have reason to be grateful to helpful staff in other libraries as well, not least the Library of the University of Sydney, the resources of which were equal to all but the most esoteric of George Eliot's demands.

Work on the edition was made possible by the award of an Australian Research Council Large Grant (1991–2) to Margaret Harris and Judith Johnston. Jennifer Moore, as Research Assistant funded by this grant, made an important and inimitable contribution to the edition. Margaret Harris was also awarded the John D. and Rose H. Jackson Fellowship at the Beinecke Library in 1993. The Department of English at the University of Sydney, and also the Department of English at the University of Western Australia, have supported the project in various ways over time: in particular, and in alphabetical order, we thank Amanda Collins, Marion Flynn, Pat Ricketts and Maree Williams in Sydney, and Denise Hill and Sue Lewis in Perth.

Criticism, encouragement, and other forms of assistance have been supplied by Rosemary Ashton, William Baker, Gillian Beer, Virginia Blain, Peter Edwards, Hilary Fraser, Constance Fulmer, Penny Gay, Beryl Gray, Jennifer Gribble, Barbara Hardy, Pamela Law, Judith Maitland, Joanne Shattock, Michael Slater, John Sutherland, Martha Vicinus, Michael Wheeler, and Joseph Wiesenfarth. The professional commitment of Andrew Brown and Josie Dixon at Cambridge University Press has been exemplary. It has been a particular privilege to have the editor of the Clarendon edition of *Romola* associated with our work on the journals: his suggestion that potential difficulties of annotation be addressed by way of an explanatory index proved to be the right one despite the problems of implementation. Colleagues, friends and relatives have borne with us and the project with seeming cheerfulness and evident fortitude. Special thanks to John Burnheim, David Overett, and Marjorie Overett.

We dedicate this edition to our daughters, Catherine Burnheim, Lucy Burnheim, and Mereana Johnston.

Abbreviations

[ ]
Matter supplied by the editors

Bodenheimer
Rosemarie Bodenheimer, *The Real Life of Mary Ann Evans: George Eliot Her Letters and Fiction* (Ithaca and London, Cornell University Press, 1994)

Cross
J. W. Cross, *George Eliot's Life as related in her letters and journals*, 3 vols. (Edinburgh, Blackwood, 1885)

GE
George Eliot

GHL
George Henry Lewes

Haight
Gordon S. Haight, *George Eliot: A Biography* (Oxford University Press, 1968)

Journals of GHL
The Journals of George Henry Lewes, held at the Beinecke Rare Book and Manuscript Library, Yale University

Letters
The George Eliot Letters, ed. Gordon S. Haight, 9 vols (New Haven, Yale University Press, 1954–78)

Letters of GHL
The Letters of George Henry Lewes, ed. William Baker, 2 vols (University of Victoria, English Literary Studies Monograph Series 64, 1995)

Wiesenfarth, Joseph
A Writer's Notebook, 1854–79, and Uncollected Writings (Charlottesville, University Press of Virginia, 1981)

Chronology

1819 *22 November* Born Mary Ann Evans, at South Farm, Arbury, near Nuneaton, Warwickshire, to Christiana, née Pearson, second wife of Robert Evans, estate manager.

1846 Translation of D. F. Strauss, *Das Leben Jesu* (1835–6), as *The Life of Jesus*, published anonymously. Publication of her 'Poetry and Prose from the Notebook of an Eccentric' in the Coventry *Herald*, owned by Charles Bray.

1849 Travels abroad for the first time, following the death of her father, in company with the Brays.

1851 Moves to London: lodges with John Chapman, and works with him on the *Westminster Review*.

1853 Moves from Chapman's home at 142 Strand to 21 Cambridge Street, as relationship with GHL intensifies. Ceases editorship of the *Westminster*, though still contributing to it and other journals.

Translating Ludwig Feuerbach's *Das Wesen des Christentums* (*The Essence of Christianity*).

1854 *July* Feuerbach translation, 'by Marian Evans', published. Leaves London for Germany with GHL.

1855 After seven months in Weimar and Berlin, returns to England, setting up house with GHL. GE publishes articles and reviews in *Westminster Review* and other journals, including a review of GHL's *Life of Goethe* for the *Leader*.

1856 *May–August* Visit to Ilfracombe and Tenby, mainly because of GHL's fascination with marine biology.

September Begins to write 'The Sad Fortunes of the Reverend Amos Barton'.

November Publisher John Blackwood accepts the first of the 'Scenes of Clerical Life' for *Blackwood's Edinburgh Magazine*.

1857 *January* Last contributions to the *Westminster*; first episode of 'Amos Barton' appears anonymously in *Blackwood's*. During the year, 'Mr Gilfil's Love Story' and 'Janet's Repentance' also serialised in *Blackwood's*.

March–July Visit to the Scilly Isles and Jersey, again because of GHL's 'seaside studies'.

Adam Bede begun.

1858 *Scenes of Clerical Life*, by George Eliot published in two volumes by Blackwood.

April–September Travel to Munich and Dresden.

1859 *February Adam Bede* (3 vols.) published. Amidst claims that the novel is the work of one Joseph Liggins, Marian Evans Lewes acknowledges to friends that she is GE.
July 'The Lifted Veil' published in *Blackwood's Edinburgh Magazine.*

1860 *April* Publication of *The Mill on the Floss* (3 vols.).

March–July Visit to Italy, during which GHL suggests Savonarola as the subject for a novel.

GHL's eldest son, Charles, leaves Hofwyl School in Switzerland and comes to live with GE and GHL.

1861 Publication of *Silas Marner* (1 vol.).

Second journey to Italy, mainly to do research for *Romola*, a novel which caused her immense difficulty.

1862 Publisher George Smith offers £7,000 for *Romola*, which begins publication in the *Cornhill* in July.

1863 *Romola* (3 vols., Smith, Elder). GE buys 'The Priory', Regent's Park. GHL's second son, Thornton, goes to seek his fortune in Natal.

1864 *May–June* Visit to Italy, during which GE has the inspiration for *The Spanish Gypsy*.

'Brother Jacob' (written 1860) published in *Cornhill.*

1865 Writes poetry, and articles for *Pall Mall Gazette* and *Fortnightly Review*. Begins *Felix Holt*.

August–September Visit to Normandy and Brittany.

1866 Returns to Blackwood for publication of *Felix Holt* (3 vols.).

Lewes's third son Herbert joins Thornton in Natal.

1867 *December–March* Journey to Spain.

1868 *The Spanish Gypsy* published.

1869 Working on poetry, and the beginning of *Middlemarch*.

Thornton Lewes returns ill from Natal; dies 19 October.

1871 Publication of *Middlemarch* in parts begins.

1872 Part publication of *Middlemarch* continues: four volume edition comes out in December.

1874 Publication of *The Legend of Jubal and Other Poems*.

Working on *Daniel Deronda*.

1875 Herbert Lewes dies in Natal.

1876 *February–September Daniel Deronda* published in monthly parts: four volume edition follows in December.

1878 *30 November* GHL dies.

1879 *Impressions of Theophrastus Such* published.

GE prepares the final volume of GHL's *Problems of Life and Mind* for publication.

1880 *6 May* Marries John Walter Cross.

22 December Dies.

Introduction

George Eliot was equivocal about posterity. On 28 November 1880 – almost the second anniversary of the death of her beloved George Lewes, and the day before she and her husband John Cross were to move from Witley in the Surrey countryside to their new London residence in Cheyne Walk – she wrote to Cara Bray:

> I think you are quite right to look over your old letters and papers and decide for yourself what should be burnt. Burning is the most reverential destination one can give to relics which will not interest any one after we are gone. I hate the thought that what we have looked at with eyes full of living memory should be tossed about and made lumber of, or (if it be writing) read with hard curiosity. I am continually considering whether I have saved as much as possible from this desecrating fate.[1]

She had made such decisions about Lewes's papers after his death. Her diary for 1879 shows her obsessive yet therapeutic reading and re-reading of many of Lewes's manuscripts and published writings as she undertook the commemorative task of completing his *Problems of Life and Mind*, and records that on the first anniversary of his death she prepared his letters to be buried with her. She can hardly have failed to consider ways of disposing of her own manuscripts during the painful process of arranging her personal and business affairs that extended from Lewes's death to hers.

At all events, the manuscript journals that are published here in full for the first time have survived, along with other notebooks and miscellaneous papers, some of them already published.[2] We believe that the journals are a set of texts as

1 *The George Eliot Letters*, ed. Gordon S. Haight (9 vols., New Haven, Yale University Press, 1954–78), vol. 7, pp. 340–1: subsequently cited as *Letters*. Cf. a letter of 1874 which refers to Dickens and to Mill's *Autobiography*: 'Is it not odious that as soon as a man is dead his desk is raked, and every insignificant memorandum which he never meant for the public, is printed for the gossiping amusement of people too idle to read his books?' (vol. 6, p. 23); and another of 1877 where she speaks of 'my repugnance . . . to autobiography, unless it can be so written as to involve neither self-glorification nor impeachment of others' (p. 371).

2 For example, *Quarry for 'Middlemarch'* (Berkeley, University of California Press, 1950), ed. Anna Theresa Kitchel; *Some George Eliot*

complex as any of George Eliot's writings, which – *pace* their author – are indeed to be 'read with hard curiosity'. The curiosity she feared was prying intrusion, perhaps even simple inquisitiveness; but these texts deflect seekers after the scandalous and sensational. The curiosity the journals invite is a subtler inquiry, rewarded both by immediate gratifications, such as the effulgence of George Eliot in love in the Weimar diary, and by cumulative satisfaction gained from the perspectives on her writing life that variously emerge.

Far from being quaint 'curiosities', the journals form a substantial addition to the canon of George Eliot's work. More than a quarter of the text of the journals has never been published before: for instance, none of 'Italy 1864' and only two sentences of 'Normandy and Brittany 1865' have been published (*Letters*, vol. 4, p. 202 n.); while large sections or episodes in other journals are unpublished – such as the wonderful account of a picnic with Keats and wine in 'Recollections of Weimar'. Even familiar pieces like 'Recollections of Ilfracombe', substantially published soon after her death in *George Eliot's Life as related in her letters and journals, arranged and edited by her husband J. W. Cross*,[3] and subsequently reprinted in more or less complete versions, read differently in the context of the other journals.

The extant journals begin as Marian Evans (not yet George Eliot) elopes to Germany with George Henry Lewes in July 1854, and continue almost to her death in December 1880. Pages have been torn from the earliest manuscript volume: internal evidence indicates that the first entries were made in Geneva in the winter of 1849.[4] The journal entries are most copious in the period before George Eliot began to publish fiction in the late 1850s – indeed, in these years, they *were* her writing, distinguished by much lively description and

Notebooks: An Edition of the Carl H. Pforzheimer Library's George Eliot Holograph Notebooks, MSS 707, 708, 709, 710, 711, 4 vols. (Salzburg, Universität Salzburg, 1976–85), ed. William Baker; *George Eliot's 'Middlemarch' Notebooks: A Transcription* (Berkeley, University of California Press, 1979), eds John Clark Pratt and Victor A. Neufeldt; *George Eliot. A Writer's Notebook, 1854–79, and Uncollected Writings* (Charlottesville, University Press of Virginia, 1981), ed. Joseph Wiesenfarth; and *George Eliot's 'Daniel Deronda' Notebooks*, ed. Jane Irwin (Cambridge University Press, 1996).

3 *George Eliot's life as related in her letters and journals, arranged and edited by her husband J. W. Cross*, 3 vols. (Edinburgh, Blackwood, 1885); subsequently cited as Cross.

4 Haight conjectures that Cross removed forty-six leaves (*Letters*, vol. 1, p. xv).

anecdote. They become more laconic particularly after the publication of *Romola* in 1863, though her chronicling of the composition of that novel is extended and excruciating. Not all the gaps are the result of erratic intervals between entries. For example, George Eliot kept a journal of the expedition to Spain early in 1867, which has disappeared,[5] and so has her diary for 1878. (We have used the terms 'diary' and 'journal' loosely and to some extent interchangeably – 'diary' is preferred for daily entries, 'journal' for longer, more formal compositions. In this edition, 'diary' entries are generally printed without justification of the righthand margin, while the 'journal' entries have righthand justification.)[6]

There are six manuscript volumes, containing three groups of material. The first consists of diaries, journals of daily record, in four books, 1854–61, 1861–77, 1879, 1880. The second group is travel diaries, which replace the regular diary on a particular journey, in two volumes. One was used for 'Germany 1858', and at the other end, for 'Recollections of Italy 1860'; with similar economy, the notebook used for 'Italy 1864' did double duty for 'Normandy and Brittany 1865'. The third group consists of more formal retrospective essays – the 'Recollections' of Weimar, Berlin, Ilfracombe, Scilly and Jersey, together with 'How I came to write Fiction' and 'History of *Adam Bede*' – and these were written in from the back of the 1854–61 diary.

There is nothing to suggest that these journals were composed for publication, though George Eliot herself reworked her accounts of Weimar in 1854 for two articles in *Fraser's Magazine*.[7] In effect, they were first edited by John Cross, whose pencilled markings and occasional annotations appear on the

5 Gordon S. Haight, *George Eliot* (Oxford University Press, 1968), p. 402n. reports that GE's Journal of her Spanish travel, 26 January–7 March 1867, was sold at Sotheby's, 27 June 1923, at the same time as her Notebook for *The Spanish Gypsy*, which 'was broken up and bound with some MS letters into volumes of *The Works of George Eliot*, large paper ed., 25 vols (Boston and N.Y., Houghton Mifflin, 1924), to form a limited ed.' While sections of the notebook and related memoranda have been traced, the journal has not turned up.

6 Judy Simons, *Diaries and Journals of Literary Women from Fanny Burney to Virginia Woolf* (London, Macmillan, 1990), recognises the issue: 'Although strictly speaking "diary" can be used as a generic term to cover both a daily record of engagements and more intimate writing, while "journal" tends to refer more specifically to a personal chronicle, writers themselves do not always keep to such nice distinctions.' (p. 7) Simons's discussion, particularly her opening chapter, 'Secret Exhibitionists: Women and their Diaries', provides a helpful context for reading George Eliot's journals.

7 See headnote to 'Recollections of Weimar'.

manuscripts, made during his extensive use of them, along with her letters and other notebooks, for *George Eliot's Life.* Much later, George Eliot's American champion, Gordon S. Haight, drew on the journals not only in his monumental edition of *The George Eliot Letters* but also for the biography, *George Eliot* (1968).[8] Each of these devotees had his own agenda which determined his use of the journal material, though both print some journals virtually complete. In this edition, the headnotes to each journal include a brief description of the use Cross and Haight have made of it.

The journals have evident biographical significance. They display George Eliot's extremes of emotion, from her happiness with Lewes in Weimar in 1854 (Diary 1854–1861) to her grief at his death (Diary 1879). They tell us how George Eliot and Lewes spent their time – reading, writing, walking, travelling; entertaining and going to theatre, opera and concerts. They show constant concern about the health of one partner or the other, and almost as constant attention to family commitments. They graph George Eliot's extension of her knowledge of natural and physical science, history and languages, and the development of her taste in art and music.

The journals challenge received biographical readings of George Eliot, for instance in their demonstration of her competence in practical matters of finance and business after Lewes's death. She adhered to certain conventions about what she recorded, without being as systematic in her journalising as Lewes ('journalising' is his word). Lewes's diaries (the first extant is numbered 'X', and begins mid-1856) frequently complement hers in giving details about particular social engagements or domestic arrangements. On the evidence of the journals, it might seem that George Eliot is not interested in current affairs: they contain only a couple of references to the Crimean War, the Indian Mutiny is mentioned by implication, there are merely hints of the volatile political situation in Italy in 1860, and no attention to the American Civil War – though on 31 December 1870, she comments on the Siege of Paris 'where our fellow-men are suffering and inflicting horrors', and in the late 1870s refers to the Eastern Question. But it would be erroneous to assume that she turned aside from such issues and events. She more frequently displays concern about

8 A complete listing of published journal material would include *Essays of George Eliot*, ed. Thomas Pinney (London, Routledge, 1963); *Selected Essays, Poems and Other Writings*, eds. A. S. Byatt and Nicholas Warren (Harmondsworth, Penguin, 1990); and *Selected Critical Writings*, ed. Rosemary Ashton (Oxford University Press, 1992).

national and international events in letters than in her journals, and that concern finds complex expression in her fiction especially from *Felix Holt* on. Moreover, as the journals show, the Leweses did not always have a daily newspaper, at least in their early years together, but they certainly kept up with the weeklies and quarterlies that were major organs of opinion (often of course Lewes was writing for them). Not surprisingly, George Eliot's vision is Eurocentric. North America does not figure prominently, and colonies such as South Africa and Australia are places to send difficult progeny (Lewes's sons) or in which to invest for profit.

Just as her awareness of events in the public domain is rarely documented in the journals, neither is her personal life fully recounted. The abrupt entry for 9 April 1880, 'Sir James Paget came to see me. My marriage decided', is the most notorious example of her withholding major personal events from even this private record. There are notable reticences in the journals – about such mundane matters as food and dress, on the whole, and more generally about relationships and emotional reactions.

The principal interest of the journals must be their relation to George Eliot's writing life. The early material can be read as prelude to the fiction, and there is some symmetry between the dwindling bulk of the journals and the growing production of stories and novels. Throughout, the journals provide evidence of her ways of working. There are parallel texts within the journals, which among other things cast light on her processes of composition: for instance the diary for Weimar in 1854 parallels 'Recollections of Weimar', and later versions appeared in the *Fraser's* articles already mentioned. There is an extraordinary parallel, discussed later, between the diary from December 1857 to June 1859, and the journal we have called 'The Making of George Eliot'. Another kind of parallel is provided by letters, both of George Eliot and George Lewes. At times our commentary draws attention to a relevant letter, but generally we assume that an interested reader will turn up Haight's edition to find how letters amplify or qualify the narrative of the journals.

The commentary points out particular connections between the journals and other of George Eliot's writings – not only the novels and letters, but also other notebooks. Some of these are dedicated to preparation of particular works, while the one edited by Joseph Wiesenfarth as *George Eliot: A Writer's Notebook, 1854–1879*, was kept concurrently with the journals. It is conspicuous that the journals provide few literal 'keys' to the novels. Locations, yes – Prague for *The Lifted Veil*, Florence for *Romola*, Rome for *Middlemarch*, the Jewish quarter in Frankfurt for *Daniel Deronda*, and so on. Occasionally, personages who later appear as characters in the novels pass through the journals: the young musician Rubinstein, encountered in Weimar in 1854, matures into Klesmer in *Daniel Deronda*; the painter, Overbeck, visited in Rome in 1860, is transposed into Naumann in *Middlemarch.* It may even be that a trace of 'the social life at Scilly' in 1857, where George Eliot 'was repeatedly told, in order to make me aware who Mr. Hall was, that he married a Miss Lemon' ('Recollections of the Scilly Isles'), persisted into *Middlemarch: A Study of Provincial Life*, where Rosamond Vincy is irremediably characterised as 'the flower of Mrs Lemon's school' (chapter 11). It is not as a source book for the fiction but as a site for observation of the processes of authorship that the journals have most to offer.

There was a time when George Eliot contemplated an autobiography: Lewes noted in his diary for 22 November 1870 (her fifty-first birthday) 'Ordered greatcoat, cigars, & bought Polly a Lockup book for her Autobiog.'[9] There is now no trace of such a volume, nor of such a work, unless it is *Impressions of Theophrastus Such* of which the opening chapter, 'Looking Inward', explicitly addresses the challenge of autobiography: 'It is my habit to give an account to myself of the characters I meet with: can I give any true account of my own?'[10] She saw possible value in an autobiography of a writer, but held express reservations about biography:

> The best history of a writer is contained in his writings– these are his chief actions. If he happens to have left an autobiography telling (what nobody else can tell) how his mind grew, how it was determined by the joys, sorrows and other influences of childhood and youth–that is a precious contribution to knowledge. But Biographies generally are a disease of English literature. (*Letters*, vol. 7, p. 230)

It is noteworthy that these remarks relate to a question about whether there is to be a biography of Lewes (himself the author of *The Life and Works of Goethe*), and George Eliot's concern that his work be properly valued.[11]

9 G. H. Lewes Diary 1870, Beinecke Rare Book and Manuscript Library, Yale University.

10 George Eliot, *Impressions of Theophrastus Such* (1879; Edinburgh, Blackwood, 1884), p. 3.

11 The record of reading throughout the journals shows that the metaphorical biography 'disease' was one to which the Leweses,

Cross, of course, claimed to be producing an autobiography:

> With the materials in my hands I have endeavoured to form an *autobiography* (if the term may be permitted) of George Eliot. The life has been allowed to write itself in extracts from her letters and journals. Free from the obtrusion of any mind but her own, this method serves, I think, better than any other open to me, to show the development of her intellect and character. (Cross, vol. 1, p. v)

His claim that 'The life has been allowed to write itself' is severely qualified in his comments on his treatment of the letters: 'Each letter has been pruned of everything that seemed to me irrelevant to my purpose – of everything that I thought my wife would have wished to be omitted.' (Cross, i. vii) The widower took upon himself the charge of ministering to the image of a George Eliot who led almost exclusively a life of the mind. The project presented some difficulties, and her relationship with Lewes was a particular embarrassment. Though the younger man had been on good terms with Lewes in his lifetime, he appears almost obsessive in eliminating references to Lewes from *George Eliot's Life.* A small but telling example is the diary entry for 23 April 1855, 'Fixed on our lodgings at East Sheen', which Cross emends to read 'Fixed on lodgings at East Sheen' (i. 381). Haight diplomatically accounts for Cross's procedures: 'Having known her only in the last decade of her life, in her "sibylline years," he naturally chose the more sententious passages and excluded the spontaneous, trivial, and humorous remarks', in the process frequently conflating letter with letter and letter with journal (*Letters*, vol. 1, p. xiii).

Haight has amply shown just how far short of acceptable twentieth-century standards of scholarship Cross's methods fell. Haight's own scholarship is exceptional, and his edition of the *Letters* an unsurpassable resource for all students of George Eliot – a resource to which our work is greatly indebted. In the *Letters*, he includes certain of the journals complete ('Recollections' of Ilfracombe, Scilly and Jersey,

Footnote 11 (*cont.*)
notoriously prone to physical ailments, frequently exposed themselves. One of the first books mentioned in the diary is Moore's *Life of Sheridan*, 'a firstrate specimen of bad biographical writing', and subsequently there are noted numerous biographies, particularly of literary figures. Significantly, George Eliot read Elizabeth Gaskell's *Life of Charlotte Brontë* almost immediately it came out in 1857, and turned to it in January 1858 to compare the reception of *Scenes of Clerical Life* with that of *Jane Eyre*.

'How I came to write Fiction', 'History of *Adam Bede*'). He includes quotations from the diaries in places, often a sentence or so in a footnote to confirm or elucidate a reference in a letter. But he too was in thrall to an image of George Eliot, derived from Charles Bray's observation that 'She was not fitted to stand alone.'[12] That reductive image governs his reading of George Eliot, the person, and her texts. His biography, while factually authoritative, is not as durable as the *Letters*. Precedence must now be given to two complementary studies. Rosemarie Bodenheimer's *The Real Life of Mary Ann Evans: George Eliot Her Letters and Fiction* (1994), by reading the letters alongside and against the fiction, explores the ways George Eliot wrote her self and life. Though not a conventional biography, this study addresses with subtlety and conviction major crises in George Eliot's life, including her conflicts with her father, her adoption of a pseudonym, and the decision to marry Cross. Rosemary Ashton's more orthodox *George Eliot: A Life* provides formidable literary and intellectual context, delineating an ambitious, anxious subject to whom even so is attributed a robust commonsense connected with her provincial background, and whose avatar in her fiction, rather than any of the Dorotheas, may be the scholar Casaubon: 'Here is strong egoism, a "fastidious yet hungry ambition", pride and self-doubt, and the terrible experience of "laborious uncreative hours" spent in paralysing fear of a "chilling ideal audience"'.[13] Certainly some of these characteristics emerge in George Eliot's journals, of which she, her own most critical and unsparing reader, was the principal audience.

The journals give considerable evidence of George Eliot as reader of and commentator on her own text. On 31 December 1857 appears the first of what becomes a fairly regular passage of the past year in review, summarising its events, and typically testifying to the empowering strength of her bond to Lewes. This entry comes significantly as she awaits the book publication of *Scenes of Clerical Life*, and while it is largely 'personal', describing her role as woman rather than as writer, her work has an important place in it. Later there is evidence of her

12 Bray, *Autobiography*, p. 75, quoted in Haight, *George Eliot*, p. 51.

13 Rosemary Ashton, *George Eliot: A Life* (London: Hamish Hamilton, 1996), p. 325: the internal quotations are from *Middlemarch*, book 1, chapter 10. F. W. H. Myers records that George Eliot herself acknowledged an affinity with Casaubon. She was asked '"But from whom . . . did you draw Casaubon?" With a humorous solemnity, which was quite in earnest, nevertheless, she pointed to her own heart.': 'George Eliot', *Century Magazine*, 23 (November 1881), p. 60.

using the journals not only for stocktaking, but for comfort and reassurance. During the awful time when she was struggling with *Romola*, she wrote, 'This evening I have been reading to G. some entries in my note-book of past times in which I recorded my *malaise* and despair.' (31 January 1862). Late in 1870, 'suffering from headache and depression . . . I look into this little book now to assure myself that this is not unprecedented'; and again on Christmas Day 1875, she uses her diary record for assurance.[14] These occasions support Rosemarie Bodenheimer's comment that 'her mind reorganized autobiographical material in conceptual ways'.[15] At times there is a willed quality in her working through emotional and intellectual challenges, as if she is testing the belief in which Tennyson supports Goethe:

> That men may rise on stepping-stones
> Of their dead selves to higher things.[16]

Her self-appraisal is sometimes quite formal. When each of the two diary volumes that has been kept over a number of years is full, George Eliot offers both retrospect and prospect. On 19 June 1861, she aspires to 'produce *better* work than I have yet done', as she declares 'This is the last entry I mean to make in my old book in which I wrote for the first time at Geneva, in 1849.' On 31 December 1877, in a different vein of resolution: 'Today I say a final farewell to this little book which is the only record I have made of my personal life for sixteen years and more . . . I am going to keep a more business-like diary. Here ends 1877.'

This body of material, made up of discrete and various pieces of writing, constitutes a discontinuous text. We suggest that George Eliot's division and placement of material is at times purposeful, while at other times it is marked by the seeming haphazardness common in such informal writing. For all their reticence, these journals are the least formal and guarded of her writing that survives. While they do not encourage the construction in retrospect of a unified identity out of fragmented experiences, there is none the less a case for reading them as an autobiography of George Eliot. The name

14 Judy Simons, *Diaries and Journals*, p. 10, gives examples of other writers, notably Virginia Woolf, similarly engaging with their textual selves in their diaries.

15 Rosemarie Bodenheimer, *The Real Life of Mary Ann Evans: George Eliot Her Letters and Fiction* (Ithaca and London, Cornell University Press, 1994), p. xv.

16 Alfred, Lord Tennyson, *In Memoriam*, 1.3–4 in *The Poems of Tennyson*, ed. Christopher Ricks (London, Longman, 1969 p. 864.)

'George Eliot', chosen when she began to publish fiction, was only one of the names taken by the woman born Mary Ann Evans, though it is the one about which the journals have most to tell, for the journals, which render abruptly or incidentally some of George Eliot's major life passages, patently document the launching of her authorial identity.

In Diary 1854–1861, at the end that begins on 20 July 1854, there are entries running from 6 December 1857 to 9 May 1859. At the other end, already used for various 'Recollections', appears 'How I came to write Fiction', dated 6 December 1857, then a succession of entries all to do with *Scenes of Clerical Life*, 'History of Adam Bede' and further dated entries to do with the fortunes of that novel. In June 1859 she inadvertently writes her regular diary entry at this end, and continues so to 19 June 1861 when she signs off from this book, now full. By June 1859, *Adam Bede* had been published, and she was beginning to acknowledge to her friends that Marian Evans Lewes was George Eliot. In the time during which she is establishing her authorial signature with the publication of her fiction in book form, there is in her concurrent use of the two ends of the volume a definite separation of the construction 'George Eliot' and the account of the public reception of George Eliot's work, from the 'private' narration of the journals. This phenomenon is discussed more fully in the headnote to 'The Making of George Eliot', and is the most striking instance of her authorial self-consciousness at work in the journals.

The publication of the journals entire restores George Eliot as the speaking subject. They are as much acts of self-representation in writing as her letters and fiction. We can consider *her* self-construction in them, rather than the contribution of a partial version of the journals to someone else's construction of her. The enactment of her claiming authority is the most striking single illumination provided by these journals. Elsewhere, though, George Eliot's dialogical processes of self-writing are to be discerned in moods as different as the exhilaration of seaside recreation at Ilfracombe in the 1850s, the dreary detail of research for *Romola* in the 1860s, and the contentment and occasional cantankerousness in the early 1870s. There were times in our work on this edition when we echoed her exclamation on receiving applications for the George Henry Lewes Studentship, 'wonderful out of all whooping!' (5 October 1879). This author, in whichever of her guises, has endless capacity to surprise and move her readers.

The Journals of George Eliot

I. *Diary 1854–1861*

Signing off from this volume in 1861, GE described it as 'my old book in which I wrote for the first time at Geneva, in 1849.' Although pages covering the period from 1849 to July 1854, when the extant text begins, have been lost, the volume remains the earliest and most extensive of George Eliot's journals. She never again writes with such amplitude and animation in her journals as during the years recorded here.

Because of its length, this diary has been presented in three sections: the first covers GE and GHL's journey to and stay in Weimar, 20 July – 3 November 1854; the second, 4 November 1854 – 13 March 1855, deals principally with their time in Berlin; and the third runs from their return to England from Germany, 13 March 1855, to 19 June 1861. GE rewrote the first of these sections as 'Recollections of Weimar' and the second as 'Recollections of Berlin'; while sequences in the third section correspond to the 'Recollections' of Ilfracombe, the Scilly Isles, and Jersey, and to the essays on authorship, 'How I came to write Fiction' and 'History of Adam Bede'. In addition, the journals 'Germany. 1858' and 'Recollections of Italy. 1860' were interpolated in the chronological span of this diary, when GE used a separate notebook to record a particular expedition.

1. Weimar, 20 July–3 November 1854

The diary begins with an elopement. On 20 July 1854, Marian Evans, journalist and translator, left her London lodgings to embark on the 'Ravensbourne' to cross the Channel to Antwerp en route to Germany. She was embarking also on a union with George Lewes, journalist and man of letters, husband and father, that endured to his death in 1878. The opening, then, is literally an account of what her widower, John Walter Cross, declared to be 'the most important event in George Eliot's life – her union with Mr George Henry Lewes'[1], although Cross excluded from his pious biography her amusingly self-deprecatory description of the rendezvous. This section – from the description of the Scheldt in the first

1 *George Eliot's Life as related in her letters and journals, arranged and edited by her husband J. W. Cross*, 3 vols. (Edinburgh, Blackwood, 1885), vol. 1, pp. 325–6.

paragraph to the idyllic rambles and picnics in Weimar – is the diary of a honeymoon, and the joyousness of GE's account of the months they spent in Germany in 1854–5 recurs only occasionally later in her journals.

The marriage of George Lewes and Agnes Jervis, contracted in 1841, had been fruitful and harmonious for some years. Agnes entertained, undertook some literary tasks on her own account, and bore five children, two of whom died in infancy. In the early 1850s, Agnes took up with their friend and Lewes's partner in publishing ventures, Thornton Hunt, and though the Leweses continued to live together until 1852, Agnes had a son and three daughters to Hunt between 1850 and 1857. Because Lewes allowed these children to be registered as his, he was held to have condoned his wife's adultery, and divorce was impossible. After the breakdown of the marriage, GHL continued to take financial and eventually custodial responsibility for the three surviving sons, whose presence and prospects figure increasingly in GE's journal from the late 1850s.

GE and GHL had become acquainted in the radical intellectual circles in which they both moved in London in the early 1850s. Just when acquaintance became intimacy is not clear – perhaps as early as the winter of 1852–3. Certainly by October 1853 when GE moved into the lodgings in Cambridge Street to which she 'said a last farewell' in the first surviving sentence of her journal, their relationship had progressed to the point where GE was helping GHL with proofs, and when he fell ill in April 1854, she took over his *Leader* reviewing. This interaction in their working lives was to be an important feature of their relationship, chronicled in the journals. At this stage GE's work took second place to GHL's, but with the success of *Adam Bede* and then *The Mill on the Floss*, the balance in the partnership shifted and there developed an explicit recognition that the demands of GE's career had priority. Lewes's role as manager and minder is even more fully documented in letters than in the journals, as the involvement of each in the work the other had in train continued to the last.

The relationship was one of sustaining devotion and great happiness (as GE frequently reiterated in her journals), though especially in the early years her consciousness of its unhallowed status made her anxious to avoid scandal. She never disavowed the relationship, but held back from announcing it even to close friends, and took pains to avoid offence, for instance by refusing invitations, and not extending them either, especially to women. From Weimar, she forthrightly asserted 'I have done nothing with which any person has a right to interfere . . . But I do not wish to take the ground of ignoring what is unconventional in my position.'[2] Concern about reactions to their union is muffled in the diary, but in these early weeks can be tracked in GE's references to letters received and written (particularly where letters survive, such as those to John Chapman of 15 October, and to Charles Bray, 16 October).[3] Her first correspondents included women: her widowed sister Chrissey Clarke, who was not aware of GE's relationship with GHL, and the energetic young reformer Bessie Parkes, who was and wrote despite her parents' remonstrances.[4] On 11 October 1854, GE noted 'A painful letter from London caused us both a bad night'. This letter was from Thomas Carlyle, whose good opinion and influence were of particular importance to Lewes's work on Goethe which occasioned the visit to Weimar. A flurry of correspondence ensued, culminating in a fervid letter from GHL to Carlyle on 19 October, thanking him for accepting GHL's account of his liaison with GE as one which succeeded the breakdown of his marriage rather than being the cause of it.[5]

GE's diary exposes the marked difference in social mores between the Continent, where she went quite freely into society, and England, where she could not. Her meeting in Weimar with the Princess Wittgenstein, openly living out of wedlock with Liszt, was timely. A letter to her Coventry friend and mentor Charles Bray describes their journey and experiences since arriving in Weimar in terms similar to those in the diary, with a particular inflection in the remark 'Above all Liszt is here. He

2 *The George Eliot Letters*, ed. Gordon S. Haight, 9 vols. (New Haven, CT, Yale University Press, 1954–78), vol. 8, p. 124. The most subtle – and persuasive – account of GE's choice of GHL and her methods of justifying it is that of Rosemarie Bodenheimer, *The Real Life of Mary Ann Evans: George Eliot Her Letters and Fiction* (Ithaca and London, Cornell University Press, 1994), chapter 4, 'The Labor of Choice'.

3 *Letters*, vol. 8, pp. 123–5, and vol. 2, pp. 178–9 (the date given is that established by Gordon S. Haight in *George Eliot* (Oxford University Press, 1968), p. 164n.).

4 Rosemary Ashton, *G. H. Lewes: A Life* (Oxford, Clarendon Press, 1991), pp. 158–9. See also Ashton's discussion in *George Eliot: A Life* (London, Hamish Hamilton, 1996), chapter 5, 'Life with Lewes: Weimar and Berlin 1854–5'.

5 *Letters*, vol. 2, pp. 176–8. Carlyle endorsed this letter in terms which indicate residual reservations (177n.). The intensity of gossip about the relationship may be gauged from letters between the Brays and the Combes (vol. 8, pp. 119–31, *passim*). GE's fullest documented self-justification was to Cara Bray, later (4 September 1855, vol. 2, pp. 213–5), a letter of which much is made by Cross, vol. 1, pp. 325–6, and much more by Bodenheimer, *Real Life*, pp. 96–9.

lives with a Russian Princess, who is in fact his wife, and he is a Grand Seigneur in this place' (*Letters*, vol. 2, p. 171).

Bray was one of the very few people GE told of her intention to go off to Germany together with Lewes: indeed, he undertook practical arrangements about payment of her allowance. The Coventry manufacturer, his wife Cara, and her sister Sara Hennell, provided GE with intellectual and emotional sympathy from the beginning of their acquaintance in 1841, when she moved into Coventry with her father. Despite GE's failure in frankness with the women about her relationship with GHL, these friendships continued to be close. Attempts to orchestrate a gradual revelation of the liaison were not very successful. In some cases reactions were hostile, or the process of acceptance was painful. If GE and GHL had decided how to comport themselves when they met acquaintances, they probably did not expect to be put to that test at the very beginning of their new shared life. But on the cross-Channel steamer, they ran into Robert Noel who had introduced the work of the German philosopher Feuerbach to the Bray-Hennell circle, and more recently quibbled about details of GE's translation of *Das Wesen des Christenthums*: criticism which GE had shrugged off, since 'Mr Noel is not a reading man and, I know, has no clear idea of the contents of Feuerbach's works' (*Letters*, vol. 2, pp. 144, 164). However, in telling Bray of this encounter, GE declared 'Mr. R. Noel was a very pleasant companion in the steamboat to Antwerp' (p. 171).

Curiously, another chance meeting was with Dr R. H. Brabant, who had been responsible for GE's undertaking the first of her two major translations from the German. He had also been responsible for involving her in sexual impropriety. GE had met Brabant, a medical man practising in Devizes, through the Brays: his daughter Rufa married Charles Hennell, Cara Bray's brother, in 1843. During GE's visit to the Brabants after the wedding, a relationship developed between the 62 year-old physician and the guest, barely 24, which led the blind Mrs Brabant to terminate the visit. What combination of flattery and fascination was at work in GE can only be conjectured. Brabant is a well-supported contender for the position of prototype of the dessicated scholar Edward Casaubon in *Middlemarch*: though unlike Casaubon he had good German and was well informed about the Higher Criticism. In his zeal to inform others, he persuaded Rufa to undertake the translation of D. F. Strauss's momentous work of critical theology, *Das Leben Jesu*, published in German in 1835–6. When Rufa had to give up in 1844, GE took over the translation, which was published as *The Life of Jesus* by Chapman Brothers on 15 June 1846. GE, none of whose names appears on the titlepage, was paid £20.

Brabant arranged a meeting with Strauss in Cologne, which GE described as 'rather melancholy. Strauss looks so strange and cast-down, and my deficient German prevented us from learning more of each other than our exterior which in the case of both would have been better left to imagination' (*Letters*, vol. 2, p. 171). They met again in Munich in 1858, when GE 'was very agreeably impressed by him' compared to 'when I saw him in that dumb way at Cologne' (p. 472). Though uncomfortable in itself, the meeting with Strauss secured additional introductions to people in Weimar, and just as the encounter with Brabant picks up a thread of perceived sexual scandal in the histories of both GE and GHL, so the meeting with Strauss reinforces the importance of their respective roles in making German literature and thought accessible in Britain.

GE's study of German began in 1840: she read Heine and Schiller particularly. The Strauss translation had been followed by a second translation from the German. Ludwig Feuerbach's *Das Wesen des Christenthums*, like Strauss's a work of radical theology, was published as *The Essence of Christianity* by Chapman in early July 1854, on the eve of GE's departure for Germany. The title-page declared this translation to have been done 'By Marian Evans, Translator of "Strauss's Life of Jesus"': the only occasion on which her given name appeared on a titlepage. Strangely, 'Marian Evans' was announced as the translator of one work, and acknowledged as the translator of another, at the point at which she was about to relinquish that name in favour of 'Marian Lewes'. None of her published work carries the name Lewes, though she insisted on being addressed by it. After their arrival in Weimar, GE continued to work at translation, often for GHL's Goethe biography, as well as at periodical essays and reviews.

This was GE's second journey out of the British Isles: after her father's death in May 1849, she had been taken off to the Continent by Charles and Cara Bray. They went first to Paris, then to the south of France and northern Italy, and so to Geneva, where GE decided to spend the winter. She was escorted back to England by her Swiss host, D'Albert Durade, in March 1850; and based herself with the Brays at their home Rosehill in Coventry until early 1851, when she moved to London. This move was decisive in the process of developing the provincial bluestocking into a powerful intellectual presence in the metropolis, and subsequently into a major English novelist. Before long GE was involved in a passionate relationship with John Chapman, the nominal editor of the *Westminster Review*, of which she was effectively editor from mid-1851 to 1854. Such an initiation into the London literary world made her a thoroughly professional woman of letters, though her major articles for the *Westminster Review* were written after her editorship.

GHL was more widely travelled, especially in Germany and France. His childhood had been spent partly in France and Jersey; he had divided most of the year 1838–9 between Berlin and Vienna; and during the 1840s he had made lengthy visits both to Paris and Berlin. Lewes's interest in German literature, stimulated by Thomas Carlyle's enthusiastic advocacy, had been manifested in articles on German and French literature and thought in various journals, together with his *Biographical History of Philosophy* (1845–6), particularly designed to win approval for the philosophies of Auguste Comte, but treating also Hegel, Kant, Lessing, Herder, Schelling, and Goethe among others.

GHL's versatility was already a legend by 1854. His achievements were extraordinary, even within the sphere of journalism. Carlyle called him 'the Prince of Journalists',[6] an epithet earned not only by the volume and range of his periodical contributions, but by his work as editor and advisor (some of which can be followed in later phases of GE's journals). In 1850 he had founded a weekly newspaper, the *Leader*, jointly with Thornton Hunt, which raised a strong radical voice on such issues as parliamentary reform and international republicanism. GHL despatched a number of pieces to the *Leader* from Germany though his involvement with the paper was to lessen from this time on.

His career had not been confined to journalism: he had published books of biography and dramatic criticism, novels, and plays. He was now returning to a study mooted as early as 1846, published as *Life and Works of Goethe* in 1855, dedicated to Carlyle, and the work for which he is best known. But his other interests, particularly in the theatre, were kept alive: GE refers in this section of the journal to his adaptation of a French farce. In the late 1840s Lewes had entertained thoughts of going on the stage professionally, after performing with Dickens's amateur company and also with a professional company in which he had played Shylock – experiences to be borne in

6 Quoted by Ashton, *G. H. Lewes*, p. 4.

mind when GE records his Shakespearean readings in her journal.

The journey of GE and GHL to Weimar was dictated by the needs of GHL's work, as other of their expeditions both in Britain and abroad were to be. His health was another consideration. Although GE's journals chronicle many of their travels, they are not in the full sense travel writing, designed to bring home the exotic and unfamiliar to an English audience. Her observations do not build up to a comprehensive survey or analysis of the foreign scene, although this section of the diary, and its companion piece 'Recollections of Weimar', intermittently depict it in pen and at times also pencil sketches (here, of items of women's dress) to an implied English reader. Now and then traces of prejudice are discernible, for GE apparently expected dirt, smells, and boorish behaviour to be prevalent on the Continent. But she is far from the traveller admonished by successive editions of Murray's *Handbook* to 'divest himself, as soon as possible, of his prejudices, and especially of the idea of the amazing superiority of England above all other countries, in all respects.'[7]

Their route to Weimar was fairly direct though they proceeded in a leisurely fashion, taking nearly two weeks to reach their destination. GE's description of dawn on the Scheldt may not have the finesse of later nature descriptions in the journals and in the novels, but it is imbued with the euphoria of the dawning of their life together. When they reached Antwerp, their schedule approximated the conventional tourist itinerary enunciated by Thackeray's Lady Kicklebury: 'We propose to rest here; to do the Rubens's; and to proceed to Cologne tomorrow.'[8] The pattern of inspecting the main features of the town, with an emphasis on studying works of art, becomes very familiar through the journals. GE's knowledge of painting and sculpture at this time was limited, and her ability to offer comment on works of art fairly rudimentary. She read the Rubens paintings she saw in Antwerp in terms of the situations and characters depicted, rather than in terms of composition, colour and so on (the difference from the

7 *A Handbook for Travellers on the Continent: being a Guide to Holland, Belgium, Prussia, Northern Germany, and the Rhine from Holland to Switzerland* (10th edn., London, John Murray, 1854), pp. xv-xvi.

8 William Thackery, *The Kickleburys on the Rhine* (2nd edn., London, Smith Elder, 1866), p. 25. The most comprehensive discussion of GE's taste and education in the visual arts is Hugh Witemeyer, *George Eliot and the Visual Arts* (New Haven and London, Yale University Press, 1979).

professional and technical observations of Sir Joshua Reynolds, quoted in Murray's *Handbook*, is marked). The extension of her knowledge of the visual arts, and her increasing sophistication in discussion of them, can be followed through the span of the journals.

On they went to Brussels. Though she had announced to Sara Hennell on 10 July 'I am preparing to go to "Labassecour"' (*Letters*, vol. 2, p. 165), Charlotte Brontë's version of Brussels in *Villette* is nowhere alluded to in the diary. They saw the main sights in their three days, but did not attempt the almost obligatory excursion to Waterloo perhaps because of the heat. When they visited Brussels again in 1866, on their post-*Felix Holt* tour, they went 'to see our favorite spots (13 [actually 12] years ago! You may imagine the memories!)'.[9]

From Brussels they went via Namur and Liège to Cologne, and then by boat down the Rhine to Mainz, and by train to Frankfurt. The description of this leg of the journey includes one of the few intrusions of current events into the diary, in the form of discussion of the escalating hostility between Turkey and Russia which has gone down in history as the Crimean War (GE and GHL joined in celebrations of the peace with Russia during a seaside holiday in 1856, described in 'Recollections of Ilfracombe').

At last, in the early hours of Thursday 3 August, the travellers reached Weimar, the capital of Saxe-Weimar-Eisenach, perhaps best known in England at this time through Thackeray's parody of it as Pumpernickel in *Vanity Fair* (1848). At the death of Goethe in 1832 its days of glory under the patronage of Duke Karl August were already receding, but in 1854 it was still home to a distinguished group of artists and intellectuals, of whom Franz Liszt was the most notable. GE and GHL explored a town essentially created by Goethe for his patrons, the ducal family. He had landscaped the park and was responsible for various elements of the design of public buildings as well as of his own residences. Some of the places GE and GHL went, and some of their new acquaintances, are more fully described in 'Recollections of Weimar'. At times, especially in accounts of expeditions to particular Goethe shrines, there are parallels between GE's diary and GHL's *Life of Goethe*, which are more pronounced in the extended descriptions of the 'Recollections'.

GHL had letters of introduction to a number of people in Weimar, such as Adolf Schöll, Director of the Free Art Insti-

9 GHL to his mother, quoted by Haight, *George Eliot*, p. 386.

tute, who assisted GHL in his research as well as making social openings for them both. The musician Franz Liszt, whom Lewes had met in Vienna in 1839, was another point of entrée into the society of Weimar. At Liszt's house, the Altenburg, GE and GHL met artists and intellectuals, the French ambassador, and the various members of Liszt's household. They heard Liszt play his own 'fantaisies'; they also heard Clara Schumann play; they met the young Russian composer Anton Rubinstein (with whom they were to renew acquaintance in London in 1876, by which time GE had already drawn on him for the character of Klesmer in *Daniel Deronda*).[10] The inveterate Lewes turned the contact with Liszt into column inches for the *Leader*. Music, long a passion of GE, was a major element in their social life, not only at Liszt's house, but also at the opera (where he was conducting that summer) and other venues. Like Lewes, GE was to turn her experience to account in revising 'Recollections of Weimar' (itself a reworking of the diary) as two articles for *Fraser's Magazine*.

They had professional reasons for being in Weimar, after all. 'They were pleasant days these at Weimar and Berlin,' Cross conceded, 'and they were working days' (Cross, vol. 1, p. 373). This section of the journal prefigures the years to follow in its record of the prodigious amounts of reading and writing both GE and GHL got through, here mostly material needed for reviews or for Goethe. GE refers to the commission from Chapman to review Victor Cousin's book which formed the core of a major piece for the *Westminster Review*, 'Woman in France: Madame de Sablé'. This essay also bears on her own situation, at least in the following passage which might be read as self-justification:

> Heaven forbid that we should enter on a defence of French morals, most of all in relation to marriage! But it is undeniable, that unions formed in the maturity of thought and feeling, and grounded only on inherent fitness and mutual attraction, tended to bring women into more intelligent sympathy with men.[11]

These writing tasks were not undertaken altruistically. GE declared 'economy is our first law' (*Letters*, vol. 2, p. 180; see also her anxious enquiries of Bray about her investment income: pp. 178 and 184). Concern about money breathes through the notes on the cost of their food and lodging, even though the

10 G. S. Haight, 'George Eliot's Klesmer', in *Imagined Worlds*, ed. M. Mack (1968), pp. 205–14; also Haight, *George Eliot*, p. 490.

11 *Westminster Review*, 62 (October 1854), p. 449.

cost of living was much less than in England. One Prussian dollar or thaler consisted of thirty silver groschen, and was worth three English shillings, so that the monthly rents of nine thalers in Weimar, and 28 thalers in Berlin, contrasted favorably with the nine pounds a month GE had been paying in Cambridge Street.

Despite the demands of work, and the constraints of ill health (another recurrent theme throughout the journals), GE experienced much physical pleasure that Weimar summer. They walked enthusiastically, as she wrote to Bray: 'the immense park and plantations with labyrinthine walks are a constant source of new pleasure, and there are charming evening or morning excursions to be made to Belvedere, Tieffurt and Ettersburg, the grand Duke's summer residences.' (*Letters*, vol. 2, p. 171) The charm of these sorties, so evident in GE's contemporary account, did not diminish with time. In 1867 they travelled again to Dresden and Ilmenau, from where GHL wrote:

> From Eisenach we came to Arnstadt & thence in an open carriage here. Again we had sun for this pleasant trip. But more than all sunshine was the sweet memories of 13 years ago when we came on foot. This route – every rood of which came back to us with vivid distinctness so that at particular turns in the road we could say – Here we plucked the plums from the roadside trees – Here I saw such a dog, or told such an anecdote – Here we rested & had coffee etc.[12]

The treatment of this diary by Cross and Haight respectively is characteristic. Cross, intercalating the diary and 'Recollections', concentrates on presenting a sober and studious GE. From this section of the diary, he uses GE's account of her embarkation and Channel crossing, without any allusion to the presence of GHL; quotes two brief paragraphs on Rubens's 'Crucifixion' in Antwerp, a snatch from Cologne and then nothing till the travellers reach Weimar, meet Liszt, and follow up Goethe associations. GE's account of other activities in Weimar is severely curtailed.

Haight in the *Letters* extracts brief snatches as notes, but quotes extensively from the sequence in which Liszt plays the piano at his breakfast party. He quotes more liberally from this section of the diary in *George Eliot*, chapter 6, '"Some One

12 *The Letters of George Henry Lewes*, ed. William Baker, 2 vols. (University of Victoria, English Literary Studies Monograph Series 64, 1995), vol. 2, p. 122.

to Lean Upon": Weimar and Berlin', in which his treatment dwells on the anxiety of GE about her irregular union. His conviction of her emotional dependence occasionally leads him to make statements not supported by the evidence: for instance, GE's account of the Channel crossing gives no warrant for his suggestion that 'Like Maggie and Stephen Guest aboard the Dutch vessel, Marian paced up and down the deck, leaning on George's arm' (p. 148).

This section of the diary was used by GE as the basis for 'Recollections of Weimar', the first of the journals written 'at the wrong end' of this same book; and the 'Recollections' in turn formed the basis of two *Fraser's Magazine* articles: see headnote to 'Recollections of Weimar'.

I. Diary 1854–1861

1. Weimar, 20 July–3 November 1854

July 20th 1854
I said a last farewell to Cambridge street this morning and found myself on board the Ravensbourne, bound for Antwerp about 1/2 an hour earlier than a sensible person would have been aboard, and in consequence I had 20 minutes of terrible fear lest something should have delayed G.[1] But before long I saw his welcome face looking for me over the porter's shoulder, and all was well. The day was glorious and our passage perfect. Mr R. Noel happened to be a fellow-passenger. The sunset was lovely but still lovelier the dawn as we were passing up the Scheldt between 2 and 3 in the morning. The crescent moon, the stars, the first faint blush of the dawn reflected in the glassy river, the dark mass of clouds on the horizon, which sent forth flashes of lightning, and the graceful forms of the boats and sailing vessels painted in jet black on the reddish gold of the sky and water, made up an unforgettable picture. Then the sun rose and lighted up the sleepy shores of Belgium with their fringe of long grass, their rows of poplars, their church spires and farm buildings.

The first view of Antwerp is dull [three or four words illegible] but the tower of the cathedral gives it majesty and under the morning sun the sloping roofs of the houses glittered as if they had a coating of silver. After the usual ennui of having our boxes inspected [a word or two illegible] got safely lodged in the Hôtel du Rhein, a comfortable German house close by Quai du Vandyck. After a rest we went out to find the Cathedral [two words illegible] with the quaint picturesque [two words illegible] of the town. The population is the most wholesome-looking I have ever seen. In the course of our walks we have scarcely seen a person whose skin and garments were not at least as clean as those of the middle class in England. The women have agreeable fresh-looking faces under the cleanest of caps, generally with long barbs. The barbed caps however are giving way to the less picturesque ribboned, round caps worn by the servants in England. A little bonnet like a flower pot with a broad rim is an indigenous article of dress to be seen here and there on the market women etc.[2] The interior of the Cathedral is less striking than the exterior. Rubens's great pictures are removed to an atelier adjoining, and there is only an altar piece by him – the Assumption of the Virgin – which did not please us much. The great treat was the sight of the *Descent from the Cross*, which with its pendant the *Elevation of the Cross* has been undergoing restoration. In the latter, the face of Jesus is sublime

1 GE almost always uses the familiar 'G.' for 'George' to refer to GHL in her journals. Occasionally in this early section, he is 'L.' for 'Lewes'.

2 These headdresses are sketched by GE on the opposite page.

1. 'A little bonnet like a flower pot with a broad rim is an indigenous article of dress'.

in its expression of agony and trust in the divine. It is certainly the finest conception of the *suffering* Christ I have ever seen. The rest of the picture gave me no pleasure. But in the Descent from the Cross, colour, form and expression alike impressed me with the sense of grandeur and beauty. A little miserable copy of the picture placed near it, served as an admirable foil. After walking through the Place Verte to look at Rubens's statue, which is very fine, we felt that we had our fill of beauty and went home to dine and rest. In the evening we saw more of the town with increasing admiration.

The Place de Meir, where are the King's Palace and other fine buildings, the neighbouring streets where there are flags hanging from the houses of consuls and ambassadors, shewed to advantage under the calm light of a lovely evening sky. After an ineffectual journey to the Zoological Gardens which we were too late to see we went home to our pleasant room from which we could enjoy the evening red melting away over the Scheldt and its shipping, the breaking out of the stars, and the itinerant concerts, which were delighting the groups of people below us.

22nd. We went to the Museum and saw Rubens's Crucifixion, even more beautiful to me than the Descent from the Cross. These two pictures profoundly impressed me with the miserable lack of breadth and grandeur in the conceptions of our living artists. The reverence for the old masters is not all humbug and superstition. At the Church of St. Paul we saw some marvellous wood carving by Verbruggen. For roundness, grace and expression I have rarely seen anything equal to it even in marble. On the outside of this church, there is an elaborate representation of Calvary – puerile, like the faith it embodies, but impressive, like everything else that attempts – even if it only attempts – to make the past vividly present. At the church of St. Jacques we saw the famous altar-piece – a Holy Family presenting portraits of Rubens, his two wives, and his Father (as Time). At the Museum, we were rather disappointed in the bull's head (in the adoration of the Magi) so much lauded by Ruskin. He dwells on the simplicity of the means by which Rubens has here produced so striking an effect – the few bold dashes of the brush by which the head is made to stand out with such reality in the picture. But on examination the texture does not appear so slight as he leads one to expect. A picture of Card-players by Valentin was the only thing that delighted us here, besides the Crucifixion. We took our coffee in the Café Français and spent our evening in listening to an excellent band which was serenading the Governor on the occasion of his being knighted.

23. Sunday. We were grilled in the Railway carriage this morning on our way to Brussels, and glad to find ourselves havened in the comfortable Hôtel de Belgique, kept by a Mlle van Stockeran. On walking out in the evening we were struck with the palatial appearance of the Haute Ville, especially in the Rue Royale, and around the Park. Standing against the statue of the Comte de Belliard, we saw the sun set behind the spire of the Hotel de Ville – a spire which reminded me of Scott's monument at Edinburgh. Then we went to a concert in the Park, and enjoyed seeing the people looking cheerful at their little tables with their glass of lemonade or sirop, or their cup of coffee.

24. We rambled about the town from breakfast till 1. St. Gudule, the principal church, is very magnificent. The front is a fine specimen of Gothic and the interior, which is very carefully and tastefully kept is rich in fine effects of painted glass, seen through labyrinthine arches. Orange trees are ranged along each side of the nave. We found the Basse Ville very picturesque – the Grand Place where stands the Hotel de Ville especially fine. A gallery or arcade of shops – La galérie de la Reine – is remarkably elegant. We strolled into the Marché aux Fleurs and there bought some cheap French novels. Our aching legs and melting bodies at last reached the Parc, where we rested under the shade a little while and then came home to dinner. A cavalry officer is the only other inmate of our hotel. In the evening we walked to the Zoological Gardens flattering ourselves that we were going to hear a concert by the band of the "Guides"; but we were only just in time to see them quit the orchestra. However we had a pretty view of houses, trees and water from the gardens, and were consoled for our disappointment by the pleasure we had in strolling through the Basse Ville by starlight. The smells in the streets are sickening.

25 and 26. Short rambles in the morning, lying melting on our beds through the middle of the day, and our one evening resort, the concert in the Park filled up these two days. We saw the famous Mannikin and took chocolate at the Café aux Milles Colonnes; went to the Messageries to inquire about our luggage with no other result than a colloquy with a hideous, uncivil man installed there as chief functionary.

27 Thursday. We rose at 5 and set off for Namur. Our companions in the 2nd class carriage were some disgustingly coarse Belgians with baboonish children. Passed a train full of soldiers who set up a hideous howl, meant for singing.

Every attempt at vocal music which we have happened to hear in Belgium has been of the same sort. When we reached Namur, it still rained a little, but after we had dined we managed to take a survey of the town, and to walk up a hill close to the fortifications from which we had a pleasant view suggestive of quiet industry. Our railway journey along the Meuse served to show us how much beauty there is on its banks, but was too rapid to allow of our enjoying it. The saloon, with its sofas and glass sides is a perfect contrivance. About 5 we reached the Hotel de l'Europe at Liège and had our tea in my bedroom, from the window of which there is an enchanting view of rich and varied foliage flanked by stately heights covered with buildings. We spent the evening in walking about Liège and were in a state of rapture at its beauty – entirely unlike anything we had seen before. The rich green everywhere breaking the lines of the picturesque houses, the amphitheatre of richly wooded hills which surround the valley of the Meuse and of which one catches sight here and there at the end of a street, the fine Boulevard leading to the river – everything we saw was beautiful. We determined to stay here through Friday and defer our departure for Cologne until Saturday morning.

28. We went the first thing to the Church of St. Jacques – perhaps the finest thing we have seen on our journey. Forms, proportions, colouring – all is harmony, and we sat for half an hour wrapt in delicious contemplation. The delicate cream colour of the stone has an effect almost equal to that of marble in beauty – perhaps quite equal in its way. We came here again in the evening to hear the organ, but the Belgian voices which accompanied it or rather overpowered it prevented us from getting much extra enjoyment out of the music. The church warden's wife told us that some English artists had been engaged for 4 years in this church and had produced a thick quarto volume of drawings from it. Next to this delight came the Palais de Justice, formerly the palace of the Prince Bishop. The interior court with its colonnade of elaborately sculptured arches in grey stone is unique in my experience. One side has been restored and shews in perfection the varied patterns of the columns. We had a drive in an open carriage through the town to the Casino, a charming place with heights from which we had a fine view of Liège and its environs. On returning we saw the statue of Grétry. In the evening after going to St. Jacques we had another drive and then a farewell walk to our beloved Palais de Justice and to the Quay.

29. We set off by the 9 o'clock train for Cologne. The country from Liège to Vervier was strikingly beautiful. At Vervier Dr. Brabant joined us in our carriage. Cologne looked very dismal as we passed through it in the omnibus on our way to the Hotel de Hollande. After dinner Dr. Brabant called to tell us that Strauss was residing in Cologne and would receive us the next morning at 9. We went with Dr. B. to see the Cathedral. When I entered it the sight of the ugly wall which shuts out the choir – the proper vista of the nave, shocked me as one would be shocked by an ugly wooden arm attached to an exquisite marble torso. In the evening we had a ramble through the town, which looked more endurable by the soft evening light – but its grand characteristics are the

multitude of churches and the multiplicity of smells. On our return we found Dr. Brabant who came to tell us that Strauss would *call on us* in the morning.

30 Sunday. We breakfasted in the public room and were joined there by Dr. B. and Strauss. After a short interview with them we went on board the steamboat which was to take us to Coblentz. I did not expect much pleasure from [the] Rhine, so I took all that came with a good grace. In Coblentz I was rather disappointed, but it had still much beauty for me. The affectionate manners of the waiter at the hotel (Trois Suisses) were amusing. The view from the bridge over the Moselle was a fine picture. So was that from our hotel windows looking on Ehrenbreitstein and the bridge of boats. We remarked the great number of deformed people here. In one short evening walk we met 10 or 12 of them.

31. We set out again by the boat at 8 this morning, and had a delightful voyage. The banks of the Rhine from Coblentz to Mainz surpassed my expectations and seemed to me really to deserve Byron's praise. I fancy we saw the vines at the right moment – their green was so vivid. When they begin to turn yellow they must look rather forlorn, but the feathery hanging woods which clothe the hills here and there would shew best in Autumn. When we landed at Mainz, it began to rain, but we were brave enough to set out on a walk through the town, and were rewarded by a sight of the Nassau soldiery exercising – richer than any caricature in Punch. We were fairly driven back to the station by the rain and the smells, so we sat quietly awaiting the time of starting by the train to Frankfurt admiring the prim architectural looking bouquets on the table of the waiting room and getting by heart the German faces about us. In the same carriage with us were a Prussian Graf, who carried a loaf of black bread on his lap and talked to every one with great bonhomie, a Dutchman, and an Austrian with his wife. They talked, like every one else of the Turks and Russians. The Dutchman declared with great emphasis that England was much less beloved by Germany than Russia because she (England) was a more formidable rival in trade! – After a 'mauvais moment' waiting for our luggage we got into the omnibus and were carried to the Weidenbusch near the Rossmarkt, a very comfortable hotel.

Aug. 1. Tuesday. The first thing we did this morning was to go and see Goethe's statue by Schwanthaler and then his home in the Hirschgraben. Next we walked to the Judengasse; a striking scene! Next to the Staedel Museum, where the one thing never to be forgotten was Hübner's picture of Job and his friends. Lessing's pictures – Ezzelin in prison and Huss before the Council of Constance – are meritorious but not thrilling. We unfortunately missed Overbeck's picture of Christianity triumphing over the Arts. We filled up our minutes before dinner by a second visit to Goethe's house, and a drive to the Bibliothek where we saw Marchesi's statue of Goethe and the portraits of Luther and his wife. In the evening we went to the Main Lust and heard some agreeable music.

2. Heavy and continuous rain kept us in our hotel till it was time to see Dannecker's Ariadne. It stands in a pavilion in the garden of Herr Bethmann, a wealthy banker. I never saw any sculpture equal to this – the feeling it excites is

the essence of true worship – a bowing of the soul before power creating beauty. At 5 o'clock we set out on our 10 hours' journey to Weimar. The second class carriage was so comfortable, and the weather so lovely after the morning rains that the first half of our journey was delightful instead of fatiguing. The splendid view we had of Marburg by the setting sun was worth the whole journey. We got a little tired and leg-achy before we reached Weimar at 1/2 past 3, but after a little difficulty we got some tolerable beds at the Erbprinz and slept away our fatigue by 9 o'clock.

3rd. It was very pretty to look out of the window, when dressing, on a garden that reminded one of an English Village. Our walk in search of lodgings made us acquainted with the physiognomy of the town, which is more like a huge village or market town than the precinct of a court. We soon obtained some lodgings and here we are at 62a Kaufgasse at the house of Frau Münderloh, on the whole as comfortable as need be. In the evening we walked to Ober Weimar to see "Der Posse als Medicin" at the "Tivoli Theater", a little wooden structure in a garden.

4. We took possession of our lodgings this morning and had enough to do before dinner in arranging our books etc. We pay 9 thalers per month for our lodgings. Our dinner at the Erbprinz is 12 1/2 groschen = about 15d. In the evening we happened, in our walk, to find the Erholung, where a concert was going forward. The walks in the garden are beautifully arched over with trees – firs chiefly which with their falling leaves make a matting that deadens the sound of one's footsteps – a great charm to me. We sat down among the company, made up almost entirely of women, most of them good-looking well dressed bourgeoises, chatting with an air of real friendliness over their knitting etc. When we came home I read some of L.'s M.S. aloud.

5 Sat. We read, wrote and walked a little before dinner. After, I read Sainte Beuve aloud. A letter from Mr. Chapman, proposing to me to write an article on Victor Cousin's Mde. de Sablé. We ordered the book at the "Hof-Buchhandlung", a modest shop in the Markt Platz. In the evening we walked to Tiefurt, and were delighted with the grounds there.

6 Sunday. We wrote our letters and then walked out. Saw the outside of Goethe's house in the Frauen Place. Dined for the first time at the Russischer Hof. Linenless, German. Our evening walk was to Belvedere, an enchanting place. A rumbling awkward carriage pronounced to be "ein hübscher Wagen".[3]

7 Monday. Rainy. A pleasant walk in the Parc, notwithstanding. Read M.S. in the evening.

8 Tuesday. L. called on Schöll, and in the afternoon he (Schöll) came and took us to the Schloss where we saw the Dichter Zimmer.[4]

3 German, 'a pretty vehicle'.

4 German, 'poets' rooms', dedicated to Goethe, Schiller and Wieland.

2. Cloak of printed cotton worn by the peasants of Weimar.

Wednesday 9. We went to the little Tivoli Theatre and saw a "star" in Kotzebue's play – *Der Arme Poet* and Numero 726 a farce known in England as "The Lottery Ticket." In the morning L. called on Liszt.

Thursday 10. About 1/2 past 10 Liszt called, and after chatting pleasantly for some time invited us to go and breakfast at his house, the Altenburg. Talking of Mde. D'Agoût, he told us that when her novel Nélida appeared, in which Liszt himself is pilloried as a delinquent, he asked her "Mais pourquoi avez vous tellement maltraité ce pauvre *Lehmann*?"[5]

On arriving at the Altenburg we were shewn into the garden, where in a saloon formed by overarching trees the déjeuner was set out. We found Hoffmann von Fallersleben, the lyric poet, Dr. Schade, a Gelehrter who has distinguished himself by a critical work on the 11,000 virgins (!), and a Herr Cornelius an agreeable looking artist. Presently came a Herr or Doctor Raff, a musician who has recently published a volume called Wagnerfrage. Soon after we were joined by Liszt and the Princess Marie, an elegant, gentle looking girl of 17, and last, by the Princess Wittgenstein with her nephew Prince Eugène and a young French (or Swiss?) artist, a pupil of Scheffer. The appearance of the Princess rather startled me at first. I had expected to see a tall distinguished looking woman, if not a beautiful one. But she is short and unbecomingly endowed with embonpoint; at the first glance the face is not pleasing, and the profile especially is harsh and barbarian, but the dark, bright hair and eyes give the idea of vivacity and strength. Her teeth, unhappily, are blackish too. She was tastefully dressed in a morning robe of some semi-transparent white material lined with orange-colour, which formed the bordering, and ornamented the sleeves, a black lace jacket, and a piquant cap set on the summit of her comb, and trimmed with violet colour. The breakfast was not sumptuous either as to the food or the appointments. When the cigars came, Hoffmann was requested to read some of his poetry, and he gave us a bacchanalian poem with great spirit. I sat between Liszt and Miss Anderson, the Princess Marie's governess, an amiable but insignificant person. L. sat next the Princess and talked with her about Goethe, whom she pronounces to have been an egotist. My great delight was to watch Liszt and observe the sweetness of his expression. Genius, benevolence and tenderness beam from his whole countenance, and his manners are in perfect harmony with it. A little rain sent us into the house, and when we were seated in an elegant little drawing room, opening into a large music-salon, we had more reading from Hoffmann, and from the French artist who with a tremulous voice pitched in a minor key, read us some rather pretty sentimentalities of his own. Then came the thing I had longed for – Liszt's playing. I sat near him so that I could see both his hands and face. For the first time in my life I beheld real inspiration – for the first time I heard the true tones of the piano. He played one of his own compositions – one of a series of religious *fantaisies*. There was nothing strange or excessive about his manner. His

5 French, 'But why have you so mistreated this poor Lehmann?'

manipulation of the instrument was quiet and easy, and his face was simply grand – the lips compressed and the head thrown a little backward. When the music expressed quiet rapture or devotion a sweet smile flitted over his features; when it was triumphant the nostrils dilated. There was nothing petty or egoistic to mar the picture. Why did not Scheffer paint him thus, instead of representing him as one of the three Magi? But it just occurs to me that Scheffer's idea was a sublime one. There are the two aged men who have spent their lives in trying to unravel the destinies of the world, and who are looking for the Deliverer, for the Light from on high. Their young fellow-seeker, having the fresh inspiration of early life is the first to discern the herald star and his ecstasy reveals it to his companions. In this young magus Scheffer has given a portrait of Liszt, but even here where he might be expected to idealize unrestrainedly, he falls short of the original. It is curious that Liszt's face is the type that one sees in all Scheffer's pictures – at least in all I have seen. In a little room which terminates the suite there is a portrait of Liszt also by Scheffer – the same of which the engraving is familiar to everyone. This little room is filled with memorials of Liszt's triumphs and the worship his divine talent has won. It was arranged for him by the Princess in conjunction with the Arnims, in honour of his birthday. There is a medallion of him by Schwanthaler, a bust by an Italian artist, and cabinets full of jewels and precious things, the gifts of the great. In the music salon stand Beethoven's and Mozart's pianos. Beethoven's was a present from Broadwood and has a Latin inscription intimating that it was presented as a tribute to his illustrious genius. In a room on the ground floor is a mask of Beethoven taken after his death, a very painful thing to see. I could not recognize the features.

Friday 11. We went to the Bibliothek with Hofrath Schöll, and looked at the portraits and busts. The most remarkable among them is one in bronze of Gluck. The rugged power of the face is given with wonderful reality, as far as possible from the feeble idealization one generally sees in busts. There is a bust of Goethe, taken during his stay in Italy, which represents him as an Apollo. It is exquisitely beautiful but I cannot believe the brow to be accurate. Lessing's head and face are small, but of a fine, delicate type. Jacobi is rather feeble looking. We walked about with Schöll till it began to rain and then sought shelter with him under a door place. He is a genial unaffected man, full of accurate knowledge on all literary and philosophical subjects, and there is no German heaviness either in his appearance or his mind. In the morning L. called on Frau von Goethe.

12 Saturday. The morning being bright, we went to spend our day at Belvedere, the Grand Duke's Summer residence. It stands on the most considerable elevation in the immediate neighbourhood of Weimar, and is surrounded with lovely gardens which one enjoys all the more because they are free to all the good people of the town. The road to Belvedere is remarkable. It is one long avenue of stately trees. Just as we were going to leave, after 5 or 6 hours of quiet happiness, we met Schöll and turned back with him. He was presently joined by his wife whom we saw for the first time.

12 [13] Sunday. Another glorious morning! But L.'s head is bad, and that makes us melancholy. We called on the Princess and strolled till dinner. Finished Cousin's book on Madame de Sablé. In the evening we walked to Ober Weimar and satisfied ourselves that the village was very ugly.

13 [14]. We devoted the day to an expedition to Ettersburg. On our return homewards the solemn grandeur of the Pine forest, in contrast with the sunbathed woods through which we had been passing, had a strong effect on us. The Chaussée has a bordering of cherry trees and mountain ashes. The bunches of coral berries gladdened our eyes.

14 [15] Tuesday. We had our names set down for the Table d'hôte at the Erbprinz, by which means our dinners will only cost us 10 silver groschen each. Our expenses here, including wine and washing are £2.6 per week. Liszt called and sat chatting for an hour with me.

15 [16] Wednesday. I wrote to my sister and to Mr. Bray.

16 [17] Thursday. Liszt dined with us at the Erbprinz and came home with us to take coffee. Much pleasant chat. Afterwards L. and I walked to Belvedere.

17 [18] Friday. Nothing particular.

18 [19] Sat. Letter from Miss Parkes. Not well.

19 [20] Sunday. L. called on Liszt, and went again in the evening.

20 [21]. Bad headache. Schöll called in the afternoon.

21 [22]. Head still bad. Walked to Belvedere and saw the Theatre in the garden.

22 [23] Wed. Better. Wrote a little. Invited to Liszt's but did not go. Went to the Vogel-schiessen in the evening and saw Punch etc.

24. Wrote all morning. Afternoon, went to Schiller's house. Stupidity of people tricking out and altering such a place instead of letting one see it as he saw it and lived in it. I played on his little claveçin, in which lay his guitar; Vogel-schiessen, Punch.

25. Goethe's House. Study and Bedroom.

30. Arthur Helps came yesterday to Weimar on his way to Dresden. L was with him all morning. He took coffee with us after dinner. In the evening we drove to Ettersburg, and he entertained us with charming stories about his Spanish travels.

Sep. 2. Saturday. I went with G. to Bercka for the first time. A little Elysium and the way to it very lovely. We dined al fresco in the presence of a pretty little meadow scene with holy oaks in the foreground. In returning, the evening was enchanting.

3 Sunday. Bad headache and unable to work. In the evening we went to Belvedere, and I saw several parts of the garden which were new to me.

4. Mr Chapman's letter came to say that my article must be ready in London by the 10th.

8. Sent off my article on Mme. de Sablé. Went to Tiefurt in the evening.

9. We went to Belvedere and spent the day there. Wrote Mr. Chapman.

10 Sunday. Wrote to Miss Parkes. Then we walked out in the fields towards Gelmeroda and sat in the sunshine. In the evening, to a party at Liszt's – Herrmann's conjuring the chief amusement. Medallion of Liszt by Rietschl very fine.

11. Walked in the Webicht, and talked of art. In the afternoon we went to Jena. Much struck by the scenery. Slept at the *Sonne*.

12. Saw Goethe's rooms at the Tanne, now occupied by Dr. Widmann and his wife, a niece of Neander's. We then walked up the Hausberg, and had an enchanting view of the little village of Lichtenhain, nestled among trees in a lovely valley. The winding walk among the pines and firs, the wild flowers, the delicious air and the unclouded sky were intoxicating. The town of Jena is unmitigatedly dull and ugly, but Nature around it is enough to reconcile one to being there a short time. As we sat on the side of the hill, in ascending, the town looked very pretty and we heard scarcely a sound except the music of a band at various distances. We came home by a *Wagen* which started from the *Sonne* at 4. I was amazed at the beauty of the road, which I had not seen well as we went, from being shut up in a close *Wagen*. The evening sky was beautiful and we had full leisure to observe it, for we did not reach Weimar till 1/2 past 7. The little town looked more bright and cheery than ever after Jena.

13 Wednesday. I was not at all well and overwalked myself by going to Belvedere in the evening. The Schölls and Sauppes were there.

14. Very unwell this morning, and glad in the afternoon to hear that Liszt wished to put off our going to him. We had a delicious walk in the open fields, came home, and finished the M.S. of Goethe's life.

16 Saturday. We went to the Weimar Theatre for the first time and heard Ernani.

17. We deferred going to Ilmenau and passed the day quietly.

18. Liszt came to dine with us at the Erbprinz and introduced M. Rubinstein, a young Russian, who is about to have an opera of his performed here.

19 Tuesday. We went to an evening party at Liszt's and heard the instrument, half organ, half piano, which he has had constructed for himself.

20. We set off for Ilmenau by railway. I read Liszt's account of "Der Fliegende Holländer" by the way. When we reached Neu Dietendorf, we had to get into the Post Wagen which turned out to be a disagreeable omnibus-like vehicle. At Arnstadt we were placed in a Beiwagen with two other passengers and had a

pleasant view of the charming country all the way to Ilmenau. But the jolting vehicles and other désagréments had made us both ill and we could only crawl to our beds about 8 o'clock.

21. We were better this morning but not equal to much walking. We rambled to a pretty stream and there sat watching a caterpillar. When it had been cut in two the fore-part set to work to devour the other half. In the afternoon we had a two hours' walk in the pine woods. They are sublime.

22. This morning we set out to find the Gabelbach. It rained a little, but still our walk was very pleasant. From the Gabelbach we went on to Kickelhahn, where Goethe's queer little wooden house stands. We wrote our names near one of the windows. The view of hills from this point is very grand. We did exploits on our way home, not knowing the road, and were amused to find ourselves at last at the spot from which we had begun our uphill walk to the Gabelbach. In the evening we turned out again and walked to Elgersberg.

23 Saturday. We went to Elgersberg and continued along the Chaussée till we came to Stutzerbach where we took a guide to Gabelbach. He took us up the hills through glorious pine and beech woods.

24 Sunday. We walked from Ilmenau to Arnstadt – a 4 hours' journey. The road is very fine and varied. Dined at the Goldene Henne, and had a boar's head splendidly decorated with green branches, a lemon in its mouth and a cross formed of carrot on its brow. We got the coupé of the Post Wagen and travelled comfortably to Neu Dietendorf, where we waited half an hour, for the train to Weimar. We reached home about half past 6 and enjoyed taking coffee snugly in our own lodgings once more. I read the Kestner letters at Ilmenau.

25. The morning looked so lovely that we were tempted to walk to Bercka, but it became very windy before we had been out long. The little valley looked more lovely than ever. We had a smart shower on setting out home, but were compensated by the sight of a lovely rainbow, which sprang from the very ground. It continued fine after this and we had a delicious evening walk.

26. In the afternoon we called at Herr Schöll's, had some pleasant chat with him and his wife, and then walked in the Park, Schöll accompanying us.

27. Mr Williams, an agreeable, unaffected young man, took coffee with us. In the evening we set out to go to Belvedere, but turned off into the open fields and found out a new walk. The sky was grand.

28 Thursday. The morning was too beautiful to be spent in doors, so we set out on the same walk that we had yesterday, and got at last to Belvedere, where we went to look at the landscapes in the glass globes.

29. In the afternoon the Princess Wittgenstein called and chatted pleasantly. G. then went to Mr. Wilson's to meet Eckermann.

30. G. dined at the Marquis de Ferrière's.

Oct. 1. In the morning I partly condensed Liszt's article on Meyerbeer for the Vivian paper. In the evening walked and read aloud the Wahlverwandtschaften.

2. Finished Liszt's article. In the evening we went to the theatre and saw "Die Journalisten". Genast, an actor of Goethe's time, was admirably humourous in the character of an obese wine-merchant. The face and tone with which he said "Es ist hübsch heute, Lotte"[6] is something to be remembered.

3 Tuesday. Mr. Marshall called and immediately after came the Marquis de Ferrière. We had an hour's agreeable talk about Byron etc. etc. and when the marquis left we had a little walk with Mr. Marshall. He spoke of Strauss with great admiration – thought the man excellent as well as the writer. At 1/2 past 6 we went to hear Tannhäuser. The overture and the first and second acts thrilled me, but the third I felt rather wearisome. The tragedy in this act is very fine, but either I was too much fatigued to relish the music, or it is intrinsically monotonous and spun out beyond any but German patience.

4 Wednesday. Translated in the morning and wrote to Mr. Chapman. In the afternoon walked to Belvedere with Mr. Marshall, met Mr Wilson on our return and took tea with him. He told us that one day when he had been walking with Carlyle who as usual had his dog with them, they were about to get into an omnibus and Carlyle drew out a horribly noisy whistle with which he summoned his dog. "Don't make that noise, man!" said the conductor of the omnibus; and Carlyle was at once silent, feeling himself rebuked.

5. Thursday. G. dined at the Marquis de Ferrière's and I read *Rameau's Neffe*.

6 Friday. Mr. Marshall and Mr. Wilson came in the afternoon and we had a long conversation about Christianity. We walked out into the open fields, and then read the Wahlverwandtschaften.

7 Saturday. G. having finished his comedy,[7] we had a long walk to Belvedere and through the grounds there. They are lovely now in their autumn dress. In the evening we went to hear "Der Markt von Richmond", an opera of Flotow's, a mere ragoût of borrowed scraps.

8 Sunday. Mr. Marshall called in the morning and walked with us. We called on Eckermann, who is interesting to look at though shattered in mind and body.

9. We had tea at Mr. Wilson's, and talked about women.

10. To Bercka. The day was lovely – warm as a July day, and the woods looked magnificent under the bright sky.

11 Wednesday. I was ill this morning and staid in doors all day. G. went to call on the Princess and had some interesting conversation with her about Madame d'Agoût and Liszt. A painful letter from London caused us both a bad night.

6 German, 'It is lovely today, Lotte.'

7 *The Fox who got the Grapes*, GHL's adaptation of Bayard and Dupin's *Alexandre chez Apelles*.

12. I was still not well enough to go out. The Marquis de Ferrière called in the afternoon, and afterwards Mr. Marshall. It rained heavily the whole day.

13 Friday. Better. G. wrote letters to Carlyle and Helps explaining his position. The rain continued all day.

14. A fine morning once more. I walked out with G. Began to read Egmont after dinner, then "The Hoggarty Diamond". Walking in the afternoon we met Schöll and he turned back with us. I received a letter from sister – with melancholy news about her boy Robert – and a letter from Mr. Chapman. G. dined with the Marquis de Ferrière.

15 Sunday. Wrote to Chrissey and Mr Chapman. G. wrote to Robert Chambers. Read the Hoggarty Diamond in the afternoon and walked out. In the evening to the Theatre to hear the "Fliegende Holländer".

16 Monday. A dismal, rainy day. The Michaelmas fair, which is going on, causes an incessant buzz of voices under our windows, not soothing to the nerves. I wrote to Mr. Bray. In the afternoon Mr. Marshall sat with us for an hour or two. The rest of the time was filled up with the "Hoggarty Diamond".

17 Tuesday. The weather has cleared up and we have had a pleasant walk once more. We have been to the Bibliothek again, that I might see the busts etc. on the upper floor. The bust of Gluck by Houdon gave me new pleasure. I never saw more reality and animation even in a portrait. The bust of Lessing too impresses one as a probable likeness. It is full of bright good sense. But one gets sceptical about all busts and portraits on comparing the cast of Schiller's skull with the head given to his bust. When the eyebrows of the bust and that of the skull are placed on a level, the departure of the artist from the true proportions is so gross that one sees it can have arisen from no mere incorrectness of perception, but only from a false principle. The same disgust at the incompetence or untruthfulness of artists is produced by the discrepant portraits and busts of Goethe; but there is one likeness of him that is really startling and thrilling from the idea it gives one of perfect resemblance. It is painted on a cup and is a tiny miniature, but the execution is so perfect that on applying a magnifying glass every minute stroke has as natural an appearance as the texture of a flower or the parts of an insect under the microscope. In a sort of cupboard with glass doors are preserved the coat in which Gustavus Adolphus was shot, Luther's gown, Goethe's court coat, and his Schlafrock,[8] etc. There are endless trifles preserved in the various rooms – toys that pleased Carl Friedrich, the last Duke – a nodding and winking figure etc. The only portraits that had any interest for me in the smaller rooms are those of the Grand Duchess Amalia and the Jagermann, Carl August's mistress. In the large Saal of the Library there is a portrait of Kant which one likes to look at in the faint hope that it may resemble him a little, but the grand objects of interest are the bust of Gluck, the portrait

8 German, 'dressing-gown'.

of Goethe on the cup, and the relics of Gustavus Adolphus, Luther and Goethe. The bust of Goethe taken when he was in Italy by Trippel is strikingly beautiful, but it is evidently so idealized on the Apollo type and so degraded by the *front fuyant*[9] which the artist has chosen to give it that one has little satisfaction in looking at it. – In the afternoon finished the Hoggarty Diamond. Mr. Marshall came to sit with us and then we went to the Theatre to see "Der verwunschene Prinz", a farce founded on Shakspeare's Christopher Sly. Hettstedt, the Christopher Sly of the piece acted with great *entrain*[10] and humour. This was followed by a vaudeville adapted from the French, "Guten Morgen, Herr Fischer", in which Franke acted the part of Doctor Hippe admirably.

18 Wednesday. Mr. Marshall brought us the Life of Sheridan and sat chatting with us and then walked out. A sombre autumn afternoon. In the evening we went to see Der Freischütz which I had never seen before, though familiar with the music. The childish construction of the drama made still more apparent by the rude bug-a-boo style in which it was put on the stage. The absence of recitative – the descent from Weber's rich melody to ordinary speaking intolerable. And set in Germany – this land of music – they even play Don Juan without recitative!

20 Friday. G. got some interesting particulars from Frau Riemer about Goethe – especially about his attachment to Minna Herzlieb, which threw light on the sad experience he declares himself to have deposited "as in a burial urn" in the Wahlverwandtschaften. I read *Egmont* in the evening. Curiously enough after we had been making up our minds in the morning that the Schölls had some reason for being cold to us, there came an invitation from them to tea at 8 o'clock. Before we went came a letter of noble sympathy from Carlyle. Our evening was very pleasantly passed at the Schölls'. Mr. Marshall and the Sauppes there.

21 Saturday. A letter from Helps the first thing this morning. In the afternoon we walked with the Schölls and Sauppe. In the morning we had had a glorious walk to Belvedere and in the grounds there. Egmont in the evening. Moore's Life of Sheridan.

22 Sunday. A letter from Mr. Bray which occupied us painfully for some time after breakfast. Then we walked. G. dined at Liszt's it being Liszt's 43rd birthday. In the evening went to hear Lohengrin but only staid out two acts.

23. Monday. I wrote to Mr. Bray. L. breakfasted with the Marquis de Ferrière. Afternoon rainy. Headache in the evening. Letter from R. Chambers.

24 Tuesday. Bad headache all day. *Gross Cophta* in the evening. Looked through Moore's Life of Sheridan in the morning – a firstrate specimen of bad biographical writing.

9 French, 'receding forehead'.
10 French, 'spirit'.

25 Wednesday. L. dined with the Marquis de Ferrière. I was not yet well.

26. Walked to the Webicht. In the evening we went to a concert rehearsal at the theatre. Heard Clara Schumann play, Mlle Genast sing, and a prelude of Liszt's played by the orchestra.

27. I read Götz in the morning. In the afternoon, Liszt, the Marquis de Ferrière and Mr. Marshall sat with us. Walked, read the "Bürgergeneral", and chatted with Mr. M. again in the evening.

28. Musical Party at Liszt's at 2 o'clock. Clara Schumann – a melancholy, interesting looking creature. Her husband went mad a year ago, and she has to support 8 children!

29. Sunday. Breakfasted quietly *en famille* with the Princess and Liszt. Saw some fine sketches from Dante by Koch.

30. I wrote to Mr. Chapman, acknowledging the receipt of the £15 for my article on Mde. de Sablé. G. dined at Mr. J. Horrocks's and in the evening we had music at Mr. Wilson's.

November 1. Wednesday. Breakfasted at Liszt's and said goodbye. The Marquis de Ferrière and Cornelius there.

2 Thursday. Packed this morning. In the afternoon Mr. Marshall, Mr. Wilson and young Osborne came to say goodbye. L. went to the Schloss in the evening, and while he was away Liszt came to say goodbye and brought me a parcel of Bon-bons from the Princess.

3 Friday. Hofrath Schöll came to say goodbye and brought me Uhland's poems as a parting present. We set off from the Weimar station at 1/2 past one, and reached Berlin at 1/2 past 9. Went to the Hôtel de l'Europe in the Taubenstrasse.

2. Berlin, 3 November 1854 – 13 March 1855

On 3 November 1854 GE and GHL left Weimar for Berlin, the capital city of Prussia. The day after their arrival, GE registered in her diary the relative sophistication of Berlin, observing that 'The people look very smart and brisk after the Weimarians'; and a week later she 'wrote a few recollections of Weimar', completed on 30 November. None the less, their life in Berlin followed a similar pattern to that established in Weimar: writing, reading, walks, visits to galleries, theatres, acquaintances. GHL described their routine in a courtly and whimsical letter to the Princess Wittgenstein:

> Our mode of life is somewhat this. We rise at eight; after breakfast read & work till between one & two; walk in the Thiergarten or pay visits till dinner, which is at 3; come home to coffee, and, when not at the theatre or in society Miss Evans reads Goethe aloud to me & I read Shakspeare aloud to her. There you have a programme of our lives.[1]

GE's diary reports in detail the busy, contented schedule summarised by GHL, without reviving the occasional ecstasy of their Weimar honeymoon. In the depth of winter, complaints about ill health are more prominent; and there is a refrain of concern about the cost of living. They kept up the practice of daily walks in the extensive Tiergarten and in the area around their lodgings close by the Brandenburg Gate, but access to the countryside was more limited than in provincial Weimar.

Their principal work was still of course the *Life of Goethe*, with Goethe's own writings dominating their reading. They continued with journalism, and to assist her partner GE also took on a good deal of translation – from German, for his work on Goethe, and from Latin, for an edition of Spinoza's *Ethica* he had been planning. She was not unprepared for this task, having translated some of Spinoza as early as 1843, and having attempted his *Tractatus Theologico-Politicus* (1670) in 1849. GE wrote to Sara Hennell in November 1854:

> I should be very glad to have my pen employed in something that would yield immediate profit, and there are plenty of subjects suggested by new German books which would be fresh and instructive in an English review. But I

1 *The Letters of George Henry Lewes*, ed. William Baker, 2 vols (Victoria, University of Victoria, English Literature Monograph Series 64, 1995), vol. 1, p. 233; cf. GE to Charles Bray, *Letters*, vol. 2, pp. 184–6.

> cannot bring myself to run the risk of a refusal from an editor. Indeed I cannot for several reasons make any proposition at present. So I am working at what will ultimately yield something which is secured by agreement with Bohn. (*Letters*, vol. 2, p. 189)

The agreement turned out to be less than secure. GE completed the Spinoza translation in February 1856, after GHL had announced it as forthcoming, 'edited by the writer of these lines', in *The Life and Works of Goethe*.[2] However Bohn reneged, and GE's translation was not published until 1981.[3] The position argued by Spinoza in the *Ethics* – that individuals' self love is checked by their sympathy for others – is consistent with the views GE developed later in her fiction.

While in Berlin GE and GHL embarked upon a comprehensive reading of Shakspeare's works, mostly aloud. There had been a proposal that GHL 'should give a course of *Lectures on Shakspeare* – say four or six – in Berlin (of course in English) giving the results of my studies of the *dramatic* art interspersed with "dramatic Readings."' (*Letters of GHL*, vol. 1, p. 228), which came to nothing. However they worked through many of the plays, *Venus and Adonis*, and some of the sonnets, at times with the actor Ludwig Dessoir: 'he comes to have long discussions about Shakespeare & acting which are generally illustrated in so lively a manner, that the neighbours must imagine two mad actors have broken loose from Les Petites Maisons, and have concealed themselves on the 1 Etage of 62!' (p. 233).

As in Weimar, GE and GHL, armed with introductions, soon found their way into the cultural and social life of the place. On their first foray into the streets they met Varnhagen von Ense (according to GHL 'one of my oldest friends'; *Letters of GHL*, vol. 1, p. 233), the distinguished critic and poet who was to provide GHL with substantial help in his Goethe work by way of introductions, personal reminiscences and loans of

2 George Henry Lewes, *The Life and Works of Goethe: with Sketches of him – his age and contemporaries from published and unpublished sources*, 2 vols. (London, Nutt, 1855), vol. 1, p. 283.

3 See *The George Eliot Letters*, ed. Gordon S. Haight (New Haven, Yale University Press, 1956–78), vol. 8, pp. 156–60 for acrimonious correspondence between GHL and Bohn. The translation was offered to A. and C. Black in 1859, and eventually appeared as *Ethics, by Benedict de Spinoza. Translated by George Eliot*, ed. Thomas Deegan (Salzburg, Salzburg Studies in English Literature: Romantic Reassessment 102, 1981). Deegan points out that 'There was no critical edition of the *Ethics* in her time', and that GE's work was that of textual editor as well as translator – she compared three Latin versions of the *Ethics*, and the French and German translations (p. vii).

books. Through Varnhagen, and at the salon of Henriette Solmar, they met many writers and intellectuals who are sketched more fully in 'Recollections of Berlin'. GE reports without comment on 6 February 'Went out in the evening first to Stahr's, who was gone to be married at last to Fanny Lewald after 9 years of waiting': the celebrated novelist Lewald and the egotistical scholar Adolf Stahr had openly lived out of wedlock all that time.

GE pursued her self-education in art not only in reading such studies as Stahr's newly published *Torso: Kunst, Künstler and Kunstwerke der Alten* (1854), but also in a practical way in studying the massive collections accessible to her in Berlin (once she had sorted out the opening times: very limited by today's standards, and frequently dependent on an introduction or similar formality): the ancient art, Egyptology, Northern antiquities, and modern paintings in the Old and New Museums, and the latest works on display in private galleries. During this time, perhaps influenced by Stahr, she manifested a particular interest in sculpture, absorbing herself in the many casts in the Berlin collections as well as the original sculptures.

In addition to fraternising with men of letters, GHL was concerned particularly to establish contacts with Berlin's scientific community through such men as the physiologist Johannes von Müller and the chemist Heinrich Magnus. He was to give unprecedented attention to Goethe's discoveries in the fields of botany and anatomy in the *Life*, and soon pursued scientific subjects in popular works such as *Sea-Side Studies* (1858) and *Physiology of Common Life* (2 vols, 1859–60).

GE and GHL left Berlin on 11 March 1855 and returned to set up house in England.

Cross draws mainly on the entries in the diary to do with GE and GHL at work; Haight quotes very little.

2. Berlin, 3 November 1854 – March 1855

4 Saturday. After Breakfast went out in search of lodgings, and at length fixed on 62, Dorotheen Strasse, at 28 thalers per month. Dined at the Hotel de l'Europe and at 6 o'clock came to our lodgings and unpacked.

Sunday 5. A bright morning. We walked out and met Varnhagen in the Linden. Dined at the Hôtel de l'Europe. In the evening G. went to Fräulein Solmar's. Berlin is very much what I expected. The people look very smart and brisk after the Weimarians.

Tuesday 7. Varnhagen called and invited us to take tea with him on Thursday. A fine looking courtly old man. He told us of his disappointment in Carlyle when after years of correspondence they at last met in the body. Carlyle was full of anathemas against the Frau von Stein. Read Vehse's Weimar in the evening.

Wednesday 8. Began translating Spinoza's Ethics. Wrote to Mrs. Robert Noel to thank her for trying to get me an introduction to Humboldt. Read Wilhelm Meister aloud in the evening.

Thursday. 9. Read Rosenkranz on the Faust Sage. Translated Spinoza. Dessoir came and staid more than an hour. Then we walked out and looked at the engravings in the Linden. At 5 o'clock went to Varnhagen's and found a very pleasant little party: Fräulein Solmar, Frau Nimsch, Doctor Ring, Dr. Vehse, Gräfin von Kalkreit, and Director Wilhelm Schadow, author of "Der moderne Vasari". We talked of Goethe; Varnhagen brought out autographs and portraits and read us an epigram of his own on the want of liberality which Goethe's family shew about opening his house to the public. He showed us a portrait of Kleist who shot himself in company with Frau Vogel near an inn on the way to Potsdam. There was no love affair between them: they were both thoroughly unhappy, he poor and hopeless for the future, and she suffering from an incurable disease. In the evening they both wrote on a single sheet of paper letters to their friends communicating their intention. (This sheet Varnhagen possesses.) Early in the morning they rose, took a cup of coffee, went to the brink of a piece of water in the neighbourhood of the inn and there shot themselves. We came away at 8. Fräulein Assing, Varnhagen's niece, lent me a volume of Heine's poems. I read aloud "Donna Clara" and then Wilhelm Meister till 10.

10 Friday. We walked through the Museum this morning and were struck with the beauty of the interior and the excellent arrangement of the works of art. Not many very valuable pictures, but still an interesting collection. Titian's daughter, Correggio's "Schweisstuch" and some portraits of Titian's school particularly impressed me. We came home and wrote a little. The day then became very unpleasant with snow and sleet. We battled our way to the Hotel de l'Europe for dinner and enjoyed the thought of getting back into our warm

rooms with the "feste Vorschlag"[1] not to turn out again. I read Wilhelm Meister aloud, and then G. read part of the Merchant of Venice.

11 Saturday. I read Heine's poems; wrote a few recollections of Weimar and translated Genealogical Tables of the Goethe family. Then we went to call on Fräulein von Solmar, who was exceedingly agreeable, and invited me to visit her when I pleased of an evening. Walked to the Wilhelmsplatz and Leipziger Platz, for the first time. In the evening went to see "Nathan der Weise". The Theatre very elegant and comfortable. Döring as Nathan excellent. The Patriarch immensely comic – "Es thut nichts, der Jude wird verbrannt",[2] the essence of the dogmatic spirit. Both thrilled by the grandeur of the sentiments. I felt that it was a noble inspiration which dictated such writing. The scenery was excellent, particularly a street in Jerusalem and the garden in the last scene. The sky was grand on our way to the theatre – the stars bright on a sable field. I began Lessing's Laocoon in bed.

12 Sunday. Wrote to Mr. Bray. Walked till dinner. Went to Kroll's – a wonderful kind of Casino, where there are concerts, theatricals, balls, and dinners. Read Wilhelm Meister and G's MS.

13 Monday. Letter from Mr. Noel enclosing a letter for Humboldt. Read Laocoon. Translated Spinoza. Du Bois-Reymond called just as we came in from Dinner. He spoke very decidedly of the German civilization as inferior to the English. A handsome, young looking man. He spoke English very well, and accounted for it by telling us that he had an English wife. In the evening came Gruppe – a cordial, lively man. He gave us an interesting account of his work on the Cosmic systems of the Greeks.

Tuesday. We took tea at Fräulein von Solmar's. General Pfuhl, Varnhagen and his niece (Fräulein von Assing), Baron Sternberg, Drs. Crepet, and Vehse. In the morning Dessoir came, and after dinner Johannes von Müller called.

Wednesday. 15. G. called on Fanny Lewald. In the evening we went to Spargnapini's, and had some chocolate and read the papers. G. finished reading allowed [sic] the Merchant of Venice, and I the first vol. of Wilhelm Meister.

Thursday 16. Fanny Lewald called. Letter from Herbert Spencer.

Friday 17. We strolled into the Museum and looked at the Flemish pictures. The beauty of detail and the marvellous painting of still life in some of the pictures which belong to a low development of art is very remarkable. Here is the original of Vandyke's famous portrait of Charles the 1st's children.

Saturday. Ill all day and unable to go out. G. finished Romeo and Juliet.

Sunday 19. Finished Lessing's Laocoon – the most un-German of all German books that I have ever read. The style is strong clear and lively, the thoughts

1 German, 'firm proposal'.
2 German, 'It doesn't matter, the Jew will burn'.

acute and pregnant. It is well adapted to rouse an interest both in the classics and in the study of art. After working as usual, we walked in the Thier-garten and saw many new spots. In the evening we went to Fräulein von Solmar's.

Tuesday 21. Wrote to Herbert Spencer. Letters from Coventry.[3] In the evening went to Gruppe's. Amusing simplicity with which he played the schoolboy's trick with the three lumps of sugar under three hats. He drew some Jews' faces with a pen admirably. We attempted "Brag" or "*Pochen*", but Gruppe presently became alarmed at G's play and said "Das würde an zwölf groschen reichen!"[4] Then G. diverted them with tricks and so concluded the evening rather brilliantly.

Wednesday. Wrote letters to Coventry and to my brother. In the evening went to the theatre to see Emilia Galotti. The acting bad with the exception of Dessoir's (Masinelli). The play seems to me a wretched mistake of Lessing's.[5] The Roman myth of Virginius is grand, but the situation transported to modern times and divested of its political bearing is simply shocking. Read Nathan on coming home.

Thursday 24 [23]. Began "Briefe über Spinoza". Walked a couple of hours in the Thiergarten. The snow beautiful on the trees for the first time. Translated and wrote Recollections till dinner. In the evening Rauch, the sculptor came – the finest old man I ever saw and the most charming. His head is noble, his features harmonious and his expression extremely winning. He told us many interesting things about Goethe whom he knew well, and thoroughly agreed with G's quotation from Jung Stilling. Rauch is tall and finely formed; his beautiful head is surmounted with silky, wavy white hair, and when he is standing he is really grand. It was a sort of cordial to look at him, his face was so beaming.

Friday 25 [24]. Went to Mlle. Solmar's in the evening to meet a cousin of Frau von Goethe's, who however was not there. Varnhagen, as usual very agreeable and Dr. Vehse very noisy. In the morning a letter from Mr. Noel introducing Dr. Fischer.

Saturday. The weather continues disagreeable and the streets dirty. Read Jacobi's Briefe über Spinoza. Wrote to Dr. Fischer. Translated Spinoza, on final causes. Walked out to the Neue Museum, but found we were too late, so came back and lounged in a bookshop. Home for half an hour and read Nathan der Weise. "Wandlungen" at Dinner. Wilhelm Meister aloud. About 1/2 past 6 the Gruppes came, sat with us some time and asked us to go to see them on Tuesday

3 From Charles and Cara Bray: see *Letters*, vol. 2, pp. 178–90.

4 German, 'That amounts to 12 groschen'.

5 Cf. GHL's article for the *Edinburgh Review*, 82 (1845), pp. 451–70 where he writes of Lessing's 'radical error in the conception' of *Emilia Galotti*: *George Eliot: A Writer's Notebook*, ed. Joseph Weisenfarth (Charlottesville, University Press of Virginia, 1981), p. 48.

and meet *Waagen*. G. read Julius Cæsar aloud, as far as Cæsar's appearance in the senate house. Very much struck with the masculine style of this play and its vigorous moderation compared with Romeo and Juliet.

Sunday. After working, we walked till dinner time in the Thiergarten. I read aloud Wilhelm Meister and then G. finished Julius Cæsar. At 9 o'clock we turned out to Spargnapini's, to have chocolate and see the papers. Gruppe sent to invite us for to-morrow instead of Tuesday.

Monday. Waited at home for Dr. Fischer who didn't come. Then walked in the Thiergarten half an hour alone. In the evening went to Gruppe's. Dr. Waagen, his wife and daughters were there. He is an intelligent, lively man. His wife serious looking because of bad teeth. Amusing judgment passed on Goethe – that he was "Kein dummer mann!"[6] Capital story of a lady who went to see him as an intellectual adorer, and began to spout to him, as his masterpiece, "Festgemauert in der Erden"[7] etc.

Tuesday. Wrote to Chrissey. A clear, lovely morning.

Wednesday. Finished *Minna von Barnhelm*. Finished *Wilhelm Meister*. G. began Antony and Cleopatra. Snowy and wet. Magnus the chemist called.

Thursday. Finished Recollections of Weimar. Began the *Italiänische Reise*.

Friday. Not well in the morning. Finished Fanny Lewald's *Wandlungen*. In the evening went to the theatre to see "Die Königin von Navarre", a translation of a French piece. Poor and badly acted.

Saturday. Bad headache. In the evening to the Theatre to see Othello. Dessoir as Othello, Döring as Iago, Frau Hoppe as Desdemona.

Sunday. Shocking weather still. Walked in the Thiergarten. Dispute with our landlord. Looked at Scherr's Deutsche Cultur und Sitte. In the evening read *Italiänische Reise* – residence in Venice. G. read Antony and Cleopatra.

Monday. Dec. 4. Took coffee at Varnhagen's – Frau von Treskow, Frau von Solmar, Prof. Dirikles and his wife, Prof. Stahr and Fanny Lewald. I talked principally with Prof. Stahr, about German style, Lessing, Spinoza, History of Jesus etc.

Tuesday. G's head bad. So we went to Magnus's, saw his portraits and had an agreeable chat with him. A man whose ideas are bornées,[8] but acute, straightforward and amiable. Portraits of Thorwaldsen, Mendelssohn and Sontag. As we were returning home, Dessoir called out "Bon jour" behind us and came in with us. Discussed his Othello. He said he found himself inevitably

6 German, 'Not a stupid man'.

7 German, 'Solidly built on earth', the first line of Schiller's 'Song of the Bell'.

8 French, 'limited, shallow'.

led into sing-song declamation by Schiller, but with Shakspear it was impossible to be declamatory. "'Shakspear,' he said, 'ist mein Gott – ich habe keinen anderen Gott.'"[9] Magnus, the other day, told us a rich story about Carlyle. At a dinner party given by Magnus in honour of Carlyle, Wiese and Cornelius were deploring Goethe's want of evangelical sentiment. Carlyle was visibly uneasy, fumbling with his dinner napkin. At last, he broke out thus: "Meine Herren, kennen Sie die Anekdote von dem Manne, der die Sonne lästerte weil sie ihn seine Cigarre nicht anstecken liess?"[10] In the evening we read the Italiänische Reise – the residence in Rome. A beautiful description of Rome and the Coliseum by moonlight – a fire made in the Coliseum sending its smoke, silvered by the moonlight, through the arches of the mighty walls. Amusing story of his landlady's cat worshipping Jupiter by licking his beard – a miracle in her esteem, explained by Goethe as a discovery the cat had made of the oil lodging in the undulations of the beard.

Wednesday. 6. G's head not well, so at 1 o'clock we set off to the Thiergarten, and explored a part we had not seen before. Talked about the factitious admiration of the Old English dramatists got up by Charles Lamb's selections – Schlegel and his criticisms etc. Walked back only just in time to dine at the British Hotel. The dinner splendid, but too dear for our pocket – 20 groschen each. Read Italiänische Reise – Residence in Naples. Pretty passage about a star seen through a chink in the ceiling as he lay in bed. G. read Henry IV, and about 1/4 past the Gruppes came. They staid chatting till after 10.

Thursday. I have begun Scherr's Geschichte Deutschen Cultur und Sitte. Worked at Spinoza. Walked in the Thiergarten. Dined at Pietsch's, and then went into Kranzler's where G. was to wait for Magnus the Chemist, who had promised to take him to the Sitz of the Akademie. However he soon came back to me, having wisely given up the Sitz in favour of a party at Prof. Olfers', where he was to go with Magnus the painter. I read the Italiänische Reise till it was time for him to dress. It is remarkable that when Goethe gets to Sicily, he is for the first time in Italy enthusiastic in his descriptions of natural beauty. G. went at 8 and I spent the evening alone for the first time since we have been at Berlin. I read G's Farce – Robson's adventure with a Russian Princess. Letter from Mr. Chapman – a chef d'œuvre of bad taste.[11]

Thursday [Friday]. Read Scherr – worked at Spinoza – walked in the Thiergarten. A lovely morning. We talked of Keely and Macready. Came home and wrote a little, then went to dine at the Hotel de l'Europe. I took Iphigenia to read. Italiänische Reise until Dessoir came. He read us the opening of Richard the 3rd and the scene with Lady Anne. Then Shylock, which G. afterwards read.

9 German, 'Shakespeare is my God – I have no other God'.

10 German, 'Gentlemen, do you know the story of the man who railed at the sun because it would not light his cigar?'

11 GE's reply of 9 December 1854 is perfectly cordial however: see *Letters*, vol. 8, pp. 131–2.

Dessoir told us an amusing story out of his early experiences among strolling actors, and imitated admirably Aldridge's mode of advancing to kill Duncan – like a wild Indian lurking for a not much wilder beast. Finished 1st act of Iphigenia.

Saturday. Miserably wet day. Read Scherr – Mythology of the Germans. Worked at Spinoza. Wrote to Mr. Chapman. Read Italiänische Reise aloud. G. read Henry IV.

Sunday. 10. Read Scherr. Worked at Spinoza. Called on Fräulein von Assing. Finished Italiänische Reise. G. Finished Henry IV First Part.

Monday. Scherr – Spinoza – Thiergarten. MS. of Goethe's Life. Fräulein von Solmar's. Letter from Rosehill enclosing one from my Brother.

Tuesday. Scherr. Spinoza. Dessoir walked with us in the Thiergarten and told us an amusing story about his early days. When he was a youth of sixteen or seventeen acting at Spandau, he walked to Berlin (about 9 miles) and back in the evening accompanied by a watchmaker named Naundorf, an enthusiast for the theatre. On their way Dessoir declaimed at the top of his voice and was encouraged by the applause of his companion to more and more exertion of lungs and limbs, so that people stared at them and followed them as if they thought them two madmen. This watchmaker was Louis XVII! Dined at the Hotel de l'Europe and read Iphigenia. Looked into the Xenien and amused ourselves with their pointlessness. Read Hermann and Dorothea – 4 first books. G. read 2nd Part of Henry IV.

Wednesday. Scherr. Head not clear, so I did not get through much of Spinoza this morning. Dined by Dessoir's invitation at Diets's, to meet Hofrath Förster and Professor Roetscher. The former served in the Prussian army at Waterloo – Theodor Körner died in his arms.

Thursday. Bad headache. A regularly wet morning. Read the Athenæum and Leader and finished Iphigenia. In the evening finished Hermann and Dorothea. Read Henry IV 2nd part. Still headachy.

Friday. Wretched weather – impossible to walk out. Read Scherr. Worked at Spinoza. Read G's MS. – Weimar period. Went to the Opera for the first time to hear "Die Stumme von Portici". Very well put on the stage, and the orchestra good, but the singing bad. Formes, the tenor, is a stumpy man with neither voice, execution, nor dramatic talent. His wife acted Fenella prettily. We left at the end of the third act, and enjoyed walking about in the fresh air. When we came in, G. finished Henry IV 2nd part. A letter from Mrs. Noel telling me that her husband is called to join his militia regiment.

Saturday. 16. Scherr. Spinoza. At 12 I went to take a warm bath. Then wrote to Mrs. Noel and we walked till dinner. At the Hôtel de l'Europe. Began Tasso aloud. G. read two acts of *As you like it*.

Sunday. Scherr. Worked well at Spinoza. From 1 to 2 we walked in the Thiergarten and enjoyed greatly the clear air and sunshine, which has been so long wanting. Came home and worked an hour longer – then went to dine at the Hôtel de l'Europe. On our way home Dessoir overtook us and came with us. He staid till 8 o'clock talking chiefly of Hamlet and discussing the question of madness or affectation of madness. Read Scherr.

Monday. 18. Read Scherr. Finished revising Part I of Spinoza's Ethics. Walked till dinner. Read a little of Tasso and then we went to Prof. Gruppe's and spent a pleasant evening with him, his wife and her naïve sister. G. acted a little of Shylock for them. I was amused to see that the young women's feeling towards the Jews was not much above that of Gratiano and co. Frau Gruppe when running through the wonderful speech "Hath not a Jew eyes" etc turned round to us and said "They don't feel – they don't care how they are used". Gruppe read us a translation of one of the Homeric Hymns – Aphrodite – which is really beautiful. It is a sort of Gegenstück to "Der Gott und die Bayadere".[12] He has struck out 150 lines which he believes to be interpolated and the connection of the poem appears perfect. Gruppe's theory of the numerous interpolations found in ancient authors is, that booksellers or rather publishers foisted them in order to recommend their new editions as possessing something new.

Tuesday. Scherr. Began Part II of Ethics. Walked into the town and in the Thiergarten. Came in and wrote. In the evening we expected Magnus but he didn't come. I began to read aloud the Wanderjahre. G. read 'As you like it'. Tasso.

Wednesday. Scherr. Spinoza. Tasso to dinner. Began Heine's Geständnisse and immensely amused with his wit. Went to Frau Solmar's and had a very pleasant evening.

Thursday. Scherr – much interested in his sketch of German poetry in the Middle Ages. Copied the appendix to 1st book of Ethics. We walked out determined to explore the town a little and went along the Friedrichstrasse to the Oranien thor, a ridiculously ugly structure. Passing through this gate we pursued a road which brought us within sight of a high bronze column surmounted by a column. We thought this worth going to and found that it is dedicated to those who fell for "Gott, König und Vaterland"[13] in 1848 and 1849. It is really a splendid monument. There is a sort of court round it on the walls of which polished granite tablets contain in golden letters the names of the "martyrs" to whom the column is dedicated. The King of Prussia's unpleasant face stands in medallion over the inscription in front of the column – speaking

12 German, 'counterpart to *The God and the Hindu Dancing Girl*'. Gruppe is presumably referring to Goethe's work *Der Gott und die Bayadere*.

13 German, 'God, King and Fatherland'. A quarrel over the price of potatoes led to the Revolution of 1848 in Berlin, in which 200 people were killed.

very ill for the God with whom he makes common cause. If this fine monument had been dedicated to some real heroism how it would have thrilled us! – Finished Tasso. After coffee, finished aloud Heine's Geständnisse. The wit burns low after the first 50 pages and the want of principle and purpose make it wearisome. G. finished "As you like it". He then went to Prof. Olfers', and I wrote at Spinoza.

Friday. Scherr, Spinoza, walk in the rain. Began Lessing's Hamburgische Briefe at dinner. Read aloud Heine's "Götter im Exil" and some of his poems. G read Lear. Copied out some translation for G.

Sat. 23. Scherr. Spinoza. A lovely day once again. We had a delightful walk in the Thiergarten. An uncomfortable letter came for G. from London. G. went with Dessoir to call on Roetscher so I came home alone and turned over the Dichtung und Wahrheit. When G. came in again read Wanderjahre *à mourir d'ennui*.[14]

Sunday. Read Scherr – Scholasticism, Universities and Roman law. Worked at Spinoza. Walked to the Neue Museum, but failed to get in. Came home and copied Goethe's Discourse on Shakspeare. Read, at dinner, his wonderful observations on Spinoza. Particularly struck with the beautiful modesty of the passage in which he says he cannot presume to say that he thoroughly understands Spinoza. After Coffee read aloud G's M.S. of the Leipsic and beginning of the Strasburg Period. G. finished Lear – sublimely powerful!

Monday. Christmas day. Miserably wet. Read Scherr – Birth of the modern drama in the Mysteries. Made little way in Spinoza from inclination to headache. Wrote to Mr. Bray. Read Wanderjahre. Taming of the Shrew.

Tuesday. Scherr. Spinoza. Long walk in the Thiergarten. Read Wanderjahre and Taming of the Shrew.

Wednesday. Scherr. Translated passages from the Kestner Briefe. Very wet again, so we did not walk long. Read a little in Wanderjahre and then read Heine's "Allemagne" in the German edition. G finished Taming of the Shrew. Letter from Princess Wittgenstein.

Thursday. Translated passages from the Kestner letters. It was a lovely morning and we enjoyed walking 2 hours, first in the Thiergarten and afterwards in the town. As we were coming in we met Stahr and Fanny Lewald who had been calling on us and we agreed to go to see them tomorrow evening. Read at dinner Goethe's account of his relations with Herder at Strasburg in Dichtung und Wahrheit. Continued aloud Heine's *Salon*. G. read Knight's Studies of Shakspeare. Twaddling in the extreme.

14 French, 'to die of boredom'. GHL writes 'it is unintelligible, it is tiresome, it is fragmentary, it is dull' (*Life of Goethe*, vol. 2, p. 418).

Friday 29. A fine frosty morning. Wrote to Mr. Noel and to my Sister. Worked a little at Spinoza but not well enough to do much. Read a little of Scherr. Read aloud Heine's Salon. Then we went to Prof. Stahr's and spent the evening there. A remarkable miniature of Schiller of which there is no engraving. We talked of the Wahlverwandschaften, amongst other things. Stahr finding fault with the dénouement which I defended. (Concession or license)

Saturday. Rainy again. After breakfast we went to the Bank and then on to Rauch's Atelier, where we found the beautiful old man superintending the modelling of a statue of *Moses praying with Aaron and Hur holding up his arms*. This was the first visit I ever paid to a sculptor's atelier. It was very interesting to me to see the small clay model done by Rauch himself – the wonderful expression thrown into the bit of clay forming the face of Moses. We also saw his model for a statue of Kant. Rauch himself saw Kant in 1789. When we went into the other rooms on the opposite side of the court we were joined by M. Crepet the good-looking Frenchman who is writing a book about Prussia. Some workmen were finishing in marble the figure of the King of Hanover, to be placed on a sarcophagus. There was a Danaïd in marble – not striking. A monument of the Queen Luise in another room was all that had any interest for us. We paddled home through the rain and were in again at 1 o'clock. Rauch is 75 or 77. A curious black silhouette of Kant interested me extremely. – G's head bad in the evening so that we had little reading.

Sunday. Dec. 31. Translated passages from Kestner's letters. Began Stahr's Torso. Read, after coffee, G's MS. Then we went to Fräulein Solmar's – not at home. Came back and G read Coriolanus. I read some of Stahr to him, but we found it too long-winded a style for reading aloud.

Monday 1 [January 1855]. Read Stahr. Worked at Spinoza. Read Heine in the evening – on German Philosophy. G. read Coriolanus.

Tuesday 2. Stahr. Spinoza and bit of Kestner letters. Warm bath, walk and dinner, with Athenæum. In the evening read a bit of Heine and then went to the Opera to hear Johanna Wagner in Gluck's Orpheus and Eurydice. Delighted with the music and with her singing and acting, but irritated by the stupid ballet-girl groups in Elysium and in the last scene before the temple of Love. The Greek shades in the back ground in Elysium looked like butchers in women's chemises. Tuczek, who was *Amor*, and sang very well, had a headdress which made her look like a shop-girl, and the Eurydice who sang disagreeably was such a scarecrow that she made the long act between her and Orpheus almost ludicrous. We talked about *symbolism* – how far it prevailed among the Greeks. I got a dreadful headache from the bad air and rushed to bed when we reached home.

Wednesday 3. My head was better so that I was able to work well at Spinoza all morning. Then we walked out and turned into the Museum to glance at the pictures – Titian's daughter, Correggio's Semele, and a charming "Weibliche

Figur"[15] in a brown mantle. Read Heine in the evening and felt my headache returning. G. finished Coriolanus. Went to bed with a bad headache.

Thursday 4. Head still bad – unable to work. Took a bath and walked a little till dinner. Read Heine. Walked in the avenue leading to Kroll's, which looked pretty, lighted with gas. G. then went to Prof. Olfers'. I went to bed early, not being well yet.

Friday 5. Better. Read a little of Stahr and worked a little at Spinoza. At 12 Gruppe surprized us and staid chatting nearly an hour. Thinks Shakspear more extensively sold in Germany than any other works except the Bible and Schiller! Read Hamburgische Briefe at dinner. G. went to Dessoir's and at 6 o'clock returned with Dessoir, who read some of Hamlet to us and staid talking till 8. Then we went to Fräulein Solmar's. Glad to see the old General Pfuhl once again. G. read Shylock, but seemed to be very imperfectly understood.

Saturday. Dr. Fischer called and brought me Kugler's History of Painting with a pamphlet by himself. Then Magnus came and chatted for an hour or so. I finished Heine's *Salon*. G read some of Twelfth Night, but his head got bad and he was obliged to leave off.

Sunday. Not well this morning and made little way in my work. We had a long walk in the Thiergarten. G was to have gone to Graf York's in the evening, but felt poorly, so he staid at home. Read Goethe's Maxims in the Wanderjahre. Then we compared several scenes of Hamlet in Schlegel's translation with the original. It is generally very close and often admirably well done but Shakspear's strong concrete language is almost always weakened. For example, "Though this hand were *thicker than* itself in brother's blood" is rendered "auch *um und um* in Bruder's Blut *getauct*".[16] The prose speeches of Hamlet lose all their felicity in the translation.

Monday. Stahr on the Eginetan sculptures. Spinoza. Walked in the Thiergarten. Came back and wrote a little before going to dinner. Read Dr. Fischer's pamphlet. Read Wanderjahre – Die Neue Melusine. Stahr.

Tuesday. Not well. We walked out till nearly 1. Then G. dictated article on Mrs Austin's book. Finished Wanderjahre, skippingly. G. read Twelfth Night. We walked out at 9 for half an hour. Came in and read Stahr. – I felt deeply the beauty of the wintry woods this morning -

> "Shadows brown that Sylvan loves".[17]

15 German, 'womanly figure'.

16 German, 'plunged further and further in brother's blood'.

17 'And shadows brown that Sylvan loves'. John Milton, 'Il Penseroso', l. 134 in *Poetical Works of John Milton*, ed. Helen Darbishire (Oxford University Press, 1958).

Wednesday. Read Stahr and finished translating the 2nd Book of Ethics. We walked in the Thiergarten by sunshine – the first we have had for many days. Began the West-Östliche Divan. Walked out under the Linden. Came in and read Stahr etc.

Thursday 11. We went in the evening to Gruppe's. He read to us parts of a poem "Ferdusi" still in M.S. which is to be read to the King. Received letters from my sister and Mr. Chapman.

Friday. We went to hear "*Fidelio*". After returning I wrote to Mr. Chapman and Miss Hennell.

Saturday 13. Staid at home this evening and read G's MS. Book 3. Took a little walk under the Linden and afterwards read Twelfth Night.

Sunday. Stahr. Spinoza. We had a delightful two hours' walk in the frosty air towards Charlottenburg. Talked about Spinoza. Read Hamburgische Briefe at dinner about Voltaire's Mérope. Read G's MS. *Measure for Measure.*

Monday 15. Stahr – Spinoza – Walk in the Thiergarten. West-Östliche Divan – Measure for Measure. Bitterly cold.

Tuesday. Stahr. Spinoza. Walked in the Thiergarten and saw the skaters. Went to the Opera and heard Gluck's Iphigenia in Tauris. Very grand. The drama as in Euripides.

Wednesday. Stahr. Little done at Spinoza, as I was not well and went to have a bath. We walked in the Thiergarten and being too late for our usual dining-place went into a new one in the Charlotten Strasse. Finished the poetry of the West-Östliche Divan. Finished Measure for Measure.

Thursday 18. Very cold. Read Stahr. Revised Spinoza. We walked in the town, bitten by the keen air. Read G's M.S. Not well. G. began Midsummer Night's Dream. I went to bed early.

Friday 19. Still very poorly. The cold more and more intense. Tried reading the 2nd Part of Faust aloud, but gave it up, as it was too difficult for G. to follow it rapidly enough. Read a little of Gervinus on Shakspeare, but found it unsatisfactory. Read some of Stahr's "Ein Jahr in Italien". The description of Florence excellent. Midsummer Night's Dream. Very poorly all day.

Saturday 20. Finished the revisal of Book II of Spinoza. We walked a little before dinner, but suffered terribly from the cold. Read the wondrously beautiful "Römische Elegien" again and some of the Venetian Epigrams. G. began "Winter's Tale". Wrote to his dictation an article on Gluck and Johanna Wagner. Received a letter from Mr. Chapman requesting me to prepare an article on Vehse's Court of Austria for the next No. of the Westminster.

Sunday 21. The snow has fallen at last and it is a little milder. Wrote to Mr. Chapman agreeing to write the article on Vehse and to my sister proposing to send her £10 this year for Emily's school bill. This evening we went to Mlle. Solmar's. A Frenchman there amused us by saying that he found in Meyerbeer's Huguenots the whole spirit of the epoch of Charles IX. "Lisez les Chroniques" – de *Froissart*, suggested Mlle. Solmar – "Oui quelque chose comme ça, ou bien les Chroniques de Brantome ou de *Merimée*, et vous trouverez que Meyerbeer a parfaitement exprimé tout cela – du moins c'est ce [que] je trouve moi."[18] I said: "Mais, peutêtre Monsieur, c'est votre génie à vous qui a fait entrer les idées dans la musique."[19] He answered with complacent deprecation. G. looked immovably serious; but was inwardly tickled by the audacity of my compliment and the evident acceptance of it.

Monday. Read Stahr. Called on Miss Assing to try and borrow Vehse's book from Varnhagen. He does not possess it, so G. called on Vehse and asked him to lend it me; he was very much pleased to do so. In the evening read G's MS., finished the Venetian epigrams, read the "Zueignung"[20] to the "Gedichte" and several of the Ballads. G. read Winter's Tale.

Tuesday 23. Read Stahr and two first vols. of Vehse. Called at Vehse's for the other volumes. Encountered *Vivier* in our walk. He came to us at 5 and chatted until 6. Then we went to hear the reading of Gruppe's Ferdusi. But the reading was bad and the room insufferably hot. So we came away and read Shakspeare at home.

Wednesday. Read Vehse. In the afternoon some of G's M.S. and *Goethe's Ballads*. Then we went to Gruppe's and finished the evening.

Thursday. Read Vehse. Not well. In the evening read Göthe's Ballads. G. went to Madame Olfers' and I read Stahr.

Friday. Finished Stahr. Read Vehse. Dessoir called and showed us the sketches Charles Kean had sent him for his Richard III. Read Goethe's Poems and finished Winter's Tale.

Saturday 27. Read 5th vol. of Vehse. Very poorly all morning. In the evening went to see the "Fechter von Ravenna". The Fechter is Thumelieus the Son of Arminius. Thusnelda his mother, discovers her son in this position and to save him from the dishonour of appearing as a gladiator, she kills him. Dessoir as Caligula was very good. Madame Crelinger, as Thusnelda, made the wearisome part doubly wearisome by her want of feeling. She is nearly sixty. Her voice is still fine and her declamation often good. Dr. Fischer called this morning.

18 French, "Read the Chronicles" – of Froissart, suggested Miss Solmar.

"Yes something like that, or rather the Chronicles of Brantôme or Merimée, and you will find that Meyerbeer has expressed all that perfectly – at least that is what I find."

19 French, 'I said "But perhaps, Monsieur, it is your own genius that has put the ideas into the music" '.

20 German, 'Dedication'.

Sunday 28. Continued Vehse. In the evening G. went to Graf York's.

Monday 29. Vehse. In the evening read G's MS and Richard III.

Tuesday 30. Read Goethe's Poems. Magnus the painter came and spent an hour or two with us. Then G. read Richard III.

31. Wednesday. Bitterly cold again. G went to Dessoir's, and afterwards to Rauch's.

Feb 1. Thursday. Not very well. Wrote part of article on Stahr. G.'s head wretchedly bad, so we had very little reading in the evening.

2 Friday. Bad headache. Read Vehse all morning. In the evening Vivier sent us tickets for his concert. Roger sang admirably – amongst other things the *Erlkönig*, with wonderful dramatic expression. Johanna Wagner sang, but not agreeably. Arabella Goddard played the Harmonious Blacksmith charmingly. Vivier's horn was delightful – he played his own music. – The King[21] was there, toothless and imbecile.

3 Saturday. Head very bad. Looked through Wraxall's Memoirs. Unable to go and see Richard III as I had hoped to do. Wrote article on Stahr.

4 Sunday. Better. Finished article on Stahr. We walked in the Thiergarten once more. In the evening began Macaulay's History of England. Richard III and G's M.S. on Goethe's scientific labours.

5 Monday. Wrote to Mr. Chapman. Went to the Bank and then to the Neue Museum. It is on a grand scale, worthy of a great nation and shames the British Museum. One room is devoted to the sculptures of the Parthenon and the Eginetan Sculptures which are admirably arranged. We saw some fine sketches by Kaulbach of the "Sage" History, Architecture etc.

6. Tuesday. I took cold at the Museum yesterday and began this morning to feel very uncomfortable from it. Wrote from Vehse. Went out in the evening first to Stahr's, who was gone to be married at last to Fanny Lewald after 9 years of waiting, then to Gruppe's who also was not at home and finally to Fräulein Solmar's. No one there besides M. Vautageux.

7 Wednesday. Cold worse. Worked at Vehse. In the evening read Macaulay and Hamlet.

8 Thursday. Still uncomfortable from my cold. Macaulay and Hamlet.

9 Friday. In the evening went to Prof. Magnus's the chemist. A large Party: Johannes Müller, Du Bois-Reymond – Prof. Ehrenberg, Mendelssohn's brother etc. etc. The rooms elegant and the supper profuse.

21 Friedrich Wilhelm IV (1795–1861) and King of Prussia from 1840.

10 Saturday, 11 Sunday, 12 Monday. Still uncomfortable from cold. The weather very severe.

13 [14] Wednesday. To Gruppe's in the evening. Played whist.

14 [15] Thursday. Worked at article on Vehse. Read G's MS. of Friendship between Schiller and Goethe.

15 [16] Friday. Went to see Richard III.

Sunday. 25. Since I last wrote in my Journal, I have been working well at my article on Vehse and have finished two thirds of it, we have spent an evening with the Stahrs and had visits from the Gruppes and Magnus. The weather is at length milder, and thick as the snow was it has almost disappeared in two days thaw – that is to say as white snow, for a great deal still remains as mud in the streets. I have been very poorly several days this week but have nevertheless managed to work. We have read Macaulay every evening, but no Shakspear. This evening I have been reading aloud G's M.S. of his last Book so far as he has done it.

Monday March 5. A great part of this week has been lost from terrible headache which came on on Tuesday and lasted till Saturday. On Thursday we went to Dr. Parthey's, formerly *Nicolai's* to see some illustrations of Shakspear by Kaulbach. We saw the original of the scene in Macbeth where he is putting on his armour and news is brought him of his wife's death, – and an engraving of the meeting of Macbeth with the witches. Also a water colour sketch by Thorwaldsen of Dante and Virgil descending into the Inferno, an admirable engraving of Albert Dürer's and a portrait of old Nicolai by Graf. G. was enraptured with a lovely engraving of the "Triumph of Galatea". On leaving Dr. Parthey's we went to the old Museum to look at the sculpture. Two Reposing Fawns, a Jupiter and an Apollo, the most remarkable things in the Rotunde. In the evening we went to see Döring's Shylock which was unmitigatedly bad. Friday and Saturday I was suffering again from my head. In the evening, however, I finished my article and yesterday (Sunday 4th) sent it to London. We walked with Dessoir in the Thiergarten and enjoyed the delicious, springlike day. In the evening I read Macaulay and wrote an article to G's dictation on Brodie's Psychological Inquiries. Today (Monday) we walked in the Thiergarten and went to Count Raczinsky's Picture Gallery – a very interesting collection which we mean to visit again. Kaulbach's *Hunnen Schlacht* and *Deutsche Sage*. Group of Italians outside St. Peter's by De La Roche. Sons of Edward IV by Hildebrand. In the evening Dessoir came and read Hamlet. G. acted Shylock.

Tuesday 6. Wrote to Varnhagen and Magnus. Went to the Neue Museum and saw the Egyptian collection and the Hall of Northern Antiquities – looked again at the Treppenhaus and then feasted on the sculptures of the Parthenon. Dined at Meinhardt's. In the evening went to the Gruppes and said good bye to them.

Wednesday 7. Walked to the Wilhelm Stadt and ascertained when we could see the Wagner'sche and Ravené'sche galleries. Then to Graf Raczinsky's gallery again. Called on the Dessoirs, dined at Meinhardt's and in the evening went to see Das Glas Wasser, a version of Scribe's "Un verre d'eau".

Thursday 8. Went to the Wagner Gallery; a collection of pictures by modern German artists. The only things that interested us at all were: a group of fishermen, one of whom is recounting to a fisherman's wife the story of her husband's wreck, by *Jordan*, an infant Christ by Hübner, a landscape by Lessing, a slave merchant with his human wares by Horace Vernet, St. Catherine carried to her grave by Angels by Mücke, and some clever Wilkie-like pictures by Hasenclever, one of them a news-room lighted with gas with readers surrounding a table. From thence we went to the Old Museum and looked at the Sculpture. It is interesting to see the statue of Napoleon who worked so much woe to Prussia placed opposite that of Julius Cæsar. We saw a beautiful Hebe of Canova's for the first time. Went into the picture gallery to have a parting look at Titian's daughter and the Correggios. Came home and packed the books. Read Macaulay. Walked out and afterwards translated and wrote for G.

Friday 9. Went to see the Ravené pictures – a small collection, chiefly landscapes, in elegant rooms. In the evening went to Fräulein Solmar's. G. read Shylock. Varnhagen, Frau von Olfers, Graf and Gräfin York, Baron Pödlitz etc.

Saturday 10. Packed and went to the Neue Museum. Before we went, Magnus called and brought us two lithographs of his paintings. Took a farewell of hearty friendliness.

Sunday. Set off in snow to Cologne. Travelling companions Madame Roger and her daughter and a queen's messenger, a very agreeable man. Spent the Night at Cologne.

Monday. From Cologne to Brussels – Hotel de Saxe, where we saw Berlioz. Travelling companions, two French artists coming from Russia.

Tuesday. From Brussels to Dover, Lord Warden Hotel.

3. England, 14 March 1855 – 19 June 1861

On their return to England from Germany, GE and GHL entered on a new phase of their relationship, in which they confronted the practical implications of their liaison: most immediately, the question of the way of life now possible for them. GE stayed at Dover for an anxious six weeks, writing 'Recollections of Berlin' and translating Spinoza, while GHL went ahead to London. They took lodgings first in East Sheen, then in Richmond, avoiding their previous haunts in central London, for economy perhaps, but more likely to secure the advantages of seclusion for work and freedom from embarrassing social interactions. GHL wrote to the Princess Wittgenstein in August 1855: 'our life is very uneventful. We live out of the world in a charming suburb & don't often mingle with Londoners, so that les jours se suivent et se ressemblent [the days follow each other and are very much alike].' (*Letters of GHL*, vol. 1, p. 238) While her diary is laconic, in letters GE yearned for 'our old habits of undisturbed companionship and work', and soon wrote glowingly of their re-establishment: 'I think we like East Sheen better and better, and are happier every day – writing hard, walking hard, reading Homer and science and rearing tadpoles.' (*Letters*, vol. 2, pp. 199, 202).

They were certainly busy. Alone at Dover GE, as always, read a good deal, continued to work at her Spinoza translation, wrote up from her Diary 'Recollections of Berlin', and began to revise 'Recollections of Weimar' for publication in *Fraser's Magazine*. During the remainder of 1855 she produced numerous reviews for several journals, among them one of GHL's *Life and Works of Goethe* for the *Leader*. The diary entries, briefer and more sporadic than in Germany, portray a journalist at work, writing for her living. Her tallies of earnings, beginning with a balance sheet for 1855, document both her businesslike habits, and increasing affluence when she begins to publish fiction.[1] She declared, 'You don't know what a severely practical person I am become, and what a sharp eye I have to the main chance. I keep the purse and dole out sover-

1 The memoranda in the diary are complemented by her literary receipt book at Princeton, and GHL's in the Berg collection, New York Public Library: transcribed by Haight, *Letters*, vol. 7, pp. 361–83. Late in life, she remarked 'Those figures which tell of distribution are the criticism of my books which I most care about' (p. 250)

eigns with all the pangs of a miser.' (*Letters*, vol. 2, p. 233) Later diaries, especially those for 1879 and 1880, after GHL's death, show that she continued to be 'severely practical' throughout her life. Her punctiliousness in money matters is most succinctly demonstrated in her letter of 5 January 1869, reminding Barbara Bodichon to repay a shilling borrowed from a servant for a cabfare months earlier, which has all the moral principle of a Caleb Garth or an Aunt Glegg (vol. 5, p. 3; cf. Haight's comments in vol. 1, p. xlviii). In any case, the satisfaction which pervades the entry in this diary for 28 November 1860 about her investment of £2000 in East Indies stock is thoroughly intelligible.

It did not escape notice in the late 1850s that GE and GHL appeared better off: Barbara Bodichon, reporting gossip about the identity of the author of *Adam Bede*, included the observation that 'the Lewes style of living was changed.' (*Letters*, vol. 3, p. 103) Their prosperity is nicely plotted in this diary, not only in actual earnings but in changes of residence: at the beginning of 1859, advances for *Adam Bede* in hand, they took a seven-year lease on Holly Lodge, Wandsworth, so progressing from being lodgers to the status of householders. The next year they moved back to central London – to Harewood Square in September and then to Blandford Square in December – in part to accommodate Charles Lewes, finished with schooling at Hofwyl in Switzerland, who came to live with them. Clearly, a metropolitan residence was now feasible, since confirmation of the success of GE's fiction with the publication of *The Mill on the Floss* in some degree counteracted her notoriety as Lewes's mistress.

The diary shows the extent of GE's reclusiveness in the late 1850s. It appears that GHL made 'rare visits to town' (1 November 1858), and even more rarely GE accompanied him (for instance, to buy a microscope, on 23 September 1856, or to have photographs taken on 26 February 1858). Their visitors were few and mostly male, though GE's woman friends were loyal: the first woman to call on them was Rufa Hennell (widowed in 1850, she married in 1857 Wathen Mark Wilks Call), while Sara Hennell and Cara Bray maintained their correspondence; as did Bessie Parkes and Barbara Leigh Smith (who visited them at Tenby in 1856, and married Dr Eugene Bodichon in 1857). With the move to Wandsworth early in 1859 came a friendship with the Congreves that was to be important, as the heartfelt, troubled entry for 3 May 1859 shows. A more active social life developed almost immediately they settled in London in 1860: GE records attendance at concerts and the theatre, and a growing circle of acquaintance, though impatience with certain kinds of social demand is evident for instance in her account of the whitebait dinner at Greenwich in June 1861 (GE's account is slightly equivocal, but not John Blackwood's: 'George Eliot was extremely delighted with the whole affair, which she caused others to enjoy so much', *Letters*, vol. 9, p. 347). Whatever reservations she had, such outings were now possible: Arthur Helps's report of the Queen's approval of her work on 20 November 1860 is a relevant indicator of GE's respectability. Yet on 28 November she laments 'the loss of the country has seemed very bitter to me'. None the less, on the evidence of this section of the journal, and the 1861–77 volume, Haight's proposition that 'her equivocal marital state' brought on depression in London is an overstatement.[2]

Family considerations, particularly to do with Charles Lewes's career, provided the immediate reason for the significant move to central London. GHL was a devoted father to his sons, though at a distance for most of the time. Charles Lee (1842–91), Thornton Arnott (1844–69), and Herbert Arthur (1846–75), were all educated at the Hofwyl School near Bern. This school, where Edward and Robert Noel had been pupils, was recommended by Sara Hennell. GHL approved its Pestalozzian educational principles, which included emphasis on modern languages and outdoors activity, and may well have also appreciated its low cost relative to English schools. After GHL's revelation to them in 1859 of his liaison with GE, the boys, who addressed Agnes as 'Mamma', opened correspondence with their stepmother as 'Mother'. Before long, as Rosemarie Bodenheimer points out, GE found her signature in their second language, *Mutter*.[3] (GHL was 'Pater' to his sons.)

GE met the lads for the first time in 1860, when she and GHL on their way home from Italy collected Charles to bring him to London. GE's growing fondness for them, and her personal and financial involvement in Lewes's family matters, emerge in the diary, in counterpoint with estrangement from her own family. On 22 June 1857, she stoically refers to but does not dwell on her brother's response to her declaration (after almost three years) that she is living with GHL (Isaac Evans had turned the family lawyer Holbeche on her: see *Letters*, vol. 2, pp. 331–2, for GE's letter to Isaac, pp. 346, 349–50 for Hol-

2 Haight, *George Eliot*, p. 338. It appears that GHL may have looked into getting a divorce abroad: *Letters*, vol. 3, pp. 366–7.

3 Bodenheimer, *Real Life*, p. 192.

beche's letter to her and her reply, and p. 354 for Holbeche's covering note to Isaac). The pain of estrangement comes through in concern about her sister Chrissey and her family, most strongly at Chrissey's death, recorded on 15 March 1859. Some contact was maintained with the Evanses and Clarkes, despite the censoriousness of Isaac. GE had a particular fondness for Chrissey's daughter Emily, singled out in 1859 ('I have four children to correspond with – the three boys in Switzerland, and Emily at Lichfield', *Letters*, vol. 3, p. 229), and left £5000 in GE's will.

Naturally enough, however, the dominant concerns of the diary are day-to-day activities. In September 1855 they took a break by the sea, at Worthing. GHL's interest in marine biology was evidently taking hold: GE notes 'Long walk on the beach; but not a mollusc to be seen!' By the summer of 1856, the interest had become a passion, and they spent three months in Devon and South Wales, at Ilfracombe and Tenby. Cheaper lodgings were to be had in these coastal resorts than in London, and there were advantages for the often precarious health of both. This was a happy and profitable time, described in several texts by each of them: in addition to GE's letters, diary and journal, there are GHL's Diary (of which the first extant volume begins on 24 July 1856), his letters, and his essays, *Sea-Side Studies*, the first of which appeared in *Blackwood's* in August 1856. Altogether it was a formative passage in the life of GE.

'Recollections of Ilfracombe' (dated 'Tenby, July 22. 1856') was written up from the diary for 8 May–26 June 1856. Their time at Tenby (26 June–8 August), though enjoyable, apparently did not warrant such treatment. Both the Ilfracombe journal, which refers to having 'a great deal of work before me', and the diary, speak of a pressure to produce. On 20 July, she looked back to the previous entry in her diary, a fortnight earlier, and observed, 'I have done no *visible* work' – that is, not counting a review, the Ilfracombe essay, and some other bits and pieces. (Cross pencilled 'Note' in the margin of the diary at this point.) Later in the same entry, the force of her observation emerges: she is disinclined to accept Chapman's invitation to write for the *Westminster Review* for the coming quarter, because 'I am anxious to begin my fiction writing'. Which she did six weeks after their return to Richmond: 'Began to write "The Sad Fortunes of the Reverend Amos Barton", which I hope to make one of a series called "Scenes of Clerical Life".'

But she also overcame her disinclination to write for the *Westminster Review* just then, and completed 'Silly Novels by

Lady Novelists' on 12 September. All her writing at this time conspired to the same end: both the important review of Ruskin's *Modern Painters* which had appeared in the April issue of the *Westminister*, and 'The Natural History of German Life' in the July issue, bear on her theories of life and literature. 'Silly Novels' (published in the October number) is by way of being a manifesto, while 'Recollections of Ilfracombe' is the overture to her writing fiction.

From the point at which she began 'Amos Barton', comment on the progress of her fiction is constant in her diary. This particular diary volume sees the composition and publication of *Scenes*, *Adam Bede*, 'The Lifted Veil', *The Mill on the Floss*, and *Silas Marner*: she also wrote the tale later published as *Brother Jacob*, and began *Romola*, a novel which was to cost her immense and protracted pain. Much of the diary record is matter-of-fact, though on 16 November 1858 appears for the first time a particularly engaging mode of exclamation: 'Wrote the last word of Adam Bede, and sent it to Langford. *Jubilate!*' (She exults in the despatch of both *The Mill on the Floss* and *Silas Marner* with *'Magnificat anima mea!'* Cross usually denies her these triumphant phrases.)

There are, as always, significant reticences in the diary, not least – for all the record of progress in composition – about the genesis of the writing identity 'George Eliot'. The period from late November 1857 to June 1859 was particularly significant: during this time, from just before the publication of *Scenes* in book form (with *Adam Bede* already under way), through its positive reception, to the hugely successful publication of *Adam Bede* and the controversy over the identity of 'George Eliot' in the Liggins affair, the pseudonym was established, and its secret surrendered.

In the diary, little is made of the pseudonym. She refers in passing to Blackwood's penetration on 10 December 1857 of the identity of 'George Eliot' (the first mention in this sequence of the name by which she was to become best-known, originally offered to Blackwood on 4 February 1857 as 'a tub to throw to the whale': *Letters*, vol. 2, p. 292). Later, on 20 August 1859, there is mention of the Liggins whose claims to be the author of *Adam Bede* were so disturbing and troublesome. Her entry for 25 October 1859, describing the decision to ban discussion of her books in her own house, provides a different and somewhat sanctimonious example of her attempt to distance her self in daily interactions from the writing self.

Both these entries postdate that for 9 May 1859, 'My Journal is continued at the opposite end, by mistake, as a continuation of the History of Adam Bede'. Apparently a straightforward confession of absent-mindedness, this entry provides the principal clue in this part of the volume to what is demonstrably a deliberate separation of the private self, Marian Evans Lewes, working at her writing, from the public persona, the published author who goes under the name 'George Eliot'. This division is discussed more fully in the headnote to 'The Making of George Eliot'. The essential point is that at the other end of this manuscript volume (where various 'Recollections' had already been written), there is a section beginning with 'How I came to write Fiction' (dated '6 Dec 57') which initiates the most striking of the various parallel texts within the body of the journals.

This part of GE's diary has parallels with 'Recollections' of Ilfracombe, the Scilly Isles and Jersey, and the material we have called 'The Making of George Eliot'. In addition, separate records of travels – to Germany in 1858, and to Italy in 1860 – complement the diary. Other journeys and expeditions, both within Britain and abroad, are described in the diary sequence: they went to Paris and Switzerland in 1859, and to Italy again, especially Florence, in 1861. The pattern of going off on an expedition after the completion of a novel was begun with *The Mill on the Floss*, which earned GE the opportunity of making the long-awaited journey to Italy.

Together with the record of work in progress, GE also regularly noted her reading in the diary, though even the impressive list of books read in the study or aloud to GHL is not always a complete record of her reading. Her range was wide – a nice example, 24 November 1859, refers to an evening of 'music, Arabian Nights, and Darwin' (*The Origin of Species*, just published); or, 8 April 1857, 'We are reading Carlyle's Cromwell and Aurora Leigh again in the evenings. I am still in the Œdipus Tyrannus, with Shelley's poems, and snatches of Natural History.' She tends to provide lists, not explanations or judgments, so that it is not evident for example that the reading listed on 6 and 8 December 1857 has an emphasis on India, obviously as a consequence of the Indian Mutiny earlier in the year.

Neither Cross nor Haight quotes from this section of the diary in any discernible pattern. Cross tends to include the end-of-year summaries, Haight uses mainly short passages of a sentence or so. Both tend to include comments about her writing. 1856 and 1858 are largely unpublished.

3. England, 14 March 1855–19 June 1861

Wednesday 14. Took Lodgings 1, Sydney Place.

Thursday. 15. A lovely day. As I walked up the Castle hill this afternoon the town with its background of softly rounded hills shrouded in sleepy haze, its little lines of water looking golden in the sun, made a charming picture. I have written the Preface to the third Book of Ethics, read Scherr and Shakspeare's Venus and Adonis.

Friday 16. A still lovelier day. A brisk wind carried about great masses of cloud below an arch of clear blue. I read Shakspeare's "Passionate Pilgrim" at breakfast and found a sonnet in which he expresses admiration of Spenser (Sonnet VIII)

> "Douland to thee is dear, whose heavenly touch
> Upon the lute doth ravish human sense:
> Spenser to me, whose deep conceit is such,
> As passing all conceit needs no defence."

I must send word of this to G. who has written in his Goethe that Shakspeare has left no line in praise of a contemporary. [*inserted later*: (G. writes that this sonnet is Barnwell's)] I could not resist the temptation of walking out before I sat down to work. Came in at 1/2 past 10 and translated Spinoza till nearly 1. Walked out again till 2. After dinner read "Two Gentlemen of Verona" and some of the "Sonnets". That play disgusted me more than ever in the final scene where Valentine on Proteus' mere begging pardon where he has no longer any hope of gaining his ends, says: "All that was mine in Silvia I give thee"! – Silvia standing by. Walked up the Castle hill again and came in at 6. Read Scherr and found an important hint that I have made a mistake in a sentence of my article on Austria about the death of Franz von Sickingen. Wrote to Sara Hennell and to Miss Parkes.

Saturday 17. Received a letter from G. and the proof of the second part of my article. Corrected the latter and carried it to the post. Wrote to G. The weather cloudy and in the afternoon rainy. Read Shakspeare's sonnets and part of Tempest. Walked up the hill. Read Scherr.

Sunday 18. A very boisterous day, but with intervals, of bright sunshine in one of which there was a beautiful rainbow. Read Scherr. Translated Spinoza. In the evening wrote.

Monday. 19. Read Scherr, translated Spinoza and walked before dinner. After dinner read Scherr again and was prevented from going out by rain. In the evening wrote Recollections of Berlin. A little cold in my head made me stupid.

Tuesday 20. Letter from G. and Leader. A very mild morning. Walked on the beach. Wrote Recollections and a note to G. Read Leader and Scherr. Walking out this afternoon along the beach I saw a sea fog come in with amazing rapidity

– a thick cloud seemed to gather on the cliff in a moment. Had a letter from Rosehill. Wrote a note to Mr. Chapman.

Wed. 21. A cold windy day, and I, having a cold, did not venture to go out. Read Scherr and translated Spinoza. After dinner read the "Tempest" and Scherr again. In the evening wrote Recollections of Berlin.

Thursday 22. The weather still terrible and I not well. Read Scherr, wrote Spinoza. Read Macbeth. In the evening wrote.

Friday 23. Snow. Very poorly. Finished Scherr. Read Macbeth again. Walked out a little and on returning found a letter from G. Read Nibelungenlied. Wrote a little.

Saturday 24. My head too weak for work. Read Shakspeare. Wrote to G. and carried the letter to the post. Read Romeo and Juliet.

Sunday 25. The Leader from G. and a note from Mr. Chapman in which he asks me to undertake part of the Contemporary Literature for the W. R. Had a delightful walk over the hills. Read the Leader and the Nibelungen Lied. Wrote till 10.

Monday. 26. Began Scherr again. Revised Spinoza. Read Romeo and Juliet and the Nibelungen Lied. Sewed and wrote.

Thursday [Tuesday] 27. Letter from G. Wrote to him. Revised Spinoza. Read Athenæum. Walked on the hill. Read Nibelungen and revised Spinoza.

Wednesday 28. Began work but became very bilious and obliged to give it up. Terrible headache in the evening.

Thursday. In bed till 4 o'clock. Got up and read for an hour or two then to bed again.

Friday 30. Better this morning. Wrote letters to G., to sister and Mr. Chapman. Read Scherr and Nibelungen Lied.

Saturday 31. Revised Spinoza. Finished Nibelungen Lied. In the evening wrote a couple of pages of Spinoza.

Sunday April 1. Received Westminster Review and a letter from G. Wrote to him and then walked over the hills, not being well enough to work. Read article on Dryden in W. R. and looked through the Contemporary Literature.

Monday 2. Read Scherr. Translated Spinoza and in the evening revised it.

Tuesday 3. Letter from G. and parcel of books. Letter from sister. Translated and revised Spinoza. Read Leader.

Wednesday. Read Scherr on the Ritterlich-romantische Literatur. Translated Spinoza. Read Athenæum and article in W. R. Too headachy to revise Spinoza. Read Scherr and wrote to Mr. Bray and Chrissey.

Thursday 5. Began *Reineke Fuchs*. Wrote to G. Translated Spinoza. In the evening revised it, and read Scherr.

Friday. 6. Letter from Mr. Chapman. Began Schrader's German Mythology. In the evening revised Spinoza and read Gibbon.

Saturday 7. Wrote Spinoza and a letter to G. enclosing Mr. C.'s. Read Schrader, Reineke Fuchs. Genesis of Science.

Sunday 8. Read Schrader. Spinoza. Leader and Athenæum. "Genesis of Science." Gibbon.

Monday. Painful letter which upset me for work. Walked out and then translated 2 pages of Spinoza. Read Henry V. In the evening translated again.

Tuesday. 10. Read Schrader. Translated Spinoza. Walked feeling much depression against which I struggled hard. Read Henry V and Henry VIII. Wrote to Mr. Chapman. Revised Spinoza.

Wednesday 11. Read Schrader. Finished Book III of Spinoza's Ethics. Read Henry VIII. Revised Spinoza in the evening. Letter from Rosehill.

Thursday, Friday and Saturday. Still feverish and unable to fix my mind steadily on reading or writing. Read the 1st, 2nd and 3 parts of Henry VI, and began Richard 2. Finished Herbert Spencer's "Genesis of Science". Friday and Saturday, wrote a little at my article on Weimar for Frazer [sic]. Finished Schrader – a poor book.

Wednesday 18. Came to town, to lodgings in Bayswater.

Monday 23. Fixed on our lodgings at East Sheen.

Wednesday 25. Went to the British Museum.

Saturday 28. Finished article on Weimar for Fraser.

Wednesday. May 2. Came to East Sheen and settled in our lodgings.

Wed. May 9. Finished article on Kingsley.

Monday 28. Sent Belles Lettres Section to Mr. Chapman.

Saturday June 9. Sent article on Liszt, Wagner and Weimar to Fraser.

Tuesday 12. Sent article on Menander for the Leader.

Wednesday 13. Began Part IV of Spinoza's Ethics. Began also to read Cumming for article in Westminster. We are reading in the evenings now, Sydney Smith's letters, Boswell, Whewell's History of Inductive Sciences, the Odyssey and occasionally Heine's Reisebilder. I began the second Book of the Iliad in Greek this morning.

Thursday 21. Finished article on Brougham's *Lives of Men of Letters*.

Friday and Saturday. Headache. Read Lucrezia Floriani. We are reading White's History of Selborne in the evening, with Boswell and the Odyssey.

Sunday 24. Mr. Chapman dined with us.

Sunday July 8. G. ill. I also took cold on the Monday and the week was lost to both of us. Tuesday Mr. Bray came to see us. (Wilhelm Meister and Article on Gruppe for the Leader.)

Aug. 1. G. only just beginning to enjoy life again after being ill for three weeks with a second gathering in his face. – Article on Milton for Leader.

8. G. went to Ramsgate for a week.

Aug. 22. Wrote article on Saint Marc Girardin for Leader.

24. Finished article on Cumming for Westminster.

Aug. 30. Article on Heine for Leader.

Sep. 13. Article on Michelet for Leader. We are reading Wallenstein and Schwann in the evenings.

Sep. 15. Finished article on Belles Lettres for the Westminster.

17. Wrote article on German Mythology and Legend for Leader.

19. Left East Sheen and came to Worthing. Took lodgings at 21 Steyne. The weather bright and warm.

20. Both miserably bilious and headachy.

21. Only a little better.

Sat. 22. Well this morning and bathed. The day divine.

Sun. 23. Long walk on the beach; but not a mollusc to be seen!

Sun. 30. A resolutely wet day.

Mon. Oct 1. Once more gloriously fine and mild.

Wed. 3. Came to Richmond 8, Park Shot.

Tues. 9. Wrote article on Margaret Fuller and Mary Wollstonecraft.

Frid. 12. Received a letter from Mr. Chapman asking me to write an article on *Heine* for the January No. of the Westminster. Article on Carlyle for Leader.

Sat. and Sun. Finished Part IV of *Spinoza's Ethics*.

Monday Oct. 15. Wrote part of article on "Translations and Translators" for Leader. Wrote to Mr. Bray.

Tuesday 16. Finished article. Wrote to Miss Hennell. We are reading Gall's *Anatomie et Physiologie du Cerveau* in the evening, with, occasionally, Carpenter's Comparative Physiology. "The Newcomes" as light fare after dinner.

Wed. Friday. Reading Heine.

Nov 1. The *Goethe* out. Article on it for Leader.

13. Letter from M. D'Albert. Article on Heine half done.

14. Renewed a wretched cold which I have had for a week so that work is disagreeable. We have been reading Longfellow's Hiawatha, and are continuing Carpenter.

28. Finished article on Heine. Began to read Charles Lamb after dinner.

Dec. 12. Finished and sent off article on Belles Lettres.

Dec. 24. For the last ten days I have done little owing to headache and other ailments. On the 19th I wrote a poor notice of Rachel Gray for the Leader. Began the Antigone, read Von Bohlen on Genesis, and Swedenborg. Mr. Chapman wants me to write an article on Missions and Missionaries for April No. of the Westminster, but I think I shall not have it ready till the July No. – In the afternoon I set out on my journey to see my sister, and arrived at her house about 8 o'clock, finding her and her children well.

Saturday 29. Returned to Richmond. G. away at Vernon Hill, having gone thither on Wednesday.

Sunday 30. Read the Shaving of Shagpat.

31. Wrote a review of Shagpat and sent it to Leader.

Work done in 1855

	£. s. d.
Article for Westminster on Austria	20. 0.0
Articles on Weimar for Frazer	14.14.0
Belles Lettres for W.R. July No	12.12.0
Article on Dr. Cumming	15. 0.0
Belles Lettres for Oct.	12.12.0
Article on Heine	20. 0.0
Belles Lettres for Jan.	12.12.0
Articles for Leader	12.12.0
	£119. 8.0

Jan 1. 1856. Read Kingsley's "Greek Heroes" and began review of Von Bohlen for the Leader.

5. G. came home.

6. Began to revise Book IV of Spinoza's Ethics, and continued this work through the week, being able to work but slowly. Finished Kahnis' History of German Protestantism.

16. Received a charming letter from Barbara Smith, with a petition to Parliament that women may have a right to their earnings.

Feb. 19. Since the 6 January I have been occupied with Spinoza and, except a review of Griswold's American Poets, have done nothing else but translate the Fifth Book of the Ethics and revise the whole of my translation from the beginning. This evening I have finished my revision.

Mar. 17. Sent off my article on Belles Lettres. I have resigned the subject of "Missions" to Harriet Martineau.

21. Finished article on "Torso" for the 'Saturday'.

24. Finished article on Henry Murger for ditto.

25. Began article on the Antigone.

28. Article on Gieseler.

April 5. Mr. Chapman has accepted my proposition to write an article on Young.

Ap. 7, 8. Wrote a story from Léon Gozlan, intended for the "Saturday".

9, 10. Article on Vehse's Memoirs of the Court of Austria for "Leader".

12. Article on Heine's Book of Songs for Saturday.

13, 14. Article on Waverley Novels – pamphlet by W. J. F.

15. Herbert Spencer dined with us.

18. Went to Sydenham with H. S.

22. Began article on Young.

26. Article on Margaret Fuller's letters.

29. Began to read Riehl, on which I am to write an article for the Westminster.

May 8. Set off in very cold weather for Ilfracomb [sic]. Staid an hour at Windsor on our way, and walked round the Castle. Reached Bristol about half past six and having two hours to stay before starting for Exeter, we walked through the narrow dirty streets to St. Mary Redcliff, the old church where Chatterton pretended to have found the Rowley MS. It is a remarkably fine old church. After looking at this we walked some distance along the road by the side of the river, but being both headachy, we were soon glad to turn back to the station and wait in the rather dirty room there till the Express set off for Exeter. We reached the Exeter Station (which is about a mile from the town), at ten, and were delighted to find a comfortable bedroom there, which saved our going to the town. We breakfasted at half past eight, and then strolled out in glorious sunshine to look at the town and Cathedral. A pretty, quiet road led us very soon to the upper part of the town – by handsome almshouses on one side and park-like grounds on the other to the principal street, where we noticed the market, and a fine bit of very old building now used as the Station House (Police). We made our way to the Cathedral which stands in a fine open space with tall trees round it. The two square towers individualize it among Cathedrals. We had a peep through the open door which gave me the idea of a grand interior. Back again to the station and away by the train to Barnstaple, the country through which we passed charmingly undulated and wooded. At Barnstaple we got into the Ilfracombe coach – or rather I got in and G got outside, making on our way the acquaintance of a family named Webster, who have since taken part of the same house with us here – Runnymeade Villa.

Saturday 10. We are enchanted with Ilfracombe. Today we have explored some of the rocks and have found some Actiniæ as a small beginning for our Vivarium. My head not yet well, so I have given myself up to enjoyment of the first day's exploits in rock-climbing.

Sunday 11. We have walked up several hills today and had exquisite views of the bays and distant promontories rising one behind the other. This morning I read Riehl and made a few notes for a couple of hours.

Monday 12. We had a glorious hunt this afternoon on the rocks and found two specimens of the Anthea Cereus and a red and blue spotted anemone – treasures to us.

Tuesday 13. Began my article on Riehl this morning with rather despairing prospects. Some books came from Mr. Chapman.

Wednesday 14. Went to Hele's who collects Zoophytes etc and supplies Lloyd in London. Saw some splendid anemones, beyond anything I had imagined of that kind, some Eolids and Corallines. We were pleased with his nice daughter, who seems to take a real interest in the animals quite apart from commercial considerations.

Thursday. G. called on Mr. Tugwell, the curate here, whom he found a charming young man, the author of various books – a Guide to North Devon etc.

Thursday 15. Mr Tugwell returned the call. In the afternoon we walked to Lee, a delicious spot in a deep hollow between two magnificent hills. The steep sides of one of these hills are hung with low woods, or with masses of furze now in full bloom. The primroses here quite cover the sides of some of the hills as well as the banks of the lanes. Not the least beautiful things we saw were the springs by the roadside, crystally clear, decked with liverwort and fern. We returned by a different way – through Slade, which we were told was only half a mile longer, but we found ourselves in an interminable road over the hills, and at length came to a spot where two directions seemed equally promising or unpromising of Ilfracomb. We took one, however, in the necessity of a choice and walked on and on without seeing any indication of our being in the right direction, till at last we came to a farm-house, where G. made inquiries and found that we were in the right road, but had still two miles to walk. We got home a little before six, after walking three hours and a half, and were thoroughly knocked up. In the last mile we passed a lovely hill where the rich colour of the marly soil made a beautiful contrast with the bright green pastures and the masses of furze. – In the evenings I have been reading Masson's Essays – "The Three Devils" and Chatterton's Life – and this evening I have read some of Trench's Calderon.

Tuesday 20. After writing an hour, we went out with Mr. Tugwell zoologizing, and thanks to his aid and exertions brought home a rich store of Actinia Crassicornis and other precious but less conspicuous things.

Saturday 24. My article on Riehl is rather more than half done. I have had a letter from Chrissey today telling me that Charlie is elected for the Medical College.

June 5. Finished my article on Riehl, and sent it to London. Had a delicious walk to Chambercombe Woods.

Friday. 6. Walked to Lee, Miss Webster with us. The day was glorious. Wrote to Mr. Bray.

Sat. 7. We went out zoologizing on the rocks opposite the Tunnel this afternoon. Letter came from Parker accepting the proposition about the History of Philosophy. Letter to me from Mrs. Peter Taylor. Wrote notice of Masson's Essays.

Sunday. Wrote to Mrs. Taylor. Letter from Mr. Chapman saying he likes the article on Riehl.

Tuesday. Terrible headache came on. We walked to Watermouth in bright sunshine.

Wednesday. Headache which prevented me from working all day.

Thursday. Not well, but went to work. Proof of my article.

Tuesday 17. Sent off my article on Belles Lettres.

Thursday 26. Set off by steamer from dear Ilfracombe to Tenby, where we arrived too late to secure lodgings the same evening.

Friday 27. Took our lodgings and unpacked. I was quite knocked up by my yesterday's journey, and the exertions of this morning. The weather bright, and the air perfect.

Saturday 28. We had a glorious hunt this morning in the caverns of St. Catherine's Rock. Found some specimens of the Alcyonium Digitatum, the Clavellina and the Stag's Horn Polype as well as abundance of Laomedeæ and Actiniæ.

Sunday 29. Wrote to Sara Hennell, Barbara Smith and Mrs. Croft. In the afternoon we had a delicious walk in the sunshine towards Gilbar Point, and saw for the first time a Lophius, or Fishing Frog. It was about three feet long and had been cast dead upon the sands. Presently after we saw a Rhizostoma nearly a foot in diameter, also cast on the sands.

30. We went hunting this morning in the cove on the north side of St. Catherine's, and found some polypes and sea weed, with which we were not familiar. We were both terribly tired and so did not attempt any long walk. I am reading in the evenings the Memoirs of Beaumarchais and Milne Edwards's Zoology. G. has begun to read Coriolanus aloud.

Sat. July 5. We have hunted two or three times in St. Catherine's caverns this week, and have found in addition to former spoils, a solitary Ascidian, two Eolids, and a specimen of Cellularia Avicularia, in which the Birds' heads were very active while the rest of the Polype appeared dead. The weather has been delicious every day, but G. having hurt his foot, we have not been able to take long walks. I have continued reading Milne Edwards aloud, and have also read Harriet Martineau's article on Missions in the Westminster, and one or two articles in the National. Reading to myself Harvey's Sea-side Book, and "The Lovers' Seat".

Sunday. July 6. The sun shines beautifully this morning, but we are rather depressed because G.'s head seems worse.

Sunday. July 20. Since I made the last note in my journal, I have had the comfort of seeing G. much better. The fortnight has slipped away without my being able to show much result from it. I have written a review of the "Lover's Seat" for the "Leader", and jotted down some recollections of Ilfracombe; besides these trifles and the introduction to an article already written, I have done no *visible* work. But I have absorbed many ideas and much bodily strength; indeed, I do not remember ever feeling so strong in mind and body as I feel at this moment.

On Saturday, the 12th, Barbara Smith arrived and staid here till Wednesday morning. We enjoyed her society very much, but were deeply touched to see that three years had made her so much older and sadder. Her activity for great objects is admirable, and contact with her is a fresh inspiration to work while it is day. On Tuesday evening she came to tell us of her interview with her "Aunt Patty" – a scene beyond the conception of Molière. We parted from her at the door of the "Coburg" at about 1/2 past 11.

In the meantime G. has been very industrious and has written a sea-side article for Blackwood, which was sent off yesterday. I have been reading aloud the Memoirs of Beaumarchais which yielded me little fruit, continued Milne Edwards, and have now taken up *Quatrefages* again.

Mr. Chapman invites me to contribute to the Westminster for this quarter. I am anxious to begin my fiction writing and so am not inclined to undertake an article that will give me much trouble, but at all events I will finish my article on *Young*.

Monday 21. We had a delightful walk on the North Sands and hunted with success. A sunny, happy day.

Monday 28. Mr. Pigott arrived at last, after various processes of expectation and disappointment. We drove to Lidstep in the afternoon. Yesterday I had a letter from Chrissey, which I answered today. I have engaged to write an article for the next W. R. on "Silly Women's Novels".

Sat. Aug. 2. Last evening we saw Mr. Pigott's Yacht sail in and cast anchor, and this morning we went on board. This evening G. and I have been out in a boat for an hour, and have caught about 20 Medusæ. The western light on the rippled water as we went out was glorious, and on our return we saw the lovely green phosphorescence about the net and the oars.

Sunday. 3. I went out to the Castle Hill after breakfast this morning, and the Yacht was gone. So we are once more quiet and alone.

Monday. Finished article on Meissner's recollections of Heine. Received a kind letter from Mr. Bray, in which he thanks me for my article on German Life.

Tuesday 5. Wrote an article on Mrs. Chanter's Ferny Combes.

Friday 8. Went by Steamer to Bristol, and from thence by railway to Bath, where we slept.

Saturday 9. Arrived at Richmond about 1/2 past 1 with terrible headache. Unpacked nevertheless, and enjoyed the sense of being "at home" again.

Monday 18. Wrote article on Felice Orsini. Walked in Kew Park, and talked with G. of my novel. Finished César Birotteau aloud.

Monday 25. G. set off for Hofwyl today.

Tuesday. Seized with terrible toothache which continued until Saturday, when I took chloroform and had the offender extracted. No work done all this week in consequence!

Thursday Sep. 4. G. returned. My article nearly half done.

Friday 12. Sent off my article on "Silly Novels", according to promise, but finished it under much discomfort from headache.

Friday 19. Sent off my article on Belles Lettres for W. R. Terrible cold in my head.

Sat. 20. This evening we went to see Dillon in Belphegor at the Lyceum. Came home with a distracting headache.

Monday. Better this morning. Began the Ajax of Sophocles. Also Miss Martineau's History of the Peace.

Tuesday, Sep. 22 [23]. Began to write "The Sad Fortunes of the Reverend Amos Barton", which I hope to make one of a series called "Scenes of Clerical Life".

Wednesday. We went into the city and bought a microscope.

Thursday. Went to the Zoological Gardens. Herbert Spencer was waiting for us when we came home. He dined with us and we spent a pleasant evening in chat.

Sunday Oct. 12. Expecting Barbara Smith to come and say good bye, before going to Algiers. Herbert Spencer, to our surprize, appeared at the station, when we were looking out for B. He dined with us, but no Barbara came.

Monday. Barbara and Bessie came about 5 and staid an hour. I have brought my story to the end of the 2nd chapter.

Sunday 19. Mr. Redford dined with us.

Sat. 25. Brought my story to the end of the 4th chapter and began the 5th.

Wednesday, November 5. Finished my first story – "The Sad Fortunes of Amos Barton".

Dec. 4. Sent off my article on Young.

13. Finished my article on History, Biography etc. for Contemporary Literature.

19. Finished and sent off article on Belles Lettres. I have had a pleasant letter from Barbara, saying how much she enjoys Algiers. Another great satisfaction has been a letter from Blackwood, expressing more cordially than ever his admiration of "Amos Barton", and hoping that the "great unknown" is laying the keel of other stories.

Christmas Eve. Alone at Park Shot. G. gone to Vernon Hill.

Christmas Day. Began "Mr. Gilfil's Love Story", the second of my series.

Dec. 30. Received a letter from Blackwood, with a cheque for fifty guineas for "Amos Barton", and a proposition to republish the series, either giving me a sum for it, or at half profits.

1856 from Jan. to July.
Finished Trans. of Sp. Ethics Feb. 19.

Art. on Shagpat for Leader	1. 1.0
do. Von Bohlen	1. 1.0
do. Rachel Gray	1. 1.0
do. Kahnis' Hist. of Protestantism	1. 1.0
do. Griswold's American Poets	1. 1.0
do. Stahr's Torso	1. 1.0
Art. on Belles Lettres for Westminster	12.12.0
Art. on Stahr for Sat. Rev.	2. 2.0
do. Henry Murger	2. 2.0
do. Antigone for Leader	1. 1.0
do. Gieseler	1. 1.0
Art. on Vehse's Austria	1. 1.0
Art. on Heine's Book of Songs for Sat. Rev.	2. 2.0
"Who wrote the Waverley Novels"	1. 1.0
Story from "La Folle du Logis"	1. 1.0

Art. on Marg. Fuller's Letters for Leader	1. 1.0
Article on Riehl for Westminster	17.10.0
Belles Lettres for July No.	12.12.0
	£61.12.0

Work done from July to December 1856

	£. s. d.
Article on Lovers' Seat for Leader	1. 1.0
Tale from Auerbach for do	1. 1.0
Art. on Forbes's "Sightseeing"	1. 1.0
Art. on Recollections of Heine	1. 1.0
Art. on Ferny Combes	1. 1.0
Art. on Felice Orsini	1. 1.0
Art. on "Silly Novels"	12.10.0
" " Belles Lettres	12.12.0
Article on Young for W.R.	20. 0.0
History etc. and Belles Lettres	22. 1.0
"Sad Fortunes of Amos Barton"	52.10.0
	125.19.0
Brot. over, from Jan. to July, 1856	61.12.0
	£187.11.0
Additional from W.R. for Art. on Young	5. 0.0
	192.11.0
From January to July brot. forwd.	61.12.0
	254. 3.0

Jan. 4 [1857]. Finished the Introductory part of "Mr Gilfil's Love Story".

17. Finished the 2nd chapter forming end of Part I.

18. Herbert Spencer and Mr. Chapman dined with us.

19–23. Unable to work for four days from bilious headache. Finished Macaulay's History. We are reading Carlyle's History of French Revolution in the evenings. A few days ago, I received a letter from Mr. Chapman, proposing to give me in future 12.12.0 per sheet for what I write in the W. R.

Feb. 1. Received a pleasant letter from Blackwood, telling me what was said at Edinburgh about the 1st Part of Amos. Reading Burke's "Reflections on French Revolution" and "Mansfield Park" in the evenings.

Feb. 11. Sent off to Edinburgh the first two parts of "Mr. Gilfil's Love Story", after having a delightful letter from Blackwood, impatient for more M.S. I have been suffering much from headache and general malaise for the last month, and this has retarded me and made writing heavy work.

Feb. 14. A letter from Blackwood saying that he is delighted with my M.S. and will send a proof in a couple of days. I am reading the *Œdipus Rex*.

Feb. 28. Finished Part III of "Mr. Gilfil's Love Story", and received cheque from Blackwood for Part I (£21.0.0).

March 2. Wrote to M. d'Albert, from whom I received a letter a week or two ago. Herbert Spencer came, walked with us in the Park, and dined with us. I wrote to Sara, also, this morning telling her my impressions from her book just published – "Christianity and Infidelity".

March 15. Sunday evening. We set off on our journey, at 9 o'clock, and slept at the Paddington Station.

16. Travelled by express from London to Plymouth. It was a delicious sunshiny day, and I enjoyed the simple English landscape in the early part of our way – the little willow-bordered streams, blue as sapphires, the soft brown uplands, and the villages with their tiled roofs, yellow and olive-coloured in the sunlight, from their coating of lichen. We reached Plymouth a little after five, and went to the Globe Hotel, from which the Truro coach starts. Before our *Thé dinatoire* we walked to the Hoe and saw the Harbour, the breakwater, and Drake's island. Plymouth is a cheerful, clean place, with the finest site I remember to have seen for a sea-port, except Genoa.

17. We set off by coach to Truro at 10$^{1}/_{2}$ under a cloudy sky. We had the back places outside, and, hard seats excepted, a very agreeable journey. Our travelling companions were a stout elderly gentleman who had travelled a great deal, bald and benevolent; an old Scotch sailor, who had come over in the vessel where the drunken captain had flogged a boy to death, and who was now travelling from Dundee to Penzance, to give his evidence in the captain's trial; a pretentious, vulgar young man with smart clothes, dirty nails, and original information on physiology; and, for part of the way, a Devonshire lass who shook hands with us all round at parting, and a Devonshire lad with scarlet flowered plush waistcoat and yellow and flowered silk neckerchief, who ate buns industriously from the time we started till his large stock was exhausted. The old sailor was a fine specimen of a simple, brave, kind-hearted man – a natural gentleman. For part of our way, until after we reached Bodmin, the country was charming – clear, rushing, winding streams, great hills, their sides clothed with woods hoary with grey lichen, and deep valleys which the unfinished railway spanned with its viaducts. But by and bye we got into the dreariest scenery of Cornwall: treeless, rough wastes, the relics of former mines; works for the preparation of the white clay used in making porcelain, where the chief objects were hovels for packing the blocks of dried, purified clay, as white as chalk, and oblong tanks where the clay is put to be purified; and throughout all this region of mines and clay works, the streams are thick and coloured or

else milky white. At St. Austel, where there is a fine church tower, we got inside, and found an intelligent companion, who told us something of the miners and their customs. At St. Probus, a little village through which we passsed, there is another exquisite church tower, but the landscape all the way is bare and dreary. It was nearly dark when we reached Truro and exchanged our stage coach for the railway. We arrived terribly weary at Penzance, about half past eight.

18. The morning was so dismal – the rain pouring down and the wind reported to be 'due west' – that we gave up our voyage to the Scilly Isles, and persisted in spite of the Captain's testimony to the good character of the wind. When the rain abated we set out to look for lodgings and, owing apparently to the glorious freedom of our will, chose the worst. However, we spent the evening pleasantly, in spite of ailing bodies, reading Mrs. Gaskell's pretty Cranford.

19. This morning the sun shines again, and we have sat down to our desks in home fashion. Reading, in the evening, "Poor Peter".

20. I was not well enough to take a long walk yesterday, but today, we went to Marazion, the pretty, clean village opposite St. Michael's Mount. The day was not bright; still, the view of the mount was beautiful – its graceful pyramidal form finely crowned by the irregular outline of the old castle.

21. Today we found a charming walk inland, along roads bordered with clear, rushing streams, avenues of elms here and there, and stone built banks under the hedge-rows. Began "The Scarlet Letter".

22. Sunday. A sunny day. We had a glorious walk, that reminded us of Ilfracombe – the roads leading over hills from which we had a view of other, distant hills, purple with the shadows of the many clouds that floated in the blue sky. I noticed the bright red tips of the trees which were most abundant in the hedge-rows, and we learned from a Cornish man, in his Sunday clothes, whose appearance promised us "good civility" that these trees were the "Cornish Elm".

23. So calm today, we could not hear the waves from our room in the morning. The sea is smooth as a lake. But there have been some hail showers, and the air is sharp. We had a delicious walk in the afternoon, clear running brooks everywhere; road-side carpeted with the heart shaped leaves of the celandine, the golden flowers peeping up here and there. I began to read Miss Catlow's Botany.

25. Packed up last night, hoping to cross to Scilly this morning, but the wind was against us, so we spent a loitering day.

26. We were called at six this morning to go on board the Ariadne. There was a delicious light from the lately risen sun over the waters and St. Michael's Mount, and the first minutes on board were very enjoyable, but we soon went below out of the rain and were glad to lie down in our berths. After a 6 hours' voyage which in spite of illness, seemed short, we landed on St Mary's, got comfortable lodgings at the Post Office, and went out on the hill to look at the

lovely prospect – the blue sea breaking in white foam against little violet-coloured islands.

April 8th. Since I made the last entry in my journal we have had many delicious walks and seen many beautiful sights – on clear days the smaller islands with their lovely colouring specking the blue sea, the white foam prancing round them; on more sombre days the grand rocky coast of the southern side of St. Mary's – Peninis, the Giant's Castle etc. Or we have walked over the furze and heath clad hills and heard the air ringing with larks.

Since we came here Chrissey has lost her pretty little Fanny, and I am still waiting anxiously for news of Katy and herself – both ill of fever when I last heard. News, too, has come from Barbara in Algiers – the probability of her marrying Dr. Bodichon, a French army physician.

Today I have finished "Mr. Gilfil's Love Story". We are reading Carlyle's Cromwell and Aurora Leigh again in the evenings. I am still in the Œdipus Tyrannus, with Shelley's poems, and snatches of Natural History.

8th. A letter from my brother this evening tells me that Chrissey and her Katy are better, but not yet out of danger.

9. Wrote nothing this morning. At 1/2 past eleven we went out hunting on Carne Thomas, but without much success. I was feeling poorly and unable to exert myself. In the evening I began the "Life of Charlotte Brontë" aloud. Deeply interesting. My head was terribly bad.

10. Still headache – unable to write, or to enjoy reading.

11. Headache again, but went out for a glorious hunt on the rocks. No letter about Chrissey.

16. No letter again. The weather has been cold and dreary and I have been constantly ailing. Pleasant letter from Sara. They are all settled now in their new home – Ivy Cottage, having said goodbye to pretty Rosehill. Last night I finished Currer Bell's Life. Today I have finished the Œdipus Rex.

18. I have begun my third story – the title not yet decided on. A letter from Sarah with news that Chrissey is still very ill, and Katie too.

22. Letter from my Brother saying Chrissey is worse. I am deeply depressed and feeling the ills of life more than the blessings, though these are so many. A letter from Barbara too. Reading the Œdipus Coloneus and Shelley. I have begun Draper's Physiology, too but rarely have spirit and clearness of brain for it. Tonight we finished Aurora Leigh for the second time.

May 2. Received letters saying Chrissey is out of danger and Katie doing well. Also letters from Blackwood, expressing his approbation of Part 4 of Mr. Gilfil's Love Story. He writes very pleasantly, says the Series is attributed by many to Bulwer, and that Thackeray thinks highly of it. This was a pleasant fillip to me, who am just now ready to be dispirited on the slightest pretext.

May 11. Left St. Mary's, Scilly, in the Ariadne at 2 o'clock p.m. and reached Penzance about 10. Spent a comfortable day at Dingley's, taking a walk among the pretty fields and lanes in the morning, and having a long chat with Mr. Conch, who called, in the evening.

13. Went to Falmouth outside the omnibus – a sufficiently pleasant drive, though cold. Got down at the Green Bank, lunched and walked to the Castle, and read "Emma" in the evening.

14. From Falmouth to Plymouth by steamer. Dined at Mrs. Downton's, and went on board again for Jersey at 6.

15. Reached Jersey at 10 a.m. and went to Jeune's, the Union Hotel in Royal Square. After resting we walked to St. Aubin's looking out for lodgings, but came to the conclusion that the place offered no advantages for a zoologist, so returned without engaging ourselves.

16. To Gorey in search of lodgings again, and found them at Rosa Cottage, where we established ourselves this evening (Saturday).

21. A letter from Nutt saying Brockhaus will give £50 for the Goethe – the best news the post has brought us since we left Richmond. The other day we had a pleasant letter from Spencer saying that he had heard "Mr Gilfil's Love Story" discussed by Baynes and Dallas, as well as previously by Pigott, all expressing warm approval, and curiosity as to the author. I am still writing the First Part of "Janet's Repentance", the third story.

26. Wrote to my Brother and Sister Fanny. Received a pleasant letter from Blackwood, enclosing one from Archer Gurney to the "author of Mr. Gilfil's Love Story". Read G. the three first chapters of Janet's Repentance. We are reading Draper's Physiology in the evenings.

30. Finished Part 1 of "Janet's Repentance".

June 22. My mind has been too intensely agitated and occupied during the last three weeks, for me to have energy left to make entries in my journal, though I have often been regretting that the days pass by without registering the beauties we see in our walks. In the interim I have had an interesting correspondence with Blackwood, have received a letter from Mr. Holbeche inquiring about my marriage, and have given him a full and explicit answer, have had letters from my sisters and from Rosehill and have been writing my second part of "Janet". The wild flowers are in great beauty just now, and I notice that everything is earlier here than in the calendars for England. The walks are endless and all enchanting, though for the last week or so we have enjoyed them less because of the harsh east winds. A letter from Barbara, received long after it was written announced to us that she was to be married on the 15th of this month.

June 27. Finished the second Part of "Janet's Repentance".

July 8. They are hay making now in all the meadows, and the lovely grasses will soon only be left in fringes on the roadsides and under the hedgerows. The weather has become windy and disagreeable again, and the trees have the monotonous dark green tint of high summer.

July 24th. Said good bye to Gorey at 6 o'clock this morning: travelled by steamer to Southampton and thence to London, where we arrived about 10 p.m. Slept at the Craven Hotel.

25th. Came on to Richmond, unpacked, and were settled in our old home as usual by 6 o'clock.

27th. Lucrezia Borgia, and Ristori as Lady Macbeth in the sleep-walking scene.

31. Sara Hennell came and staid all night. We received a letter from Varnhagen with a book by Fräulein Assing, his niece – a biography of the Countess of Ahlefeldt, the friend of the poet Karl Immermann.

August 1. Finished Part 3 of "Janet's Repentance", and read it to G. in the evening. Aug. 4. Dr. Bodichon and Barbara came.

Aug. 12. Finished the Electra of Sophocles and began Æschylus – Agamemnon.

Aug. 24. G. set out for Hofwyl with Bertie.

Sep. 2. Put the last stroke to Janet Part IV, deferred owing to headache.

Sep. 3. Finished Buckle's History of Civilization in England vol. I which I began a fortnight ago. G. at home again. Read to him Janet Part IV in the evening.

Friday. 4. Sent off Part IV to Blackwood.

Friday. Oct. 9. Finished "Janet's Repentance".

10. Sent off the Fifth Part of "Janet" to Blackwood.

Thursday. 22. *Began my new novel, "Adam Bede".*

- 29. Received a letter from Blackwood, offering me £120 for the first Edition of "Scenes of Clerical Life".

Nov. 6. Received my first proof of the 'Scenes', to be published in two vols.

Nov. 28. A glorious day, still autumnal and not wintry. We have had a delicious walk in the park and I think the colouring of the scenery is more beautiful than ever. Many of the oaks are still thickly covered with leaves of a rich yellow brown; the elms golden, sometimes still with lingering patches of green. On our way to the Park, the view from Richmond hill had a delicate blue mist over it that seemed to hang like a veil before the sober brownish yellow of the distant elms. As we came home, the sun was setting on a fog-bank and we saw him sink into that purple ocean. The orange and gold passing into green above the fog-bank – the gold and orange reflected in the river in more sober tints.

The other day as we were coming home through the park after having walked under a sombre, heavily clouded sky, the westering sun shone out from under the curtain, and lit up the trees and grass, thrown into relief on a background of dark purple cloud. Then as we advanced towards the Richmond end of the park the level reddening rays shone on the dry fern and the distant oaks and threw a crimson light on them. I have especially enjoyed this autumn the delicious greenness of the turf in contrast with the red and yellow of the dying leaves.

Sunday, Dec. 6. Finished the Agamemnon today. In the evenings of late, we have been reading Harriet Martineau's sketch of The British Empire in India, and are now following it up with Macaulay's articles of Clive and Hastings. We have lately read H. M.'s Introduction to the History of the Peace and have begun the History of the Thirty Years' Peace.

8. We have been reading the last two evenings, the Christmas number of Household Words – "Perils of certain English Prisoners" – by Wilkie Collins and Dickens. I am reading "Die Familie" by Riehl, forming the third volume of the series, the two first of which "Land und Volk" and "Die Bürgerliche Gesellschaft", I reviewed for the Westminster.

10. Major Blackwood called – an unaffected agreeable man. It was evident to us when he had only been in the room a few minutes that he knew I was George Eliot.

Thursday. 17. Read my new story to G. this evening as far as the end of the third chapter. He praised it highly. I have finished "Die Familie" by Riehl, a delightful book. I am in the Choephoræ now. In the evenings we are reading History of Thirty Years' Peace and Béranger. Thoroughly disappointed in Béranger.

Dec. 19. Saturday. Alone this evening, with very thankful solemn thoughts – feeling the great and unhoped for blessings that have been given me in life. This last year especially has been marked by inward progress and outward advantages. In the Spring, George's History of Philosophy appeared in the New Edition – his Sea-side Studies have been written with much enjoyment and met with much admiration and now they are on the verge of being published, with bright prospects. Blackwood has also accepted his Physiology of Common Life; the 'Goethe' has passed into its third German edition; and best of all, G's head is well. I have written the Scenes of Clerical Life – my first book – and though we are uncertain still whether it will be a success as a separate publication, I have had much sympathy from my readers in Blackwood, and feel a deep satisfaction in having done a bit of faithful work that will perhaps remain like a primrose root in the hedgerow and gladden and chasten human hearts in years to come.

Christmas Day. George and I spent this lovely day together – lovely as a clear Spring day. We could see Hampstead from the park so distinctly that it seemed to have suddenly come nearer to us. We ate our turkey together in a happy 'solitude à deux'.

Sat. Dec. 26. G. set out today at 12 o'clock for Vernon Hill for a week's holiday.

Dec. 31. The last night of 1857. The dear old year is gone with all its *Weben* and Streben.[1] Yet not gone, either; for what I have suffered and enjoyed in it remains to me an everlasting possession while my soul's life remains. This time last year I was alone, as I am now, and dear George was at Vernon Hill. I was writing the Introduction to Mr. Gilfil's Love Story. What a world of thoughts and feelings since then! My life has deepened unspeakably during the last year: I feel a greater capacity for moral and intellectual enjoyment, a more acute sense of my deficencies in the past, a more solemn desire to be faithful to coming duties, than I remember at any former period of my life. And my happiness has deepened too: the blessedness of a perfect love and union grows daily. I have had some severe suffering this year from anxiety about my sister and what will probably be a final separation from her – there has been no other real trouble. Few women, I fear have had such reason as I have to think the long sad years of youth were worth living for the sake of middle age.

Our prospects are very bright, too. I am writing my new novel. G. is full of his "Physiology of Common Life" which Blackwood has accepted with cordial satisfaction; and the first part, on "Hunger and Thirst" appears in the January No. of Maga. He has just finished editing Johnston for which he is to have 100 guineas. And we have both encouragement to think that our books just coming out – "Sea-side Studies" and "Scenes of Clerical Life" will be well received.

So goodbye, dear 1857! May I be able to look back on 1858 with an equal consciousness of advancement in work and in heart.

Money received for work in 1857

	£. s. d.
"Mr. Gilfil's Love Story", Part 1. March	21. 0.0
Do. Parts 2 & 3, April & May	45. 0.0
" Pt. 4. June	22.10.0
" Pt. I of "Janet's Repentance"	27. 0.0
" Pt. II " "	24. 0.0
" Pt. III " "	20. 0.0
" Pt. IV " "	21. 0.0
" Pt. V " "	30. 0.0
"Amos Barton"	52.10.0
	£263. 0.0
First Edition of Clerical Scenes	120. 0.0
	£383. 0.0
Additional Sum in consideration of 250 copies	60. 0.0
	£443. 0.0

1 German, 'activities and endeavours'.

Jan. 2 [1858]. G. returned from Vernon Hill, and I read to him, after the review of my book in the "Times", the delicious scenes at Tetterby's with the "Moloch of a baby" in the "Haunted Man".

Jan. 5. Herbert Spencer came to walk and dine with us.

6. The "Scenes of Clerical Life" came today bound in two goodly volumes. Finished Chapter 4 of my novel.

13. G. went today into the city to see Langford about the "Clerical Scenes". 750, including 100 sent to Edinburgh, already disposed of to the libraries and booksellers. Letter from Blackwood the other day saying he should have the pleasure of making me both payments together.

Sunday. Cold and sore throat, but enjoying the writing of my 5th chapter. I have begun the Eumenides, having finished the Choephoræ. We are reading Wordsworth in the evenings – at least G. is reading him to me. I am still reading aloud Miss Martineau's history.

20. Letter from Dickens. Read aloud the additional dialogue in the chapter of "The Hall Farm". G. admired it very much.

Jan. 31. Finished Chapters 7 and 8 – the dialogue between Dinah and Mr. Irwine, and the rest up to the arrival of the Rector and Captain at Adam's cottage. Headachy since yesterday. Letter from Barbara, at last!

Feb. 1. My Headache continuing, G. proposed we should go out for an excursion, the morning being brilliant. We went to Windsor, but the cold was so bitter that we were glad to return home at half past two, after walking along the great avenue towards the Forest, and seeing the Royal Chapel. The Chapel is not satisfactory to the eye, from the flatness of the roof.

2nd and 3rd. Unable to work still, so that I have lost 3 days. Gave up Miss Martineau's History last night after reading some hundred pages in the second volume. She has a sentimental, rhetorical style in this history which is fatiguing and not instructive. But her history of the Reform Movement is very interesting. G. has finished The Excursion, which repaid us for going to the end by an occasional fine passage even to the last. He has now begun the other poems of Wordsworth. This morning I finished the Eumenides. Wrote to Barbara, 79, East Fifteenth Street, New York. Bessie Parkes has written to me wishing me to contribute to the "English Woman's Journal", a new monthly which, she says, "We are beginning with a £1000 and great social interest".

Feb. 10. Finished Chapter 9. Reading Macaulay in the evening. The "Prometheus" in the morning.

16. Wretched with headache for several days since the 10th and my work has been almost at a stand still.

Friday. 26. We went into town for the sake of seeing Mr. and Mrs. Call, and having our photographs taken by Mayall.

28. Mr. John Blackwood called.

March 4. He came again, and I gave him my M.S. to the end of the second scene in the wood.

7. We went into town again and did errands. I wrote my will, and signed it in the presence of Mr. Chapman and Mr. Birt.

8. Wrote Chapter 14 up to the going to bed.

Ap. 1. Received a letter from Blackwood, containing warm praise of 'Adam Bede', but wanting to know the rest of the story in outline before deciding whether it should go in the Magazine. I wrote in reply, refusing to tell him the story.

Ap. 3. I pack up this journal now, since it is not empty enough to be companion [sic] on my second visit to Germany, whither we set out next Wednesday, the 7th.

Oct. We reached Munich on the 11th of April, and remained there until the 7th of July, when we set out on our journey to Dresden by way [of] Vienna. We reached Dresden, I think, on the 18th of July, and remained there until the 30th of August. We staid two nights at Leipsic on our way home, where we arrived on the night of Sep. 2nd. Such record as I made of our time in Germany is contained in another book.[2]

Sep. 8. I finished the second volume of Adam Bede and sent it off to Blackwood.

Oct. 29. George took the M.S. of the third volume up to p. 216 to town, to be dispatched to Edinburgh. I finished this morning Horace's Epistle to the Pisos, which I have been reading at intervals.

Sunday. 31. A rather misty, yet fine day, this last of October. Barbara came (accompanied by Bessie) to bid us Good-bye before her departure to Algiers, whither her husband, Dr. Bodichon is gone before her to provide a house for them. We walked by Ham Common through the Park.

November 1. I am alone to-night, G. being gone on one of his rare visits to town. I have begun Carlyle's Life of Frederic the Great, and have also been thinking much of my own life to come. This is a moment of suspense, for I am awaiting Blackwood's opinion and proposals concerning Adam Bede.

November 4. Received a letter from Blackwood containing warm praise of my 3rd volume and offering £800 for the copyright of Adam Bede for four years. I wrote to accept.

5. Herbert Spencer came to dine with us and brought the unpleasant news that Dr. Chapman had asked him point blank if I wrote the Clerical Scenes. I wrote at once to the latter to check further gossip on the subject.

2 See 'Germany 1858'.

Nov. 10. Wilkie Collins and Mr. Pigott came to dine with us, after a walk by the river. I was pleased with Wilkie Collins – there is a sturdy uprightness about him that makes all opinion and all occupation respectable.

Nov. 16. Wrote the last word of Adam Bede, and sent it to Langford. *Jubilate!*

Nov. 25. Corrected the first four sheets of proof this morning. Afterwards, we had a visit from Mr. Bray, who told us much that interested us about Mr. Richard Congreve, and also his own affairs – his unpopularity among the Coventry artisans, etc. etc.

27. Herbert Spencer came to dine with us, and consult us about a letter of John Mill's, which he proposed to use as a testimonial in seeking an appointment as Foreign Consul.

30. I received the other day an offer from Tauchnitz for the English reprint of "Clerical Scenes" – £30. I may also note, by way of dating the conclusion of an acquaintance extending over eight years, that I have received no answer from Dr. Chapman to my letter of the 5th, and have learned from Mr. Spencer that the circumstances attending this silence are not more excusable than I had imagined them to be. I shall not correspond with him or willingly see him again.

Christmas Day. George and I spent this wet day very happily alone together. We are reading Scott's Life in the evenings with much enjoyment. I am reading through Horace in this pause.

Monday Dec. 27. George left me today to pay a short visit at Vernon Hill.

30th. Received a letter from Dr. Chapman.

31st. The last day of the dear old year which has been full of expected and unexpected happiness. Adam Bede has been written, and the second vol. is in type. The first No. of George's "Physiology of Common Life" – a work in which he has had much happy occupation – is published to-day, and both his position as a scientific writer and his inward satisfaction in that bent of his studies have been much heightened during the past year. Our double life is more and more blessed – more and more complete.

For Work in 1858

	£
Copyright of Adam Bede for four years	800
American Reprint	30
German Reprint of Clerical Scenes	30
do. of "Adam"	50
Additional in considn. of success	800
German Translation	25
Dutch Reprint	10

[1859] The New Year opened with rain, but brought me back my dear husband in safety. I corrected today the last sheets of the second vol. of Adam Bede, and wrote a brief answer to Dr. Chapman.

Jan. 12. We went into town today, and looked in the Annual Register for cases of *inundation*. Coming home we saw Erasmus Wilson who had been reading "Hunger and Thirst", and expressed great value for it. Letter from Blackwood today speaking of renewed delight in Adam Bede, and proposing 1st February as the day of publication. Read the article in yesterday's *Times* on George's Sea-side Studies – highly gratifying. We are still reading Scott's life with strong interest; and G. is reading to me Michelet's book "*De l'Amour*".

Saturday 15. I corrected the last sheets of Adam Bede, and we afterwards walked to Wimbledon to see our house, which we have taken for seven years. I hired the servant – another bit of business done; and then we had a delightful walk across Wimbledon Common and through Richmond Park, homeward. The air was clear and cold – the sky magnificent.

Monday Jan. 31. Received a cheque for £400 from Blackwood, being the first instalment of the payment for 4 years' copyright of Adam Bede. Tomorrow the book is to be subscribed, and Blackwood writes very pleasantly – confident of its "great success." Afterwards we went into town, paid money into the Bank and ordered part of our china and glass, towards housekeeping.

Feb. 6. Yesterday we went to take possession of Holly Lodge, which is to be our dwelling, we expect for years to come. It was a deliciously fresh, bright day. I will accept the omen.

11. Friday. Today we entered our new home, and after two or three days of preparatory arrangement we hope to be thoroughly settled.

Saturday 12. Received a cheering letter from Blackwood, saying that he finds Adam Bede making just the impression he had anticipated among his own friends and connexions, and enclosing a parcel from Dr. John Brown "To the author of Adam Bede". The parcel contained "Rab and his Friends", with an inscription.

22. Today G. went into town and brought home the news that "Adam Bede" was moving, but at the same time said other things which depressed me. I am saddened and discouraged with life – perhaps from physical ailments and household annoyances.

24. Pleasant news from Edinburgh about Adam Bede: that Mr. Caird admires it and had forgotten time in reading it. Letter of warm acknowledgment from Mrs. Carlyle, and one from Dr. John Brown. Good news, too, about the Physiology of Common Life: the first No. having sold near upon 6000, the second 5000.

26. Very laudatory reviews of "Adam Bede" in the Athenæum, Saturday Review, and Literary Gazette.

Mar. 14. My dear Sister wrote to me about three weeks ago, saying she regretted that she had ever ceased writing to me, and that she has been in a consumption for the last eighteen months. Today I have a letter from my niece Emily telling me her mother has been taken worse and cannot live many days.

March 15. Chrissey died this morning, at a quarter to 5.

23. The M.S. of Adam Bede came this morning from Blackwood, who has had it bound in russia, before sending it to George in answer to his request.

April 26. Finished a story – "The Lifted Veil" – which I began one morning at Richmond, as a resource when my head was too stupid for more important work.

27. Resumed my new novel, of which I am going to rewrite the two first chapters. I shall call it provisionally, "The Tullivers", for the sake of a title *quelconque* – or perhaps, "*St. Ogg's on the Floss*".

May 2. G. and I went into town. He saw Simon, who examined him with the stethoscope, and declared him to be quite free from organic disease. This is a great blessing to me, for last week he fainted in his dressing-room, without any previous complaint of malaise, and since then I had been doubly anxious about him.

May 3. I had a letter from Mrs. Richard Congreve telling me of her safe arrival with her husband and sister at Dieppe. This new friend whom I have gained by coming to Wandsworth, is the chief charm of the place to me. Her friendship has the same date as the success of Adam Bede – two good things in my lot that ought to have made me less sad than I have been in this house.

May 9. George and I had a delicious drive to Dulwich, and back by Sydenham. We staid an hour in the gallery at Dulwich, and I satisfied myself that the St. Sebastian is no exception to the usual "petty prettiness" of Guido's conceptions. The Cuyp glowing in the evening sun, the Spanish Beggar boys of Murillo, and Gainsborough's portrait of Mrs. Sheridan and her sister are the gems of the gallery. But better than the pictures was the fresh greenth of the Spring – the chestnuts just on the verge of their flowering beauty, the bright leaves of the limes, the rich yellow-brown of the oaks, the meadows full of buttercups. We saw for the first time, Clapham Common, Streatham Common, and Tooting Common – the two last like parks rather than Commons.

My Journal is continued at the opposite end, by mistake, as a continuation of the History of Adam Bede.[3]

June 1. At p. 85 of my new novel.

3 The entries from 1 June 1859 to 19 June 1861 are written at the 'opposite end' of this journal volume, following on from the material printed in 'The making of George Eliot'.

Sunday, 5. Blackwood came and we concocted two letters to send to the Times, in order to put a stop to the "Liggins" affair.

June 20. We went to the Crystal Palace to hear the "Messiah", and dined afterwards with the Brays and Sara Hennell. I told them I was the author of Adam Bede and Clerical Scenes, and they seemed overwhelmed with surprize. This experience has enlightened me a good deal as to the ignorance in which we all live of each other.

July 9. George and I started for Switzerland, and reached Paris at 10 o'clock at night. Slept at the Hotel du Danube.

10. Sunday. We spent a delightful day in Paris, in spite of heat and headache. To the Louvre first, where we looked chiefly at the Marriage at Cana, by Paul Veronese. This picture, the greatest I have seen of his, converted me to high admiration of him. Next, we took a carriage and drove to the Bois de Boulogne, getting down on our return at the Palais de l'Industrie, where we saw poor statues, and took abominable ices. Afterwards we strolled in the Palais Royale and looked at the shops, took a carriage in the evening along the Boulevards, and so passed the time till we went to the railway, on which we were to journey through the night to Strasburg.

11. Arrived at Strasburg about 10 in the morning, washed and breakfasted at the Maison Rouge, then went to look at the glorious cathedral, of which we bought a print. To the railway again in the afternoon, and at Bâle in the evening: I, feeling very ill, and fit only for bed.

12. Up at five and on the railway to Lucerne. Much relieved by the cooler morning air, and able to look out on the landscape with some enjoyment the latter part of the way. A broadchested man, with coloured tickets stuck out round his hat came into our carriage: he was to be one of the competing shooters with the rifle at the approaching Zurich festival, and had purchased these tickets at a high price, as a sign of the right to shoot for as many prizes. At 9 or 10 o'clock we got to Lucerne, glad to make a home at the charming Schweizerhof on the banks of the lake. G. went to call on the Congreves, and in the afternoon Mrs. Congreve came to chat with us. In the evening we had a boat on the Lake.

13. Wednesday. G. set off for Hofwyl at five o'clock, and the days were passed by me, till his return on Saturday, in quiet chats with the Congreves and quiet resting on my own sofa.

16. Saturday. G. came back to me about 9, and in the evening we had a walk to the Drei Linden, a very fine point for a view of the lake and mountains.

17. Sunday. We went up the lake in the steamer, dined at Fluellen, and returned in the evening to join the Congreves in their sunset view from the Linden.

18. In the evening, we went to Bâle on our way home.

19. Spent the morning in Bâle, chiefly under the chesnut trees near the Cathedral, I reading aloud Flouren's sketch of Cuvier's labours. In the afternoon on the railway.

20. From Bâle to Paris all night. Coffee at 6 o'clock opposite the station where we were to start for Boulogne. Reached Boulogne at 1 o'clock, and rested there.

21. From Boulogne homeward. Found a charming letter from Dickens, and pleasant letters from Blackwood: nothing to annoy us. Magnificat anima mea![4]

Before we set off we had heard the excellent news that the fourth edition of Adam Bede (5000) had all been sold in a fortnight. The fifth edition appeared last week.

July 29. *Pug came*!

Aug. 11. Received a letter from an American – Mr. T. C. Evans – asking me to write a story for an American periodical. Answered, that I could not write one for less than £1000, since in order to do it, I must suspend my actual work.

12. Mr T. C. Evans wrote again, declaring his willingness to pay the £1000, and asking for an interview to arrange preliminaries.

15. Declined the American proposition which was, to write a story of 12 parts (weekly parts) in the New York "Century", for £1200.

17. Received a letter from Blackwood with a cheque of £200, for 2nd edition of Clerical Scenes.

20. Letter from the troublesome Mr. Quirk of Attleborough, still wanting satisfaction about Liggins. I did not leave it unanswered, because he is a friend of Chrissey's; but G. wrote for me.

25. In the evening of this day we set off on our journey to Penmaenmawr. We reached Conway at 1/2 past 3 in the morning, and finding that it was hopeless to get a bed anywhere, we walked about the town till the morning began to dawn and we could see the outline of the fine old castle and battlemented walls. In the morning we went to Llandudno, thinking that might suit us better than Penmaenmawr. We found it ugly and fashionable. Then we went off to Penmaenmawr which was beautiful to our hearts' content – or rather discontent; for it would not receive us, being already filled with visitors. Back again in despair to Conway, where we got temporary lodgings at one of the numerous Jones's. This particular Jones happened to be honest and obliging and we did well enough for a few days in our indoor life, but out of doors there were cold winds and rain. One day we went to Abergele, and found a solitary

4 Latin, 'my soul doth magnify the Lord': utterance of the Virgin Mary (Luke 1: 46–55) and often used by GE from now on to mark such occasions as the completion of a major writing task.

house called Beach House, which it seemed possible we might have at the end of a few days. But no! and the winds were so cold on this northerly coast that George was not sorry, preferring rather to take flight southward. So we set out again on the 31st and reached Lichfield about 1/2 past 5. Here we meant to pass the night, that I might see my nieces – dear Chrissey's orphan children – Emily and Kate. I was much comforted by the sight of them, looking happy, and apparently under excellent care, in Miss Eborall's school. We slept at the Swan, where I remember being with my father and mother when I was a little child, and afterwards with my father alone in our last journey into Derbyshire. The next morning we set off again and accomplished our journey to Weymouth. Here again we found difficulty in getting lodgings, this being the fullest moment of the season, but at last we settled ourselves at 39, East Street, with some good Wesleyans, honest and kind. Many delicious walks and happy hours we had in our fortnight there. A letter from Mr. Langford informed us that the subscription for the 6th edition of Adam Bede was 1000. Another pleasant incident was a letter from my old friend and schoolfellow Martha Jackson, asking if the author of Adam Bede was *her* Marian Evans.

Friday Sep. 16. We reached home about 4 o'clock, and found letters awaiting us – one from Mr. Quirk, finally renouncing Liggins! – with tracts of an ultra-evangelical kind for me, and the Parish Mag. etc. – from the Rev. Erskine Clark of St. Michaels, Derby, who had written to me to ask me to help him in this sort of work.

Sunday 18. A volume of devotional poetry from the authoress of "Visiting my Relations", with an inscription admonishing me not to be beguiled by the love of money: *In much anxiety and doubt about my new novel.*

October 7. Since the last entry in my journal, various matters of interest have occurred. Certain new ideas have occurred to me in relation to my novel and I am in better hope of it. At Weymouth I had written to Blackwood to ask him about terms supposing I published in Maga. His answer, offering me £3000 for publishing in Maga and four years' copyright, determined me to decline. On Monday the 26th we set out on a three days' journey to Lincolnshire and back – very pleasant and successful both as to weather and the objects I was in search of. A less pleasant business has been a correspondence with a *crétin* named Bracebridge, a Warwickshire Magistrate who undertakes to declare the process by which I wrote my books – and who is the chief propagator and maintainer of the story that Liggins is at the bottom of the Clerical Scenes and Adam Bede. It is poor George who has had to conduct the correspondence, making his head hot by it, to the exclusion of more fructifying work. Today in answer to a letter from Sara, I have written her an account of my interviews with my Aunt Samuel. This evening comes a letter from Miss Brewster: full of well-meant exhortation.

16. Sunday. Yesterday, as I lay in bed ill from the exertion of walking about in the Zoological gardens, whither we went for the sake of George's health, came a pleasant packet of letters: one from Blackwood saying that they are printing a

seventh edition of Adam Bede (of 2000), and that Clerical Scenes will soon be exhausted, and an anonymous letter asking me for a sequel to "Adam", telling all about Hetty, the silk handkerchief and the locket and earrings! I have finished the first volume of my new Novel, "Sister Maggie", have got my legal questions answered satisfactorily, and when my headache has cleared off must go at it full speed.

Tuesday 25. The day before yesterday Herbert Spencer dined with us, and there was talk – for the last time, I hope – about my books. We have made a resolution that we will allow no more talk in our own house on the subject. I find it destructive of that repose and simplicity of mind which is the only healthy state in relation to one's books: it has the same effect as talking of one's religion, or one's feelings and duties towards one's father, mother, or husband.

We have just finished reading aloud "Père Goriot" – a hateful book. This evening I am at p. 31 of my 2nd vol.

I have been reading lately and have nearly finished Comte's Catechism. We have also read aloud "Tom Brown's School Days" with much disappointment. It is an unpleasant, unveracious book.

Friday 28. Received from Blackwood a cheque for £400, the last payment for Adam Bede in the terms of the agreement. But in consequence of the great success, he proposes to pay me £800 more at the beginning of next year. Yesterday Smith the publisher called, to make propositions to G. about writing in the Cornhill Magazine.

November. 10. Dickens dined with us today, for the first time, and after he left I went to the Congreves', where George joined me and we had much chat – about George Stephenson, religion etc.

11. I received today a charming letter from Mrs. Gaskell, in which she says "Since I heard, from authority, that you were the author of "Scenes of Clerical Life" and "Adam Bede", I have read them again; and I must, once more, tell you how earnestly, fully, and humbly I admire them. I never read anything so complete and beautiful in fiction, in my life before". Very sweet and noble of her! – I have been very poorly almost all this week, and sticking terribly in the mud so far as my writing is concerned.

18. On Monday, Dickens wrote asking me to give him, after I have finished my present novel, a story to be printed in "All the Year round" – to begin four months after next Easter, and assuring me of my own terms. The next day G. had an interview by appointment with Evans (of Bradbury and Evans) and Lucas, the editor of "Once a week", who after preliminary pressing of G. himself to contribute, put forward their wish that I should give them a novel for their Magazine, promising higher terms than Blackwood would give. They were to write and make an offer, but have not yet done so. We have written to Dickens saying that *Time* is an insurmountable obstacle to his proposition as he puts it. – Today G. has been into town again to see the attorney, Mr. Sheard, about our wills. – I am reading Thomas à Kempis.

Saturday 19. Mr. Lockhart Clarke and Mr. Herbert Spencer dined with us.

Sunday 20. A headache this morning induced us to give up work and walk in Richmond Park, where there is still much beauty of tint from the red brown of the ferns and the yellow elm leaves. George called at Professor Owen's, and I walked home alone. We are reading aloud Huber's History of Bees, and the Life of Charlotte Bronte for the second time.

21. Mr. Sheard brought our Wills for signature, and I consulted him about the legal affairs of my novel.

22. We have been much annoyed lately by Newby's advertisement of a book called "Adam Bede, Junior, a Sequel", and today Dickens has written to mention a story of the tricks which are being used to push the book under the pretence of its being mine. One Librarian has been forced to order the book against his will, because the public have demanded it! Dickens is going to put an article on the subject in Household Words, in order to scarify the rascally bookseller. The Blackwoods are slow to act in the matter – hitherto, have not acted at all: not being strongly moved, apparently by what is likely to injure me more than them. Several persons have expressed their surprize at the silence of the Blackwoods.

23. We began Darwin's work on "The Origin of Species" tonight. It seems not to be well written: though full of interesting matter, it is not impressive, from want of luminous and orderly presentation.

24. This morning I wrote the scene between Mrs. Tulliver and Wakem. G. went into town, and saw Young Evans (of Bradbury and Evans), who agreed that it would be well to have an article in Punch on this scoundrelly business of "Adam Bede, Junior". A divine day! I walked out and Mrs Congreve joined me. Then music, Arabian Nights, and Darwin.

25. Not having been quite pleased with Blackwood's behaviour of late, I have written to have a clear understanding from him whether he wishes to continue to be my publisher. – I am reading old Bunyan again after the long lapse of years, and am profoundly struck with the true genius manifested in the simple, vigorous, rhythmic style.

26. Letter from Lucas, editor of "Once a week", anxious to come to terms about my writing for said periodical. The three boys have all written us charming letters this week.

27–29. Mr. Meredith brought his boy to see me – a nice little fellow; and we had a Sunday walk together. On the 29th I sent off a packet of letters for the boys.

30. Yesterday a letter came from Blackwood proving that he had been under the supposition that I did not intend to publish my next book with him. I wrote again, explaining. Also a letter to the "Times" and to Delane about Newby.

December 1. Bradbury and Evans have offered me £4500 for my new novel, i.e. for publication in "Once a Week" and for two subsequent editions.

3. Finished the third Book of my story and read it aloud to George, who is delighted.

5. A Batch of letters this morning: – one from M. d'Albert, telling me of the death of Dr. Chaponnière – one from Barbara with good news about herself, and one from Blackwood, who is coming to us the day after to-morrow, when we shall discuss the publication of my book.

6. Wrote to Sara, Barbara, and M. d'Albert.

7. Mr John Blackwood came, and took away my MS. to read.

9. Tauchnitz, the Leipzig publisher, called, on a visit of homage – a tall fresh-complexioned, small-featured, smiling man, in a wig.

10. We went into town to-day to make purchases, and I returned thoroughly tired.

11. A dense fog, and a sense of ailing kept me indoors. I read the Life of Francois de Sales.

15. Blackwood proposes to give me £2000 for 4000 copies of an edition at 31/6, and after the same rate for any more that may be printed at the same price. £150 for 1000 at 12/- – and £60 for 1000 at 6/-. I have accepted.

Christmas Day. We all, including Pug dined with Mr. and Mrs. Congreve, and had a delightful day. Mr. Bridges was there too.

Jan. 11 [1860]. Since Xmas Day, I have had a letter from Barbara asking me to lend her £100 in June to give to Dr. Elizabeth Blackwell, and have answered her. I have had a very delightful letter of sympathy from Professor Blackie of Edinburgh, which came to me on New Year's morning, and a proposal from Blackwood to publish a third edition of Clerical Scenes at 12/-. George's article in the Cornhill Magazine – the first of a series of "Studies in Animal Life" is much admired and in other ways our New Year opens with happy omens.

16. Finished my 2nd Volume this morning, and am going to send off the M.S. of the 1st vol. tomorrow. We have decided that the title shall be "The Mill on the Floss". We have been reading "Humphrey Clinker" in the evenings and have been much disappointed in it, after the praises of Thackeray and Dickens. Today, being a clear bright day, we have walked from Richmond through the dear old Park; and I have read aloud this evening the last of Heyse's "Vier neue Novellen". On Thursday (12th) Herbert Spencer dined with us and we discussed his plan of publishing his series of works by subscription in quarterly parts.

Jan. 26. Mr. Pigott, Mr. Redford and Mr. F. Chapman dined with us and we had a musical evening, Mrs. Congreve and Miss Bury joining us after dinner.

31. This last day of January, after nearly a week of headache, I have finished the second chapter of Vol. III, p. 38.

Feb. 4. Came, this morning, a letter from Blackwood announcing the dispatch of the first eight sheets of proof of "The Mill on the Floss", and expressing his delight in it. Tonight G. has read them and says "Ganz famos!" Ebenezer![5]

Feb 12. *Sunday*. G. went yesterday for a little holiday to Lymington, so I am alone for two days – the first time in this house. I have today finished correcting proofs up to p. 256 of the 1st vol. and am at p. 117 M.S. of my 3rd vol.

23. Sir Edward Lytton called on us – Guy Darrell in propria persona.

29. G. has been into town today and has agreed for £300 for "the Mill on the Floss" from Harpers of New York. This evening too has come a letter from Williams and Norgate, saying that Tauchnitz will give £100 for the German reprint: also that "Bede Adam" is translated into Hungarian. At p. 213 of M.S.

March 5. On Saturday the 3rd, a letter came from Emily at Lichfield saying that dear little Katie is dead. I was ill with bilious headache which continued yesterday and prevented me from working. Yesterday, Mr. Lawrence, the portrait painter lunched with us, and expressed to G. his wish to take my portrait.

9. Oppressed every day with threatening headache, hampering my power of work. No farther than 251 p. of my M.S. this morning, in consequence. Yesterday a letter from Blackwood expressing his strong delight in my 3rd Vol. which he had read to the beginning of "Borne on the tide". Despatched 50 more pages. Today Young Blackwood called: told us among other things, that the last copies of Clerical Scenes had gone today – 12 for export. Letter came from Germany announcing a translation of G.'s Biographical History of Philosophy.

11. Today the 1st vol. of the German translation of Adam Bede came. It is done by Dr. Frese, the same man who translated the Life of Goethe. At p. 268 of M.S. this evening.

20. Prof. Owen sent me his Palæontology to-day. Have missed 2 days of work from headache and so have not yet finished my book. At p. 307.

21. Finished this morning "The Mill on the Floss" – writing from the moment when Maggie, carried out on the water, thinks of her mother and brother.

We hope to start for Rome on Saturday, 24th.

Magnificat anima mea!

July 1. We found ourselves at home again in Holly Lodge, after three months of delightful travel to Rome first – then to Naples, Florence, Bologna, Padua, Venice, Verona, Milan, Como, Splugen, Zurich, Berne and Geneva. From Bern we brought our eldest boy Charles, to begin a new period in his life, after four

5 German, 'Quite splendid, first rate, capital'. Ebenezer was the Stone of Help raised by Samuel. See 1 Samuel 7: 12.

3. A page from Diary 1854–1861, recording the period from 4 February to 1 July 1860, which includes completion of *The Mill on the Floss*, and a brief account of the journey to Italy described in detail in 'Recollections of Italy. 1860'.

years at Hofwyl. During our absence "The Mill on the Floss" has come out (April 4) and achieved a greater success than I had ever hoped for it. The subscription was 3600 (the number originally printed was 4000, and shortly after its appearance, Mudie having demanded a second thousand, Blackwood commenced striking off 2000 more, making 6000. While we were at Florence I had the news that these 6000 were all sold and that 500 more were being prepared). From all we can gather the votes are rather on the side of "The Mill", as a better book than "Adam".

July 27. We are full of anxiety and trembling hope just now about Charley who is preparing to pass a competitive examination for a supplementary clerkship in the Secretary's department of the Post Office, the nomination having been kindly procured for him by Mr. Anthony Trollope.

August 21. Since I wrote the last entry, Charlie has passed his examination and has achieved the triumph of being first on the list of competitors. He has already been at his post for a week as a supplementary clerk, commencing with a salary of £80. This is a great addition to our comfort – to have him well-placed for the present, with a reliable prospect of future advancement.

Aug. 28. We have succeeded in letting our house at last, and are now searching and considering as to our future residence. I have sat today for the eighth time for my portrait to Laurence who still demands another sitting. I feel much depressed just now with self-dissatisfaction and fear that I may not be able to do anything more that is well worth doing.

Sep. 4. We have been making repeated journeys to town lately, trying to find a suitable house. Today we have made an offer of £1600 for a house in Park Village West.

27. Today is the third day we have spent in our new home here at 10, Harewood Square. It is a furnished house in which we do not expect to stay longer than six months at the utmost. Our books are all in order now, and we are expecting Thornie home from Hofwyl this evening, to be taken in a few days to Edinburgh for a year's study at the High School. – Since our return from Italy I have written a slight Tale – "Mr. David Faux, confectioner" – which G. thinks worth printing. – Today I have received from Blackwood the first cheque (£1000) for the "Mill on the Floss."

Sep. 30. This evening G. set off with Thorney by express to Edinburgh, in order to place him at the High School, under Dr. Schmitz.

Oct. 5. My time since G's departure has been chiefly spent in illness. Last night he returned, much satisfied with his visit to Edinburgh, and with the arrangements he has been able to make about Thorney. That is another step taken in life's duties.

Nov. 28. Since I last wrote in this journal I have suffered much from physical weakness accompanied with mental depression. The loss of the country has seemed very bitter to me, and my want of health and strength has prevented me from working much – still worse, has made me despair of ever working well again. I am getting better now by the help of tonics, and I should be better still if I could gather more bravery, resignation and simplicity of striving. In the meantime my cup is full of blessings: my home is bright and warm with love and tenderness, and in more material vulgar matters we are very fortunate. I have invested £2000 in East Indies Stock, and expect shortly to invest another £2000, so that with my other money, we have enough in any case to keep us from beggary.

Last Tuesday, the 20th, we had a pleasant evening. Anthony Trollope dined with us, and made us like him very much by his straightforward, wholesome *Wesen*.[6] Afterwards Mr. Helps came in, and the talk was extremely agreeable. He told me the Queen had been speaking to him in great admiration of my books, especially the Mill on the Floss. It is interesting to know that Royalty can be touched by that sort of writing – and I was grateful to Mr. Helps for his wish to tell me of the sympathy given to me in that quarter.

Today I have had a letter from M. d'Albert, saying that at last the French edition of Adam Bede is published. He pleases me very much by saying that he finds not a sentence that he can retrench in the first vol. of "The Mill".

I am engaged now in writing a story, the idea of which came to me after our arrival in this house, and which has thrust itself between me and the other book I was meditating. It is "Silas Marner, the weaver of Raveloe". I am still only at about the 62nd page, for I have written slowly and interruptedly of late.

Dec. 17. We entered today our new home – 16, Blandford Square, which we have taken for three years, hoping by the end of that time to have so far done our duty by the boys as to be free to live where we list.

31. On this last day of the old year, I have received a cheque for £1300, being £1000 for the second instalment for "The Mill" and £300 for the 12/- editions of Adam Bede and Clerical Scenes.

This year has been marked by many blessings, and above all by the comfort we have found in having Charles with us. Since we set out on our journey to Italy on March 25 the time has not been fruitful in work: distractions about our change of residence have run away with many days, and since I have been in London my state of health has been depressing to all effort. May the next year be more fruitful!

6 German, 'character, nature'.

Money for "The Mill on the Floss", 1860

	£
For 4000 copies in 3 vols	2000.0.0
American Reprint	300.0.0
German do	100.0.0
Dutch translation	10.0.0
2500 additional copies of "The Mill"	1250.0.0
German Translation	25.0.0
	3685.0.0
For "Silas Marner", 1861	
4000 copies at 12/-	800.0.0
American reprint	100.0.0
Dutch do	10.0.0
German reprint	50.0.0
4000 additional Copies	800.0.0
	5345.0.0
Cheaper Editions in 1860	
2000 of "Adam" and Cl. Sc.	300.0.0
2000 of "the Mill"	300.0.0
	5945.0.0
Received for "Adam" etc. 1859	1942.0.0
For Clerical Scenes, 1857	443.0.0
	£8330.0.0

Feb. 1 [1861]. The first month of the New Year has been passed in much bodily discomfort – making both work and leisure heavy. I have reached p. 209 of my story, which is to be in one volume, and I want to get it ready for Easter; but I dare promise myself nothing with this feeble body.

The other day I had charming letters from M. and Mde. d'Albert, saying that the French "Adam" goes on very well, and showing an appreciation of the "Mill" which pleases me.

13. This last fortnight has been almost uninterruptedly filled with bodily discomfort. On the second, both G. and I were so poorly that we determined to run away to the country for a few days. Charles went with us on the Saturday afternoon to Dorking, leaving us on Sunday evening. On Monday the morning was brilliant, and we enjoyed a long walk. The country air had quite cured me already. In the afternoon we drove to Leatherhead and round home by several villages and a fine common. But the weather seemed already to threaten a change, and we resolved to return home the next day. In the morning we saw Deepdene, and returned home by railway to dinner, much strengthened and refreshed by our draughts of fresh air. But yesterday and today I have been as ill as ever – incompetent from biliousness either to work or to enjoy. On Monday we went to a concert at St. James's Hall, and heard a grand quartett of

Beethoven's, and the Kreuzer Sonata, played by Vieuxtemps and Miss Goddard.

March 10. Finished "Silas Marner", and sent off the last 30pp. to Edinburgh. Magnificat anima mea!

Sunday. 16 [17]. Tomorrow we are to set off to Hastings, for the refreshment of our souls and bodies, after nearly six months of town.

April 19th. We set off on our second journey to Florence, through France, and by the Cornice. Our weather was delicious, a little rain on our way from Toulon to Vidauban, and a storm on our way to Cannes being the only interruptions to our sunshine; and we suffered neither from heat nor from dust. Dear Florence was lovelier than ever on this second view, and ill health was the only deduction from perfect enjoyment. We had comfortable quarters in the Albergo della Vittoria on the Arno; we had the best news from England about the success of "Silas Marner"; and we had long letters from our dear boy to make us feel easy about home. I was too ill with a severe cold even to go out for nearly a week after our arrival, and after that George was constantly ailing with sore throat or cough, making him dread the breeze in driving, so that for the first three weeks of our stay our expeditions were confined to walks about the town; the most interesting of all expeditions, however. Later on we visited Pistoia, and the old points of view – San Miniato, Galileo's Tower, Bello Sguardo and Fiesole. Our only new drive was to Coreggi, and we were so delighted with the place and the view from it that we went a second time. At the end of May, Mr. T. Trollope came back from England and persuaded us to stay long enough to make the expedition to Camaldoli and La Vernia in his company. We arrived at Florence on the 4th of May, and left it on the 7th of June: – thirty four days of precious time spent there: will it be all in vain? Our morning hours were spent in looking at streets, buildings and pictures, in hunting up old books at shops or stalls, or in reading at the Magliabecchian library. Alas! I could have done much more if I had been well – but that regret applies to most years of my life. – We returned by steamer from Leghorn to Genoa; then by railway to Lago Maggiore, which we traversed from Arona to Magadino in the steamer; then, the next morning with post horses on our way to the St. Gothard as far as Airolo; then, the next day, under rain, over the snowy pass, and through the narrow vallies to Fluelen [sic] on the Lake of Lucerne (the latter part of the way with brightening skies). We persevered, after the passage along the Lake, in getting to Olten the same night, so that the next morning about eleven we arrived at Berne, where we rested at the pleasant Bernerhof and had Bertie with us till we started for Bâle at half past nine the next morning. The dear boy is improved, and we had excellent testimony about him from Dr. Müller, so that here also we have grounds of comfort. – We travelled right on to Paris, reaching it at 1/2 past 5 in the morning. Our day there was spent partly at the Louvre and partly in resting; our evening in seeing very unsatisfactory acting at the Gymnase.

The next day, June 14th, we reached home, and found all well there. Blackwood, having waited in town to see us, came to lunch with us, and asked me if I would go to dine at Greenwich on the following Monday, to which I said "Yes" by way of exception to my resolve that I will go nowhere for the rest of this year. He drove us there with Colonel Stewart, and we had a pleasant evening – the sight of a game at Golf in the Park, and a hazy view of the distant shipping with the Hospital finely broken by trees in the foreground. At dinner Colonel Hamley and Mr. Skene joined us: Delane who had been invited, was unable to come. The chat was agreeable enough, but the sight of the gliding ships darkening against the dying sunlight made me feel chat rather importunate. I think, when I give a white bait dinner I will invite no one but my second self, and we will agree not to talk audibly.

This morning for the first time I feel myself quietly settled at home. I am in excellent health, and long to work steadily and effectively. If it were possible that I should produce *better* work than I have yet done! At least there is a possibility that I may make greater efforts against indolency and the despondency that comes from too egoistic a dread of failure.

This is the last entry I mean to make in my old book in which I wrote for the first time at Geneva, in 1849. What moments of despair I passed through after that – despair that life would ever be made precious to me by the consciousness that I lived to some good purpose! It was that sort of despair that sucked away the sap of half the hours which might have been filled by energetic youthful activity: and the same demon tries to get hold of me again whenever an old work is dismissed and a new one is being meditated.

June 19th. 1861

II. *Diary 1861–1877*

Of all GE's journals, this diary most closely documents her processes of composition, and the list of 'Order of Writings' in the front of the book (evidently written in 1876 or '7) provides a stocktake of her career. The diary opens in the thick of research for *Romola*, and records the alternation of her exhilaration in tracking down sources, together with her despondency at the pain of composition, in a manner that underlines the force of Lewes's injunction to John Blackwood: 'When you see her, mind your care is to discountenance the idea of a Romance being the product of an Encyclopaedia.'[1] Some of the notes she describes herself as taking are to be found in other manuscript notebooks she was keeping at this time.[2] There are references to her dealings with George Smith about publication of this novel and with Frederic Leighton about the illustrations, but only a brief formal statement concerning the break with Blackwood for the publication of *Romola.* Both the separation and the reconciliation are documented in letters, rather to the advantage of the Blackwoods (*Letters*, vol. 4, pp. 33–9 and 44; pp. 240–8).

The span of this diary covers the composition not only of *Romola*, but of *Silas Marner, Felix Holt*, poetry including the verse drama *The Spanish Gypsy*, her brief re-engagement with writing for periodicals in the mid-1860s (when Lewes was involved with the *Cornhill*, *Fortnightly Review* and *Pall Mall Gazette*), and finally *Middlemarch* and *Daniel Deronda*. Though *Daniel Deronda* was as earnestly researched as *Romola*, the diary gives relatively little evidence of that research, nor of her studied preparation for both *Felix Holt* and *Middlemarch* (there are, of course, separate 'quarries' and other notebooks for all three novels and *The Spanish Gypsy*). Once *Middlemarch* begins to take

1 *The George Eliot Letters*, ed. Gordon S. Haight, 9 vols (New Haven, Yale University Press, 1954–78), vol. 3, p. 474

2 Andrew Brown discusses GE's notes for *Romola* in his introduction to the Clarendon edition of the novel (Oxford University Press, 1993): 'Five of her surviving notebooks contain material relevant to *Romola*, though only two of them are devoted exclusively to it' (p. xxi). These are 'Quarry for Romola', Princeton University Library, Parrish Collection AM 14959, and 'Florentine Notes', British Library Add. MSS 40768. Brown shows the nature and extent of GE's use of her preparatory reading in the novel, and provides a full account of the composition of the novel and negotiations about publishing it.

shape, poetry is abandoned and so is the diary. The months of silence are a provocative contrast to the almost daily record of despair in the painful writing of *Romola*, and George Eliot is reticent also about the resounding success of *Middlemarch*.

Beyond the record of work accomplished, there are in addition tantalising references to projects which seem never to have eventuated: indeed, the diary closes with the comment that 'Many conceptions of works to be carried out present themselves . . . my mind is embarrassed by the number and wide variety of subjects that attract me'. This diary relates to a phase of experiment in GE's career: *Romola* represents a change of genre (to historical fiction) and mode of publication (serial), as well as of publisher; she works in poetry, drama, periodical essays; opens a new vein of fiction in *Felix Holt* and *Middlemarch*, and in *Daniel Deronda* produces the most original of all her novels. There was further experiment in forms of publication with the half-volume parts in which *Middlemarch* and *Daniel Deronda* were originally issued. Yet while this is a period of experiment, it is also one of consolidation, as her work goes through new editions and impressions, with the collected Cabinet edition in preparation as this diary closes.

The diary includes some occasions of self-conscious reflection on the significance of the record it contains: for instance, on 31 January 1862, she notes:

> I have been reading to G. some entries in my note-book of past times in which I recorded my *malaise* and despair. But it is impossible to me to believe that I have ever been in so unpromising and despairing a state as I now feel. – After writing these words, I read to G. the Proem and opening scene of my novel and he expressed great delight in them.

(Surely a fair example of what Lewes described to John Blackwood as 'an art of ingeniously self tormenting', *Letters*, vol. 5, p. 246: though on another occasion, the shrewd Blackwood commented to his brother 'I think Lewes fidgets her in his anxiety both about her and her work and himself', *Letters*, vol. 6, p. 253). Her habit of reading back over her journals persisted at intervals almost to the end of her life, as later diaries show. Edith Simcox reports her referring in 1879 to what is identifiably the diary entry for 1 January 1865 (*Letters*, vol. 9, p. 266).

Eliot used this diary with even less regularity than her earlier one. The entries are generally more staccato, with hardly any of the description and anecdote found previously. They become very much more spasmodic after the death of Thornton Lewes in 1869, marked in the diary by a moving formal tribute, ending with the *memento mori*, 'This death seems to me the beginning of our own'. She did not resume diary entries for seven months, and then worked in from the other end of the volume.

The Lewes sons are very much a presence throughout, especially London-based Charles. The purchase of the lease of The Priory at Regent's Park for £2000 in August 1863, after a succession of earlier attempts to find an acceptable central London residence, was nominally on Charles's account. At about the same time, the engaging but difficult Thornton was despatched to Natal: he had threatened to go 'out to Poland to fight the Russians', a plan his exasperated father described as 'too preposterous' (*Letters*, vol. 4, p. 102). Bertie followed him in 1865: he died there in 1875, leaving a widow and two children, ingratiatingly named Marian and George, to be provided for. After his marriage in 1865, good-natured Charles continued to be a kind of factotum for his parents. Music brought him close to GE, and he gave her substantial support after GHL's death in 1878.

GE's involvement with the Leweses extended well beyond GHL and his sons – among others, GHL's widowed sister-in-law Susannah and her son Vivian appear in this journal. GHL was himself a thoughtful son to his mother, visits to and from whom until her death in 1870 are noted by GE. More than familial socialising was involved: these relationships with various Lewes connections (including Lewes's wife Agnes) represented a substantial ongoing financial commitment.

While GE's professional life is now the dominant one, her journal records GHL's publishing activities, as editor (*Fortnightly Review*, 1865–6) or editorial adviser (*Pall Mall Gazette*, 1865–8), and as author (*Studies in Animal Life* came out in 1862, *Aristotle, A Chapter from the History of Science* in 1864, revised editions of the *Life of Goethe* in 1864 and of *Biographical History of Philosophy* in 1867 and 1871, three volumes of *Problems of Life and Mind* from 1874). There are inklings also of his role as her business manager, more conspicuously documented in correspondence.

Money still rates a mention, mainly in the careful recording of sales figures and payments, and in ways which indicate the relative affluence of the household now, such as the casual reference to an investment of £1000 in October 1861, and expenditure of £4 on a volume of Savonarola on 13 December that year. GE does not record John Cross's assumption in 1872–3 of his role as the Leweses' man of business, though Cross appears in GHL's diary giving advice on purchase of a carriage (*Letters*, vol. 5, p. 469 and n.). London outings and company feature: GE's literary success has consequences for her social life as well. She has conspicuously more contact with women, adding to the faithful friends of her own generation a circle of younger women, such as Georgiana Burne-Jones, and fervent admirers like Elma Stuart and Edith Simcox, both of whom made her acquaintance in 1872. Edith's 'The Autobiography of a Shirt Maker', begun in May 1876, provides in its jealous narrative of GE's last years a fuller account of GE in person than any other.

GE and GHL were often on the move in these years. They made frequent expeditions within Britain, usually represented as escapes from London, and took a third trip to Italy in 1864; then to Paris in January 1865 and to Normandy and Brittany in the summer of that year; to Germany and the Lowlands in 1866, and later to Spain, returning in March 1867. They travelled again to Germany in 1867 and to Germany and Switzerland in 1868, and made a fourth visit to Italy in 1869. While they were in Rome on that occasion, they met up with the Cross family, known previously to GHL through Herbert Spencer. The Crosses lived at Weybridge in Surrey, and while it was the young banker John whose entry into the lives of GE and GHL was to be most significant, the whole family circle turned out to be a congenial one. GE's journal makes no mention of this meeting, though a disconcerting entry in GHL's does. On 18 April, after a wet morning

> When a break in the clouds tempted us out we took umbrellas and walked to the Coliseum. Read Cellini. In the evening Mrs Cross with son and daughter came for an hour.
> *My FiftySecond Birthday*. Both Polly and I had entirely forgotten it.

Rosemarie Bodenheimer points out that after this 1869 journey, the Leweses developed a practice of spending the summer in the country, alternating the increasing busyness of London life with relative solitude.[3] By the early 1870s they had begun a search for a country house, which the increasingly indispensible John Cross brought to a satisfactory conclusion when he found The Heights at Witley for them in 1876. Journeys out of England continued in the 1870s, generally of shorter duration than previously (weeks rather than months). With travel now

3 Rosemarie Bodenheimer, *The Real Life of Mary Ann Evans: George Eliot Her Letters and Fiction* (Ithaca and London, Cornell University Press, 1994), pp. 243–4.

a regular experience, GE's practice of keeping a separate travel diary seems to have fallen away. The latest of such journals extant are those dealing with the Italian expedition of 1864 and that to Normandy in 1865. There is no reason to suggest that journals for the other expeditions ever existed, with the exception of that for the venture to Spain early in 1867. This loss is in any case a matter for regret, and the more so since the letters of both GE and GHL during their travels, and GHL's journal, provide exuberant accounts of perhaps their most enterprising itinerary.

The staples of this diary remain the same as in the 1854–1861 volume: work and worry – notably increasing concern about GHL's state of health, as well as GE's own miserable metabolism. We conjecture that some of her complaints may relate to menopause: the asterisks which appear from 12 July 1861 through to early 1868 seem to refer to her menstrual cycle (and some symptoms indicate premenstrual syndrome).

Use of the material in this volume by Cross and Haight is sparing. There are some pencilled markings in the margins of the manuscript which may relate to Cross's selection of material.

II. Diary 1861–1877

Order of Writings[1]

Amos Barton, 1856. Article on Young.
Mr. Gilfil's Love Story 1857.
Janet's Repentance 1857.
Adam Bede, 1858, published February 1859. The Lifted Veil April 1859.
The Mill on the Floss, published February 1860. Brother Jacob.
Silas Marner, published March 1861. Romola begun January 1862.
Romola ... finished June 9, 1863.
First draught of Spanish Gypsy, begun 1864, in September.
Felix Holt, begun, March 1865. A Minor Prophet finished January 1865.
Spanish Gypsy, finished April 29, 1868.
Agatha, finished, January 23, 1869.
How Lisa loved the King, finished February 15, 1869.
Brother and Sister, finished August 1, 1869.
Middlemarch (Vincy and Featherstone part) begun August 1869.
Legend of Jubal finished January 13, 1870.
Armgart finished, September 1870.
"Miss Brooke" begun, November 1870.
Middlemarch finished, September, 1872. Arion, April 1873.
Stradivarius, September, 1873.
Sketches towards Daniel Deronda, January and February 1874.
A Symposium, March and April 1874.
Daniel Deronda, Vols I and II finished. August 17, 1875.
" " Vol. III finished February 7, 1876.
" " Vol. IV beginning of June 1876.

Diary: July, 1861

1. Finished reading the four last volumes of the *Histoire des Ordres Religieux*. Began *La Beata*, a story of Florentine Life, by T. A. Trollope. I am also reading Sacchetti's Novelle, and Sismondi's History of the Italian Republics.

2. Desultory morning, from feebleness of head. Osservatore Fiorentino and Tenneman's Manual of Philosophy. In the evening La Beata.

3. Read Sismondi. Mr. Langford came and brought me *Le Moyen age illustré* and The Monks of the West.

1 This list is written in the purple ink which GE first uses in this volume in 1873, and was presumably made after June 1876. Approximately 5 cm. has been cut from the page.

4. Began Montalembert's "Monks of the West". Mr. Clark, of Cambridge, and Mr. Anthony Trollope dined with us. *Mrs. Browning died on the 29th.*

5. Continued the Monks of the West. Read in Sismondi, concerning the constitutions or forms of government of the Italian cities when they first emerged into historical notice. The first introduction of the Carroccio coincident with the increased importance of the infantry. Finished *La Beata*. In the afternoon, went to a concert of Hallé's, at which he played three Beethoven sonatas.

6. Read "Le Moyen Age", chiefly on Popular superstitions; looking also through other parts to see if it is worth while for me to keep the work. George was very poorly all morning, and lay on the sofa behind me. In the afternoon we walked to see Nursie. Read, in the Athenæum, an interesting article on Bishop Colenso's (of Natal), Letter to the Archbishop of Canterbury on the toleration of Polygamy in converts to Christianity. In the evening, read the "Monks of the West".

Sunday 7. Read the Monks of the West. In the afternoon went to the Zoological gardens. Read the Introduction to Savonarola's poems, by Audin de Rians, the Spectator and Athenæum. Played Beethoven with Charley. Busied myself with a plan of rational mnemonics in history.

8. Received cheerful letters from Cara and Sara. Promised to subscribe two guineas to Mr. Bray's Philosophy of Necessity.

9. Finished the first vol. of "Monks of the West". Read Comte on the Middle Ages. In the evening a bad headache came on.

10. Read the Cornhill, and Orley Farm, as *distraction* under a bad headache. Mrs Congreve came to lunch with us.

11. Headache still. Mrs. Bodichon came in the morning. In the evening, Miss Parkes; to learn my decision about contributing to the Victoria Regia. My decision is – "No".

*12. Wrote to Sara. Read 2nd vol. of Montalembert.

13. Read "Histoire des Ordres Religieux" and Monks of the West; finishing both.

Sunday 14. Not well enough to work much. Professor Blackie called. G. was very poorly.

*15. Read Sismondi. In the evening read Renan Etudes d'Histoire religieuse aloud to G.

16. Read Sismondi – vicissitudes of Florentine Government. Colonel Hamley called.

17. Sismondi. Began Virgil's Eclogues again. Went with G. to see Pictures at British Institution.

18. Finished 3rd vol. of Sismondi: began Buhle's History of Modern Philosophy. Virgil and Sacchetti.

19. Read 4th vol. of Sismondi, and G's article on Mad Dogs which he was going to send to Edinburgh.

20. 5th vol. of Sismondi. Went to see the Exhibition of the New Society of Water colours, where Corbauld's pictures from Adam Bede are hanging. A letter came from Mr. and Mrs. Trollope. We also went to Broadwood's to look at the grand pianos.

21. 6th vol. of Sismondi. Buhle. In the evening Dr. and Mrs. Bodichon were with us.

22. Read Hallam on the study of Roman law in the Middle Ages. Finished Virgil's Eclogues. Walked with G. and Dr. Bodichon toward Hampstead. Charlie distressed me by telling me of a little disappointment in his hopes at the Post Office.

23. Read nothing this morning, being occupied with thinking. Terribly depressed and hopeless.

24. Read Gibbon on the revival of Greek learning and Buhle on Ficinus. Walked with George over Primrose Hill. We talked of Plato and Aristotle.

25. Read Buhle on the philosophy of Ficinus. Savonarola's Sermons.

26. In the morning Thornton came home from Edinburgh and we were occupied with him. In the evening G. and I went to see Fechter as Hamlet, and sat next to Mrs. Carlyle.

27. Headache in the morning. In the evening Mrs. Bodichon came and the time passed agreeably.

28. Went with Mrs. Bodichon to the Unitarian Chapel in Little Portland Street; enjoyed the fine selection of collects from the Liturgy, but was rather wearied by a common place sermon by an elderly gentleman who, to our disappointment, was a substitute for James Martineau. Mr. Schütz Wilson lunched with us. In the evening I read Barbara's letters from Brittany.

29. Read Buhle on the Jewish and Alexandrian philosophy. Dr. Schmitz came to lunch with us, and talked of Thornie. Afterwards, G. and I went to Hampstead, where we found the ponds disappointingly shallow; but we brought home some embryonic and vermicular treasures in the glass jar and phial, and enjoyed the fresh air and wide view.

30. Read little this morning – my mind dwelling with much depression on the probability or improbability of my achieving the work I wish to do. I struck out two or three thoughts towards an English novel. G. and I have had the pleasure of dining alone, the boys being gone together to see their schoolfellow Empson. G. has been to Dr. Brinton to-day to consult him about his health which is still

unsatisfactory. I am much afflicted with hopelessness and melancholy just now: and yet I feel the value of my blessings. Before breakfast I have been reading Savonarola's Discourse on Government, and have looked into his Sermons on the Epistle of John and on the Psalm *Quam Bonus*.

31. Not well today. Mrs. Bodichon came in the evening and showed us her little sketches of scenes in Brittany.

August 1. Began Lastri – Osservatore Fiorentino – this morning, intending to go regularly through it. In the afternoon walked with G. to see Nursie surrounded by her little scholars. Struggling constantly with depression.

2. Read the 2nd and 3rd volumes of Lastri. Looked into the *Marmi* of Doni. Walked in the park with George. Read Sacchetti and Boccaccio's capital story of Fra Cipolla – one of his few good stories – and the Little Hunchback in the Arabian Nights, which is still better. Read Nardi in the evening.

3. Third vol. of Lastri. Sacchetti. In the evening we went to the Marybone Theatre and saw the Pirate of the Savannah!

*4. Went with Barbara to St. Margaret's church. In the afternoon to the Zoological gardens with Pater and boys. Miss Nannie Smith called to say good-bye in the evening. I have begun Bulwer's Rienzi, wishing to examine his treatment of an historical subject.

5. Read 4th vol. of Lastri. Had a bad headache most of the day.

6. Read Roscoe's Life of Lorenzo de' Medici. Headache still. Read some of Sacchetti's stories and spent the evening alone with G.

7. Still feeble and headachy. Continued Roscoe, with much disgust at his shallowness and folly.

8. Roscoe. Young Blackwood lunched with us. My head became worse again, and I was forced to lie down. In the evening music with the boys.

9. Read again Burlamacchi's Life of Savonarola. In the evening played to the boys' singing.

10. Walked with G. who had a headache, and enjoyed the morning lights in the Park. We talked of my Italian novel. Grandmamma came. In the evening, Mr. Pigott and Mr. Redford.

11. Sunday. Went with Barbara to the church in Vere Street, hoping to hear F. D. Maurice; but we heard only a curate, who, however, preached a sensible sermon.

12. Got into a state of so much wretchedness in attempting to concentrate my thoughts on the construction of my story, that I became desperate, and suddenly burst my bonds, saying, I will not think of writing! Read Sacchetti and began Pulci.

13. Looked over Catalogue of London Library, and finished with Roscoe's volumes. Began again the Life of Savonarola by Villani. Read of "Ecstasy".

14. Read "Savonarola". Went with George to the Zoological Gardens. In the evening Nursie came.

15. Looked into the Novellieri Scelti. Discussed the plot of my novel with G. and in the course of our conversation I struck out an idea with which he was thoroughly satisfied as a "backbone" for the work. After lunch we went to the London Library and looked over some books. In the evening Dr. Bodichon came in, and afterwards I began Mrs. Jameson's Sacred and Legendary art.

16. George has been very poorly to-day as well as yesterday – unable to work the whole morning – feeble and suffering. He is taking Dr. Brinton's prescriptions. Dr. B. tells him that the proximate cause of his bad health is a relaxed mucous membrane. I have never before seen him so feeble. Read Mrs. Jameson's "Legendary Art".

17. A letter from Miss Hennell gives me a painful sense that my old friends at Coventry are feeling more acutely than hitherto the pressure of their straitened circumstances, expecting to leave their pretty cottage, where they have lived these six years. – Read the 5th vol. of Lastri. Went to the Marybone theatre with Thornie to see Elkanah the Prophet. On our return, found Mr. Pigott and Mr. Redford, who gave us some music.

18. *Sunday*. Read the 6th vol. of Lastri and the Life of Savonarola. Walked with Pater and Charles to the Hampstead fields. Read Mrs. Jameson.

19. Walked in the morning with G. who was not well. Played on the piano throughout the evening.

20. Thornie started for Switzerland. This morning I conceived the plot of my novel with new distinctness.

21. Read Savonarola, and then ran through "Rienzi" to survey the treatment.

22. Spent most of my morning in meditating on my novel, and making out special wants. Walked with G. in Hyde Park. In the evening read Mrs. Jameson.

23. and 24. Read Savonarola, copied extracts on medical superstitions and read Mrs. Jameson. On the evening of 24, Mr. Pigott and Mr. Redford came, and we had music. These have been flaccid ineffective days, my mind being clouded and depressed.

25. Read Savonarola: remodelling of the Government. Yesterday, G. brought me Hymni and Epigrammata of Marullus which I had despaired of seeing except at the British Museum. Also Politian's Epistles, and Marchesei's works. In the afternoon we drove to Hampstead and returned by Highgate. Barbara came in the evening, and afterwards I read Mrs. Jameson.

26. Read Savonarola. Went with Barbara to her school and spent the afternoon there. G. very poorly today, with severe headache.

27. G. again suffering; so we went to Windsor, to try the effect of fresh air. In the evening Barbara and the Doctor came.

28. Read Tiraboschi and Rock's Hierurgia. Walked to Primrose Hill with G. Finished Vol. 1 of Sacchetti, and began Marullus. In the evening read Pettigrew on Medical Superstitions.

29. Read Tiraboschi on the Discovery of Ancient MSS., and *Manni*, Vite etc. Walked with G. in Hyde Park. Read Marullus. In the evening played with Charles and read Mrs. Jameson.

30. Read Tiraboschi and Manni's Life of Burchiello, copying extracts. Walked with G. to the Zoological Gardens, and came home with an inclination to headache. Barbara came in the evening.

31. Headache this morning. Read some of Tiraboschi and copied out the Lives of some saints from Mrs. Jameson. Walked in the Park with G. In the evening came Mr. Pigott and Mr. Redford and we had some music.

September 1. Sunday. Headache still so that the morning passed by with little profit. G. was poorly and we walked out together. I was better in the evening and read aloud to G. an article in National on the discoveries of Bunsen and Kirchoff. G. very poorly.

*2. Not well this morning, so that I was not able to read effectively. Read on Vestments in Rock's Hierurgia and corrected Adam Bede. Walked with G. to Primrose Hill. In the evening, read Mrs. Jameson and Orley Farm.

3. Mary Lee came to meet Mrs. Bodichon about taking the situation of Cook and Housekeeper, and my morning was broken by them. Wrote out the Ecclesiastical Vestments from Rock. In the evening Nursie came.

4. Read Legendary Art and wrote from it this morning. Walked into town with G. and packed. Tomorrow morning we start for Malvern, for the sake of George's health.

Sep. 18. Yesterday we returned from Malvern, with very promising results after a week's trial of the water cure there. During our stay I read Mrs. Jameson's book on the Legends of the Monastic orders, corrected the first vol. of Adam Bede for the next edition and began Marchese's Storia 'di San Marco. This morning, having headache I continued correcting Adam Bede and wrote to Miss Hennell.

23. Monday. I have been unwell ever since we returned from Malvern, and have been disturbed from various causes in my work, so that I have scarcely done any thing except correct my own books for a new edition. On Saturday G. returned from a two days' walking expedition with Mr. Spencer, and the latter dined with us along with Mr. Williams of Birmingham. Yesterday, George, Charlie, and I took a long walk to Hampstead chiefly in the rain, for the benefit of my head and spirits, and the experiment answered. Today, I am much better and hope to begin a more effective life tomorrow. Mr. Williams has been with us this evening, and consumed our hours in chat.

24. Thornie returned from Switzerland this evening. In the morning I wrote to my nephew Charlie and sent him ten shillings.

25. Finished correcting "The Mill on the Floss". Received from Blackwood a cheque for £1000 making up £1600 for 8000 copies of Silas M.

26. I began to correct the "Clerical Scenes". Walked with George to the Zoo. and saw a puppy Jaguar.

*27. Continued correcting Clerical Scenes. In the afternoon we went to Kirkman's to choose a piano. In the evening, ill.

28. Finished Clerical Scenes and began Silas Marner. In the evening Mr. Spencer, Mr. Pigott and Mr. Redford came. We talked with Mr. Spencer about his chapter on the Direction of Force, i.e. Line of least resistance.

29. Sunday. Finished Silas Marner. I have thus corrected all my books for a new and cheaper edition and feel my mind free for other work. Walked to the Zoo. with the boys. Read the newspapers, and in the evening played duets.

30. Took up again the MSS. connected with my Italian novel, and made various arrangements towards work. In the evening Thornie left us to go to Edinburgh.

October 1. An irregular morning, partly spent in playing on the piano. G. went into town to see about investments for £1000, and I walked out a little alone. In the evening I read aloud Charlie's compositions, which show very good sense in their effort to arrive at exactness of expression about common things.

2. Spent the morning in arranging the plot of my novel, and walked after lunch in Hyde Park with G. In the evening read Nerli. The coupons for Victoria Bonds came.

3. Today our new grand piano came – a great addition to our pleasures.

4. My mind still worried about my plot – and without any confidence in my ability to do what I want. Not well in the evening so that I read nothing but an article on the Mormons in the W. R.

5. Looked into the Archivio Storico and read some *Ricordi*, and "Lives" by Vespasiano. Grandma came to lunch with us. In the evening Mr. Redford and Mr. Spencer came and we had much music.

6. A wet and foggy day. Read about the prophecies of Savonarola. Walked round the Park with G. and C. In the evening read newspapers and the National and Westminster. In the latter, an interesting article on the Mormons.

7. Continued reading of Savonarola's prophecies. Began the first chapter of my novel. G. went into town, and I practised and had a bath. Afterwards Mary Lee came to say that Captain Willim had offered to give her equal wages with those offered by Mde. Bodichon, and it was concluded, owing to Mrs. B's kind consent, that she should go to Grandmamma's. In the evening played duets with C. Read Tiraboschi on Abate Girachimo, and Sismondi on the XVth Century. G. bought me a copy of Vasari.

8. Read on the Government of Florence. Walked into town with G. going into old bookshops, and to Gower St. to buy note-books. Read Ginguéné in the evening.

9. Read *Nerli*. Went to the Zoological gardens with G. and Herbert Spencer. At least I did so yesterday – for I have reversed the record of our afternoon walks. In the evening G. went to the Soirée of the Microscopic Society and I had a good practice on the piano.

10. Finished my reading of *Nerli*; walked to Hyde Park with G. Read a chapter on the Roman Law in the Middle Ages in Guizot's History of Civilisation in France. Played a long while with Charles in the evening and read Ginguéné.

11. Read Nardi's History of Florence. In the afternoon walked with Barbara, and talked with her from lunch till dinner time.

12. Having been excited and perturbed by the question of selling my copyrights, I was not able to read this morning, so I spent it at the piano. In the evening, we had our usual Saturday mixture of visitors talk and music, an agreeable addition being Dr. McDonnell of Dublin.

14. Read Nardi. Then G. being poorly, walked with him before lunch into the Hampstead fields to hunt. Read the newspapers, and then went with Barbara to her school to hear the children sing. In the evening G. was ill, so that we could not go to Mrs. Nutt's Ragged School as we intended.

15. Read Nardi. In the afternoon, Latin. In the evening Ginguéné.

16. Finished Nardi. Looked through Machiavelli's works. In the evening read Ginguéné.

17. Read Villari, making chronological notes. Then Muratori on Proper Names. G. was out, so I played on the piano, then walked out for an hour, and on returning, in consequence of a letter from Bradbury and Evans, wrote to Blackwood, declining to sell my copyrights for which he had offered £3000. Played all the evening till 10 and then read Ginguéné.

18. Walked with G. and Mr. Spencer to Hampstead and continued walking for more than five hours. It was a lovely October day.

19. My head inactive from excessive walking the day before. In the evening we had music: Dr. Baetcke, Mrs. Bodichon and Miss Parkes were our additional visitors.

20–24. Read Marchese's Storia di San Marco; began Politian's letters, and read Giannotti on the Government of Florence. On the 24 a sore throat I had had for a day or two turned into a severe catarrh, and I went to bed feeling very ill.

25. Ill in bed all day.

26. Better, but with headache still. Nevertheless I played a great deal in the evening, with Mr. Redford and Dr. Baetcke who were our only guests.

27. Headachy still. Read some of Sacchetti and Boccaccio. Walked out in the morning with G. and played duets in the evening. – This week I have had a further correspondence with Blackwood about the terms for the cheap editions of my books.

28–30. Not very well. Utterly desponding about my book.

31. Still bilious with an incapable head – trying to write, trying to construct, and unable.

Nov. 1. Friday. Went with G. to Mortlake and had a glorious walk through our dear old Park to Richmond. In the evening Charlie left us to spend his month's holiday at Hofwyl.

2. Spent my morning in brooding – producing little. In the afternoon went with G. into town to Regent St. and Holborn. In the evening Mr. Redford was our only guest.

3. Read Manni. Miss Nannie Smith came to bid me good by before starting for Rome. In the evening read the Newspaper, and an article on Renan in Blackwood.

4. Not well: did little, in consequence except reading Manni and Tiraboschi.

5. Read Cicero de Officiis, and began Petrarch's letters. Walked with G. into town, and looked at old books. *Dreadfully depressed about myself and my work*.

6. Received a letter from Charlie saying that he had arrived without accident at Hofwyl. So utterly dejected that in walking with G. in the Park, I almost resolved to give up my Italian novel.

7. Went to the Zoological Gardens with G. and found almost all the lovely golden fish, with winglike caudal fins, had disappeared.

8. Read Politian's Letters and Petrarch's. – Then Corniani and Manni. In the afternoon went shopping with G. to Redmayne's and then to the London Library where I looked through Selden's Titles of Honour and brought away *Monteil*, XVth century.

9. A lovely day! Walked in Hyde Park. In the evening Dr. Baetcke and Mr. Kunze the sculptor.

10. Sunday. New sense of things to be done in my novel, and more brightness in my thoughts. Yesterday, I was occupied with ideas about my next English novel; but this morning the Italian scenes returned upon me with fresh attraction. Walked in Regent's Park with G. and talked over my ideas with him. In the evening read Monteil – a marvellous book: crammed with erudition, yet not dull or tiresome.

11. We went to see Fechter in Othello.

12. Having heard on Friday from Charlie of his safe arrival, wrote to him in reply.

13. Wrote to Thornie.

14. Went to the British Museum Reading Room for the first time.

15. Bad headache. To the British Museum, looking over Costumes.

16. To the British Museum. In the evening Mr. Redford, Mr. Pigott and Mr. Colyter came. We had music, but my head was bad.

*17. Bad headache. Finished the Pirate.

18. Ditto. Arrivabene came yesterday.

19. My head better this morning. I reviewed my notes on costume. Meier's. Savonarola came. After lunch we went shopping. Read *La Tancia*, and Ginguéné, Roman Epic.

20. I read Craik's History of English Literature. Mrs. Congreve, Miss Bury and Mr. Herbert Spencer came to lunch, and staid the afternoon. In the evening read Craik up to end of XVth Century.

21–23. Received a letter from Sara on the 22nd and wrote to her in reply. On the 23rd (Saturday) we had friends and music in the evening, as usual.

24. *Sunday*. G. went to see Grandmamma today. I was not very well from a slight cold.

25–29. This week I have read a satire of Juvenal, some of Cicero *De Officiis*, part of Epictetus' Enchiridion, two cantos of Pulci, part of the Canti Carnascialeschi, and finished Manni's Veglie Piacevolé, besides looking up various things in the classical antiquities and peeping into Theocritus.

30. The last day of November! I have a tiresome little cough, which makes me rather low, and dull. Read Epictetus, and the sixth Satire of Juvenal, with part of a vol. of the Osservatore Fiorentino. In the evening we had Wilkie Collins, Mr. Pigott, and Mr. Spencer, and talked, without any admixture of music.

Dec 1. My cough became very bad last night and this morning, and my head being much shaken I spent the morning in reading Orley Farm and the newspapers. In the evening read Goldwin Smith's answer to Mansel. Charlie came home!

2. Monday. Read Epictetus and Politian's letters. In the evening Bekker's Charikles.

3–7. I continued very unwell until Saturday, when I felt a little better. In the evening, Dr. Baetcke, Mr. Pigott and Mr. Redford.

8. Sunday. G. had a bad headache, so we walked out in the morning sunshine. I told him my conception of my story, and he expressed great delight. Shall I ever be able to carry out my ideas? Flashes of hope are succeeded by long intervals of dim distrust. Finished the 8th vol. of Lastri, and began the IXth chapter of Varchi in which he gives an account of Florence.

9. Finished the Encheiridion of Epictetus. Wrote sketches of scenes. Finished the IXth chapter of Varchi, which contains many passages highly interesting to me. There came from the library Hody de Graecis Illustribus, in which I looked at the life of Marullus; Middleton's Free Inquiry, which is not the book I wanted, namely, the Letter from Rome; and Poggiana. G. brings me word from the British Museum, that Filelfo's letters are translated into Italian.

10. Wrote to Mr. and Mrs. Trollope. Went to the British Museum. Found some details in Ammirato's Famiglie Nobili Fiorentini. Filelfo's supposed "translated letters" was all a mistake. However coming home we bought a little copy of his letters which we found at Baldock's. In the evening I read Muratori on the Confraternità.

11. Received from Holbeche £47.11.0. Went to the British Museum after lunch and read in Litta's "Famiglie". Made notes in the evening from Marullus' Life in Hody. In the morning wrote a scheme of my plot.

*12. Read Sacchetti and the Letters of Filelfo. Finished writing my plot, of which I must make several other draughts before I begin to write my book.

13. Read Poggiana and finished looking through Filelfo's letters. In the afternoon walked to Molini's and brought back Savonarola's Dialogue, *de veritate Profetica*, and *Compendium Revelationum*, for £4! In the evening looked over the 9th Book of Varchi again.

14. Read half through the dialogue de Veritate Profetica. Read the Newspapers. In the evening came Mr. Huxley, Mr. Pigott and Mr. Redford.

15. Sunday. Read through Middleton's Letter from Rome, and finished de Veritate Profetica.

16. Read the Compendium Revelationum. In the evening Lastri.

17. Studied the topography of Florence. Read the IXth vol of Lastri, and some of Sacchetti.

18. Read Sacchetti, Macchiavelli's History, and Heeren on the XVth Century. Began Lastri X.

19. Read Theocritus, and Politian's Letters, and Sacchetti. Miss Allen came in the evening. The Aldine Edition of Politian came.

21. Walked toward Hampstead, in the morning.

22. Read Politian's Lamia, and the Osservatore. Mr. Blackwood came to lunch with us. Then we walked to Nursie's. In the evening wrote notes, and read Osservatore.

23. Continued Politian's Lamia. Read XIII and XIV vols of Lastri. Mr. and Mrs. Blackwood came. Read Sacchetti, and Lastri in the evening.

24. Walked into town bookhunting, and bought Ammirato and Malmantile.

25. *Christmas day*. We spent this day with all blessings surrounding us. Only our trio to eat the turkey and plum pudding. We had asked poor Miss Allen if she would be alone, and if so we would have had her join us; but she was going to her mother's. Mr Spencer, our other lonely friend had got his brother with him, so that we could have the pleasure of being simply en famille without prickings of conscience for our selfishness.

26. Read the Malmantile. Reviewed my notes. Received a letter from "Jane Evans" asking me for a negative photograph of myself to aid her in building a school. Wrote in answer. Read Sacchetti, and Luigi Pulci's novel, and part of Lasca's story of Lorenzo and the Medico Manente.

27 and 28. Read Marullo's epigrams, and studied details about Florence. On Saturday rather a dull evening with Mr. Spencer, Mr Pigott and Mr. Redford.

29. Sunday. Read passage from Du Bois Reymond's book on Johannes Mueller, à propos of visions. Finished Libro 1 of Machiavelli's Istorie. Read Blackwood and wrote out notes on the Monastic orders.

30 and 31. Read Topography and Chronology. Walked into town with G. to the Bank. Read Sacchetti and Machiavelli.

1862. Jan 1. Mr Blackwood sent me a note enclosing a letter from Montalembert about Silas Marner, and a few hours after a china *Pug* as a memorial of my flesh and blood Pug, lost about a year ago.

I began my Novel of Romola.

2. Mr. Blackwood called. I wrote part of an Introductory chapter.

3. 4. A slight sore throat. A stupid evening on Saturday. Only Dr. Baetcke and Mr. Pigott. G. going poorly to bed.

5. Sunday. An unproductive morning, from inefficiency of brain. Mr. Spencer came after lunch and chatted for an hour. Then I walked with Charlie. My cold became worse.

*9. Much troubled by my cold since Sunday. G. also poorly. Made index to Osservatore, and read Juvenal, Pulci, Macchiavelli etc.

11. A dreadful headache made the prospect of company a heavy one. Mrs. Peter Taylor and Miss Remond were of our party, Mr. Spencer and his father, Dr. Baetcke etc.

12. Sunday. My head still very bad. Read newspapers only. Blackwood came in the afternoon.

13. Letters from Sara and Cara, telling their pleasure in Mr. Noel's visit to them. My head was still too feeble for me to work efficiently. In the evening I read the Apocrypha and Müller's book on Language. Finished *Macchiavelli's Istorie*.

14. My head better at last. I wrote a continuation of my introductory chapter. In the evening read Macchiavelli. G. very poorly.

18. Saturday. We had an agreeable evening. Mr. Burton and Mr. Clark of Cambridge made an acceptable variety in our party.

19. My head became very bad, and I was unable to write or read.

20. Head still bad, producing terrible depression. Read Müller.

21. My head a little better in the evening, when I finished Müller's Lectures on Language.

22. Able to write again. Looked at the Chronicle of the conquest of the Morea yesterday, and into Finlay's History of Medieval Greece.

23. Wrote again, feeling in brighter spirits. Mr. Smith the publisher called and had an interview with G. He asked if I were open to "a magnificent offer". This made me think about money – but it is better for me not to be rich.

24. Our heads being frail, we walked to the British Museum, and I wrote out Antonio Pucci's poem on the Mercato Vecchio.

25. We went to the British Museum through the rain, and I made some notes from Cambi. Came home to lunch. Read Newspapers. In the evening our usual party and music.

26. Sunday. Detained from writing by the necessity of gathering particulars: 1°. about Lorenzo de' Medici's death; 2°. about the possible retardation of Easter; 3°. about Corpus Christi day; 4°. about Savonarola's preaching in the Quaresima of 1492. Walked with Mr. Spencer to the zoological gardens. Finished La Mandragola, second time reading for the sake of Florentine expressions, and began La Calandra. Yesterday we received a letter from Mr. and Mrs. Trollope.

Jan. 31. The last day of this month! This evening I have been reading to G. some entries in my note-book of past times in which I recorded my *malaise* and despair. But it is impossible to me to believe that I have ever been in so unpromising and despairing a state as I now feel. – After writing these words, I read to G. the Proem and opening scene of my novel and he expressed great delight in them.

* Feb. 3. On Saturday we went to Drury to see the Pantomime at 2 o'clock. G and I walked home but felt rather poisoned all the evening by the theatre air. Mr. Burton was of our party in the evening, with Mr. Spencer and Mr. Redford. On Sunday we walked to Nursie's in the afternoon. In the morning I had written some dialogue and done a fair bit of work, but the rest of the day I was very feeble, unable to do more than read newspapers. This morning was brilliant and G. tempted me out to walk to Hampstead. We returned at $^{1}/_{2}$ past 11 and I wrote till lunch. This evening Charley has read to us the 12th No. of Orley Farm, which is interesting so far as it pursues the main path of the story – the fortunes of Lady Mason.

7. A week of February already gone! I have been obliged to be very moderate in work, from feebleness of head and body; but I have re-written with additions the first chapter of my book. I have done little reading in the last week. At present I am running along with Pulci, and have got interested in the paladins, but I find him less full of point and idiom than I expected after the first Canto or two. The other day Mr. G. Smith called and offered me 250 guineas for my story of the Idiot Brother, which George mentioned as lying by me. I am not quite certain yet whether I shall accept. Today we have been to the London Library and I have read J. Mill's article on "The American Contest". Mrs. Hooper called and brought me her little book.

10. Sunday. I was very ill with headache and sickness.

11. We set off to Dorking, and took up our old quarters at the White Horse. The day was lovely, and on arriving, we at once set out on a walk through Mr. Hope's Park to Betchworth, then returned to our inn and dined at 1/2 past 4. In the evening I read aloud von Sybel's Lectures on the Crusades.

12. The day was grey, but the air was fresh and pleasant. We walked to Wootton Park – Evelyn's Wootton – lunched at a little roadside inn there and returned to Dorking to dine. I continued von Sybel in the evening.

13. There had been rain in the night, so we determined to come home by the 1/2 past eleven train; but this allowed us time for a little walk. We arrived at home at 1/2 past 1, and found Charlie's long-missing box, just come before us – a very welcome sight. During our stay at Dorking I have finished the first 12 cantos of Pulci.

Feb. 17. Monday. I have written only the two first chapters of my novel besides the Proem, and I have an oppressive sense of the far-stretching task before me, health being feeble just now. On Saturday, Dr. Wyatt, Mr. F. Chapman, and Mr. Boner from Munich were our visitors. I was much fatigued and consequently not well on Sunday. We walked to Hampstead in a very cold wind. Today there has been constant rain and fog, and I have not been out of doors.

19. This evening I read aloud to G. again, at his request the first 45 pages of my romance, Charlie also being present. The rain has been constant all day. Nevertheless we have been to the British Museum, and I have picked some details from Manni's life of Bartolommeo Scala – also from Borghini's Discorsi, about the simplicity of the Florentine table equipage.

I have lately read again with great delight Mrs. Browning's Casa Guidi Windows. It contains amongst other admirable things a very noble expression of what I believe to be the true relation of the religious mind to the Past.

26. I have been very ailing all this last week and have worked under impeding discouragement. I have a distrust in myself, in my work, in others' loving acceptance of it which robs my otherwise happy life of all joy. I ask myself, without being able to answer, whether I have ever before felt so chilled and oppressed. On Saturday pleasant Mr. Williams from Birmingham joined our

party. Yesterday, G. and I went to Egham by railway and walked on to Englefield Green to see a house which is to be let there. We were pleased to have found out a beautiful country where we may, if we like, have lodgings at the Barley Mow Inn. I have written now about 60 pages of my romance. Will it ever be finished? – ever be worth anything?

27. George Smith, the publisher, brought the proof of G.'s book "Animal Studies", and laid before him a proposition to give me £10,000 for my new novel – i.e. for its appearance in the Cornhill and the entire copyright at home and abroad.

March
*1. Saturday. The idea of my novel appearing in the Cornhill is given up, as G. Smith wishes to have it commenced in May, and I cannot consent to begin publication until I have seen nearly to the end of the work. In the evening we had Mr. Scharf, Mr. Desmond, Mr. Burton, Mr. Pigott and Mr. Redford, with Mr. Spencer as usual. I was not well, but got through the evening better than I expected.

3. Still very feeble, and unable to write. The day turned out fine, after signs of oncoming snow, and we walked in the Park and Zoological Gardens. Finished Vol. 2 of the Morgante.

11. On Wednesday last, the 5th, G. and I set off to Englefield Green where we have spent a delightful week, and have returned this afternoon. I have finished Pulci there, and read aloud the Chateau d'If to G.

24. Monday. After enjoying our week at Egham I returned to protracted headache and discomfort. G. too, has been, and is, very ailing. Miss Hennell paid us three visits after our return: another incident was a bit of unwonted dissipation – our going to the theatre to see an amusing piece in which Mr. Frank Matthews was *admirably* disagreeable as an intimate friend. Last Saturday we received as usual, and our party was joined by Mr. and Mrs. Noel. I have begun the Fourth Chapter of my novel, but have been working under a weight. During the interval I am noting down Mr. Simpson has been, from Edinburgh and has brought us a pleasing account of Thornie.

*27. I have been lately reading some books on the mediæval condition of Greece, sent by Mr. Clark from Cambridge, and this morning not being well enough to write I have been running through Wordsworth's Greece and studying the geography.

28. Finished Wordsworth's Greece.

29. Saturday. In the evening we had only Mr. Scharf and Mr. Redford.

30. Wrote very little having a head-ache threatening me.

31. Again wrote little. In the evening went to a concert at St. James's Hall and heard Joachim.

April 1. Rainy weather. My head very infirm, so that I could do nothing in the evening.

2. Better this morning, writing with enjoyment. At the 77th page. Read Juvenal this morning, and Nisard – Poetes Latins de la Décadence in the evening.

16. As I had been very ailing for a fortnight and more, we resolved to go to Dorking and set off today.

May 6. We returned from Dorking after a stay of three weeks, during which we have had delicious weather. The first Saturday Charlie came down to see us. He is since gone on his holiday to Geneva, and we are alone in Blandford Square this evening, feeling much better and stronger for our furlough from town, and hoping to work well.

9. Yesterday we heard from Charles of his safe arrival at Geneva. Mr. G. Smith the Publisher came, and it was agreed that George should assist with his advice in the administration of the Cornhill, at £50 per number.

10. At p. 149 of my novel. This afternoon we went to the rehearsal of the New Philharmonic.

*17

23. Since I wrote last very important decisions have been made. I am to publish my novel of *Romola* in the Cornhill Magazine for £7000 paid in twelve monthly payments. There has been the regret of leaving Blackwood, who has written me a letter in the most perfect spirit of gentlemanliness and good feeling. – We have had one painful disappointment – more painful than almost anything that has occurred to us for years, namely, a letter from Mr. Trollope telling us that Charles is not thought well of as a worker at the Post Office. We have yet to learn how far he is himself conscious of any ground for complaint.

Yesterday, Mr. Leighton the artist came to see me about the illustrations to my novel which he is going to undertake. Today Mr. T. Trollope came to see us, on his arrival from Florence.

26. Received a pleasant letter from Mr. Leighton. In the afternoon we went to the Exhibition of Water Colours and saw Mr. Burton's admirable heads.

27. Mr. Helps, Mr. Burton and Mr. T. Trollope dined with us.

31. Saturday. Finished the *second part*, extending to page 183. Charles came home at night.

*June 10. Since the last record, we have been so far comforted about Charles, that we find there has been no conscious slackness in duty on his part, and that his character is very generally liked by his comrades and superiors. There is only slowness of apprehension and of execution. I have not made quite so much way in my new part as I had hoped to do in these first 10 days.

13. At p. 211. 22. Read the third part to G. ending with Tessa's marriage.

23, 24. Made a few additions to the part, having a headache which prevented me from working vigorously.

25. Yesterday afternoon G. took the 3rd Part to the printers, and this morning I begin the 4th.

Thornton came from Edinburgh for his Examination on the 21.

June 30. I have at present written only the scene between Romola and her brother in San Marco towards Part IV. On Friday we went to the International Exhibition with Mrs. Bodichon, and in the evening to the Opera to hear the Huguenots: On Saturday Evening Mrs. Bray came to see us. And this morning I had a delightful, generous letter from Mr. Anthony Trollope about Romola.

July 6. *. The past week has been unfruitful from various causes. I have not been sufficiently determined in my resistance to sensational and external hindrances. The consequence is, that I am no further on in my MSS. and have lost the excellent start my early completion of the 3rd Part had given me.

10. A dreadful palsy has beset me for the last few days – I have scarcely made any progress. Yet I have been very well in body. G. has had a severe bilious attack, but today is better. Thornton has started for Switzerland yesterday and today I have been reading a book often referred to by Hallam: Meiners' Lives of Picus von Mirandola and Politian. They are excellent. They have German industry and are succinctly and clearly written.

11. At p. 30 of Part IV.

17. *G. set off for Spa.*

21. At p. 59 of Part IV.

31. Finished Part IV, pp. 94.

*August 2. *This evening G. returned bright and well from Spa.*

6. Having had a new scene to insert in Part IV and not having been well, I have not yet begun Part V. – 10. Thornie came back for 3 days.

24. Read aloud Part V to G. up to p. 45. On the 5th or 6th came to us the news that Thornie had passed his examination.

25. Bad headache.

26. Altered Chapter 1 of Part V.

*28. Not being very well my writing has halted a little this week.

30. Grandma lunched with us, and we drove in Hyde Park.

Sep. 3. Sent Part V to press. Packed in preparation for going to Worthing. Last evening we went to see Charles Mathews.

*23. Returned from our stay in the country – first at the Beach Hotel, Little Hampton, and for the last three days at Dorking. At p. 54 of Part VI. *Dante v. I.*

26. At p. 62. Yesterday a letter came from Mr. T. Trollope full of encouragement for me. *Ebenezer*! – Pitti, Istorie. Boccaccio.

30. The last day of the month. At p. 72 – not yet at the end of my December part. After 3 days of horrible fog and rain, a clear sky. We walked towards Hampstead, but were overtaken by rain. Read Savonarola on Amos.

October 1. A delicious, clear day. We walked to Hampstead.

2. At p. 85. Scene between Tito and Romola.

3. Finished Part VI.

6. Monday. Began part VII having occupied the intermediate days in planning.

13. Monday. Read aloud to G. up to p. 37 of Part VII. – Mr Spencer lunched with us and we walked with him to the Zoo. to see the Catfish and the Limulus. Reading once again the *Processi* of Savonarola, and Vol. III of Boccaccio.

*18. An unfruitful week. Only at p. 45 of Part VII.

20. Wrote nothing because of indisposition. Began "Il Principe". 22. Received £180 from Blackwood for Adam Bede. 6/- ed.

24. Only at p. 51, having rejected a chapter which I had begun, and determined to defer it to the next Part.

25. We had friends to dinner, and in the evening were joined by Mr. Williams etc.

26. An unfruitful morning, consequent on the excitement of the evening.

Oct 31. Finished Part VII having determined to end at the point where Romola has left Florence.

Nov. 10. Only at p. 18, not being in working order.

*14. Finished reading Boccaccio through for the second time.

17. Read the Orfeo and Stanze of Poliziano. The latter are wonderfully fine for a youth of 16. They contain a description of a Palace of Venus which seems the suggestion of Tennyson's Palace of Art in many points.

18. At p. 42 of Part VIII. Read it aloud to G.

25. At p. 59. Read aloud the scene between Romola and Savonarola.

28. Wretched headache.

30. Sunday. Finished Part VIII. Mr. Burton came.

December 9. Tuesday. Violent attack of sick headache.

*10. Still headache. Letter from Mr. Craik.

11. do.

12. Still too ailing to work.

13. Able to write a little. Mr. Spencer came in the evening.

16. Writing but without inspiration. In the evening Browning paid us a visit for the first time.

17. At p. 22 only. I am extremely spiritless – dead, and hopeless about my writing. The long state of headache and disordered liver has left me in depression and incapacity. The constantly heavy, clouded and often wet weather, tends to increase the depression. I am inwardly irritable and unvisited by good thoughts. Reading the Purgatorio again, and the Compendium Revelationum of Savonarola . . . After this record, I read aloud what I had written of Part IX to George, and he to my surprize entirely approved it.

19, 20. Wretched hemicrania beset me again and prevented me from working.

21. This shortest day of the year there was a bitterly cold wind. I was a little better.

22. At p. 33. Finished Compendium Revelationum for the second time.

24. Mrs F. Malleson brought me a beautiful plant as a Christmas offering. In the evening we went to hear the Messiah at Her Majesty's Theatre. Mrs. Harrison, who sat behind us, told us of Mr. Congreve's severe illness. I enjoyed the Messiah greatly in spite of a rather unsatisfactory performance – no organ and an ill-trained chorus.

25. We had a happy Christmas Day – dining alone with the Boy. In the evening Pater sang Mozart for two hours. The day was sunshiny and mild.

26. Very good for nothing in health, and consequently depressed about my work. Wrote to Bertie.

27. Making little way. Only at p. 44!

31. Last day of the kind old year. Clear and pleasantly mild. At p. 58 of my 9th Part which I think will be the dullest that has yet come. Yesterday a pleasant message from Mr. Hannay about Romola.

We have had many blessings this year – opportunities which have enabled us to acquire an abundant independence, the satisfactory progress of our two eldest boys, various grounds of happiness in our work, and ever growing happiness in each other. I hope with trembling that the coming year may be as comforting a retrospect: with trembling, because my work is not yet done. Besides the finishing of Romola, we have to think of Thornie's passing his final examination, and, in case of success, his going out to India: of Bertie's leaving Hofwyl: and of our finding a new residence. G.'s health has been very variable and frequently infirm. I have had more than my average amount of comfortable health until this last month in which I have been constantly ailing and my work has suffered proportionately.

1863. January 1. Grandmamma came to lunch with us and we drove her round Hyde Park. My head was infirm all day, so that I could do little. The weather is still very mild, but the year has entered like a lion, with roaring winds.

3. At p. 66 of Part IX, hoping to finish it tomorrow. A clear day. G. and I walked towards Hampstead.

4. Finished Part IX. Read it aloud in the evening, and brought on a dreadful headache, which lasted nearly all the next day. Pleasant words from Anthony Trollope.

*6. Spent the morning in planning, having a feeble head. Read the Purgatorio in the evening.

7. We went in the evening to Exeter Hall to hear Judas Maccabæus, and were thrilled by Sims Reeves's fine singing of "Sound an alarm!"

8. G. went to dine at Theodore Martin's and met Helps. He brought me the encouraging word that Theodore highly enjoys Romola, and thinks it the finest thing I have done. Finished the Purgatorio second time.

10. Began Part X. In the evening came Mr. Redford and Mr. Pigott and we had singing.

11, 12. Made little way, not being well. Wrote a letter to Blackwood about the third vol. of my "Works".

22. We had Browning, Anthony Trollope, Mr. Burton and Mr. Scharf to dine with us.

23. Feeling very poorly we set off to Dorking in the morning, and had a delicious walk there before dinner. I felt better with only a few hours of country air and quiet.

26. Monday. We returned from Dorking, and found all well at home. I have still about 25 pages of my Xth part to write.

*30. Having deferred a portion of what I have written I am thrown back a little in my Part.

Feb. 1. At p. 39.

2. 43. Very encouraging news about Romola came through Mr. Smith this morning. Millais reported that at a party at Lady de Grey's she said it was the finest book she had ever read: the expression of opinion passed round the company and it was unanimous in the same sense. Ebenezer!

Feb. 4. Finished Part X.

6. Charles set off for Switzerland yesterday evening. Not well, or else blamable, for I did nothing effective this morning. Mr. William Blackwood called yesterday about Clerical Scenes and Silas Marner, and I wrote to Mr. John Blackwood on the subject this morning.

7. Browning came and sat with us through the evening. In the afternoon we went with Herbert Spencer to the Zoological Gardens.

8. Sunday. Mr. Burton called and we took him to the Zoo. I was not well in the evening and could do nothing.

11. At p. 22 of Part XI. After lunch we went to the National Gallery. Mr. Smith brought pleasant news about Romola, saying that the opinion of it in high quarters was getting fast downwards, two of the papers this week having called it a "masterpiece".

13. My head was frail and I wrote little. After lunch we went into the city to receive a dividend at the Bank. Mr. and Mrs. Hooper called, and after that I was very ill with headache and vomiting.

14. No writing this morning. Corrected proof and wrote to Mrs. Congreve. In the afternoon we went in a brougham to Hampstead with Herbert Spencer, and had a walk on the heath. A glorious, clear day!

15. Sunday. G. went to call on Mrs. Charles Knight who had not seen him for many years and said she should not have known him. I had uneasy incapacitating sensations all day.

22. At p. 41. Not well. We drove to Wimbledon to see Mr. and Mrs. Congreve.

*23. Wretchedly squandered day, from malaise. Unable even to read. G. went into town to sign his mother's trust deed.

24. We started for Dorking this afternoon. While there I received a letter from Miss Faithfull asking me to write a story for a new Magazine of hers.

March 3. We returned from our week's stay at Dorking. I had headache as usual, as my introduction to town life. Finished Part XI.

8. Sunday. Charles returned from Switzerland. Last week a letter from Miss Nannie Smith at *Palermo*.

16. Only at p. 22 of Part XII. Wretchedly oppressed and ailing – feeling as if I should never get my work done so as to satisfy me. G. went today to see his sister-in-law Susannah, who is very ill from anxiety and attendance on her boy. On Sat. 14, Mr. Burton came and sat with us in the evening.

*20, 21. Oppressed with bodily ills; making no progress in writing.

22. Better: wrote up to p. 32.

*23. Monday. We went to Dorking, where G. left me the following day. I was ill and alarmed about myself lest I should get incapable of work. But by the end of the week I recovered from my worst ailments, still infirm in head however, and little able to write. George came back to me on Saturday the 28th and we returned home on the Monday – I with violent sick headache. Through the week I was in incessant malaise from indigestion producing Hemicrania, until Saturday, April 4, when I seemed to turn the corner and get a better prospect.

Ap. 6. Yesterday, Sunday I finished Part XII and read to G. in the evening, who was highly contented – Ebenezer! – Miss Parkes came for an hour and chatted pleasantly.

13. Only at p. 13!

*16. At p. 20.

*18. George's 46th Birthday.

May 6. We have just returned from Dorking whither I went a fortnight ago, to have solitude while George took his journey to Hofwyl to see Bertie. The weather was severely cold for several days of my stay, and I was often ailing. That has been the way with me for a month and more and in consequence I am backward with my July number of Romola – the last part but one.

7. At the 37th page, having made a large excision of matter for the sake of rapidity.

10. Sunday. Wrote this morning the beginning of the Trial by Fire. I am very feeble, finding the latter half of the day all weariness.

*14. Read Part XIII to G. up to the moment when Spini gives the order about Tito.

16. Finished Part XIII. Killed Tito in great excitement! – Went to see the Priory, North Bank, a house we think of buying.

18. Began Part XIV – the last! Yesterday George saw Count Arrivabene, who wishes to translate Romola, and says the Italians are indebted to me.

20. Mr. and Mrs. Bray lunched with us.

24. Sunday. We went to St. Mary's Moorfields in the morning, and heard Beethoven's Mass in C and Cardinal Wiseman's wretched Sermon on the Day of Pentecost. Coming home, we found Mrs. Bray waiting for us. Drove her to Hampstead.

25. Heavy and good for nothing. Only at p. 18.

June 1. I have not yet finished Romola, and am made stupid and depressed by a slight cough. I have written up to the moment when Tessa and the children are taken home by Romola.

June 6. We had a little evening party, with music, intended to celebrate the completion of Romola, which however is not absolutely completed, for I have still to alter the Epilogue.

7. Sunday. Ill with hemicrania, unable to do anything all day.

*8. Still suffering from my cough and headache.

9. Tuesday. Put the last stroke to Romola.

Ebenezer!

Went in the evening to hear La Gazza Ladra.

16. G. and I set off to the Isle of Wight where we had a delightful holiday. The only drawback during the first week was my cough which made the cold breezes unwelcome. On Friday the nineteenth we settled for a week at Niton, which, I think, is the prettiest place in all the island. On the following Friday, we went on to Freshwater, and failed from threatening rain, in an attempt to walk to Alum Bay, so that we rather repented of our choice. The consolation was that we should know better than to go to Freshwater another time. On the Saturday morning we drove to Ryde and remained there until Monday the 29th. I am much strengthened by the change and have quite lost my cough.

July 3. Thornie came home from Edinburgh yesterday, looking very well and cheerful in the prospect of his final examination for India.

4. Went a second time to see a house in Circus Road, which divides our choice with the Priory. Went to see Ristori in Adrienne Lecouvreur, and did not like it. I have had hemicrania for several days, and have been almost idle since my return home.

12. Went to the Princess's to see the French actress, Stella Colas in Juliet. The two Mr. Trollopes called in the morning, and after lunch we went with Mr. Spencer to the Zoo. and heard some music. I am now in the middle of G's Aristotle, which gives me great delight.

July 23. Reading Mommsen, and Story's Roba di Roma. Also Liddell's Rome, for a narrative to accompany Mommsen's analysis.

*28. Last evening Browning came to see us and brought me a photograph of his wife, taken from a portrait of her as a very young girl. Bertie returned from Hofwyl.

29. We drove Nursie to Hampstead in the afternoon. In the evening we went to Covent Garden to hear Faust for the third time. On our return we found a letter from Frederick Maurice – the greatest, most generous tribute ever given to me in my life.

Aug. 10. I have been feeling very ill and depressed – partly in consequence of agitation about Thornie who has failed to pass his examination for the Indian Civil Service, partly I suppose from the effect of London air and London circumstances. So on this day G. took me to Worthing and staid with me till Wednesday evening. On Saturday he returned to me having sent me in the meanwhile a sweet letter from Mrs. Hare wife of Julius Hare, and Maurice's sister. Yesterday – the 18th – we returned home. I am much invigorated by my week of change, but my spirits seem to drop, as usual, now I am in London again.

*22. Last evening Mr. James Doyle came to spend an hour or two with us. Today, Charlie went with us to the Zoo.

24. Mr. and Mrs. Congreve lunched with us.

Sep. 15. I went to Richmond for a fortnight, during which we were in much anxiety about Thornie. G. went to Knebworth on the 19th to talk to Sir E. Lytton about sending T. to one of the Colonies.

26. We came home from Richmond. Mrs. Bodichon having recommended Natal and offered to further Thornie by writing on his behalf to her friends there, we think now of sending him thither.

Oct. 17. *Thornton left us for Natal.*

Nov. 5. We moved into our new home – The Priory, 21 North Bank. I was still suffering from the remains of a severe cold which had attacked me a week before.

Nov. 14. We are now nearly in order, only wanting a few details of furniture to finish our equipment for a new stage in our life's journey. I long very much to have done thinking of upholstery and to get again a consciousness that there are better things than that to reconcile one with life.

24. *Charlie's 21st Birthday*.

Dec. 25. Bertie with us, delighting us by the improvement in him after his three months of Scotch farming. Our life is made up of blessings.

1864
Jan. 17. *Sunday. Two months and seventeen days since we moved into our new home.

30. We had Browning, Dallas and Burton to dine with us and in the evening a gentleman's party.

Feb 4. Mr. Anthony Trollope and Mr. Theodore Martin dined with us.

Sunday 7. Mr. and Mrs. Theodore Martin called on us.

8. We went to see Laura Bateman in "Leah".

*14. Sunday. G. went to see Helen Faucit on business of mine. Mr. Burton dined with us and asked me to let him take my portrait.

Mar. 5. Went to see Sothern in Lord Dundreary and Bunkum Muller.

Mar. 6. Sunday. Mrs. Martin brought me her portrait.

8. Received cheque of £150 from Blackwood.

*11. Went to hear Judas Maccabæus with Mr. Burton.

27. Mrs. Bray spent the day with us and in the evening G. and I set out on a journey to Glasgow.

April 2. We returned from Glasgow, having seen Bertie in his home at Hillhead, Covington, on our way back.

4. Had a delightful letter from Thornie dated Jan. 28 from Pietermaritzburg, Natal. Then G. and I went to see Mr. Leighton's pictures in his Studio.

*6. Wednesday. Mr. Spencer called for the first time after a long correspondence on the subject of his relation to Comte.

9. Went with Mr. Owen Jones to the Kensington Museum to see Mulready's pictures and the Indian Courts.

10. Grandmamma dined with us.

18. We went to the Crystal Palace to see Garibaldi.

19. George went into Herefordshire.

May 4. We started for Italy with Mr. Burton.

June 20. Arrived at our pretty home again after an absence of seven weeks.

July 17. Horrible scepticism about all things – paralyzing my mind. Shall I ever be good for anything again? – ever do anything again?

July 19. Reading Gibbon vol. 1 in connection with Mosheim. Read about the Dionysia. Also Gieseler, on the condition of the world at the appearance of Christianity.

Aug. 6. G. having been into town came back with the news that the Cornhill Magazine was a loss. I am nearly at the end of Gibbon vol. II, and am reading a little in Philology, much interrupted by visitors etc.

14. Sunday*. Mr. Pigott and Mr. Burton dined with us. George very feeble and delicate just now.

Sep. 6. George still feeble, thinner and thinner, giving me great anxiety. *I am reading about Spain and trying a drama on a subject that has fascinated me – have written the prologue, and am beginning the First Act. But I have little hope of making anything satisfactory.*

13. George and I started for Harrogate.

23. Went from Harrogate to Scarbro', seeing York Minster on our way.

Oct 1. Saturday. We returned home, having broken our journey by staying a night at Peterbro'. George is much benefited by the change.

2. Sunday*. I returned to my drama, but did not write much because G. called me away to go and see Mother.

5. Finished the first draught of the First act and read it to George.

8. Saturday. I have rewritten up to the Entrance of Fedalma. As Mrs. Congreve is coming to stay a night with us, I shall miss my morning's work to-morrow. The last two mornings I have had a dubious head which has prevented me from doing as much as I could have done if I had been quite well.

12. Began Act II. I have been feeling very unwell for the last few days, and the days have not been fruitful.

17. Went to see Helen Faucit as Imogen at Drury Lane.

18. Horrible theatre headache. Went to the Maestro for a "sitting".

19. Headache continued so that I could write nothing. In the afternoon went to see the Miss Gillies.

20. G. set off for Malvern, to try fresh air and the water cure.

24. Monday. We have had a letter today from Thornie, after a long interval during which he was "up country". It is altogether cheering and I have sent it on to George. The excitement of this pleasure disturbed me too much to let me work, as I was not very well beforehand.

Nov. 3. G. returned from Malvern, much benefited by the Water Cure.

4. Read my 2nd Act to George. It is written in verse – my first serious attempt at blank verse. G. praises and encourages me.

10. I have been at a very low ebb body and mind for the last few days, sticking in the mud continually in the construction of my 3, 4, and 5 acts. Yesterday Mrs. Congreve and her sisters came. Browning also to tell us of a bust of Savonarola in terra-cotta just discovered at Florence. Yesterday I settled my 3rd and 5th acts. This morning I must determine the 4th.

*14–18. Ill and obliged to keep perfectly quiet. I read Prescott again and made notes.

20. Sunday. G. went to consult with the people concerned in the management of the Reader.

25. For the last two or three days I have been disordered by dyspepsia, and unfitted for doing anything well. I am still only a little way in my Third Act.

Dec 5. During the last week I have been worse than ever – with continual bilious headache. But yesterday and today I seem to be emerging from this swamp of miseries. I have written to the 16th page of the Third Act. The other day I read to George and he approved it highly.

15. Amidst much malaise and feebleness, yet gradually recovering, I have struggled on to the 33rd page. Last week Mr. Trollope and Mr. F. Chapman dined with us and there was talk of a new periodical of which it is possible G.

may be the editor. Also, he has had an arrangement with Mr. Smith as to the part he is to take in a new journal.[2]

*18. Sunday. Mr. Pigott dined with us. There is deepish snow on the ground and the cold is severe. I wrote a letter to Barbara in answer to one she sent me the other day from Algiers.

24. A Family party in the evening – Grandmamma, the Miss Gillies, Gertrude, Lizzie, Miss Marshall, and Bertie, who is with us for his Christmas holiday.

25. I read the third act of my drama to George, who praised it highly. Dr. Stummer paid us a long call; then G. and I went to call on Grandma; Miss Parkes and Miss Craig called between 4 and 5, and after that we spent a perfectly quiet evening, intending to have our Christmas day's jollity on Tuesday when the boys are at home. This week G. has determined against accepting the editorship of the new Journal or Review.
End of 1864.

1865
Jan. 1. The last year has been unmarked by any trouble except bad health. George has suffered much more malaise than in the two or three previous years, but now he is returned to his usual condition of delicacy without more than occasional ailments that incapacitate him from doing his morning's work. The bright spots in the year have been the publication of "Aristotle" and our journey to Venice. With me the year has not been fruitful. I have written three acts of my drama and am now in a condition of body and mind to make me hope for better things in the coming year. The last quarter has made an epoch for me by the fact that for the first time in my serious authorship I have written verse, and George declares it to be triumphantly successful. We have had good news from Thornie in Natal; Bertie is with us for his holiday, delighting us by the improvement in his mind and health; and Charlie is happy in the prospect of his marriage in April. In each other, we are happier than ever: I am more grateful to my dear husband for his perfect love, which helps me in all good and checks me in all evil – more conscious that in him I have the greatest of blessings.

Sunday Jan. 8. Mrs. Congreve staying with us for a couple of nights. Yesterday we went to Mr. Burton's to see my portrait, with which she was much pleased. Since last Monday I have been writing a poem, the matter of which was written in prose 3 or 4 years ago – My Vegetarian Friend.

10.* A headache came on disabling me for two days.

13. We had packed up and were to set off for Paris tonight, but the high winds forbade.

2 Lewes was editor of the *Fortnightly Review*, published by Chapman and Hall, from its inception in 1865 to 1866; he acted as adviser to George Smith's *Pall Mall Gazette* from 1865 to 1868, for £300 a year.

15. Sunday. Set off for Paris at 1/2 past 9, and had a fair though rather long passage to Boulogne. Arrived at Paris at 11, but did not reach the Hotel de Lille till 1.

25. Reached home in comfort and safety at 7 this evening.

28. Finished my poem on Utopias.[3] Mr. Trollope called.

29. Mr. Beasley called, and the Maestro dined with us.

30. Much depressed in the morning, feeling my work worth nothing. In the evening, talking over my 4th act with George, I recovered some hope.

31. Last day of January! Sixteen days or more of the month have been robbed from work by our visit to Paris, by sickness, and by Mrs. Congreve's visit to us. The remaining fifteen have only produced my little poem of 400 lines.

Feb. 6. I have only just written in verse the opening of my 4th act.

7.* Gertrude with us last evening, staid all night perhaps her last visit of this kind, before her and Charlie's marriage, which is to take place at the beginning of April.

*11. At p. 10 – having been disabled by sickness.

12 Sunday. I get on slowly from feebleness of body. Mr. and Mrs. Noel called in the afternoon and Miss Margaret Gillies: and the Maestro dined with us -

17. Mrs. Congreve came to see us, and brought me a pretty present from her sister Emily.

18. Our first Evening party since last winter!

19, 20, 21. Ill with bilious headache, and very miserable about my soul as well as body. *George has taken my drama away from me.*

Mar. 1. Poor Nelly Bray died, after a long illness from consumption. I wrote an article for the Pall Mall Gazette, "A Word for the Germans".

Mar. 12. Went to Wandsworth, to spend the Sunday and Monday with Mr. and Mrs. Congreve. Feeling very ailing – in constant dull pain, which makes all effort burthensome.

Mar. 20. *Charlie and Gertrude were married.*

25. During this week the commencement of the Fortnightly Review, of which George has been prevailed on to be the Editor, has been finally decided on. I am full of vain regrets that we did not persist in original refusal, for I dread the worry and anxiety G. may have. About myself I am in deep depression feeling powerless. I have written nothing but beginnings since I finished a little article for the Pall Mall on the Logic of Servants. Dear George is all activity, yet is in very

3 'A Minor Prophet', published in *The Legend of Jubal and Other Poems* (1874).

frail health. How I worship his good humour, his good sense, his affectionate care for everyone who has claims on him! That worship is my best life.

29. Sent a letter on Futile Lying from Saccharissa to the Pall Mall. *I have begun a Novel.*4

May 4. Sent article on Lecky's History of Rationalism for the Fortnightly. For nearly a fortnight I have been ill, one way or other.

10. Finished a letter of Saccharissa for the P. M. G. Reading Æschylus, Theatre of the Greeks, Klein's History of the Drama etc.

May 28. Finished Bamford's Passages from the life of a Radical. Have just begun again Mill's Political Economy, and Comte's Social Science in Miss Martineau's Edition.

June 7. Finished Annual Register for 1832. Reading Blackstone. Mill's Second article on Comte to appear in the Westminster, lent me by Mr. Spencer. My health has been better of late, and I am anxious to use the precious hours well. I have finished correcting the sheets for the cheap edition of Romola.

13.* We went to Her Majesty's to hear Cherubini's *Medea*.

14. Relieved by hearing news of Thornie dating March last. Miss Bury lunched with me, but the day was spoiled by headache.

15. Read again Aristotle's Poetics, with fresh admiration.

20. Read the opening of my novel to G. Yesterday we drove to Wandsworth, walked together on Wimbledon Common in outer and inner sunshine, as of old; then dined with Mr. and Mrs. Congreve, and had much pleasant talk.

25. Sunday. Reading English History, Reign of George III. Shakspeare's *King John*. In the afternoon we had Barbara and the Doctor, Maestro, Colonel Pelly and his friend Mr. Jeffery the Conchologist, and Mr. Neuberg. Later, Danby Seymour. Then we went to see Mother, who has returned from the Sea-side in a sadly weak condition. Yesterday G. dined at Greenwich with the multitude of so-called writers for the Saturday. He heard much commendation of the Fortnightly especially of Bagehot's articles, which last is reassuring after Mr. Trollope's strong objections. Tyndal told G. that he dined with Lecky at Longman's and on going home read my article, which seemed to him to give a thoroughly just conception of the man – to "hit him off exactly". Thinks he will do nothing better. I am glad to have this testimony that I have not in this case done any injustice. 26. Maestro dined with us.

27. Finished the 1st vol. of Mill's Political Economy.

28. We went to hear Mr. and Mrs. Wigan read Tennyson and "The Rivals" at Apsley House.

4 *Felix Holt* (1866).

*July 2. Sunday. We had an agreeable gathering. Mrs. Bodichon, H. Spencer, Lord Edward S., Maestro, Mr. Warren, Colonel Pelly, Mr. and Mrs. Bain.

3. Went to hear the Faust at Covent Garden: Mario, Lucca, Attri and Graziani. I was much thrilled by the great symbolical situations and by the music – more, I think, than I had ever been before.

7. The children, Miss Gillies and Grandmamma spent the evening with us. Poor Grandma has had a sad half year of illness and had not been with us before, since Christmas Eve.

9*. Sunday. We had Browning, Huxley, Mr. Warren, Mr. Bagehot and Mr. Crompton, and the talk was pleasant.

12. Ill for three days – with bad headache. Finished Mill's Political Economy.

16. Mlle. Bohn, niece of Prof. Scherer called. She said certain things about Romola, which showed that she had felt what I meant my readers to feel. She said she knew the book had produced the same effect on many others. I wish I could be encouraged by this.

17. Mr Doyle to dinner, and we had a musical evening. The Maestro joined us after dinner.

20. To the Royal Academy with Barbara to see a new Velasquez – the dead knight – from the Portalis Collection.

21. With Barbara to the Royal Academy for a last glance.

22. Sat for my portrait, I suppose for the last time.

23. We have at last had letters from Thornie – on Wednesday the 19th they arrived. The news is middling, except that he is in good health. There has been a monetary crisis in the colony, which has made his trading expedition of doubtful result. He says it is of no use to send Bertie out without a little capital, and discourages the prospect of farming in Natal, so that we must now think of Bertie's being a trader. Today we had a good group of visitors and some pleasant talk. George is not yet well; he has been ailing ever since Saturday week! I am going doggedly to work at my novel, seeing what determination can do in the face of despair. Reading Neale's History of the Puritans.

26. Mr. Doyle dined with us, and the Maestro. We had music, but I was not well.

29. Read Æschylus before breakfast. Had a bath and wrote a little. Mrs. Congreve came to lunch with us and we went to the Zoological Gardens. I was weary, not being well. After Mrs. C. was gone in the evening, I read G's article on Grote's Plato.

Aug. 2. Finished the Agamemnon, 2nd time. Mr. A. Trollope and his brother dined with us – the first time we have seen Mr. T. Trollope since his wife's death, which happened in March last.

5. Mr. Doyle spent the evening with us, and we filled it with music.

6. Our last Sunday at home for some time. We intend on Thursday to set off for a month's excursion into Normandy and Brittany. I have been reading Villemarqué's "Contes populaires des Anciens Bretons."

Sep. 7. We returned home after an expedition into Brittany. Our course was from Boulogne to St. Valéry, Eu, Dieppe, Rouen, Caen, Bayeux, St. Lô, Vire, Avranches, Dol, St. Malo, Rennes, Auray and Carnac – back by Nantes, Tours, Le Mans, Chartres, Paris, Rouen, Dieppe, Abbeville and so again to Boulogne.

Oct. 14. At p. 74 of my novel. The last fortnight has been almost unproductive from bad health.

15. Sunday. In the evening walked home with Browning, went into his house, and saw the objects Mrs. Browning used to have about her, her chair, tables, books etc. An epoch to be remembered. Browning showed us her Hebrew Bible with notes in her handwriting, and several of her copies of the Greek dramatists with her annotations.

20*. p. 92. Went into town with G. to make some purchases.

31. At p. 107. Headache – unable to work.

Nov. 1. News from Mrs. Congreve that Emily Bury who has been dangerously ill of fever is slowly recovering.

15. During the last three weeks George has been very poorly, but now he is better. I have been reading Fawcett's Economic condition of the Working Classes, Mill's Liberty, looking into Strauss's Second Life of Jesus, and reading Neale's History of the Puritans of which I have reached the fourth volume. Yesterday the news came of Mrs. Gaskell's death. She died suddenly while reading aloud to her daughters.

*16. Writing Mr. Lyon's story, which I have determined to insert as a narrative. *Reading the Bible.*

22. Sara Hennell lunched and dined with us. At the end of Chapter VII.

24. Finished Neale's History of the Puritans: began Hallam's Middle Ages.

Dec. 4. Finished 2nd volume of Hallam. The other day read to the end of Chapter IX of my novel to George, who was much pleased and found no fault. 8. Concert at Exeter Hall.

11.* For the last three days I have been foundering from a miserable state of head. I have written chapter X. This evening read again Macaulay's Introduction.

15. Today is the first for nearly a week on which I have been able to write anything fresh. I am reading Macaulay and Blackstone. This evening we went to hear the Messiah at Exeter Hall.

24. At p. 146. For two days I have been sticking in the mud, from doubt about my construction: I have just consulted G. and he confirms my choice of incidents. Bertie came home yesterday for his Christmas holiday.

27. We had our family party in which our friend Mr. Williams joined.

28, 29. Ill, unable to do anything. At p. 257.

31. Sunday. The last day of 1865. I will say nothing but that I trust – I will strive – to add more ardent effort towards a good result from all the outward good that is given to me. My health is at a lower ebb than usual; and so is George's. Bertie is spending his holiday with us and shows hopeful characteristics. Charles is happy. Poor Thornie is under a cloud, and our pity for him is our chief trouble.

1866. New Year's Day. Maestro dined with us, and Bertie. The sun shone; but I was suffering from bodily ailment and depression.

** Jan. 9. Prof. Huxley, Prof. Beesly, Maestro, and Mr. Spencer dined with us. Mr. Harrison in the evening.

20. For the last fortnight I have been unusually disabled by ill health. At p. 296. I have been consulting Mr. Harrison about the law in my book with satisfactory result – George is also sadly ailing – thinner and thinner, and less and less able to digest even the plainest food.

24. Today Bertie set off for Warwickshire, and we being thus at liberty from our cares about him set off for Tunbridge Wells.

Feb. 7. We returned home, both still feeble, I especially suffering from a bilious attack which pulled me back in the last days of my stay at Tunbridge Wells. We were glad to be at home again.

9. At p. 300. George and I both ailing still.

March 7. Both of us have been benefited by change of weather – a week or so of frost – and by Dr. Brinton's prescriptions, but G. is still far from being comfortable in body. We have so much happiness in our love and uninterrupted companionship, that we must accept our miserable bodies as our share of mortal ill.

Last night, at p. 374. I am reading Mill's Logic again, Theocritus still, and English History and Law.

*8. Mr. A. Trollope lunched with us and brought us the result of the Fortnightly council – a request that G. would not resign the Editorship.

9. p. 388. We drove to Highgate to see Susanna.

17. p. 430. To St. James's Hall, hearing Joachim, Piatti and Hallé in glorious Beethoven music.

25. Sunday. Without visitors except the Maestro.

Mar. 26. Read my MS. to George up to p. 468. He was delighted with it.

*29. We walked in Hyde Park together.

31. Last day of the month! Sickness has hindered me for the last fortnight. I am only at p. 484, commencing the scene at Duffield.

April 12. Finished vol. II.

16. Horrible headache lasting for three days has hindered me. I began my 3rd vol. today only.

21. Sent MS. of two volumes to Blackwood at p. 41.

25. Blackwood has written to offer me £5000 for Felix Holt. I have been ailing and uncertain in my strokes, and yesterday got no farther than p. 52.

Ap. 29. Sunday. Dr. Müller came to see us, before returning to Switzerland. At p. 80.

May 1. We went to the Rookery Farm, Westcott, near Dorking, intending to stay a fortnight. But I was not well and found the new circumstances unfavourable to work, so we came back on Monday, 7th.

15. Blackwood came to lunch with us and I gave him the MS. of Vol. III to p. 139. I was very far from well, and unable to do a good morning's work, from having overdone myself the previous day.

16. Wrote to p. 168. Corrected proofs in the evening.

17. Bad hemicrania. Did nothing but write mottoes to my proofs, and then walked with G. to the Water Colour and French Exhibitions. The only thing that rejoiced us was Henriette Browne's "Nun".

*18. Not well and unable to write much. Translated mottoes from Sophocles etc.

22. Horribly ill. Finished the scene in the prison between Felix and Esther to p. 196.

31. *Finished Felix Holt.*

June 7. Set off on our journey to Holland, etc.

August 3. Returned home.

Aug. 17. Bertie came home from Warwickshire in consequence of a letter from Thornie in which he tells us that he has a grant of 3000 acres of land on the Orange River, and wishes Bertie to join him as soon as possible.

30. I have taken up the idea of my drama, "The Spanish Gipsy" again, and am reading on Spanish subjects – Bouterwek, Sismondi, Depping, Llorente etc.

September 6. We went with Bertie to Sydenham, as a farewell visit for him.

9. Sunday. Bertie parted from us to go to Natal.

15. Finished Depping's "Juifs au Moyen Age". Reading Chaucer, to study English. Also, reading on acoustics, musical instruments etc.

24. *Today the sad news came that Gertrude had lost her little baby.*

Oct. 15. Monday. Recommenced "The Spanish Gipsy", intending to give it a new form.

*Nov. 6. George has been ill lately, but is better now. He is to give up the Editorship of the Fortnightly Review after the appearance of the next number – for December, 1866, and when he has finished his work on the new edition of his History of Philosophy, he must devote himself to getting well.

20. Reading Renan's Histoire des Langues Sémitiques. Ticknor's Spanish Literature.

22. *Read the opening 3 or 4 pages of Introduction of my poem to George.*

Dec. 6. We returned from Tunbridge Wells where we have been for a week, hoping that George would profit by the change. I have been reading Cornewall Lewis's Astronomy of the Ancients, Ockley's History of the Saracens, Astronomical Geography, and Spanish Ballads on Bernardo del Carpio.

Dec. 11. Ill ever since I came home, so that the days seem to have made a muddy flood, sweeping away all labour and all growths.

27. Set off in the evening on our journey to the South, for the sake of George's health, which has been continually declining.

1867. March 16. This Evening we got home again after a journey to the South of Spain, which has restored George's health. He has now to finish the new edition of his History of Philosophy, which has been delayed on account of his illness, and then he will be free from all but self-imposed work. I go to my Poem and the construction of two prose works – if possible.

21. Received from Blackwood a cheque for £2166.13.4, being the second instalment of £1666.13.4, towards the £5000 for Felix Holt, together with £500 as the first instalment of £1000 for ten years' copyright of the Cheap Edition of my novels.

April 5. The first number of the Illustrated Edition of Adam Bede came to me.

May 1. Read a portion of my poem to G. He was much pleased with it.

Sunday. May 5. We went to Bouverie St. to hear the first of a course of lectures on Positivism delivered by Dr. Congreve. There were present 75 people, chiefly men.

May 7. George finished the writing for the new edition of his History of Philosophy.

8. We went to Kensington to see the collection of Historical Portraits.

*11. We had Mr. and Mrs. Call to dine with us, and an evening party afterwards.

12. We went to hear Dr. Congreve's second lecture. The morning was thoroughly wet – the audience smaller, but still good.

19. Third Lecture – chilling. New faces in great part.

26. Lecture – rather better.

27. Went with G. to the Academy Exhibition. Then to see Maestro, who has recently gone through a great crisis in his life.

29. Went to the Exhibition of French pictures – very agreeable and interesting.

30. Went to see Maestro, and read him the good article on Blank verse in an old Cornhill.

June 1. Saturday. Wrote up to the moment when Fidalma appears in the Plaça.

*

June 5. Blackwood dined with us and I read to him my poem down to p. 56. He showed great delight.

11. Finished the scene in the Plaça.

20. We went to Eton to spend the day with Mr. Oscar Browning.

24. Finished the scene between Fidalma, Isidor and Silva.

June 26. We went to Niton for a fortnight, returning July 10.

July 16. Received £2166.13.4 from Blackwood, being the final instalment for Felix Holt and copyright for 10 years.

19. Finished the scene between Silva and Fedalma down to p. 93.

29. We went to Dover this evening as the start on a journey into Germany (North).

Oct. 1. We returned home after revisiting the scenes of cherished memories – Ilmenau, Dresden, and Berlin. Of new places we have seen Wetzlar, Cassel, Eisenach and Hanover. At Ilmenau I wrote Fidalma's soliloquy after her scene with Silva, and the following dialogue between her and Juan. At Dresden I rewrote the whole scene between her and Zarca.

Oct. 8. Finished the Prior's soliloquy.

9. Fixed the development of my poem. Reading "Los Judios en España", "Percy's Reliques", "Isis", occasionally aloud.

10. Began the scene in the Gypsy Camp. Reading the Iliad, book III. Finished Los Judios en España, a wretchedly poor book.

11. Began again Prescott's Ferdinand and Isabella.

*19. George returned last evening from a walking expedition in Surrey with Mr. Spencer. Today the children dined with us and I read (in continuation of a former reading) my poem down to the scene with Juan and the Gypsy girls.

30. We dined at Highgate with Mr. and Mrs. F. Lehmann. In the morning I finished a scene between Juan and Pepita.

31. Upset by fatigue and unable to work. In the evening Mr. G. Smith came and we consulted about a series of poems.

I have now inserted all that I think of for the First Part of The Spanish Gypsy. On Monday I wrote three new Lyrics. I have also rewritten the first scenes in the Gypsy camp, to the end of the dialogue between Juan and Fidalma. But I have determined, to make the commencement of the second part continue the picture of what goes forward in Bedmár.

Nov. 1. Began this morning Part 2. "Silva was marching homeward" etc.

9. Received the present of a cast of the Æsculapius head from the British Museum.

22. Began an address to the working men by Felix Holt, at Blackwood's repeated request.

Dec. 4. Sent off the MS. of the address to Edinburgh.

*Dec 13. Ill until today – able to do very little.

Dec. 21. Finished reading "Averroës and l'Averroisme", and "Les Médecins Juifs". Reading "First Principles".

25. George and I dined happily alone; he, better for weeks than he had been all the summer and autumn before; I, more ailing than usual, but with much mental consolation, part of it being the delight he expresses in my poem, of which the First Part is now in print.

1868

Jan 1. George absent at Bonn. The servants having a little festival. The day was clear and dry – a bright beginning. I walked to Grossmutter's and read her a letter of G.'s. Reading *Munk, Mélanges de Philosophie juive et arabe*.

Sunday, Jan 5. Finished the first draught of the scene between Silva and Sephardo.

Wednesday 8. George came back in safety and health.

10. Finished the scene in the hall of the castle, in prose.

ˣ12. Finished the scene in the Market place.

21. Finished the scene between Fidalma and Hinda. Finished Max Müller's Essays.

25. Wrote as far as p. 101, Part III – in the scene between Zarca and Silva, with Fidalma.

27. Monday. I was feeling so poorly that G. urged our going to Tunbridge Wells for a couple of days. I corrected part of my Proof there.

29. Returned home this evening, much better for the change.

31. Wrote to End of p. 105, part III.

Feb. 7. Put the last lines to Part III.

13. Since the seventh I have been ill, and done nothing but correct my Proof, finished this morning. I am now free to begin Part IV.

27. Returned last evening from a very pleasant visit to Cambridge. I am still only at p. 5 of Part IV, having had a wretched month of malaise.

Mar. 1. Sunday. Finished Guillemin on the Heavens and the 4th Book of the Iliad. I shall now read Grote.

6. Finished the description of Silva's watch. Part IV, p.15. Reading Lubbock's Prehistoric ages.

*8. Saturday concert – the 5th – Joachim and Piatti with Schubert's Ottett.

9. Mr and Mrs. Byrne [sic] Jones lunched with us.

10. Went to the Lyceum to see Narcisse.

17. We travelled to Torquay, and put up at the Queen's Hotel on the "Strand".

19. Entered our Lodgings – Carslew – our landlady being a Mrs. Powers.

April. 16. Returned home – bringing Book IV finished, and Book V, p. 4 – too much shaken by the journey to work until the 20.

Saturday 18. Went with Mr. Pigott to see Holmann [sic] Hunt's great picture – Isabella and the pot of Basil.

22. I am writing the final scene between Fedalma and Silva, but am feeling very languid and depressed. Sent the MS. of Book IV to Edinburgh.

Sat. 25. Finished the last dialogue between Silva and Fedalma. Mr. and Mrs. Burne Jones dined with us.

29. *Finished "The Spanish Gypsy".*

May 26. We set out this evening on our journey to Baden, spending the night at Dover and setting off by the packet the next morning. Our route was by Tournay, Liège, Bonn and Frankfurt to Baden, where we stayed nine days: then to Petersthal, where we stayed three weeks: then to Freiburg, St. Märgen, Basle, Thun and Interlaken. From Interlaken we came by Fribourg, Neuchâtel, Dijon, Paris and Folkstone.

July 23. *Arrived at home* again.

30. Sent corrections for the reprint of the Spanish Gypsy.

Aug. Reading; First book of Lucretius, 6th book of the Iliad; Samson Agonistes, Warton's History of English Poetry; Grote 2nd vol; Marcus Aurelius; Vita Nuova; vol. IV, Chapter 1 of the Politique positive; Guest on English Rhythms, Maurice's Lectures on Casuistry.

September 19. We returned from a visit to Yorkshire. On Monday we went to Leeds and were received by Dr. Clifford Allbutt, with whom we stayed till the middle of the day on Wednesday. Then we went by train to Ilkley, and from thence took a carriage to Bolton. The weather had been grey for two days but on this evening the sun shone out and we had a delightful stroll before dinner, getting our first view of the Priory. On Thursday, we spent the whole day in rambling through the woods to Barden Tower and back. Our comfortable little inn was the Red Lion, and we were tempted to lengthen our stay. But on Friday morning the sky was threatening, so we started for Newark, which we had visited in old days on our expedition to Gainsborough. At Newark, we found our old inn, the Ram, opposite the ruins of the Castle, and then we went for a stroll along the banks of the Trent, seeing some charming quiet pictures – Frith landscapes. This morning we walked again for an hour and then prepared to start by the train to Peterborough where we paused again and had a second view of the Cathedral. Then back to the train among a crush of market people, and so home to dinner at 1/2 past six.

October 22. Received a letter from Blackwood saying that the Spanish Gypsy must soon go into a third edition. I sent my corrections for it.

Nov. 3. Went to dine and sleep at Dr. Congreve's Wandsworth.

4. We set off for Sheffield where we went over a great iron and steel factory under the guidance of Mr. Benzon. On Saturday, the 7th, we went to Matlock and stayed till Tuesday. I recognized the objects which I had seen with my Father nearly 30 years before – the turn of the road at Cromford, the Arkwright's house and the cottages with the stone floors chalked in patterns. The landscape was still rich with autumn leaves.

Nov. 22. The return of this Saint Cecilia's day finds me in better health than has been usual with me in these last six months. But I am not yet engaged in any work that makes a higher life for me – a life that is young and grows, though in my other life I am getting old and decaying. It is a day for resolves, and determination. I am meditating the subject of Timoleon.

Dec 30. I make today the last record that I shall enter of the old year 1868. It has been as rich in blessings as any preceding year of our double life, and I enjoy a more and more even cheerfulness, and continually encreasing power of dwelling on the good that is given to me, and dismissing the thought of small evils. The chief event of the year to us has been the publication, and friendly reception by the public, of "The Spanish Gypsy". The greatest happiness (after our growing love) which has sprung and flowed onward during the latter part of the year, is George's interest in his psychological inquiries. I have perhaps gained a little higher ground and firmer footing in some studies, notwithstanding the yearly loss of retentive power. We have made some new friendships, that cheer us with the sense of new admiration of actual living beings whom we know in the flesh, and who are kindly disposed towards us. And we have had no real trouble. I wish we were not in a minority of our fellow-men! – I desire no added blessing for the coming year but these: that I may do some good, lasting work, and make both my outward and inward habits less imperfect, that is, more directly tending to the best uses of life.

1869.

Jan 1. A bright frosty morning! And we are both well. The servants are going to have their little treat, and we are going to see Mr. and Mrs. Burne Jones and carry a book for their little boy. I have set myself many tasks for the year – I wonder how many will be accomplished? A Novel called Middlemarch, a long poem on Timoleon, and several minor poems.

Jan. 23. Since I wrote last I have finished a little poem on Old Agatha. But the last week or two I have been so disturbed in health that no work prospers. I have made a little way in constructing my new Tale, have been reading a little on philology, have finished the 24th Book of the Iliad, the first book of the Faery Queene, Clough's poems, and a little about Etruscan things in Mrs. Grey and Dennis. Aloud to G. I have been reading some Italian, Ben Jonson's Alchemist and Volpone, and Bright's Speeches, which I am still reading – besides the first four Cantos of Don Juan. But the last two or three days I have seemed to live under a leaden pressure – all movement mental or bodily is grievous to me.

In the evening read aloud Bright's 4th speech on India, and a story in Italian. In the Spectator some interesting facts about loss of memory, and "double life". In the Revue des Cours a lecture by Sir W. Thomson of Edinburgh on the retardation of the earth's motion round its axis.

27. The last two days I have been writing a rhymed poem on Boccaccio's story of Lisa. Aloud I have read Bright's speeches and "I promessi sposi". To myself I have read Mommsen's Rome.

Feb. 6. The last few days I have been looking through Matthew Arnold's poems, and find his earlier ones very superior to the later. Yesterday I wrote the song of Minuccio in Lisa. Today at verse 404, "who meetly told that lovetale meet to know". We went to the third concert, which was rather spoiled by Piatti's absence and the inferiority of his substitute Pezzi. Madame Schumann played finely in Mendelssohn's Quintett, and a Trio of Beethoven's. As a solo she played the Sonata in D minor. In the evening I read aloud a short speech of Bright's on Ireland, delivered 20 years ago, in which he insists that nothing will be a remedy for the woes of that country unless the Church Establishment be annulled: after the lapse of 20 years the measure is going to be adopted. Then I read aloud a bit of the "Promessi Sposi", and afterwards the Spectator, in which there is a deservedly high appreciation of Lowell's Poems.

Feb. 11. Miss Hennell and Mr. Spencer dined with us.

13. The concert was spoiled for me by headache which has made these last two days barren.

14. Finished the poem from Boccaccio. We had rather a numerous gathering of friends today, and among the rest came Browning who talked and quoted admirably à propos of versification. The Rector of Lincoln thinks the French have the most perfect system of versification in these modern times!

15. I prepared and sent off "How Lisa loved the King" to Edinburgh. In the afternoon I stayed at home to receive the Maestro, who had requested an interview. In the evening I read "I promessi sposi" aloud, and some Roman History to myself.

16. Very tremulous and ailing all day, so that I achieved nothing but the writing of some letters – one to the Ladies of the "Sorosis" at New York, who proposed to make me an honorary member of their society – I declined. Mrs. Senior came to lunch with us, and then we walked. G. finished reading "Séraphime" aloud to me.

20. Sat. A glorious concert, Hallé, Joachim and Piatti, winding up with Schubert's Trio.

21. Mr. Deutsch and Mrs. Pattison lunched with us, he in farewell, before going to the East. A rather pleasant gathering of friends afterwards; Charlie staying to dinner.

22. Sleet and rain, bitterly cold. G. went into the city and saw Trübner, who is negotiating for Ticknor and Field of Boston to publish a library edition of all my books.

24. Mrs. Pattison came to say goodby before going back to Oxford. I am reading about plants, and Helmholtz on music. A new idea of a poem came to me yesterday.

March 3. We started on our fourth visit to Italy, via France and the Corniche.

May 5. We reached our home after our nine weeks' absence. In that time we have been through France to Marseilles; along the Corniche to Spezia; then to Pisa, Florence, Naples, Rome, Assisi, Perugia, Florence again, Ravenna, Bologna, Verona; across the Brenner Pass, to Munich; then to Paris via Strasburg. In such a journey, there was necessarily much interest both in renewing old memories and recording new; but I never had such continuous bad health in travelling as I have had during these nine weeks.

On our arrival at home I found a delightful letter from Mrs. H. B. Stowe, whom I have never seen, addressing me as her "dear friend".

Saturday 8. *Poor Thornie arrived from Natal, sadly wasted by suffering.*

Monday 24. Sold "Agatha" to Fields and Osgood, for the "Atlantic Monthly", for £300.

July 3. Finished my readings in Lucretius. Reading Victor Hugo's "L'Homme qui rit". Also the Frau von Hillern's novel "Ein Arzt der Seele". This week G. and I have been to Sevenoaks, but were driven home again by the cold winds and cloudy skies. (Sonnets on Childhood: five finished.)

10. Saturday. I wrote to Mrs. Stowe, in answer to a second letter of hers accompanied by one from her husband.

14. *Returned from Hatfield, after two days' stay.*

15. Began Nisard's History of French Literature – Villehardouin, Joinville, Froissart, Christine de Pisan, Philippe de Comines, Villon.

July 16. Read the articles Phœnicia and Carthage in Ancient Geography. Looked into Smith's Universal History again for Carthaginian religion. Looked into Sismondi's Littérature du Midi, for Roman de Rose, and ran through the first chapter, about the formation of the Romance Languages. Read about Thallogens and Acrogens in "the Vegetable World". Drayton's Nymphidia – a charming poem. A few pages of his Polyolbion. Re-read Grote v-vii on Sicilian affairs down to rise of Dionysius.

18. Sunday. Miss Nannie Smith came – after a long absence from England; Prof. Masson and Dr. Bastian, Madame Bodichon, and Dr. Payne. Some conversation about Saint-Simonism, àpropos of the meeting on Woman's Suffrage the day before, M. Arlès Dufour, being uneasy because Mill did not in his speech recognize what women owed to Saint Simonism.

19. Monday. Writing an introduction to *Middlemarch* I have just reread the XVth Idyll of Theocritus, and have written three more Sonnets. My head uneasy. We went in the afternoon to the Old Water Colours, finding that the Exhibition was to close at the end of the week. Burne Jones's Circe and St. George affected me by their colour, more than any of the other pictures: they are poems. In the evening read Nisard on Rabelais and Calvin and Marot.

20. To the Academy Exhibition in Burlington House. Came home with a bad headache and went to bed early.

21. In bed half the day with a bad headache.

22. Only a little better. Read Reybaud's book on Les Reformateurs Modernes. In the afternoon Mrs. P. Taylor came and saw Thornie, who has been more uneasy this week, and unwilling to move or come out on the lawn.

23. Read Theocritus Idyll 16. Meditated characters for Middlemarch. Mrs. F. Malleson came.

24. Saturday. Still not quite well and clear-headed, so that little progress is made. In the afternoon G. and I went to Hyde Park. Found Mr. Pigott on our return. Charlie came and sat with Thornie in the evening. I read about Fourier and Owen, and thought of writing something about Utopists.

25. Sunday. Read Plato's Republic, in various parts. After lunch, Miss N. Smith, Miss Blythe, Mr. Burton and Mr. Deutsch. In the evening I read Nisard, and Littré on Comte.

Aug. 1. Since last Sunday I have had an uncomfortable week from mental and bodily disturbance. I have finished eleven Sonnets on "Brother and Sister", read Littré, Nisard; part of 22nd Idyll of Theocritus, Sainte Beuve aloud to G. two evenings. On Thursday: the evening was occupied with Gertrude and Charles, Monday evening with looking through Dickson's Fallacies of the Faculty. On Tuesday afternoon we went to the British Museum to see a new bronze, and I was enchanted with some fragments of glass in the Slade Collection, with dyes of sunset in them. Yesterday, sitting in Thornie's room I read through all Shakspeare's sonnets. *Poor Thornie has had a miserably unsatisfactory week, making no progress*. After lunch came Miss N. Smith and Miss Blythe, Mr. Burton, Mr. and Mrs. Burne Jones and Mr. Sanderson.

2. Began *Middlemarch* (The Vincy and Featherstone parts).

[x]August 5. Thornie during the last two or three days gives much more hopeful signs, has been much more lively, with more regular appetite, and quieter nights. This morning I finished the first chapter of Middlemarch. I am reading Renouard's History of Medicine.

8. Thornie has had a sad relapse:- during all last night in incessant pain. I have had two rather fruitless days; on Friday from being interrupted by Thornie's coming downstairs, yesterday from my own ailments.

9. Sir Henry Holland believes that Thornie has had paraplegia. The lower part of his body is quite helpless.

19. Since I wrote last I have been constantly ailing. Poor Thornie has nearly recovered the use of his limbs but looks more wasted. Yesterday, Charlotte left us on account of ill health, and a new nurse took her place.

29. Thornie is much better, but is still not able to walk. At p. 40 of Middlemarch.

Aug 31. We went to Weybridge, walked on St. George's Hill, and lunched with Mrs. Cross and her family.

Sep. 1. Wednesday. I meditated characters and conditions for Middlemarch which stands still in the beginning of Chapter III.

X 2. We spent the morning in Hatfield Park, arriving at home again at $^1/_2$ past 3.

10. I have achieved little during the last week except reading on medical subjects – Encyclopædia about the medical colleges – Cullen's life – Russell's Heroes of Medicine etc. I have also read Aristophanes Ecclesiazusæ, and Macbeth.

11. I do not feel very confident that I can make anything satisfactory of Middlemarch. I have need to remember that other things which have been accomplished by me, were begun under the same cloud. G. has been reading Romola again, and expresses profound admiration. This is encouraging. *At p. 50 – end of Chapter III.*

15. George and I went to Sevenoaks for a couple of nights, and had some delicious walks.

17. Returned home in the afternoon just in time to receive a call from Mr. John Blackwood. Poor Thornie struck me as looking distressingly haggard; still he feels better.

21. Finished studying again Bekker's Charikles yesterday, the morning was spent walking with G. because his head was not well. I am reading Maundeville's Travels. As to my work, *im Stiche gerathen.*[5] Mrs Congreve and Miss Bury came, and I asked Mrs. Congreve to get me some information about provincial Hospitals, which is necessary to my imagining the conditions of my hero.

22. We went down to Watford for a change.

24. Returned home this morning because of the unpromising weather. It is worth while to record my great depression of spirits, that I may remember one more resurrection from the pit of melancholy. And yet what love is given to me! – what abundance of good I possess. All my circumstances are blessed; and the defect is only in my own organism. Courage and effort!

Oct. 5. Ever since the 28th I have been good for little, ailing in body and disabled in mind. On Sunday an interesting Russian pair came to see us, M. and Mde Kovilevsky: she, a pretty creature with charming modest voice and speech, who is studying Mathematics (by allowance through the aid of Kirchhoff) at Heidelberg; he amiable and intelligent, studying the concrete sciences, apparently – especially geology; and about to go to Vienna for six months for this purpose, leaving his wife at Heidelberg! – *I have begun a long-meditated poem: "The Legend of Jubal"*, but have not written more than 20 or 30 verses.

13. Yesterday Mr. Clark of Cambridge came to see us, and told of his intention to give up his oratorship and renounce his connexion with the Church. I have read rapidly through Max Müller's History of Sanskrit Literature and am now reading Lecky's History of Morals. I have also finished H. Spencer's last number of his Psychology. My head has been sadly feeble and my whole body ailing of

5 German, 'stuck'.

late. I have written about 100 verses of my poem. *Poor Thornie seems to us in a state of growing weakness.*

Oct. 19. 1869. This evening, at half past six o'clock our dear Thornie died. He went quite peacefully. For three days he was not more than fitfully and imperfectly conscious of the things around him.

He went to Natal on the 17th of October, 1863, and came back to us ill, on the 8th of May, 1869. Through the six months of his illness, his frank impulsive mind disclosed no trace of evil feeling. He was a sweet-natured boy – still a boy though he had lived for 25 years and a half. On the 9th of August he had an attack of paraplegia, and although he partially recovered, from it, it made a marked change in him. After that, he lost a great deal of his vivacity. But he suffered less pain. This death seems to me the beginning of our own.

May 20th. 1870.[6] I am fond of my little old book in which I have recorded so many changes, and shall take to writing in it again. It will perhaps last me all through the life that is left to me. Since I wrote in it last, the day after Thornie's death, the chief epochs have been our stay at Limpsfield, in Surrey, till near the beginning of December (I think we returned on the 21st November); my writing of Jubal, which I finished on the 13th of January; the publication of the poem in Macmillan's Magazine (May No.); and our journey to Berlin and Vienna from which we returned on the 6th of this month, after an absence of eight weeks. This is a fortnight ago, and little has been done by me in this interim. My health is in an uncomfortable state, and I seem to be all the weaker for the continual depression produced by cold and sore-throat which stretched itself all through our long journey. My teeth have teazed me a great deal since Xmas, and these small bodily grievances make life less desirable to me, though every one of my best blessings – my one perfect love, and the sympathy shown towards me for the sake of my work, and the personal regard of a few friends – have become much intensified in these latter days. I am not hopeful about future work: I am languid, and my novel languishes too. But tomorrow may be better than today.

Wednesday, May 25. We started for Oxford at 1/2 past 9, and arrived at Lincoln College, where we were to stay with the Rector and his wife about 12. After luncheon, G. and I walked alone through the town, which on this first view was rather disappointing to me. Presently we turned through Christ Church into the Meadows and walked along by the river. This was beautiful, to my heart's content. The buttercups and hawthorns were in their glory, the chestnuts still in sufficiently untarnished bloom; and the grand elms made a border towards the town. After tea, we went with Mrs. Pattison and the Rector to the croquet ground near the Museum. On our way we saw Sir Benjamin Brodie; and on the ground Professor Rawlinson, the "narrow-headed man", Mrs. Thursfield, and

6 In resuming her diary entries after a lapse of seven months, GE turned the book over and worked in from the other end to that where she began the diary in 1861.

her son who is a fellow (I think of Corpus), Miss Arnold, daughter of Mr. Tom Arnold, and Prof. Phillips, the Geologist. At supper we had Mr. Bywater and Miss Arnold, and in chat with them, the evening was passed.

26. G. and I went to the Museum, and had an interesting morning with Dr. Rolleston who dissected a brain for me. After lunch, we went again to the Museum, and spent the afternoon with Sir Benjamin Brodie, seeing various objects in his laboratories, amongst others the method by which weighing has been superseded in delicate matters by *measuring* in a graduated glass tube. After, Mrs. Pattison took me a drive in her little pony carriage round by their country refuge – The Firs, Haddington, and by Littlemore, where I saw J. H. Newman's little conventual dwellings. Returning we had a fine view of the Oxford towers. To supper came Sir Benjamin and Lady Brodie.

27. In the morning we walked to see the two Martyrs' Memorial, and then took a cab to Sir Benjamin Brodie's pretty place near the river and bridge. Close by their grounds is the original ford whence the place took its name. The Miss Gaskells were staying with them, and after chatting some time, we two walked with Sir Benjamin to New College, where we saw the gardens surrounded by the old City wall; the chapel where William of Wykeham's crozier is kept, and the cloisters, which are fine but gloomy, and less beautiful than those of Magdalen which we saw in our walk on Thursday, before going to the Museum. After lunch we went to the Bodleian, and then to the Sheldonian Theatre, where there was a meeting apropos of Palestine Exploration. Captain Warren, conductor of the Exploration at Jerusalem read a paper, and then Mr. Deutsch gave an account of the interpretation, as hitherto arrived at, of the Moabite Stone. I saw "squeezes" of this stone for the first time, with photographs taken from the squeezes. After tea we went – Mrs. Thursfield kindly took us – to see a boat-race. We saw it from the Oriel barge, under the escort of Mr. Crichton, fellow of Merton, who on our return took us through the lovely gardens of his college. At supper were Mr. Jowett, Prof. Henry Smith, Miss E. Smith his sister, Mr. Fowler, author of "Deductive Logic", and Mr. Pater, writer of articles on Leonardo da Vinci, Morris etc.

28. After a walk to St. John's College, we started by the train for London and I arrived at home about 2 o'clock, delighted to be under our own roof again.

29. Mr. Spencer, Mrs. Burne Jones and Mr. Crompton came. I read aloud No. 3 of "Edwin Drood".

30. We went to see the autotypes of Michael Angelo's frescoes at 36, Rathbone Place. I began Grove on the Correlation of the Physical Forces, needing to read it again with new interests after the lapse of years.

31. We walked to Hampstead to see mother in her new lodgings. Mr. and Mrs. Lytton called, and Mr. and Mrs. Call. In the evening, G. being very weary, I read him some of Rossetti's poems. Continuing Grove.

End of May

August 4. Two months have been spent since the last record! Their result is not rich, for we have been sent wandering again by G's want of health. On the 15th of June, we went to Cromer; on the 30th, to Harrogate, and on the 18th of July to Whitby, where Mrs. Burne Jones also arrived on the same day. On Monday August 1 we came home again, for a week only, having arranged to go to Limpsfield next Monday. To-day, under much depression, I begin a little dramatic poem the subject of which engaged my interest at Harrogate.

Oct. 27. On Monday the 8th of August we went to our favourite Surrey retreat, Limpsfield and enjoyed three weeks there, reading and walking together. The weather was perfect, and the place seemed more lovely to us than before. Aloud I read the concluding part of Walter Scott's Life which we had begun at Harrogate, two volumes of Froude's History of England, and Comte's correspondence with Valat. We returned on Monday the 29th. Before our return we had had a letter from Bertie telling us, to our joy, that he was engaged to a "well-educated young lady, Eliza Stevenson Harrison", and we agreed to write to the young lady's father on the subject to see if any provision could be made for their early marriage.

During our stay at Limpsfield I wrote the greater part of "Armgart", and finished it at intervals during September. Since then I have been continually suffering from headache and depression, with almost total despair of future work. I look into this little book now to assure myself that this is not unprecedented.

Dec. 2. I am experimenting in a story, which I began without any very serious intention of carrying it out lengthily. It is a subject which has been recorded among my possible themes ever since I began to write fiction, but will probably take new shapes in the development. I am today at p. 44.

I am reading Wolf's Prolegomena to Homer. In the evening aloud, Wilhelm Meister again!

Dec. 10. *George's Mother died this morning, quite peacefully as she sat in her chair.*

17. Reading Quintus Fixlein aloud to G. in the evening. Grote on Sicilian history.

Dec. 31. On Wednesday the 21st we went to Ryde to see Madame Bodichon at Swanmore Parsonage, a house which she had taken for two months. We had a pleasant and healthy visit, walking much in the frosty air. On Christmas day I went with her to the Ritualist Church which is attached to the Parsonage and heard some excellent intoning by the delicate-faced tenor-voiced clergyman Mr. Hooker Wicks. On Wednesday last, the 28th, Barbara came up to town with us. We found the cold here more severe than at Ryde, and the papers tell of still harder weather about Paris where our fellow-men are suffering and inflicting horrors.[7] Am I doing anything that will add the weight of a sandgrain against the persistence of such evil?

7 GE is referring to events in the Franco–Prussian War of 1870–1.

Here is the last day of 1870. I have written only 100 pages – good printed pages – of a story which I began about the opening of November, and at present mean to call "Miss Brooke". Poetry halts just now.

In my private lot I am unspeakably happy, loving and beloved. But I am doing little for others.

Sunday, March 19. 1871. It is grievous to me how little, from one cause or other, chiefly languor and occasionally positive ailments, I manage to get done. I have written about 236 pages (print) of my Novel, which I want to get off my hands by next November. My present fear is that I have too much matter, too many "momente".

Dec 1. This day the first Part of "Middlemarch" was published. I ought by this time to have finished the fourth Part, but an illness which began soon after our return from Haslemere has robbed me of two months.

20. My health has become very troublesome during the last three weeks, and I can get on but tardily. Even now, I am only at p. 227 of my fourth Part. But I have been also retarded by construction which, once done, serves as good wheels to progress.

1872. It is now the last day but one of January. I have finished the Fourth Part. i.e. the 2nd volume of Middlemarch. The First Part published on Dec. 1. has been excellently well received, and the second Part will be published the day after tomorrow.

About Xmas a volume of extracts from my works was published under the title "Wise, Witty and Tender Sayings in Prose and Verse". It was proposed and executed by Alexander Main, a young man of 30, who began a correspondence with me by asking me how to pronounce Romola, in the summer when we were at Shotter Mill. Blackwood proposed that we should share the profits, but we refused.

May 8. I have been reposing for more than a week in the hope of getting stronger – my life having been lately a swamp of illness with only here and there a bit of firm walking. In consequence of this incesssant interruption almost every week having been half nullified for me so far as my work has been concerned, I have only finished the Fifth Book, and have still three Books to write – equal to a large volume and a half.

The reception of the book hitherto has been quite beyond what I could have believed beforehand, people exalting it above everything else I have written. Kohn is publishing an English Edition in Germany; Duncker is to publish a translation; and Harpers pay me £1200 for reprinting it in America.

Jan. 1. 1873. At the beginning of December the eighth and last book of Middlemarch was published, the three final numbers having been published monthly. No former book of mine has been received with more enthusiasm –

not even Adam Bede, and I have received many deeply affecting assurances of its influence for good on individual minds. Hardly anything could have happened to me which I could regard as a greater blessing than this growth of my spiritual existence when my bodily existence is decaying. The merely egoistic satisfactions of fame are easily nullified by toothache, and *that* has made my chief consciousness for the last week. This morning, when I was in pain and taking a melancholy breakfast in bed, some sweet natured creature sent a beautiful bouquet to the door for me, bound round with the written wish that "every year may be happier and happier, and that God's blessing may ever abide with the immortal author of Silas Marner". Happily my dear husband is well and able to enjoy these things for me. That he rejoices in them is my most distinct personal pleasure in such tributes.

Monday May 19. We paid a visit to Cambridge at the invitation of Mr. Frederick Myers, and I enjoyed greatly talking with him and some others of the "Trinity Men". In the evenings we went to see the Boat race and then returned to supper and talk – the first evening with Mr. Henry Sidgwick, Mr. Jebb, Mr. Edmund Gurney; the second, with young Balfour, young Lyttleton, Mr. Jackson, and Edmund Gurney again. Mrs. and Miss Huth were also our companions during the visit. On the Tuesday morning we breakfasted at Mr. Sidgwick's with Mr. Jebb, Mr. G.W. Clark, Mr. Myers, and Mrs. and Miss Huth.

22. We went to the French play at the Princess's and saw Plessy and Desclée in "Les idées de Mde. Aubray". I am just finishing again Aristotle's Poetics which I first read in 1856.

Nov. 7. In the beginning of June we paid a visit to Mr. Jowett at Oxford, meeting there Mr. and Mrs. Charles Roundell then newly married. We stayed from Saturday till Monday, and I was introduced to many persons of interest – Prof. Green, Max Müller, Thompson, the Master of Trinity College, Cambridge and Mr. Wordsworth, the grandson of the poet, who had spent much time in India and a host of others "too tedious to mention".

Soon afterwards we went abroad – stayed a few days at Fontainebleau, then went by easy stages to Plombières where we stayed three weeks – then to Luxeuil for a week – then, hurried on by alarm about G's deafness, to Frankfort, and thence to Homburg. Home again through France. On our way to Plombières we had seen Troyes and Nancy; on our way back we saw Mainz, Metz, Verdun, Rheims and Amiens.

We remained only a week at the Priory and then went down to Blackbrook, near Bickley, which we had taken prospectively before going abroad, intending to hold it for a year on trial. But we found it advisable to give it up at the end of the two months from Sep. 4 to Oct. 31, the house being too ill garrisoned with furniture and too ill fortified against the cold. But we left it with regret, having learned to love the neighbourhood and the secluded grounds where we were shut in from all ugliness and intrusion.

Now we are in our London home again expecting to keep stationary through the winter. The first volume of my dear husband's work "Problems of Life and Mind" – the Studies for which have made a chief epoch in his life, having included the becoming acquainted with Mathematics in his 6th decade – is about to be published. And we are entirely happy, save that his health has flagged sadly during the last seven or eight months.

I am in tolerable bodily comfort, but not good for much in mind, and slow to concentrate myself.

1874. January 1. The happy old year in which we have had constant enjoyment of life notwithstanding much bodily malaise, is gone from us for ever. More than in any former year of my life, love has been poured forth to me from distant hearts, and in our own home we have had that finish to domestic comfort which only faithful, kind servants can give. Our children are prosperous and happy, Charles evidently growing in mental efficiency; we have abundant wealth for more than our actual needs; and our unspeakable joy in each other has no other alloy than the sense that it must one day end in parting. My dear husband has a store of present and prospective good in the long work which is likely to stretch through the remaining years of his intellectual activity, and there have not been wanting signs that what he has already published is being appreciated rightly by capable persons. He is thinner than ever and is only just getting the better of much dyspeptic discomfort that has beset him since the beginning of November, but still he shows wonderful elasticity and nervous energy.

I have been for a month rendered almost helpless for intellectual work by constant headache and nausea, but am getting a little more freedom. Nothing is wanting to my blessings but the uninterrupted power of work. For as to all my unchangeable imperfections I have resigned myself.

Jan. 17. 1874. I received this morning from Blackwood the accounts of Middlemarch and of the Spanish Gypsy for 1873. Of the guinea edition of Middlemarch published in the spring 2,434 copies have been sold. Of the *Spanish Gypsy* 292 copies have been sold during 1873, and the remaining copies are only 197. Thus out of 4,470 which have been printed, 4,273 have been distributed.

May 19. This month has been published a volume of my poems – "Legend of Jubal and other poems". George continues to have tolerable health and is far on in the preparation of his second volume. On the 1st of June we go into the country, to The Cottage, Earlswood Common, for 4 months, and I hope there to get deep shafts sunk in my prose book. My health has been a wretched drag on me during this last half year. I have lately written, *A Symposium*.

Jan. 13. 1875. Here is a great gap since I last made a record! But the time has been filled full of happiness. Yesterday I received from Blackwood the last year's account of Middlemarch, Jubal and the Spanish Gypsy, amounting to £860. Of Jubal a second edition was published in August and the 4th edition of the

Spanish Gypsy is all sold. This morning I received a copy of the 5th edition. The amount of copies sold of Middlemarch up to Dec. 31 is between 19 and 20,000.

Yesterday I also received the good news that the engagement between Emily Cross and Mr. Otter is settled.

The last year has been crowded with proofs of affection for me and of value for what work I have been able to do. This makes the best motive or encouragement to do more; but as usual I am suffering much from doubt as to the worth of what I am doing and fear lest I may not be able to complete it so as to make it a contribution to literature and not a mere addition to the heap of books. I am now just beginning the part about Deronda, at p. 234.

June 15 or 17 we went to a house we had taken at Rickmansworth. Here in the end of July we received the news that *our dear Bertie had died on June 29th.* Our stay at Rickmansworth, though otherwise peaceful was not marked by any great improvement in health from the change to country instead of town – rather the contrary. We left on Sep. 23 and then set off on a journey into Wales which was altogether unfortunate on account of the incessant rain. After our return I grew better and wrote with some success – G. worse, and consequently he consulted Dr. Reynolds, whose prescriptions seem to have answered so that he has recovered his usual power of enjoying work.

For the last three weeks, however I have been suffering from a cold and its effects so as to be unable to make any progress. Meanwhile, the 2 first volumes of Daniel Deronda are in print and the first Book is to be published on Feb. 1. – I have thought very poorly of it myself throughout, but George and the Blackwoods are full of satisfaction in it.

Each part as I see it before me *im werden*[8] seems less likely to be anything else than a failure, but I see on looking back this morning – Christmas Day – that I really was in worse health and suffered equal depression about Romola – and so far as I have recorded, the same thing seems to be true of Middlemarch.

I have finished the vth Book, but am not far on in the vith as I hoped to have been, the oppression under which I have been labouring having positively suspended my power of writing anything that I could feel satisfaction in.

1876.

Jan 1 [1876]. All blessedness except health!

Ap. 12. On February 1 began the publication of Deronda, and the interest of the public, strong from the first, appears to have increased with Book III. The day before yesterday I sent off Book VII. The success of the work at present is greater than that of Middlemarch up to the corresponding point of publication. What will be the feeling of the public as the story advances I am entirely doubtful. The Jewish element seems to me likely to satisfy nobody. I am in rather better health, having perhaps profited by some eight days' change at Weybridge.

8 German, 'in the process of development'.

June 3. Book V published a week ago. Growing interest in the public and growing sale, which has from the beginning exceeded that of Middlemarch. The Jewish part apparently creating strong interest.

June 10. We set off on our journey, intending to go to San Martino Lantosca in the Maritime Alps. But I was ill at Aix, where the heat had become oppressive and we turned northwards after making a pilgrimage to Les Charmettes – stayed a few days at Lausanne, then at Vevey where again I was ill, then by Berne and Zurich to Ragatz, where we were both set up sufficiently to enjoy our life. After Ragatz to Stachelberg, the Klön-Thal, Schaffhausen, St. Blasien in the Black Forest, and then home by Strasburg, Nancy, and Amiens, arriving Sep. 1.

Oct. 20. Looking into accounts à propos of an offer from Blackwood for another ten years of Copyright I find that before last Xmas there had been distributed 24,577 copies of Middlemarch. Magnificat anima mea!

Dec. 1. Since we came home at the beginning of September I have been made aware of much repugnance or else indifference towards the Jewish part of Deronda, and of some hostile as well as adverse reviewing. On the other hand there have been the strongest expressions of interest – some persons adhering to the opinion, started during the early numbers, that the book is my best – delightful letters have here and there been sent to me, and the sale both in America and in England has been an unmistakeable guarantee that the public has been touched. Words of gratitude have come from Jews and Jewesses, and there are certain signs that I may have contributed my mite to a good result. The sale hitherto has exceeded that of Middlemarch as to the £2/2s four-volumed form, but we do not expect an equal success for the guinea edition which has lately been issued.

11. We have just bought a house in Surrey, and think of it as making a serious change in our life, namely, that we shall finally settle there and give up town.

15. At the beginning of this week I had deep satisfaction from reading in the Times the report of a lecture on Daniel Deronda delivered by Dr. Hermann Adler to the Jewish Working Men, a lecture showing much insight and implying an expectation of serious benefit. Since then, I have had a delightful letter from the Jewish Theological Seminary at Breslau written by an American Jew named Isaacs, who excuses himself for expressing his feeling of gratitude on reading Deronda, and assures me of his belief that it has even already had an elevating effect on the minds of some among his people – predicting that the effect will spread.

I have also had a request from Signor Bartolommeo Aquarone, of Siena, for leave to translate Romola, and declaring that, as one who has given special study to the History of San Marco and has written a life of Fra Jeronimo Savonarola, he cares especially that 'Romola' should be known to his countrymen for their good. He afterwards found that a previously existing translation was a hindrance, though out of print. Magnificat anima mea!

And last night I had a letter from Dr. Benisch, Editor of the Jewish Chronicle, announcing a copy of the paper containing an article written by himself on reading 'Deronda' (there have long ago been two articles in the same journal reviewing the book) and using strong words as to the effect the book is producing. I record these signs, that I may look back on them if they come to be confirmed.

31. We have spent the Christmas with our friends at Weybridge, but the greater part of the time I was not well enough to enjoy greatly the pleasures their affection prepared for us.

Farewell, 1876!

1877

Jan. 1. The year opens with public anxieties, first about the threatening War in the East,[9] and next about the calamities consequent on the continued rains.

As to our private life, all is happiness – perfect love and undiminished intellectual interest. G's third volume is about halfway in print.

March 16. Since I wrote last G. has had an illness of rheumatic gout, and I have had a visitation of my renal disorder from which I am not yet free.

April 22. The improvement in my health which had begun has been checked for a week by an attack of influenza ending in bilious sickness and headache, from which I have not been free till the last twenty-four hours. Since I wrote last, G's third volume has been published. Also I have had some delightful evidence of the effect wrought by 'Deronda', especially among Jews.

The Priory, 21 North Bank
November 10. We went to the Heights, Witley at the beginning of June, after a delightful visit to Cambridge, and returned to this old home on the 29th. We are at last in love with our Surrey house and mean to keep it. The air and abundant exercise have quite renovated my health, and I am in more bodily comfort than I have known for several years. But my dear husband's condition is less satisfactory, his headaches still tormenting him.

Since the year began several little epochs have marked themselves. Blackwood offered me £4,000 for another ten years' copyright of my works, the previous agreement for ten years having expired. I declined, choosing to have a royalty. G's third volume has been well received and has sold satisfactorily for a book so little in the popular taste. A pleasant correspondence has been opened with Professor Kauffmann, now principal of the Jewish Theological Seminary at Pesth, and his "Attempt at an appreciation

9 In 1876 Turkish troops killed many Orthodox Christian rebels against Ottoman rule in Bulgaria. Russia threatened to make war on Turkey. Britain, needing to protect its routes to India, wanted neither to condemn Turkey nor fight Russia. The Eastern Question was live from 1876 to 1880.

of Daniel Deronda" has been translated into English by young Ferrier, son of Professor Ferrier.

A new Cabinet Edition of my Works, including 'Romola', has been decided on and is being prepared, and there have been multiplied signs that the spiritual effect of 'Deronda' is growing. The 7/6 edition has lately appeared. In America the book is placed above all my previous writings.

Our third little Hampstead granddaughter has been born and was christened Saturday the 3rd – Eleanor.

Yesterday, Mr. Macmillan came to ask me if I would undertake to write the volume on *Shakspeare* in a series to be issued under the title, "Men of Letters". I have declined.

26. The other day we saw in the Times that G's name had been proposed for the Rectorship of St. Andrews. Blackwood writes me that in less than a month they have sold off all but 400 of the 5250 printed. And in October were sold 495 of the 3/6 Adam Bede. Magnificat anima mea!

Our friend Dr. Allbutt came to see us last week, after we had missed each other for 3 or 4 years.

Dec. 31. Today I say a final farewell to this little book which is the only record I have made of my personal life for sixteen years and more. I have often been helped by looking back in it to compare former with actual states of despondency from bad health or other apparent causes. In this way a past despondency has turned to present hopefulness. But of course as the years advance there is a new rational ground for the expectation that my life may become less fruitful. The difficulty is, to decide how far resolution should set in the direction of activity rather than in the acceptance of a more negative state. Many conceptions of works to be carried out present themselves, but confidence in my own fitness to complete them worthily is all the more wanting because it is reasonable to argue that I must have already done my best. In fact, my mind is embarrassed by the number and wide variety of subjects that attract me, and the enlarging vista that each brings with it.

I shall record no more in this book, because I am going to keep a more business-like diary. Here ends 1877.

III. *Diary 1879*

The diary for 1879 has significant differences from the earlier ones. GE announced a resolution in signing off from the volume she kept from 1861 to 1877: 'I shall record no more in this book, because I am going to keep a more business-like diary. Here ends 1877.' The diary for 1878 – and it seems fair to assume that there was one – has disappeared, so that 1879 is the first of the two surviving 'more business-like' diaries. She chose a commercial printed diary – Beeching's Annual Diary, a brand favoured by GHL since 1873 – which includes data of various kinds about saints' days and bank dividends, and alternates plain leaves with pages printed to provide a designated space for each daily entry. There are sections ruled to allow for keeping accounts, which GHL did in his diary up to his death, GE taking over in this 1879 diary. While information about her investment income and various expenditures has a certain interest, these extensive financial memoranda have not been reproduced in the text of this journal, nor have shorter records of dividend income and the like been annotated.

Her entries on the whole are short, and sometimes entries under a particular date appear to have been made at different times, since one may be in pencil, the others in ink. We have made no attempt to transcribe these variations, which generally explain apparent oddities like that concerning Mrs Congreve and lunch on 11 November. The sometimes cryptic brevity of many entries must be ascribed at least in part to the layout of the printed diary page.

Only in part. The entries in this extraordinary diary mainly concern GE's devastation following the death of GHL on 30 November 1878. Here is a discontinuous narrative, in which the manuscript mutely offers blank days (the printed diary headings of day and month have been omitted from the transcript where there is no entry). The narrative tells the great grief of 'a bruised creature',[1] who initially finds some controlled expression of her suffering in the words of fellow writers, and before long sets about the therapeutic memorial activity of preparing her partner's unfinished work for publication.

1 *The George Eliot Letters*, ed. Gordon S. Haight, 9 vols. (New Haven, Yale University Press, 1954–78), vol. 7, p. 93.

As is the case elsewhere in the journals, some gaps and reticences are up to a point supplied by other texts, including her letters. Charles Lewes's descriptions of her prostration in the first weeks of mourning, and Edith Simcox's anxious, loving notes (*Letters*, vol. 7, pp. 87–8, 90; vol. 9, pp. 250–1), for example, confirm the agony apparent in the diary.

In signing off from her old diary in 1877, GE cannot have anticipated that within the year Lewes's death would oblige her to take over much of the business of which he had borne the brunt. The management of two sizeable establishments (the Priory in Regent's Park, and the Heights at Witley), her own literary affairs and Lewes's, investments, and the payment of allowances to relatives on both sides of the family, were all involved. The daughter of Robert Evans betrays no trace of resentment or incapacity in the diary. Other evidence is conflicting: Edith Simcox implies that practical responsibilities of this kind were welcomed as occupation and even as a scourge (*Letters*, vol. 9, p. 267). To Elma Stuart, some months later, GE permitted herself to complain: 'For as I have no one now to write business letters and notes of politesse, I find my time much drawn upon by these details of social duty, at which I grumble the more, perhaps, because I am not easy unless they are immediately fulfilled.' (vol. 7, p. 249)

Some of the business has to do with her work. Where the diary has laconic notes, her letter of 5 April 1879 to John Blackwood, on matters to do with the publication of *Theophrastus Such*, shows hard-headed command of both general strategy and particular detail of negotiations, which she asks the publisher to pursue: 'You see I have been so used to have all trouble spared me that I am ready to cast it on any willing shoulders. But I am obliged now to think of business in many ways.' (*Letters*, vol. 7, p. 126)

In such matters she was well-prepared, and well-supported. In other matters, Lewes's death exposed her to indignity. Bank account, investments, and property were all in GHL's name. Though 'Mary Ann Evans, spinster' was the sole executrix of his will, which left his copyrights to his sons, and everything else to her, several legal manoeuvres were necessary before she came into possession, including the macabre move of her changing her name by deed poll to Mary Ann Evans Lewes on 31 January 1879.[2] It is inconceivable that this business could have been conducted without her feeling

2 Gordon S. Haight, *George Eliot* (Oxford University Press, 1968), p. 523.

humiliated. There is a glimpse of GE's suffering at having to endure legal process to get access to her wealth in her calculations in GHL's account book, which shows the extent to which her earnings had contributed not only to his maintenance, but also to the support of Agnes and her children and several other Lewes relations. 'I make these memoranda to show that the property extant is far below the results of my work, and is therefore justly to be pronounced as placed out in trust for me', she wrote (*Letters*, vol. 7, p. 383). Various entries through this diary, as well as in the detailed accounts not reproduced here, make plain the extent of GE's ongoing commitment to members of the large and extraneous Lewes family (for a start, £100 a year to Agnes, GHL's estranged wife, designated by 'K.' for Kensington, where she lived, and £200 to Eliza, Bertie's widow).

While this is predominantly a volume of lamentation, it is also one of celebration and healing. The first entry in the diary proper is simply lugubrious: the quotation from Shakespeare, 'Here I and Sorrow sit' (*King John*, 3. 1. 73), leads off a substantial anthology of morbid verse, much of it from Tennyson's *In Memoriam*. The affective response may seem excessive, even by Victorian standards, but GE's mourning was mediated by her intellect. Already on 1 January she was addressing herself to work on GHL's unfinished *Problems of Life and Mind*, reading back through his earlier publications and manuscripts (thus on 13 January, 'Worked at M. S. Read Physical Basis – and dear Journal of our Seaside work'). Gradually, GE comes out of seclusion to a less stricken life. She finds energy and resolution to complete and see through the press the last two volumes of GHL's *Problems of Life and Mind, The Study of Psychology. Its Object, Scope, and Method* (published in May by Trübner) and *Mind as a Function of the Organism* (December).[3] The fact that there is frequent reference to particular chapters or topics explains what might otherwise be bizarre entries (say, that for 6 June). For a time, this work takes precedence over correcting the proofs of her own *Impressions of Theophrastus Such*, which GHL had despatched to Blackwood only a week before he died, and which was published – not without authorial misgivings – in May.

3 K. K. Collins, 'G. H. Lewes revised: George Eliot and the moral sense', *Victorian Studies*, 21 (1978), pp. 463–92, shows the extent to which GE worked over GHL's manuscripts. Collins's 'Reading George Eliot reading Lewes's obituaries', *Modern Philology*, 85 (1987), pp. 153–69, glosses the diary references to articles by James Sully and Joseph Delbœuf in particular.

The first reference in the diary to the proposal to set up a scholarship in GHL's memory is as early as 19 January, and discussions about the matter continue through to its award in October. Her exclamation on reading the applications on 5 October, 'wonderful out of all whooping!', is back to old form.

Emergence from the initial shock of her bereavement is more pronounced from 8 February, when she drove out for the first time. By April she was again well in touch with friends, and active not only with Lewes's proofs but with other business and family matters – for instance, she was concerned for the welfare of Bertie's widow Eliza and her children – 'the Africans' (*Letters*, vol. 7, p. 160) – in Natal and then in England when they arrived at the end of April. Acknowledgement of Eliza's incompatibility can be traced in the letters, but not in the diary, which reports endearing family errands (on 5 May, 'Went into town to buy toys for the children and then took them up to Hampstead') and wonderful agglomerations like that on 8 September. She receives and sends telegrams (she had been with GHL to a demonstration of the telephone in 1878, and knew of the phonograph – pp. 16 and n., 7).

She experienced considerable physical as well as emotional suffering in the course of the year. The endpapers and 'Memoranda' pages carry notes of addresses, the mails to Natal – and a single personal entry: 'Weight July 1st. 7 st. 5 1/2 lbs.'. Her thinness was much remarked, for instance by Barbara Bodichon (pp. 159, also 180), and was evidently due to general debility, exacerbated by severe attacks of kidney stone between June and August (even then she was 'able to write my letters and read my proofs', p. 183). Champagne was prescribed (see pp. 174–5, 179, 182), and the diaries take stock of her cellar in February and November.

But sorrow was never far off. The death of John Blackwood on 29 October was noted without comment, though letters testify to her grief at the loss of this stalwart friend and publisher. On 29 November the imminent anniversary of GHL's death occasioned a haunting entry that is tantamount to a prediction of her own death.

The strangest silence of the diary has to do with John Cross and his role in GE's life. There are certainly no explicit revelations, and it is tempting to read as anticipations of their marriage such cryptic notes as those of 2 and 16 May, 'Crisis'; 21 August, 'Decisive conversation'; 25 November, 'Another turning point'. Cross saw her sooner than most people, on 23 February (when Herbert Spencer was not received), and thereafter visited frequently, sometimes in company with others, or as on 6 March, 'to consult about investments'. On 18 March she referred to him familiarly as 'J. W. C.', but there is no inkling in the diary that by the end of the year she was writing him very loverlike letters (*Letters*, vol. 7, p. 211–12). Haight asks in respect of the entry for 8 October, 'Joy came in the evening': 'Is Joy a unique abbreviation for Johnny or a term of endearment?' (*George Eliot*, p. 529). Shoshana Knapp answers him, that the entry may be read as a play on Psalms 30:6, 'Weeping may endure for a night, but joy cometh in the morning'.[4] The account of the marriage in the 1880 diary is less forthcoming even than this.

Both Cross and Haight quote isolated passages.

4 '"Joy came in the evening": a note on a serious joke in George Eliot's diary', *Victorian Newsletter*, 64 (1983), pp. 1–3.

III. Diary 1879

Richard Kimpton, Wardour Street, 126 W.
H. H. Kimpton, 82 High Holborn, W. C.

Weight July 1st. 7st. 5$^{1}/_{2}$ lbs.

Direct Packet to Natal, 6th of each month.
Mail (indirect) every Thursday.
Address Sydenham, near Durban

Inv	1412	P	375
Dr	83	W	150
		C	200
	1495	H	208
		W	60
		T	30
		C&G	20
		GR	5
		G	16
		Ex	20
		P.	100
			1184

MEMORANDA, 1879.

Note in Journal 1877
Engelmann transferred his (formerly Kohn's collection) to
Karl Grädener of Hamburgh. 45 Hermann Strasse

Gas Light & Coke Company. Chief Office – Horseferry Road, Westminster S.W.
Colonial Bank 13, Bishopsgate St. Within, E.C.

Sambre et Meuse Railway 10 Moorgate Street, E.C.
South Eastern Railway, Manager & Secretary
~~Nat^{l}. Provincial B^{k}. of Eng^{d}. 112, Bishopsgate St Within~~
London Bridge Station S.E.

JANUARY 1879

Here I and Sorrow sit.[1]

1 William Shakespeare, *King John*, 3.1.73.

Einst ich wollte fast verzagen
Und ich dacht' ich trug es nie,
Und ich hab' es doch ertragen,
Aber frag' mich nur nicht wie.[2]

"Death and the Grave, that are not as they were"[3]

Du versuchst, O Sonne, vergebens
Durch die düsteren Wolken zu scheinen,
Das ganze Gewinn meines Lebens
Ist seine Verlust zu beweinen.[4]

WEDNESDAY 1

Copied stray pencilled notes.
Began to read "Principles of Success in Literature".
Feeling ill, unable to work at MS.
Mrs. Flower (née Rothschild) who has lately lost her husband sent me a basket of white flowers with a letter. Mrs. E. Gurney brought me 2 beautiful Arums. Mrs. B. Jones and the children a pot of white lilies.

'Whoso seeth me first on morrow
May sayne he hath met with sorrow
For I am sorrow and sorrow is I.' Chaucer[5]

"She being now removed by death a commensurable grief took as full possession of him as joy had done". Walton's Life of Donne[6]

Some little happiness have thou and I
(Since we shall die ere we have wished to die.)
For thou hast died ere thou didst wish to die.[7]

2 GE misquotes from Heine's *Buch der Lieder* the lines correctly quoted in her 'German Wit: Heinrich Heine', *Westminster Review*, 65 (1856), p. 29. Her own translation is 'At first I was almost in despair, and I thought I could never bear it, and yet I have borne it – only do not ask me *how*.'

3 The last line of Shelley's 'Alastor', which should read 'Birth and the Grave, that are not as they were'.

4 Lines from a poem said to have been written by Goethe on the day of his wife's death in 1816. The lines are translated as 'In vain, O Sun, you struggle /to shine through the dark clouds;/the whole gain of my life/is to bewail her loss' in GHL's *Life of Goethe* (3rd edn., 1855; London, Smith Elder, 1875), p. 533.

5 Geoffrey Chaucer, *Book of the Duchess* (1595), ll. 595–7.

6 Izaak Walton's *The Life and Death of Dr Donne* was included in the edition of Donne's *LXXX Sermons* (1640).

7 William Browne, *Britannia's Pastorals* (1613), Book 2, Song 5, ll. 819–20.

Kneeling before this ruin of sweet life,
And breathing to his breathless excellence
The incense of a vow, a holy vow,
Never to taste the pleasures of the world,
Never to be infected with delight,
Nor conversant with ease and idleness,
Till –[8]

Death
Shall give thy will divineness, make it strong
With the beseechings of a mighty soul
That left its work unfinished.[9]

Trocknet nicht, trocknet nicht,
Thränen der ewigen Liebe!
Ach, nur dem halbgetrockneten Auge
Wie öde, wie todt die Welt ihm erscheint!
Trocknet nicht, trocknet nicht,
Thränen unglücklicher Liebe.
Trocknet nicht![10]

Ah, better to be drunk with loss
To dance with death to beat the ground
Than that the victor Hours should scorn
The long result of love and boast
'Behold the man that lov'd and lost
But all he was is overworn'.[11]

THURSDAY 2

Kind letter from M. Foster of Cambridge, offering to help me on any physiological point.
Worked at M.S., but feeling ill.
Cheque from East Indian Railway.
Sent cheque to Melbourne and Hart.

FRIDAY 3

Ill, and worked only a little at M.S.

8 Shakespeare, *King John*, 4.3.65–71.

9 GE's ms reads as if these lines are part of the *King John* quotation which precede them. Their actual source eludes us. She may have composed them herself.

10 Goethe, '*Wonne der Wehmut*': 'Dry not, dry not/Tears of eternal love!/Ah, to half-dried eyes/How desolate, how dead the world seems!/Dry not, dry not/Tears of unhappy love/Dry not!'

11 Tennyson, *In Memoriam*, 1. 11–16. Tennyson's line 11 reads 'Ah, sweeter to be drunk with loss'.

SATURDAY 4

Feeling very ill all day, la mort dans l'âme,[12] but read and corrected some M.S.
Sent cheque to Harris and Sons
Cheque from Continental Gas Co.

SUNDAY 5

Walked out a little in Garden for the first time in the frosty sunshine.
Finished second reading of M.S.

MONDAY 6

Feeling ill – weary and heavy laden.
Re-read various portions of M.S. and made further corrections. Copied an addendum and wrote Title-page, etc.
Letter from a Mrs. Thomas (née Gilchrist) who knew something of my loved one in his youth.
Sent cheque to Beeching.
Mrs. Thomas's letter to be answered some time.

TUESDAY 7

Paid Brock's wages up to Feb. 3.
Reading and correcting M.S. and read Physical Basis.

WEDNESDAY 8

Re-reading M.S.
Letter from Herzen of Florence about translating Physical Basis.
Herzen, to be answered.

THURSDAY 9

Weary and heavy laden.
Reread discussion on the position of Psychology.
Calculated quantities of 1, 2, and 3 Problems.
Paid Dingley's half-yearly account up to Oct. 7/78.

FRIDAY 10

Ailing. Read M.S. 'Social Function' – and Physical Basis.
Paid Short and Chappell.

SATURDAY 11

Head miserable and heart bruised.
Letters from Mrs. Stowe and Mrs. Pfeiffer.

MONDAY 13

Worked at M.S. Read Physical Basis – and dear Journal of our Seaside work.
Letter from a Mrs. Forman of Indiana, mentioning her son Lewis Forman who is in London studying the organ with a Mr. Turpin; and from Lady Strangford.

12 French, 'sick at heart, the iron has entered the soul'.

TUESDAY 14

Sent Colonial and Sambre et Meuse to the Bank

THURSDAY 16

Too ailing to do much.

> "In every varied posture, place and hour
> How withered every thought of every joy".[13]

FRIDAY 17

Still ailing.

SATURDAY 18

Wrote to Dr. Michael Foster; and to Asher I. Myers.
Editor of Jewish Chronicle. Asher I. Myers.
Letter from Wells the dramatist asking my sanction for dramatising Adam Bede on behalf of Mrs. Hare and the Court Theatre.
Wrote refusal for Charles to copy.

SUNDAY 19

La mort dans l'âme – finished Reading 1 of Physical Basis.
Ruminating on the founding of some educational instrumentality as a Memorial to be called by his name.

MONDAY 20

Finished 'Moral Sense' and began copying Problems vol. 1.
Physiology.
Letters from Dr. Allbutt and Rector of Lincoln, the former testifying to my Darling's influence on Students.
Letter from Sir H. Maine.
Second Letter from Herzen which I answered, authorizing him to offer a French translation by him of the Physical Basis of Mind to Reinwald, the Parisian publisher.

TUESDAY 21

Finished copying 'Moral Sense' and wrote opening of chapter on Freewill.

WEDNESDAY 22

Finished for the present the revision of Problem I.

> 'Ah yet, ev'n yet, if this might be,
> I falling on his faithful heart,
> Would breathing thro' his lips impart
> The life that almost dies in me;

13 Edward Young, *Night Thoughts, On Life, Death, and Immortality*, ll. 21–2, quoted in GE's article 'Worldliness and Other-Worldliness: the Poet Young', *Westminster Review* 67 (1857), p. 26.

That dies not, but endures with pain,
    And slowly forms the firmer mind,
    Treasuring the look it cannot find,
The words that are not heard again.'[14]

Tears of a widower when he sees
    A late-lost form that sleep reveals,
    And moves his doubtful arms, and feels
Her place is empty, fall like these;

Which weep a loss forever new;
    A void where heart on heart reposed;
    And where warm hands have prest and closed
Silence, till I be silent too.[15]

THURSDAY 23

Wrote memories, and lived with him all day. Read in his diary 1874 – "Wrote verses to Polly – Wrote verses on Polly".[16]
Wrote to Blackwood about Bank. Paid Broadwoods 6/-.
Letter from some pious person signing 'A stranger' Postmark Nuneaton.

FRIDAY 24

Began Revision of Problem II. Revised Introduction.
Finished 2nd Reading of Psychological Principles.
Sent cheque to Williamsons and Sons.
Letter from a lady at Bordighera.
Letter from Miss Phelps.
Miss Phelps.

SATURDAY 25

Made Index to Introductory chapter.
Sent P.O. order to Gill and Carling, Guildford 7/5.

SUNDAY 26

Read and revised chapter II, Universality of Mind.

MONDAY 27

Revised chs III and IV, Laws of Sensibility and Organization of Impressions.
Received piece of Japanese medlar from Mrs. Pattison in sign of remembrance – with a letter.
Wrote to Sir James Paget.
'Limitations of Knowledge'.
Copied notes of the last days.

14 Tennyson, *In Memoriam*, 18. 13–20.
15 Tennyson, *In Memoriam*, 13. 1–8.
16 Entries of 10 and 12 September 1874, GHL Diary.

TUESDAY 28

Account from Blackwood – 777.12.6.
Answer from Sir James Paget.
Sent cheque to Mr. F. Malleson £2.2.
Wrote to Blackwood.
Limitations of Knowledge.

WEDNESDAY 29

Read and revised M.S. 'Sensorium'.
Mr. Warren came to get my signature etc.
Paid Burkin 1 week's wages, but omitted a second week, which I mean to pay him.
Mr. Warren. *Burkin*.
Charles brought me £20 from the Bank.
Pain in my hip sent me to bed.

Calm is the morn without a sound,
    Calm, as to suit a calmer grief
    And only thro' the faded leaf
The chestnut pattering to the ground:

Calm and deep peace on this high wold
    And on the dews that drench the furze,
    And on the silvery gossamers
That brighten into green and gold.

Calm and still light on yon great plain
    That sweeps with all its autumn bowers,
    And crowded farms and lessening towers,
To mingle with the bounding main:

Calm and deep peace in this wide air,
    These leaves that redden to the fall;
    And in my heart, if calm at all,
If any calm, a calm despair:

Calm on the seas, and silver sleep,
    And waves that sway themselves in rest,
    And dead calm in that noble breast
Which heaves but with the heaving deep.[17]

THURSDAY 30

Revised Laws of Sensibility.
Severe attack of Renal colic.

17 Tennyson, *In Memoriam*, 11.

FRIDAY 31

Relieved from pain.
Revised 'Logic of Feeling and Logic of Signs'.
Sir James Paget called to see me and gave prescription.
Spoke of Simon's scheme for Lectures at College of Surgeons.

FEBRUARY 1879

SATURDAY 1

Ill all day with headache and nausea. Unable to occupy myself in any way.

SUNDAY 2

Still thoroughly uncomfortable in body.
Sir James Paget came.

MONDAY 3

Relieved by a dose, but still uncomfortable enough to hinder work.
Wrote to Barbara, Mignon and Mrs. C.
Brock's wages paid up to this day.

TUESDAY 4

Ill again – unable to work.
Received 'Revue Scientifique' containing article by Delbœuf on my loved one.
Sent a copy to Frederic Harrison.
Read my darling's book on the Spanish Drama.

WEDNESDAY 5

Worked with difficulty all morning.
Had a severe attack of Colic.

> "When Each by turns was guide to each,
> And Fancy light from Fancy caught,
> And Thought leapt out to wed with Thought
> Ere Thought could wed itself with Speech."[18]

THURSDAY 6

Freed from pain, but feeling weak.
Finished Revision of Problem II to the end of 'Some Laws of Operation'.
Sir James Paget came. Talked of my darling.
Dreadfully depressed. Unable to do anything all the evening.

FRIDAY 7

Occupied the whole morning investigating dates of my darling's earliest work, owing to something mentioned by Sir James.
Wrote to Mrs. Thomas to ask her for the Syllabus of Lectures.

18 Tennyson, *In Memoriam*, 23.13–16.

SATURDAY 8

Drove out (on the Kilburn Road) for the first time.
Read my darling's first article on Goethe.

SUNDAY 9

Finished revision of Problem II including Consciousness and Unconsciousness.

MONDAY 10

Suffering and deeply depressed. Reading Problem III.

TUESDAY 11

Ailing and in constant pain.
More and more fainting under the anxiety of finding no satisfactory arrangement of parts in Problem III.

WEDNESDAY 12

In pain, rendering work difficult and inefficient.

> As sometimes in a dead man's face,
> To those that watch it more and more,
> A likeness, hardly seen before,
> Comes out – to some one of his race:
>
> So, dearest, now thy brows are cold,
> I see thee what thou art, and know
> Thy likeness to the wise below,
> Thy kindred with the great of old.
>
> But there is more than I can see,
> And what I see I leave unsaid,
> Nor speak it, knowing Death has made
> His darkness beautiful with thee.[19]

THURSDAY 13

Severe internal disturbance all morning. Afterwards still in pain and miserably head-weak as well as heart-fainting.

FRIDAY 14

Feeling worse and nervous, sent for Dr. Andrew Clarke, Sir James being out of town. Dr. C. came at 3 and comforted me greatly.
I was in bed all day – head aching, and unable to read anything except 'Times'.

SATURDAY 15

Ill again, but worked in dining room at M.S.

SUNDAY 16

Worked at M.S. but felt ill most of the day.

19 Tennyson, *In Memoriam*, 74.

MONDAY 17

Sir James and Dr. Clarke came: Thought the fons et origo mali[20] was renal, but that I should get better, though remain liable to renewals of the infirmity.

TUESDAY 18

Drove out at 12 but felt ill. Unable to work at M.S. so busied myself in making arrangements, finding out books etc.
Wrote to Mrs. Fields, Boston, U.S.A.

WEDNESDAY 19

Took a long drive and felt at first better, walking with more ease, but on my return at 4 felt the old pain return with more severity than usual. Felt very ill all the evening, and through a great deal of the night.

As when a soul laments which has been blest,
Desiring what is mingled with past years,
In yearnings that can never be exprest
By sighs, or groans, or tears.[21]

Let grief be her own mistress still.
She loveth her own anguish deep
More than much pleasure. Let her will
Be done – to weep or not to weep.[22]

Grief became a solemn scorn of ills.[23]

THURSDAY 20

Very unwell, but able to work a little at M.S. Wrote letters to Brock, Sarah, Jane, Mr. Sidgwick, Dr. Allbutt, Mrs. Trübner and Mrs. Pattison.

FRIDAY 21

Better. Worked all morning.
Wrote to Delbœuf.
Letter from Eliza. She has drawn £50 for the present year.

SATURDAY 22

Letter from Blackwood to Charles sending him £25 for his Father's republished stories.

SUNDAY 23

Saw Johnnie for the first time. Worked at MS.
Read Clifford's First and last Catastrophe.
Herbert Spencer called – did not see him.

20 Latin, 'source and origin of ill'.
21 Tennyson, *A Dream of Fair Women*, ll. 281–4.
22 Tennyson, 'To J.S.', ll. 41–4.
23 Tennyson, *A Dream of Fair Women*, ll. 227–8.

MONDAY 24

Worked at MS. Drove out.
Sir James Paget called.
In the evening corrected Proofs.
Letter from Delbœuf.

TUESDAY 25

Worked at MS.
Drove out and walked a little.
Received letter and supplementary sheets from Blackwood, and wrote in reply.
Corrected Proofs.

WEDNESDAY 26

Worked well at M.S. in the morning, but attacked with pain in the afternoon and obliged to go to bed.

Brett's list of Wines etc	2 doz & 4 Best Claret
	24 doz Commoner do
	2 doz & 3 Pints Champagne
	4 q^{t}. do
	1 doz & 1/2 Sherry
	5 Brandy
	1 whole Case of German Wine
	2 doz pint do
	2 doz white
	3 Huszar Bor
	1 doz Mineral Water
	4 Appollinaris
	1 doz Friedrichshall
At Witley	6 Sherry
	Claret B. 24. A18
	Rhine 3 doz.
	Brandy 7
	Apollinaris 4 doz.

THURSDAY 27

Ill with bad headache.
Unable to work.
Letter from Dr. Clifford Allbutt saying he would gladly write about what he had observed of the influence my darling's work had on young men.

FRIDAY 28

Headache still.
Mr. John Cross came. Head worse, sending me to bed, and obliging me to lie still.
Read J. S. Mill on Socialism.

MARCH 1879

SATURDAY 1

Still ailing, but better in the evening.
Letter from America from a Catholic young Lady full of affectionate ardour.
Read Proofs.

SUNDAY 2

Read half Problem IV. Johnnie came and discussed business, advising purchase of debentures.

MONDAY 3

Continued Problem IV.
Received letter from Mr. Sidgwick concerning the *Studentship*, and wrote to him in answer.
Read some reviews of Problems.
Corrected Proofs.

TUESDAY 4

Finished Problem IV.
Wrote Letters to Mrs. Ponsonby, Mrs. Grant Duff, J. W. Cross, and Walter Senior (with cheque).
Finished correcting proofs.

WEDNESDAY 5

Sent off proofs of Theo. to Edinburgh with letter to Blackwood. Wrote to Prof. Bain and to Barbara.

THURSDAY 6

Worked at Problem III. A lovely Spring day.
Drove and walked on the Kilburn Road and felt a little stronger.
Mr. John Cross came, to consult about investments.
Read Spencer's Psychology.

FRIDAY 7

Went to the lawyer's in Bloomsbury Sq. and then on into the City to the American Consul's.
Sent Subscription of £10 to the Clifford Fund.

SATURDAY 8

Worked at Problem III. Muscular Sense and Motor Perceptions and Intuitions, and Signatures of Feeling.
Gertrude and the children came to tea.
Letter from Mrs. F. Pollock and from Mrs. Congreve.

SUNDAY 9

Mr Sidgwick came to discuss the plan of the Studentship.
Wrote to M. d'Albert and to Emily.

MONDAY 10

Worked at MS. and paged Problem II having at last made up my mind about the chapters to be included in it.

TUESDAY 11

Read chapter on the affective States Problem III and wrote new page.
Sent cheque to Othen.
Johnnie came to discuss investments and brought me a register with all my investments neatly written out. I authorized him to sell San Francisco Bank, Continental Gas, and the American Coupons previously marked to the amount of £5000 – to be invested in L. and N.W. Debentures – also U.S. Funded which were about to be paid.

WEDNESDAY 12

Finished all at present included in Problem III.
Drive in the clear air and walk – *alone*.
Charles came and took away my will to carry it to the lawyer's.
Read on the colour-sense.

THURSDAY 13

Had to go to the Dentist at 10 o'clock. On return looked again over the outlying MSS.
Michael Foster came at 4 to discuss the Studentship, and we arrived at a satisfactory clearness, as to the conditions.
He mentioned as men whom he had thought of as suitable Trustees, Huxley, Pye Smith, Thistleton Dyer, F. Balfour, and H. Sidgwick.
Read Magnus on the *Farbensinn*.

FRIDAY 14

Went to the Dentist again and lost time in consequence.
Read his Diaries.
Farbensinn.

SATURDAY 15

Read over again Problem I preparatory to seeing Trübner on the subject of printing.

SUNDAY 16

Trübner came, and I arranged with him the printing of Problem I 'The Study of Psychology' to be published at the beginning of May. He brought Allen Grant's volume on the Colour Sense, of which I read the early chapters in the Evening. It settled my determination not to do anything further with the subject for the Problems.

MONDAY 17

Read Problem II intending to go through it again, before proceeding with Problem IV and the MSS on Language.

TUESDAY 18

Revised again Problem II to end of 'Range of Inner Life'.
Went to Bloomsbury Square to sign my Will.
J. W. C. came, and brought me the account of sales and purchases of stock.

WEDNESDAY 19

Problem II continued.
Mrs. Congreve came.
Grant Allen on the Colour Sense.

THURSDAY 20

Finished re-reading Problem II 4th time.
Moved into our Bedroom.

FRIDAY 21

Felt beaten with sadness.
Occupied miscellaneously with business.
Finished Grant Allen, Colour Sense.

SATURDAY 22

Revise of Theophrastus. Wrote to Blackwood.
Mrs. Congreve came again.
Mrs. Burne Jones came.
Unable to do much.

SUNDAY 23

Feeling ill in body and mind. Occupied chiefly with Theophrastus. Looked over prints and photos.

MONDAY 24

Sent off revise and wrote to Blackwood.
Wrote to Susanna with cheque.
Charles brought me £15.
Looked over Folio in Study.
Read my darling's M.S. on Language.

TUESDAY 25

Bitter weather. Snow again.
Read Part IV again. Felt it better not to print this fragment. Arranged his books and periodicals in Bookroom closet.
Read Bain on the Nervous mechanism – and looked for comparison into Foster's.
Wrote to Blackwood (William).
Signed Probate account.

WEDNESDAY 26

Weather still cruel, and my soul in deep gloom.

THURSDAY 27

Arranged Scientific apparatus and Books.
Drove out for the first time for several days.
Made list of his articles, and read His article on Philosophy in France, 1843.
First Proof of Problem I.

FRIDAY 28

Letters from Mr. Sanderson and Eliza announcing her having started for England.
Re-read Proof. Drove out in mental conflict.
Johnnie came on business.
Charles to dinner.

SATURDAY 29

Read Proof. Wrote to Mr. Sanderson.
Mrs. Congreve came.
Charles brought my Banking Book – balance £903.
Mill on Socialism.

SUNDAY 30

Re-read "Laws of Operation". Wrote letters and cheques.
Mr. Bowen came, Mr. Spencer, and Johnnie.
Read Herzen's "La Condizione fisica della Coscienza", sent to me at my request, because it criticizes my darling's standpoint.
Wrote to *Herzen* and to Mrs. L. M. Child.
Brock's wages paid up to this day.

MONDAY 31

Finished revision of Laws of Operation and numbered §§ of Problem II.
Iliad in Munro's edition.
Johnnie brought documents for signature.
Bad Headache.

APRIL 1879

TUESDAY 1

Headache continued all day.
3rd Proof came, and I corrected it

WEDNESDAY 2

Not well. Drove out in the clear morning air.
Johnnie came.
Read His writing in 1843.

THURSDAY 3

Drove out again in the morning.
Susanna came at 4.

Charles.
Read 1842.
Wretched inward struggles.

FRIDAY 4

Proof. Drove out to Highgate in the morning.
Mrs. Congreve.
Charles.
Mrs. Burne Jones.
Wrote to Mrs. Stuart.
Mathematics.

SATURDAY 5

Drove to Hampstead with Charles – saw his house for the first time.

SUNDAY 6

Johnnie came, then Charles, afterwards Mr. Trübner and finally when I was alone Mr. H. Sidgwick with whom I had a long and important conversation about the Studentship and other interesting subjects.

MONDAY 7

Going through Problem III again.
Letter from Dr. Allbutt about my darling.
Drive in the Spring air and walk.
A mental crisis.
Occupied with His writing.

TUESDAY 8

Revision and Proof.
Mrs. Stuart came.
Charles dined with me.

WEDNESDAY 9

Proof.
Went into Pr. Street with Brett, then on a cold drive along the Finchley Road.
His writings. Charles, talking.
Homer.

THURSDAY 10

Proof and Revises.
Wet. No drive. Arranged Books.
His writings.
Letter from Trübner promising last proof on Tuesday.
Homer.

FRIDAY 11

Alone all day.
Drove out before lunch. Saw Mr. Mocatta.

Heavy in body and mind.
Read 'Dwarfs and Giants' with which many memories are connected of far-off Richmond Days.
Homer.

SATURDAY 12

Proofs and Revises.
His writings.
Homer.
Daffodils and Violets sent me by post.

SUNDAY 13

Revises. Mr. and Mrs. Harrison came.
Snow. Incorporated portions into Problem III.

MONDAY 14

Cruel weather.
Incorporated Chapter on "Differences in the Triple Process".
Read again papers on Colour and Language.
Wrote to Mrs. Stuart and Susanna.

TUESDAY 15

Revises and Proofs.
Letters from Dr. Jowett and Blackwood.
Drove to Highgate.
Charles.
Homer.
Scientific articles.

WEDNESDAY 16

Sent off last Proofs.
Letters from Dr. Kaufmann and Emily.
Dr. Kaufmann writes that the Hungarian Translation of the History of Philosophy was just going to be sent in three volumes to my darling when it was heard that he had gone into the 'Friedhof der Geschichte'.[24]

THURSDAY 17

'Language' again.
Mrs. Congreve all afternoon.
Charles dined with me.
Steinthal.
Homer.

FRIDAY 18

Last Revises.
'Moral difficulty'.

24 German, 'graveyard of history'.

SATURDAY 19

Letter from Michael Foster saying he will be ready for next proofs after 16 June.

SUNDAY 20

Read Homer, Bain, Sainte Beuve.
Isaiah. Herbert Spencer in the afternoon asking advice about his autobiography.

MONDAY 21

Charles – then Vivian, to whom I promised £100, giving him 50 – to save him from reducing his capital.
Homer III.

TUESDAY 22

Letter from Vivian, returning cheque, and confessing his error.
Letter from Mde. Belloc asking me to lend her £500. Told Charles about V.
John came to advise me in the evening.
Wrote to Mde. Belloc, declining.
Homer IV. Foster, Physiology.
Mrs. Congreve at 2. Drove her home, with parcel of my grey dresses for the girls.

WEDNESDAY 23

Wrote to Vivian.
Letter from Blackwood about Harper, and price of English edition. Answered him.
Mrs. Ritchie called and I saw her.

THURSDAY 24

Headache.
Sir James Paget called.
Charles to dinner.

FRIDAY 25

Head still aching, I drove out in the morning.
'Moral difficulty' a little disentangled.
Finished Iliad IV.

SATURDAY 26

Mr. and Mrs. Hall at 4.30.

SUNDAY 27

Johnnie till 4, Mr. Bowen till 6.
Grote on the Sophists – then History of Philosophy to compare.
Began Sketch.
Life of Goethe.

MONDAY 28

News from C. that Eliza had arrived.
Went to meet him at Paddington Station and waited half an hour in vain.

Read Notes.
History of Philosophy. Pollock's Sketch of Clifford.
Life of Goethe. Homer.

TUESDAY 29

I went to Hampstead with Charles and brought Eliza and the two children to lunch. I took them back, and found Edith on my return.
Wrote a painful letter in the evening.

WEDNESDAY 30

Head bad.

MAY 1879

THURSDAY 1

Copied Notes. Headache.
Mrs. Peter Taylor came.
Went to the Cemetery.
History of Philosophy and Goethe.

FRIDAY 2

Copied Notes.
Went to the Cemetery again, and saw the Gardener. Ordered Ivy and Jessamine.
Headache.
Letter from Susanna about Vivian.
Mignon came at 6.
Crisis.

SATURDAY 3

Still Headache.
Copied notes.
Drove to Hampstead and took out Eliza and children.
Caird's Exposition of Comte.

MONDAY 5

Copied Notes.
Went into town to buy toys for the children and then took them up to Hampstead.

TUESDAY 6

Copied notes.
Mr. and Mrs. Call. Eleanor and Florence.
Goethe.
Homer.

WEDNESDAY 7

To the Cemetery.

THURSDAY 8

Water Rate.
Hung portrait.[25]
Drove to Hampstead – took out Gertrude and the children.
Burne Jones came.

FRIDAY 9

Re-read Problem IV.
To the Cemetery.
Charles.
Mrs. Burne Jones.
Dante. Goethe.

SATURDAY 10

Finished re-reading Problem IV.
Letter from Budapest.
Edith and Mr. Pigott.

SUNDAY 11

Mr Bowen came in the afternoon.

MONDAY 12

Brock's wages paid up to this day.
Drove to Hampstead to see Eliza and the children and took them [for] a drive.
Charles and Mrs. Congreve till dinner.

TUESDAY 13

Dr. Andrew Clarke came and gave me important suggestions about the Studentship of which I wrote to Mr. Sidgwick, Dr. C. having promised to see Huxley tomorrow.

WEDNESDAY 14

Wrote.
Dante. Received Duncan, Warren and Gardner's Account.

25 Edith Simcox in her diary entry for 10 May 1879 recorded a visit to GE: 'She said hurriedly as she kissed me – "Go into the dining room there is something you will like to see". – An enlarged portrait of him, framed and put over the chimney piece where her portrait used to be' (*Letters*, vol. 9, p. 128). In December 1879 GE told Elma Stuart, 'I am bitterly repenting now that I was led into buying Mayall's enlarged copy of the photograph you mention. It is smoothed down and altered and each time I look at it I feel its *un*likeness more. *Himself as he was* is what I see inwardly, and I am afraid of outward images lest they should corrupt the inward' (*Letters*, vol. 7, p. 233).

Finished reading "Life and Works of Goethe" with great admiration and delight.

THURSDAY 15

Headache.
Wet day. Did not go out.
Charles came.
Head bad all the evening.
Chose cover for Theo and wrote letter to W. Blackwood.

FRIDAY 16

Sent cheque to Duncan, Warren and Gardner.
Crisis.

SATURDAY 17

To the Cemetery.
Ill.

SUNDAY 18

Ill all day.

MONDAY 19

Still ailing and useless. But finished the packing of Books.
Charles brought copy of "Study of Psychology".
Theophrastus came.

TUESDAY 20

Severe attack of pain.
Hungarian Translation of History of Philosophy.

WEDNESDAY 21

Saw Mr. Anthony Trollope.

THURSDAY 22

Came down to Witley.
Lovely mild day.
Head bad.

FRIDAY 23

Arranged Books and Papers. Head still ailing.
Charles came down.

SATURDAY 24

Copied Draft to send to Sir James Paget.

SUNDAY 25

Made another copy of Draft.
Letters from Delbœuf and Mrs. Harrison.

Wet day (in the morning). Fine afternoon.
Drive with Charles.

MONDAY 26

Very ill with renal pain. In bed till 3.
Brock's wages paid up to this day.

TUESDAY 27

Drive in the rain to Elsted.
Touched the piano for the first time.
Letter from Michael Foster.

WEDNESDAY 28

Drove to Godalming, and opened account with Bank.
His presence came again.
Letter from Mrs. Pattison.
Letter from W. Blackwood announcing that 3000 of Theophrastus disposed of – going to press with 2nd ed.
Burkin paid up to Monday last.

THURSDAY 29

Letter from Sir James Paget about Studentship.
Wrote to Mrs. Pattison and to Prof. Josef Banoczi.

FRIDAY 30

Received a letter from Kaufmann asking for materials to help Szasz (the Hungarian translator of Life of Goethe) in preparing memorial address to the Hungarian Academy. Wrote to Charles asking him to collect articles.
Wrote letter to Dr. Foster about Studentship.

SATURDAY 31

Drove to Guildford and ordered Victoria at 12s. 6d. per week.

JUNE 1879

SUNDAY 1

Stormy.
Finished Iliad VI.

MONDAY 2

Selecting and copying Notes.
Mary, Alkie and Johnnie came. Rain!
Finished Magnin.

TUESDAY 3

Notes continued.
Drove to Godalming: got letter from Blackwood enclosing account of Edinbro' subscription to 2nd edition, and letter from Mr. Main.

WEDNESDAY 4

Letter from M. d'Albert enclosing one from M. Petavel-Ollif, a Jew, sending me a work of his Father's, who was deeply moved by D. D. having cherished similar ideas to Mordecai's.
Mrs. Evans called.

THURSDAY 5

Not well.
Morning absorbed in letters and business.
Madame Bodichon called – unable to pay the proposed visit, because of Dr. Bodichon's arrival.
Article in Times on Theophrastus Such weak and laudatory.
Paid Mrs. Brock.

FRIDAY 6

Madame Bodichon proposes to come.
Copying Notes from book marked Sensation.
Drove round by Manor House.
Reasoned Realism.

SATURDAY 7

Wet all day. Impeded in writing.
Head uncomfortable, and obliged to go to bed early.
Played on the piano.

SUNDAY 8

Wet in the morning. Drove out in afternoon.

MONDAY 9

Letter from a projector, in consequence of hearing of Theophrastus and *Merman*.
Letter from Charles.

TUESDAY 10

Drove to Waverley Abbey.

WEDNESDAY 11

Letter from Mr Bowen announcing his appointment to the Judgeship vacant on the retirement of Judge Mellor.

Extra Expenses for Half Year – ending June 1879.

Birkin's Mourning	11.11.0
Servants and Family etc. to Charles	60. 0.0
Present to Charles	50. 0.0
Melbourne & Hart	1. 4.0
Fun. Co	30. 7.6

Williamson	41.17.3
Pink	30.18.5
Maple & Co	2.16.6
Income Tax	79.12.6
Nutt	3.11.6
Othen	32. 1.9
Clifford	10. 0.0
Probate	120. 3.6
Jennings	25. 0.0
L. & N. Deb.	217. 0.0
Mayall	5.13.0
Cox & Sons	41. 0.0
Warren	164. 5.2
London & County Bank	50. 0.0
Other	22. 7.6
	999. 9.7
Other expenditure during Half year	534. 0.0

THURSDAY 12

Account of Sales of "Psychology" from Trübner: 350.
Letter from William Blackwood saying that the 2nd Edition of Theophrastus was half sold.

FRIDAY 13

Received altered Draft from Dr. Foster.
Sent off M.S. to Ballantyne Hanson and Co and wrote seven letters.

SATURDAY 14

Finished copying Notes.

SUNDAY 15

In pain most of the day.
Drew £400 from Bank of Deposit.

MONDAY 16

Pain worse. Obliged to go to bed after my drive.
Sent cheque for 364.11.10 to Mr. Warren for Fines etc on copyhold.

TUESDAY 17

Confined to bed all day.

WEDNESDAY 18

Letters from Mr. Beesly, Mrs. Stuart and Charles which I answered before rising.
Felt better and took a drive.
Sent cheque to Mr. Beesly and to Charles and drew cheque for Rates 6.

THURSDAY 19

Ill.

Severe pain. Sent for Mr. Parson; and for Sir James Paget who came, but before his arrival I had been considerably relieved.

FRIDAY 20

Ill and in bed all day.

SATURDAY 21

Ill.

SUNDAY 22

Ill.

MONDAY 23

Ill.

TUESDAY 24

Ill

WEDNESDAY 25

Ill.

JULY 1879

THURSDAY 10

Ill at ease.

FRIDAY 11

New attack of pain.
Relieved in the afternoon.

SUNDAY 13

Dr. Andrew Clarke came, and brought his wife with him. Very ill in the evening.

MONDAY 14

Brock's wages paid up to this day.
Suffering in the morning, but better afterwards.
Paged Problem III.

WEDNESDAY 16

Better symptoms today.

TUESDAY 29

Beautiful anonymous letter from New Zealand.
Deed of Studentship came for my signature.

IOT, GEORGE, ORDER NO:
ORDER DATE: 11JAN2002

THE JOURNALS OF GEORGE ELIOT / EDITED BY
MARGARET HARRIS AND JUDITH JOHNSTON.

N
T
A
S

BLACKWELL RETAIL (UK) 1998 1 VOLS
60.00 GBP CLOTH
0-521-57412-9 98-3679
LO-477171
QTY ORDERED: 001
ENG LIBR F K QTY SHIPPED: 001
EHEASLIP G4-542/0057
BLACKWELL BOOK SERVICES

OKANAGAN UNIVERSITY, COLLEGE| 122220005|

WEDNESDAY 30

For the last week I have been improving – pain reduced to something easily bearable, and strength increasing.
Letter from Sir James Paget, proposing that I should go to town to have a consultation held upon me by himself, Dr. Clarke, and a third.

THURSDAY 31

Wrote a report of myself to Sir James.

AUGUST 1879

FRIDAY 1

Telegram from Sir James Paget saying that he and Dr. Andrew Clark thought I need not go to town.

SUNDAY 3

Greatly better – feeling as if I should recover.

WEDNESDAY 6

Not thinking quite so well of my condition.

THURSDAY 7

Letters from Michael Foster and Mr. Sully expressing their Interest in Problem II. Sent off the final four sheets of this Problem to Ballantynes.

FRIDAY 8

Feeling much better.

SUNDAY 10

Letter and account of sales from Blackwood.

MONDAY 11

Brock's wages paid up to this day.

TUESDAY 12

Dr. and Mrs. Congreve came.

THURSDAY 14

Drove to Hampton Ponds for the first time this year.

FRIDAY 15

Letter from William Blackwood saying Theophrastus is all sold out, and 17 copies ordered in London, while they are still reprinting an additional 500, making in all according to the accounts received more than 6100 copies.

THURSDAY 21

Decisive conversation.
Balance at Banker's £718.

WEDNESDAY 27

Dr. and Mrs. Congreve to lunch.

SUNDAY 31

Elinor and her brother came.

SEPTEMBER 1879

MONDAY 1

Brock's wages paid up to this day.
Sent U.S. Funds Loan £45 and Midland Railway £19.1.10 to Bank.

TUESDAY 2

Received draft of Advertisement of Studentship from Dr. Foster and returned it with approval.
The Trust deed is now signed and the money transferred.
Mrs. Geddes to lunch.

WEDNESDAY 3

Drove to Godalming Bank and round by Bramley.
Sent Gaslight and Coke £66 to Union Bank.

SATURDAY 6

Charles and Gertrude came.
Drove them to Elsted.

SUNDAY 7

Rainy all morning. Drove in the afternoon.
Proof. Letter from Blackwood.

MONDAY 8

Proof. Oliphant on the Druses.
Wrote to Blackwood.
Drove to Godalming. Ordered Cocoa.
Mutiny in Afghanistan.
Darwin. Schubert.
Homer. Mrs Greville and Lady Probyn called.

TUESDAY 9

Drove by Shillinglea.

WEDNESDAY 10

Read Mr. Sully's proof of his article on my darling for the New Quarterly, and wrote to him.
Called on Mrs. Evans and at Hambledon Parsonage and left cards. Mr. Parson called.

Mrs. Stuart Hodgson called.
Wrote to Mrs. Congreve, Overton, Mrs. Greville and read proof with Foster's corrections – also proof with M.S. to p. 384.
Letter from M. Foster saying he had sent off advertisements of studentship.

THURSDAY 11

Received proof of 'Extract' from the deed of Studentship and sent it back to A. G. Dew-Smith.
Mathematics.
Finished Book XIV of Iliad.

FRIDAY 12

Letters from Emily and Mrs. Stuart.
Answered Emily.
Rain, rain.

SATURDAY 13

Drove to Godalming in the rain.

SUNDAY 14

Mrs. Greville and Mr. Pigott called.
Glorious day.

MONDAY 15

Another fine day for the Harvest.

TUESDAY 16

Sent Charles cheque for Kensington £40.
Mr. Burne Jones came. Drove him to Hinde Head.

WEDNESDAY 17

Drove to Godalming and paid cheque for £50 into the Bank.
Mrs. Evans and Miss Greenaway called.

THURSDAY 18

Mist, but no rain.
Headache.
Drove to Godalming Station.
Beaumarchais.
Lady Holland called.
2nd advertisement of Studentship in Times.

FRIDAY 19

Mist.
Headache again.
Mr. Parson called.
Drove to Godalming and called on Mrs. Greville.

Proofs and Revises.
Sent off Revises.

SATURDAY 20

A little better.

SUNDAY 21

Walked out towards the Terrace, but did not find it. Drove to Thursley.

MONDAY 22

Pain in limbs, and altogether less well.
Fine day, and harvest-work going on diligently.
Proofs coming in fast, but nothing from Foster.
Mrs. Greville called.

TUESDAY 23

Rain again, heavily through the last night, and continuing through the day.
Mrs. Congreve came to lunch.

WEDNESDAY 24

Stormy and called [sic].
Drove out towards Elsted.
Finished Voltaire's Candide again after many years' interval.

THURSDAY 25

Fine and bracing.
Wrote to Mrs. Congreve to tell her E's opinion of 'Soul of Mitre Court'.
Proofs from Mr. Sully up to the last in my possession.

FRIDAY 26

Feeling ill and depressed.
Mr. Tennyson and Hallam called.

SATURDAY 27

Still ailing.
Lady Holland called.

SUNDAY 28

Last proofs came from Dr. Foster and Mr. Sully.
Better in the afternoon.

MONDAY 29

Brock's wages paid up to this day.
Sent off last proofs.
Madame Bodichon came to stay.

TUESDAY 30

Wet day – could not drive.
Mr. Cross came to dinner with us.

OCTOBER 1879

WEDNESDAY 1

Letter from a madman in Kansas.
Drove Made. Bodichon to Thursley.
Mrs. Greville came and recited the Revenge, Delilah from Samson Agonistes, and Jeanne d'Arc.

THURSDAY 2

Letter from Michael Foster.
Madame Bodichon left at 1/2 past 11.

FRIDAY 3

Tears, tears.
Letter from Mrs. Merritt, with Etchings and copy of her husband's memoir etc.

SATURDAY 4

Vivian and Constance, Charles and Gertrude.

SUNDAY 5

Bank bill from Blackwood. Wrote to acknowledge.
Last Revises from Ballantynes.
Letter from Master of Balliol proposing to come.
Michael Foster sent packet of applications for Studentship – wonderful out of all whooping!

MONDAY 6

Ill in body and mind.
Reading Plato – Republic.
Drove to Godalming.

TUESDAY 7

Mr. Jowett expected – did not arrive.
Wrote answer to Mrs. Merritt.
Read her Recollections of H. Merritt.

WEDNESDAY 8

Letter from W. L. Bicknell, wanting to dramatize Romola.
Joy came in the evening.
Drove to Godalming Bank and got £25.

THURSDAY 9

Letter about French translation of Theophrastus. Wrote to W. Blackwood on the subject.
Choice of Hercules.

FRIDAY 10

Hebrew and Algebra.

SATURDAY 11

Drove to Bargate.

SUNDAY 12

Alone all day.
Hebrew and Plato's Republic.

TUESDAY 14

Letters from Mrs. Stuart and Edith.
Drive.
Purgatorio.

THURSDAY 16

Not well. Wrote Letters.
New Quarterly with Sully's article.
Called on Lady Holland.
Revise of Title page.

FRIDAY 17

Letter from America – Miss Watson – and from Mrs. B. Jones.
Drove on the Chillingfold Road.
Meditation on difficulties.

SATURDAY 18

Bright day.
Letter from Dr. M. Foster saying that he had chosen Dr. Roy for the Studentship.

SUNDAY 19

Wet, stormy Sunday. Walked in the garden.

MONDAY 20

Received and sent off last revise of Title page.
Wrote to Trübner and to the Master of Balliol.
Drove by Pepper Harrow to Juniper Common in the clear morning.

TUESDAY 21

Drove by Bramley in the morning air.
Finished Plato's Republic.

FRIDAY 24

Read Grote on the Sophists.

SATURDAY 25

Drove to Juniper Common in the afternoon.

MONDAY 27

Brock's wages paid up to this day.

WEDNESDAY 29

Mr. John Blackwood died.

FRIDAY 31

At Weybridge for the night.

NOVEMBER 1879

SATURDAY 1

Returned to the Priory.

SUNDAY 2

Mr. Spencer and Roland Stuart.

MONDAY 3

Occupied in unpacking etc.

TUESDAY 4

To the Cemetery.

WEDNESDAY 5

To Hampstead, to see Eliza.

Wine left at Witley
Nov. 1879 4 Brandy
6 sherry
2 doz & 5 Liebfrauenmilch
3 Claret

THURSDAY 6

Mr. Pigott called.
Charles dined with me.

FRIDAY 7

Drove in the Kilburn Road and walked up the old lane, ruminating in the sweet air. A lovely autumnal day.

SATURDAY 8

Wrote to Mrs. W. Smith, Mignon, etc etc.
Mrs. Ruck, Dr. A. Clark.

SUNDAY 9

Mr. Spencer to say Goodbye – going to Egypt.
Mr Burne Jones – about St. Mark's Venice.
Reading Jowett's Thucydides.

MONDAY 10

Letter from Mr. Sidgwick forwarded – how to pay first quarter in advance for Studentship.
Sent telegram.
Sir James Paget called and Mrs. Burne Jones.

TUESDAY 11

To Dentist's at 1/2 past 10.
Mrs. Congreve coming to lunch.
Mrs Congreve to lunch.
To the Dentist's.

WEDNESDAY 12

To Hampstead to see Eliza and children.

TUESDAY 18

Dr. Congreve and Lady Bowen.
To the Dentist's 10.30.

WEDNESDAY 19

Mrs. Hooper and Miss Simcox.
Drove to the Cemetery in clear air.

THURSDAY 20

Letter from Dr. Roy – highly satisfactory.

FRIDAY 21

Dentist at 2.

SATURDAY 22

Miss Graham and Mr. Jacobs.

SUNDAY 23

Fog and Headache.

MONDAY 24

Headache. Indoors all day.

TUESDAY 25

Dentist at 2.
Wrote to Dr. Roy.
Another turning-point.

WEDNESDAY 26

Drove into town in the morning to buy books and toys for the children.

FRIDAY 28

Went to the Cemetery.

SATURDAY 29

Reckoning by the days of the week, it was this day last year my loneliness began. I spent the day in the room where I passed through the first three months – I read his letters, and packed them together, to be buried with me. Perhaps that will happen before next November.

SUNDAY 30

Mr. Sidgwick writes.
Sent £50 to Mr Balfour for Dr. Roy.

DECEMBER 1879

MONDAY 1

~~Brock's wages paid up to this day~~
up to Dec. 8.

WEDNESDAY 3

Mr. William Blackwood.

FRIDAY 5

Mr and Mrs. Darwin.
Mr. Leslie Stephen, Mr. and Mrs. Beesly.
Miss Simcox.

SATURDAY 6

Sent cheque to Brock.
Florence Hill.
Gertrude, Charles, Eliza and the children to lunch.

MONDAY 8

Brock's wages paid up to this day.
Mr. William Blackwood.

TUESDAY 9

Mary Cross. Mr. Frederick Myers.

WEDNESDAY 10

Dr. and Mrs. Bridges. Mrs. Strachey.

THURSDAY 11

Sent Cheque to Macmillan £41.
Mr. Harrison.

FRIDAY 12

Cheque to Debenham for Witley Rates, £6.3.9.
Mr Hamilton Aidé. Charles.

SUNDAY 14

General Hamley, Sir C. Bowen, N. Grosvenor.

MONDAY 15

Drove to see Eliza.
Mr. and Mrs. Druce, Mrs. Trübner.

TUESDAY 16

Master of Balliol.
Charles to dine.

WEDNESDAY 17

Cold in the earth – and the deep snow piled above thee
Far, far removed, cold in the dreary grave!
Have I forgot, my only love, to love thee,
Severed at last by Time's all-severing wave?

Now when alone, do my thoughts no longer hover
Over the mountains, on that northern shore,
Resting their wings where heath and fern leaves cover
Thy noble heart for ever, ever more?

Cold in the earth – and fifteen wild Decembers,
From those brown hills have melted into Spring
Faithful indeed is the spirit that remembers
After such years of change and suffering!

Sweet love of youth, forgive, if I forget thee
While the world's tide is bearing me along;
Other desires and other hopes beset me,
Hopes which obscure but cannot do thee wrong!

No later light has lightened up my heaven
No second morn has ever shone for me;
All my life's bliss from thy dear life was given
All my life's bliss is in the grave with thee.

But when the days of golden dreams had perished
And even Despair was powerless to destroy;
Then did I learn how existence could be cherished,
Strengthened and fed without the aid of joy.

Then did I check the tears of useless passion –
Weaned my young soul from yearning after thine;
Sternly denied its burning wish to hasten
Down to that tomb already more than mine.

And even yet I dare not let it languish
Dare not indulge in memory's rapturous pain.

Once drinking deep of that divinest anguish
How could I seek the empty world again?

Emily Brontë[26]

THURSDAY 18

Mrs. Sotheby.

FRIDAY 19

Miss Cross.
Miss Simcox.

SATURDAY 20

Finished the Iliad.

SUNDAY 21

Mr. Cross, Sir Lewis and Lady Pelly, Mrs. A. Tennyson and Mr. Locker, Mr. Trübner.

MONDAY 22

Gas Light & Coke shares sold £1200 for 2260.

WEDNESDAY 24

Eliza and the children to lunch. Left at 4.
Lady Strangford and Dr. Congreve.

THURSDAY 25

Alone. Dense fog all day.

FRIDAY 26

Miss Simcox.

SATURDAY 27

Lady Bowen.

SUNDAY 28

Finished Weber's Indian Literature.

26 This poem was published as 'Remembrance' in *Poems by Currer, Ellis, and Acton Bell* (London, Aylott and Jones, 1846).

IV. *Diary 1880*

Again as in 1879 GE used a commercial printed diary, keeping detailed financial accounts in it (not reproduced in full), but otherwise making only brief notations – rarely more than a sentence or two. Other entries give even more than usual attention to health, as her kidney complaints worsened. In the early months of the year, her busyness in a settled routine is evident, though her entries are spare. In letters she reiterates that she is at home from 4.30 p. m. each day, and the diary records a stream of callers. She drives out to galleries, and to pay visits (on 31 March the Kensington addresses she notes are those of the painter Millais, in Cromwell Place, and Mrs Call, née Rufa Brabant, at 9 Addison Gardens South).

The extent to which the diary provides only a partial record of what is happening in her life is highlighted by the laconic note of 9 April, 'My marriage decided'. Just as the extant journal is silent on the choice of George Henry Lewes, so it is on the choice of John Walter Cross. There has been no explicit preparation for this announcement, though in retrospect some of the cryptic notes in 1879 become portentous. If GE was unforthcoming in her diary, her behaviour towards her friends was distinctly secretive: letters to Barbara Bodichon on 26 April and to Edith Simcox on 2 May make clear that she baulked at breaking the news to them.[1] The prospective bridegroom was deputed to break the news to Charles Lewes a week before the wedding, and Charles in turn was deputed to inform other people at nominated times. The day before the wedding, GE mentions arrangements for payment of Lewes[1] dependents and the servants. But also she wrote to a small number of her friends: William Blackwood, Georgie Burne-Jones, Maria Congreve, Cara Bray – and to Barbara Bodichon, with the request, 'Please tell Bessie for me, with my love to her.' (*Letters*, vol. 7, p. 269) The letter to Barbara, of all people, remained unposted until Charles Lewes retrieved it from a drawer and mailed it on 7 July. Meanwhile this most intuitive of friends had written wonderfully when she learned the news:

> Tell Johnny Cross I should have done exactly what he has done if you would have let me and I had been a man.

1 *The Letters of George Eliot*, ed. Gordon S. Haight, 9 vols. (New Haven, Yale University Press, 1954–78), vol. 7, p. 265; vol. 9, p. 305.

> You see I know all love is so different that I do not see it unnatural to love in new ways – not to be unfaithful to any memory. (*Letters*, vol. 7, p. 273)

GE's reply to Barbara on 6 June (pp. 290–1) is exemplary of the account of her marriage she purveyed to her intimates. Here is a succinct version, offered to Charles Lewes: she describes the Grande Chartreuse, expressing regret that

> the Pater had not seen it. I would still give up my own life willingly if he could have the happiness instead of me. But marriage has seemed to restore me to my old self. I was getting hard, and if I had decided differently I think I should have become very selfish. To feel daily the loveliness of a nature close to me, and to be grateful to it, is the fountain of tenderness and strength to endure. (*Letters*, vol. 7, p. 283)

Attempts to account for the marriage have ranged from the condescending (Haight's all-purpose explanation that she needed someone to lean upon) to the concupiscent. That astute reader of GE's deviousness, Rosemarie Bodenheimer, provides a convincing illumination of this fraught and complex decision as of other of GE's rites of passage. She develops the insight that in the group of letters announcing her marriage, GE is declaring 'her resignation from the position of "strong-minded woman" . . . For the sake of the friends who had come to know and revere her as George Eliot, she produced a George Eliot fable' of redemption into human community.[2] In such a reading, the absence of explanation or self-justification in the diary can be mute witness.

That the marriage brought satisfactions to the sixty-year-old bride is evident. The staccato diary entries yield to a brief formal statement about the wedding, followed by an elated account of the Channel crossing, and of Paris. After Paris, there is bald detail of the itinerary which takes the newlyweds south through France to Italy, where they spent a few days in Milan before moving on to Verona, Padua, and Venice. Among matters not mentioned in the diary is her loss of a brooch (*Letters*, vol. 7, p. 277: like the misplaced letter to Barbara, a symptom of anxiety?) and the rapprochement with brother Isaac (pp. 270, 287) who held out for his sister to be respectable before he resumed correspondence after twenty-odd years (though the Evans women had kept in touch: Isaac's

2 Rosemarie Bodenheimer, *The Real Life of Mary Ann Evans: George Eliot Her Letters and Fiction* (Ithaca and London, Cornell University Press, 1994), pp. 116–7.

wife wrote a letter of condolence when Lewes died, for example). The tone of both GE's letters, and Cross's, is that he is a novice being initiated into the finer points of travel. Cross's letter from Verona to his sister, for instance, exclaims about his growing 'knowledge of early art', repeats witticisms of 'mia Donna' (*Letters*, vol. 9, p. 311) – and among other things indicates that volumes of Murray and Kugler – regular companions of GE and GHL on their travels – were also on this tour to provide instruction and guidance. Once in Venice, it was to Ruskin they turned for tuition.

It is difficult to read the groom's reactions. Cross rather wistfully describes GE's stamina on their honeymoon:

> I had never seen my wife out of England, previous to our marriage, except the first time at Rome, when she was suffering. My general impression, therefore, had been that her health was always very low, and that she was almost constantly ailing. I was the more surprised, after our marriage, to find that from the day she set her foot on Continental soil, till the day she returned to Witley, she was never ill – never even unwell. She began at once to look many years younger.[3]

Cross's having lost weight is several times mentioned in letters (e.g. *Letters*, vol. 7, p. 294), but whether this was a symptom of the crisis that overtook him in Venice on 16 June cannot be established. The trauma of his throwing himself into the Grand Canal in (presumably) an attempt at suicide is curtly represented in the diary in details about doctors' visits and telegrams. GE's distress is betrayed by repetition of the entry about the arrival of Cross's brother Willie (18 and 19 June, with variant spellings of Willie). The received version of this episode has to do with heat, polluted canals, the Scirocco, lack of exercise.[4] The diary is unforthcoming. After a week the Cross party began a measured journey back to England, arriving at Witley on 26 July.

And thereafter the diary is simply practical, occupied as usual with social activities (including tennis) and reading (at the usual pitch to the end), and with arrangements for the move to the London house they had chosen. The final entry on

3 *George Eliot's Life as related in her letters and journals, arranged and edited by her husband J. W. Cross*, 3 vols (Edinburgh, Blackwood, 1885), vol. 3, p. 417.

4 J. W. Cross, *George Eliot's life as related in her letters and journals*, 3 vols. (Edinburgh, Blackwood, 1885), vol. 3, pp. 408–9; *Letters*, vol. 7, pp. 307–8.

4 December notes attendance at 'our first Pop. Concert' for the season. After a subsequent concert on 18 December, GE complained of a sore throat. Her condition worsened, and she died on 22 December.

Haight quotes perhaps a quarter of the entries; Cross's use of this diary is very sparse.

IV. Diary 1880

MEMORANDA, 1880

T.C. Barnett, 5. Worowzow Rd. Water Rate.
A. Head, 10 Queen's Road, Income Tax.
Phoebe's wages due July 15.

MEMORANDA, 1880

Wages due
Mrs. Dowling, Oct. 13. Jan. 13. Apr. 13. July 13.
Brett and Amelia, Sep. 1. Dec. 1. Mar. 1. June 1.

JANUARY 1880

THURSDAY 1

Kind Letter from Master of Balliol.
" " Mrs. Pears.
Drove to Hampstead in clear air and walked on the hill.
Nihilists (XIXth Century). Piano.
Monier Williams's India. Odyssey.

SATURDAY 3

Dr. Foster called.

SUNDAY 4

Mr. Trübner brought Bret Harte.
Mr. Justice Bowen came afterwards.

MONDAY 5

Brock's wages paid to this day.
Letter from Signor Pericles Tzikos asking me to write for the 'Minerva'. Wrote to decline.
Letter from Ripley, with article.
Finished Monier Williams.

TUESDAY 6

Drove to Sizer's about binding books.
Edith.
Charles dined with me. Gave him Ripley's article and letter.

WEDNESDAY 7

Thick fog.
Piano tuned.
Mr. Langford called and told me that there had been 1000 vols of my cheap editions sold since the 1st. Magnificat anima mea!
Invitation to become a Vice President of the Spelling Reform Association. Declined.

THURSDAY 8

Thick fog again. Drove to Sizer's.
Wrote to Mr Cyples, thanking him for his letter and volume.
Romanes, 'Theism'.
Tiele, History of Religions.
Odyssey.

FRIDAY 9

Dark morning again.
Mrs. Blackwood wrote – answered her.
Mr. Myers wrote to tell me of his engagement.
Answered him.
Horrible darkness. Indoors all day.
Bret Harte.

MONDAY 12

Charles – account of Ripley.
Tiele, History of Religions.

TUESDAY 13

Letter from W. Blackwood, enclosing £400.
Chaucer's Prologue.

WEDNESDAY 14

Chaucer. Prologue finished.

THURSDAY 15

Arranging books for binding.
Drove to see Eliza. Bright day.
Mrs. Sotheby called.

Pass Book. Balance £1046.
25

FRIDAY 16

Finished arrangement of Pamphlets.
Edith.
Burton's Queen Anne.

Odyssey.
Music.

SATURDAY 17

Clear day. Drove in Hyde Park.
Astronomy.
Mr. and Mrs. Austin and Mr. Kegan Paul.

SUNDAY 18

Sir Henry Maine, Mrs. Orr, Dr. Waldstein.
Miss Streeter.

MONDAY 19

Went to Exhibition of Old Masters.

TUESDAY 20

To Sizer's with Books for binding.

WEDNESDAY 21

To Offord's about Carriage.
Letter from Mrs. Streeter, thanking me.

THURSDAY 22

Mr. Clifford, artist, called to talk about East End work.
Finished Fanny Kemble's Records of a girlhood.

FRIDAY 23

Balance £1061 + 25.
Drove to Hampstead and walked.
Mignon and Phil to tea.
Letters from Mr. Justice Bowen, Mrs. Wilson (about Italian translation of Deronda) and Mrs. Westlake (about Spelling Reform).

SATURDAY 24

Went to Exhibition of Old Masters.
Miss Cross.

SUNDAY 25

Hebrew.
Mr Trübner, Bret Harte, Mr. Lyulph Stanley.

MONDAY 26

To Grosvenor Gallery with Mrs. Burne Jones.
Letter from Mr. Pigott enclosing one from Mr. S. M. Samuel about dramatizing 'Deronda'.
Pole's Music.

TUESDAY 27

Fog and severe cold. Did not go out.

WEDNESDAY 28

Continued fog and cold.
Mrs. Gurney called.

THURSDAY 29

Went to the Grosvenor Gallery again.
Mr. Gurney, Elinor, Edith.
Finished heap of pamphlets on the Jewish question in Germany.

FRIDAY 30

Prof. Croom Robertson – talked to him about disposal of Library for public purposes.

SATURDAY 31

Sent cheque for 39.19.5 to Duncan, Warren and Gardner.
Mr Samuel came about "Daniel Deronda".

FEBRUARY 1880

SUNDAY 1

General Hamley called. Hebrew. Kenilworth.

MONDAY 2

Not well.
Drove in Hyde Park and walked under a little Sunshine.
Charles and Mr. Hamilton Aïdé called.
Dante.

TUESDAY 3

Letters and cheques.
Drove to Mecklenburgh Square.
Vivian and his wife (next day). Gave him 3 boxes of cigars.
Taken rather ill with cholic.

WEDNESDAY 4

Read a heap of Jewish Chronicles.

THURSDAY 5

Probable Balance after having Sent Head for Income Tax 62.10.10 – £932.
Letter from Barbara – wrote in reply.

FRIDAY 6

Called at Mr. Clifford's Studio – not at Home.
Went on to Grosvenor Gallery.

Mr. G. Smith wrote about Édition de luxe of Romola.
Pole's music.

SATURDAY 7

Wet day – did not go out.
Hebrew.
Pole.

SUNDAY 8

Miss Streeter and Mr. Harrison.

MONDAY 9

Mrs. W. Sellar and her daughter Eppie.

TUESDAY 10

Mr and Mrs. DuMaurier.

WEDNESDAY 11

Mrs. Congreve came to lunch.
Charles called.

THURSDAY 12

Dentist and Regents Park.
Mrs. P.A. Taylor called.

FRIDAY 13

Drove to Dentist's.
Mr. George Smith called – about Romola.
Mrs. Burne Jones and Miss Florence Hill.

SATURDAY 14

Received Blackwood's account.
No. of copies of works (vols.) sold, 32,543.
Sent Brock's wages till Easter Monday.
Mr. L. Tennyson and Mr. Ernest Myers.

SUNDAY 15

Miss North brought her Indian drawings, with Miss Ewart. Mr. H. Spencer, Mde. Belloc, Mr and Mrs. Allingham.

MONDAY 16

Brock's wages paid to this day.
Read 'Hebrew Migration' – an anonymous Book, very well done – arguing that Mount Sinai is in Idumæa and is identical with Mount Hor.

SATURDAY 21

Charles and Gertrude with Blanche and Maud to lunch.

MONDAY 23

Affectionate letters from strangers.

WEDNESDAY 25

To South Kensington Museum.
Mrs. Earle.

THURSDAY 26

Letter from a German, of an effusive kind, begging me to let him know if I were coming to Germany, pronouncing my books supreme in their kind, but calling me 'a female politician, with my absurd notion of Palestina Rediviva'!

FRIDAY 27

Wrote to Emily and sent her £25.
Mr. Williams.
Mrs. R. Ritchie and Miss R.
Mrs. Geddes.
Bad headache.
Letter from "Dolores".

SATURDAY 28

Incapacitating Headache.
Children to Tea. Mr. Trollope and Mr. K. Paul with his daughter.

SUNDAY 29

Mr. and Mrs. L. Stanley and Mr. Justice Bowen.
Headache continued.

MARCH 1880

MONDAY 1

Called on Mrs. Stuart.
Mde. Belloc and Mrs. Clifford.

TUESDAY 2

Beatrice and Sophie came to lunch and I took them to the Exhibition of Old Masters.

SATURDAY 6

Drove to Dulwich Gallery.
Mrs. Orr and Mr. Bond.

MONDAY 8

Mrs. Earle and Miss Graham.

TUESDAY 9

Drove to Hampstead to see Eliza.
Mrs. and Miss Lankester and Edith.

THURSDAY 11

American letters, letters!

FRIDAY 12

Went to see Mrs. Allingham's drawings.
Taken very ill with cholic which lasted a couple of hours (after receiving Lady Ponsonby).

SATURDAY 13

Feeling much shattered.
Alice Helps and Florence Hill.

SUNDAY 14

Charles to lunch. Mde. Bodichon, Mr. and Mrs. Call, Mr. Spencer, Mr. and Mrs. Harrison, Mr. Romanes, Mr. and Mrs. Sidgwick, Mr. F. Pollock.

MONDAY 15

Walked in the Park.
Wrote to Susanna and Vivian and sent cheque.
Mrs. Greville.

TUESDAY 16

Called on Mrs. Stewart.
Mr. Pigott called, and Burne Jones.

THURSDAY 18

Miss Rintoul.
Teased with choosing curtains for Witley.

FRIDAY 19

Sad and not well.
Drove towards Kilburn in the morning.
Sir James and Lady Colvile, Mr. and Mrs. Leslie Stephen. Mr. Shadworth Hodgson and Charles.
Long letter from Miss Beneke.

SATURDAY 20

Wrote to Mr. Sully and Mr. Trübner and sent cheque to Mr. Parson.
Mr. and Mrs. Beesly and Miss Simcox.

SUNDAY 21

Mr. Justice Bowen and Mr. and Mrs. Yates Thomson.

MONDAY 22

Mrs. Clifford.

TUESDAY 23

Went to see Eliza.
Mr. Hall, Lady Lindsay, Mr. Tennyson and Hallam. Dr. Waldstein, Lady Lilford and her son Mr. Powys.

WEDNESDAY 24

To the British Museum.
Mrs. Higford Burr. Mrs. Burne Jones.
Charles to dinner.

THURSDAY 25

Drove along the Kilburn Road.
Miss Simcox, Mrs. Greville and Lady Pollock.

FRIDAY 26

Quiet day. Walked in the Park.
Mr. and Mrs. F. Pollock called, but I did not see them.

SATURDAY 27

Mrs. Congreve to lunch. Drove her home.

SUNDAY 28

Went to Weybridge.

MONDAY 29

Brock's wages paid up to this day.
Walked on St. George's Hill.
Letter from America asking me to read M.S. Revelation.

TUESDAY 30

Returned from Weybridge early.
Maud's birthday. Gertrude, Blanche and Maud to lunch.
Miss Colenso came. Much interesting talk.
Went to see Mrs. Stuart.
Letter from Mrs. Elizabeth Thompson, U.S.A.

WEDNESDAY 31

Drove to 7 Cromwell Place and to Addison Gardens.
Mrs. Burne Jones from 4.30.

APRIL 1880

THURSDAY 1

Drove to Hampstead and took cheque to Eliza.
Quiet afternoon. Finished Prose Edda, etc.
Akkadians.
Malthus.

FRIDAY 2

Balance 515.
Alice Helps.

SATURDAY 3

Went to Sydenham.

FRIDAY 9

Sir James Paget came to see me.
My marriage decided.

SATURDAY 10

To Chelsea to look at No. 4 Cheyne Walk.

MONDAY 12

Drove out Alice Helps.
Mr. W. Cross.

TUESDAY 13

Charles and Mr. Williams.

FRIDAY 16

Sir James and Lady Colvile and Miss Paul.
Charles.

SATURDAY 17

To Kew.
Mr. Paul, Mrs. Moscheles and Mr. Robb.

SUNDAY 18

Mr. and Mrs. Harrison.

MONDAY 19

Gertrude, Eliza and children. Charles. Mr. Allingham, Leslie Stephen, Mrs. Clifford, Miss Colenso.

TUESDAY 20

Went to see Mrs. Stuart.

THURSDAY 22

To Sevenoaks.

FRIDAY 23

Charles came to tell me of his promotion.
Went in the afternoon to Burne Jones's.
Sir James Paget called during my absence.
Sent Eliza her cheque for May.

SATURDAY 24

To Weybridge.

MONDAY 26

Returned from Weybridge with bad cold.
Mr. Pigott and Miss Simcox called.
Mr. Sully sent me the 'Academy' containing his article on Problems – third Series.

TUESDAY 27

Sizer sent home books from binding.

MAY 1880

WEDNESDAY 5

Draw cheque for Charles £110 on acct. of

Kensington	£25
Susanna	18.15
Eliza till Aug.	33. 6.8
Mrs. Dowling on acct. July 15,	£20
Her and Phœbe's wages July 15,	£ 9.10

THURSDAY 6

Married this day at 10.15 to John Walter Cross, at St. George's, Hanover Square. Present, Charles, who gave me away, Mr. and Mrs. Druce, Mr. Hall, Willie, Mary, Eleanor, and Florence. We went back to the Priory, where we signed our wills. Then we started for Dover, and arrived there a little after 5 o'clock.

FRIDAY 7

We crossed the Channel delightfully in a private cabin on deck, and then went on to Amiens, where we were made very comfortable at the Hotel du Rhin. We went to see the Cathedral before dinner and looked at the wondrous wood carving in the choir. In the morning we repeated our visit and had a view of the façade.

SATURDAY 8

We took a leisurely walk in the Cathedral noticing the coloured sculptures round the choir, representing the lives of St. Firmin and St. Sauve – some of the figures excellent. Came on to Paris and after a vain attempt to get rooms in the Hotel Voltaire, arrived at the Hotel Vouillemont about 5 o'clock. Here we have a pleasant sunshiny apartment.

SUNDAY 9

Wrote Letters.
Went to the Russian Church – too late.
Read Ruy Blas aloud. Afterwards saw 3 acts.

MONDAY 10

(Brock's wages paid to this day). Saw La Sainte Chapelle, which delighted J. then entered Notre Dame.
Lunched at the Café Corazza.
Drove in the Bois.
Bought Saynètes et Monologues.[1]

TUESDAY 11

Went to the Louvre from 11 till 12.30.
Corazza.
Eugénie Grandet.
Walk in the Champs Elysées.

THURSDAY 13

Morning in the Musée du Luxembourg. Feyen's little picture of a market on the coast.

FRIDAY 14

To Sens.

SATURDAY 15

To Dijon.

SUNDAY 16

Afternoon to Mâcon.

MONDAY 17

To Lyons.

TUESDAY 18

To Grenoble.

WEDNESDAY 19

To the Grande Chartreuse.

THURSDAY 20

To Chambéry.

FRIDAY 21

Walked to Les Charmettes.

SATURDAY 22

To Modane.

SUNDAY 23

To Turin.

1 French, 'comedy sketches and monologues'.

MONDAY 24

To Milan.

TUESDAY 25

To the Brera Gallery.

WEDNESDAY 26

To San Ambrogio.

THURSDAY 27

Festa – everywhere we went we found ourselves at the wrong moment.

FRIDAY 28

To San Maurizio and S. Giorgio in Palazzo.

SATURDAY 29

To Santa Maria delle Grazie.

SUNDAY 30

To Verona.

MONDAY 31

Saw the Duomo, the church of S. Zeno and the tombs of the Scaligers. Had a long drive in the environs. Went into the Amphitheatre.

JUNE 1880

TUESDAY 1

Went to the Museo and the church of S. Anastasio.
In the afternoon to Padua.

WEDNESDAY 2

Saw the Church of San Antonio, with especial attention to the two chapels of S. Antonio and S. —, the Arena Chapel, and the general aspect of the town, passing by the Palazzo Ragione. In the afternoon to *Venice*, where we looked round and into S. Marco.

THURSDAY 3

Awoke in Venice. First Visit to the Accademia.

SATURDAY 5

Bought some pamphlets of Ruskin's at Ongania's.

SUNDAY 6

Festa (Corpus Christi(?)) and procession which we went to see among a crowd of gondolas.

TUESDAY 8

To the Lido.
J. called at Mr. Bunney's and brought home other pamphlets of Ruskin.

WEDNESDAY 9

To Murano and Torcello.
To Santa Maria Formosa, to see Santa Barbara.
To the Accademia to see pictures pointed out by Ruskin: Giovanni Bellini, Tintorets, Carpaccio etc.

THURSDAY 10

San Zaccaria: Giovanni Bellini: S. Giovanni in Bragola: Baptism of Christ by Cima; S. Giov. Crisostomo; the last picture of G. Bellini – S. Cristoforo etc, and Giorgione's San Crisostomo and Saints, finished by Sebastian del Piombo.

FRIDAY 11

S. Vitales: Carpaccio's picture, over the altar. Carmine: Cima's Nativity with Tobit and Angel. Madonna dell'Orto, Cima's John the Baptist, Tintoretto's Last Judgment, St. Agnes, Worshipping the Golden Calf, and Presentation of the Virgin. Also his Tomb.
At 4 o'clock to Mr. Bunney's, who showed us his sketches.

SATURDAY 12

Into the Piazza to meet Mr. Bunney who showed us his picture of the façade of S. Marco, then went with us to S. Maria Formosa, to find my remembered Madonna spreading her robe, by B. Vivarini, then to look at the Adam and Eve Capital of the Palazzo Ducale. Afterwards we went to the Salute to look at Tintoret's Marriage at Cana. After lunch the Carmine, S. Sebastiano, S. Casciano.

SUNDAY 13

To see the Scuola di S. Giovanni, and into the Frari hearing music. At 1/2 past 5 to Mr. Bunney's to see pictures.

MONDAY 14

With Mr. and Mrs. Bunney to the Manfrini Palace and Casa de'quattro Evangelisti.

TUESDAY 15

To the Accademia seeing the Bellinis.
Did not go out after lunch.

WEDNESDAY 16

Dr. Ricchetti called.

FRIDAY 18

Dr. Cesare Vigna called in. Came at 10.30p.m.
Willie arrived in the Evening.

SATURDAY 19

Dr. Vigna twice.
Better. Wrote to the girls.
Sent Telegram.
Willy arrived in the evening.

SUNDAY 20

Better on the whole. Wrote telegram.
Dr. V. twice.

MONDAY 21

Quiet night, without chloral.
Dr. Vigna in the morning, alone.

WEDNESDAY 23

Left Venice at 9.5 a.m and travelled to Verona – 'le Due Torri'.

THURSDAY 24

To Trent – Hotel Trento.

FRIDAY 25

To Botzen – Kaiser Krone.

SATURDAY 26

Arrived at Innsprück at 2 o'clock.

SUNDAY 27

Innsprück. Rainy morning.

MONDAY 28

Innsprück.

TUESDAY 29

Innsprück.
Drove to Maria Brunn.

WEDNESDAY 30

Innsprück.
Drove along the Engadine Road.

JULY 1880

THURSDAY 1

Innsprück.
Drove 'nach Italien'.

FRIDAY 2

To Munich.

SATURDAY 3

Munich. Rainy. Saw Glyptothek and Neue Pinacothek.

SUNDAY 4

Went to the Alte Pinacothek.
To Augsburg at 5.

MONDAY 5

Augsburg.

TUESDAY 6

To Stuttgardt.
Drove in the Park.

WEDNESDAY 7

Stuttgardt.

THURSDAY 8

To Wildbad – Hotel Klumpp.

MONDAY 12

Willie left for England.

SATURDAY 17

Drove to Baden by Herrenalb.

SUNDAY 18

At Baden. Drove to the Alt Schloss.

MONDAY 19

To Strasburg.

TUESDAY 20

To Metz.

WEDNESDAY 21

To Luxembourg.

THURSDAY 22

To Brussels.

FRIDAY 23

At Brussels.

SATURDAY 24

From Brussels to Dover.

SUNDAY 25

At Dover.

MONDAY 26

Arrived at Witley, 4.10.

TUESDAY 27

Brock's wages paid up to this day.
Eleanor and Florence came.

WEDNESDAY 28

Charles and Gertrude came to dine and stay the night.

THURSDAY 29

Long drive in hired carriage by Thursley and Elstead.

FRIDAY 30

Walk in the morning with J.
Drive in the afternoon.
Began Sayce with J.

SATURDAY 31

Settled with Mrs. Dowling for account during our absence. Paid her and Brett's wages for June 1 and July 13.
Went to lunch at Weybridge.

AUGUST 1880

SUNDAY 1

Wrote to Emily Clarke with cheque for £25 and to Josiah Mills, cheque for coal.

MONDAY 2

Brock's wages paid up to this day.
Answered letters from Lady Strangford, Mrs. Strachey, Mr. Paul.

TUESDAY 3

J. went to town to see coachman etc.
Mrs. Lathbury called.

THURSDAY 5

J. to Weybridge to play tennis.

SUNDAY 8

To Sir H. Holland's to Tea.

MONDAY 9

Went to Town together.
Saw the Chelsea House, shopped and went to the Priory.

TUESDAY 10

Delicious day. Walk in the morning.
Drive to Hampton Ponds in the afternoon.
Called at Mrs. Lathbury's and Mrs. Burrowes'.
Sayce and Promessi Sposi.

WEDNESDAY 11

J. to town.
Wrote to Eliza with cheque for August, also to Susanna and Dr. Roy.

THURSDAY 12

Wrote to Charles in answer to his letter.
Received a letter from Emily acknowledging cheque for £25.

FRIDAY 13

Send account of Income Tax.
To go to Thornhill. Emily and Mr. Otter there.
Mr and Mrs. Spotteswoode to dine.

SATURDAY 14

At Thornhill. Mr. Hall joined us.

TUESDAY 17

Arrived at Witley – 5.6

TUESDAY 24

J. to town.

WEDNESDAY 25

Mary and Florence to lunch.

THURSDAY 26

To Sir H. Holland's in the afternoon, for Tennis; the de Bunsens there, Mr. Robarts, and Mr. and Miss Benson.

FRIDAY 27

J. to town: met him at Godalming. Called at Witley House on our way home.

SUNDAY 29

Started at 8.33 a.m. and went as far as Peterborough. Went round the Cathedral.

MONDAY 30

Arrived at Ranby, after pausing at Lincoln and seeing the glorious cathedral.

SEPTEMBER 1880

FRIDAY 3

Left Ranby and travelled as far as Ely, where we just walked round the Cathedral inside and outside, dined and slept at the Lamb, and started for Newmarket the next morning at 10.30.

SATURDAY 4

Henry met us at Newmarket and we had a pleasant drive to Six Mile.
Mr. and Mrs. Sidgwick to dinner.

SUNDAY 5

Mr. and Mrs. Jebb as well as the Sidgwicks at dinner.

MONDAY 6

Henry drove us to Mr. Parker Hammond's to see his wondrous plantations.
Mr. and Mrs. Robinson, Mr. Hudson and M. Bécher to dinner.

TUESDAY 7

Returned from Six Mile to Witley.

WEDNESDAY 8

J. to town.
Sent cheque to Mr. Warren, £189.19. and also to Susanna, £18.15.

THURSDAY 9

J. to town again.

MONDAY 13

To the Priory.

TUESDAY 14

J. to town. Met him at Godalming.

THURSDAY 16

J. to town. Met him at Godalming.
Mrs. Greville came and recited the Revenge and the Grandmother.

FRIDAY 17

Drove to Lythe Hall.

SATURDAY 18

Called at Mrs. J. Foster's and Mrs. Evans's.

SUNDAY 19

Not well. In the morning we read Sayce, vol. 2 and Faust. Drove out in the afternoon.

MONDAY 20

J. to town.

WEDNESDAY 22

Called in Mr. Parson, my ailments being no better.

WEDNESDAY 29

Still ailing. To Brighton.

OCTOBER 1880

SATURDAY 9

Returned from Brighton, feeling no better.

SATURDAY 16

Charles and Gertrude came to stay till Monday.

SUNDAY 17

Taken very ill in the night. Relieved from pain in the day by an opiate.

FRIDAY 22

Dr. Andrew Clarke came to see me.

WEDNESDAY 27

Came down stairs.

THURSDAY 28

Went out for a drive.

SATURDAY 30

Beginning to feel myself recovering.

SUNDAY 31

Finished the Discours Préliminaire.

NOVEMBER 1880

MONDAY 1

J. to town, to see about moving furniture from the Priory.
Played on the piano for the first time.

TUESDAY 2

Feeling much stronger.
J. cut down trees in the afternoon.

WEDNESDAY 3

Bright day again. J. to the city.
Wrote to Miss Lewis and sent her cheque.
Also to Mrs. Congreve and Mrs. Greville.

THURSDAY 4

Began Spencer's Sociology.

FRIDAY 5

J. to town. Not so well.

FRIDAY 12

J. to town, to see about the moving of furniture.

SATURDAY 13

J. to town again.

SUNDAY 14

A great storm and continuous rain.
I feel better, and am conscious of gaining strength.

MONDAY 15

Wet day again. J. to town.
Did not go out.

TUESDAY 16

Rain with gleams of sunshine. Mr. and Mrs. Otter to lunch. J. to town, still superintending the removal of furniture.

WEDNESDAY 17

Beautiful day. Books moved to Chelsea: J. to town.

SATURDAY 20

J. at home.

MONDAY 22

Fine frosty day.
Having finished Spencer's Sociology we began Max Müller's Lectures on the Science of Language.

TUESDAY 23

J. to town to meet Mr. Armitage.

WEDNESDAY 24

Read Comte and began Hermann and Dorothea.

THURSDAY 25

J. to town.
Packed Books.

MONDAY 29

Left Witley and came to London to Baileys Hotel Gloucester Road.
Read Tennyson's new vol. of poems and particularly like "The first Quarrel".

TUESDAY 30

Bailey's Hotel.
Read "My faithful Johnny" in the Cornhill.
Hermann and Dorothea and Comte.

DECEMBER 1880

WEDNESDAY 1

Bailey's Hotel. Went to the South Kensington Museum in the morning.
J. to city afternoon. Finished "My Faithful Johnny" – Tennyson's new vol. and some Hermann and Dorothea.

THURSDAY 2

Bailey's Hotel.
Shopping in the morning.
Read Comte and Hermann and Dorothea evening.

FRIDAY 3

Left Bailey's Hotel and came to Cheyne Walk.
Unpacking – after dinner began Duffield's translation of Don Quixote and Myers' Wordsworth.

SATURDAY 4

J. to city in morning. Home to lunch.
Went to our first Pop. Concert and heard Norman Neruda, Piatti etc. Miss Zimmermann playing the piano. After

V. *Recollections of Weimar 1854*

GE noted in her diary for 30 November 1854, 'Finished Recollections of Weimar'. This 'sketch which I wrote at the wrong end of my journal'[1] occupied her during the first weeks of the time she and GHL spent in Berlin. In the 'Recollections', written up from her diary, GE amplified the earlier, relatively laconic record. People who are not much more than a name in the diary, such as Schöll and the Sauppes, are more fully characterised in the essay, which also gives extended accounts of some of the expeditions undertaken by GE and GHL, like those to Jena and Ilmenau, and lays a greater emphasis on the Goethe and Schiller memorabilia. Parallels with GHL's *Life of Goethe* are also more explicit: for example, the passage about the sculpture inscribed *genio loci* has a counterpart in the *Life*, as does the description of Goethe's townhouse.

The essay provides more of a summary and an overview than the diary; impressions are assimilated and organised, modifying the narrator's initial unfavourable impression of Weimar (this narrator is never identified, nor even gendered). It emphasises the travellers' reactions to the place and the people they met, and obscures the working aspect of their visit which is so strongly marked in the diary. Though the focus is on Weimar as a centre of culture, and on the customs and characteristics of the people, the pleasures of the flesh are not disregarded. There is a good deal of comment on food (uncommon elsewhere in GE's journals, and in her fiction), on their walks (of which the picnic with wine and Keats is a high point), and such particular episodes as those of the Russian bath and the purloined plums.

Where the diary has passages of somewhat laboured comment on works of art, this essay at times makes apparently unselfconscious observations which hint at some of the aesthetic questions GE was to formulate in relation to her practice as a writer of fiction. In particular, the representation of the natural world engages her. The description of the glass globes in the park at Belvedere provides a case in point: 'how beautifully the scenery round is painted in these globes. Each is like a pre-Raphaelite picture with every little detail of grav-

1 *The George Eliot Letters*, ed. Gordon S. Haight, 9 vols. (New Haven, Yale University Press, 1954–78), vol. 2, p. 201.

elly walk, mossy banks and delicate-leaved interlacing boughs in perfect miniature.' Values of fidelity to nature, manifested in detailed observation, together with moral seriousness, characterised the Pre-Raphaelite Brotherhood which had brought together in 1848 a number of young artists including Millais, the Rossetti brothers and Holman Hunt. By 1854 its members, with whose work GE was sympathetically acquainted, were prominent and controversial participants in the English art world. Earlier in the year, she had admired Holman Hunt's *The Light of the World* at the Royal Academy exhibition, and made discriminating comments on Ruskin's letter in defence of the Pre-Raphaelite painters which appeared in the *Times* on 5 May 1854 (p. 156).[2]

The section headed 'Ana' was evidently an afterthought which includes some material collected in Berlin as well as in Weimar. It is all anecdote, whether to do with people she had met, or things she had heard. General Pfuel's anecdote she found sufficiently noteworthy to include in her commonplace book as well as here.

These 'Recollections' formed the basis of two articles published in *Fraser's Magazine*, following GHL's approach to J. W. Parker, editor of *Fraser's*, in February 1855 (the first documented occasion on which Lewes acts as GE's agent):

> would you like a delightful article *Three months in Weimar*? Miss Evans during our stay, made notes of manners, scenery, etc. which would I think shape themselves into a very amusing paper. Weimar is quite unvisited by English & has never been written about. It is very unlike the other German capitals.[3]

On 12 May 'Miss Evans' (who a few days earlier had been impressing on Bessie Parkes the need to send her letters under cover to Lewes) wrote to Charles Bray about the article in press and her pleasure at 'turning it into guineas' (*Letters*, pp. 200, 201). Her claim that she did not write in the first instance with

2 *Letters*, vol. 2, p. 156. For further discussion of GE in relation to the English Pre-Raphaelites, see John Murdoch, 'English Realism: George Eliot and the Pre-Raphaelites', *Journal of the Warburg and Cortauld Institutes*, 37 (1974), pp. 313–29, and Hugh Witemeyer, *George Eliot and the Visual Arts* (New Haven and London, Yale University Press, 1979).

3 *The Letters of George Henry Lewes*, ed. William Baker, 2 vols (University of Victoria, English Literature Studies Monograph 64, 1995) vol. 1, p. 236. The *Fraser's* pieces are 'Three Months in Weimar', 51 (June 1855), pp. 699–706, and 'Liszt, Wagner and Weimar', 52 (July 1855), pp. 48–62.

a view to publication is confirmed by the nature and extent of her re-writing. She had no need to shift the speaking position of the traveller reporting experiences in an exotic place, and concentrated more on distinctive aspects of Weimar than on purely personal detail. It is not surprising that she should have discarded the apostrophe to 'Dear Park of Weimar!', and the sweetly apologetic 'Trivial details these! but every incident is precious in the remembrance of hours made bright by the sunshine of love'; and expanded some material, including the anecdotes about their lodgings and their various theatre visits.

The *Fraser's* articles provide the only substantial instance of GE's turning journal material directly into published work. Late in her life she revised them for *Essays and Leaves from a Notebook* (1884), which Charles Lewes saw through the press: her extensive cuts are indicated in Thomas Pinney's text in *Essays of George Eliot* (1963). Pinney comments on the significance of the second article for the history of Wagner's reception, suggesting that the hostile response to his concerts with the London Philharmonia Orchestra from March to June 1855 may have 'prompted GE to add an account of Wagner to the otherwise personal recollections of her German trip'.[4] Here is a topical instance to include with other occasions on which GE interpreted or championed German culture to the English through her essays, her reviews and her translations. GE's acceptance of Wagner was always readier than GHL's, who famously pronounced in 1870 that 'The Mutter and I have come to the conclusion that the Music of the future is not for us – Schubert, Beethoven, Mozart, Gluck or even Verdi – but not Wagner – is what we are made to respond to' (*Letters*, vol. 5, p. 85), and in 1872 that Wagner's music 'remains to us a language we do not understand' (p. 317).

Both Cross and Haight begin to quote from this essay at the point almost halfway through where GE turns from her account of their domestic arrangements and the town of Weimar to describe expeditions to places associated with Goethe. Haight characteristically quotes brief passages of a sentence or two; Cross uses longer sections, playing down anecdote and personal detail in favour of an emphasis on serious tourism which cannot accommodate such passages of abandon as the picnic reading Keats.

4 Thomas Pinney, *Essays of George Eliot* (London, Routledge, 1963), p. 96.

V. Recollections of Weimar 1854

It was between 3 and 4 o'clock on a fine August morning (the 2nd) that after a ten-hours' journey from Frankfurt I woke up at the Bahnhof of Weimar. No tipsiness can be more dead to all appeals than that which comes from fitful draughts of sleep on a railway journey by night. To the disgust of your wakeful companion, who has been smiling in envious pity upon you as you have stared wildly around at every stoppage of the train and then instantly sunk into dreamland again, you are totally insensible to the existence of your umbrella and to the fact that your carpet bag is stowed under your seat or that you have borrowed his books and have tucked them behind the cushion. "What's the odds so long as one can sleep?" is your "*formule de la vie*",[1] and it is not till you have begun to shiver on the platform in the cool morning air that you are alive to propriety and its duties and to the further necessity of keeping a fast grip upon it. Such was my condition when I reached the station at Weimar. The ride from thence to the town thoroughly roused me and as usual by the time I got into a bed room I had no longer any desire for bed. The glimpse of the town which this ride gave me was in striking contrast with my preconceptions. The lines of houses looked rough and straggling and were often interrupted by trees peeping out from bits of garden. At last we stopped before the Erb-prinz, an inn of long standing in the heart of the town, and after some delay through the dreamy doubts of the porter whether we could have rooms before the "Herrschaft"[2] had departed, we found ourselves following him along heavy-looking and dark corridors and at length were ushered into rooms which overlooked a garden for all the world like one you may see in many an English village at the back of a farm house. From a walk in the morning in search of lodgings [illegible] we saw that Weimar was more like a market town than the precinct of a court. And this is the 'Athens of the north,' we said. Materially speaking, it is more like Sparta. The blending of rustic and civic life, the indications of a central government with those of drinking and smoking subjects has some analogy with the condition of old Lacedemon. No vehicles in the streets save here and there a cart bringing farm merchandise. The shops are most of them such as you would see in the back streets of a provincial English town,

1 French, 'philosophic formula'. The phrase is translated thus (the French does not appear) in the version of 'Three Months in Weimar' published in GE's *Essays and Leaves from a Note-book* (Edinburgh, Blackwood, 1884), p. 290. These essays were seen through the press by Charles Lee Lewes, whose preface implies that the selection and final revision of material in the volume was done by GE herself. We have noted when the translation given is from *Essays.*

2 German, 'the master and mistress'.

and the commodities on sale are often chalked on the door posts. The inhabitants seemed to us to have more than the usual heaviness of *Germanity;* even their stare is slow, like that of herbivorous quadrupeds. You set out with the intention of exploring the town and at every other turn you find yourself in a street which takes you out of the town or else in one which leads you back to the Markt from which you set out. One's first feeling is: How could Goethe live here, in this dull, lifeless village? The reproaches cast on him for his worldliness and attachment to court grandeur seemed ludicrous enough, and it was inconceivable that the stately Jupiter *en redingote*[3] who is so familiar to us all through a statuette which ornaments many a shop window and study in London, could have habitually walked along these rude streets and among these slouching mortals. Not a picturesque bit of building was to be seen; there was no quaintness, nothing to remind one of historical associations, nothing but the most arid prosaism. This was the impression produced on us by a first morning's walk in Weimar – an impression which very imperfectly represents what Weimar is, but which is worth noting because it is true as a sort of "back view". We soon had our impression modified when in the evening we found our way to the Belvedere Chaussée, that splendid avenue of chestnut trees – when we saw the Schloss and discovered the labyrinthine beauties of the Park; indeed every day opened to us fresh charms in this quiet little valley and its environs. To any one who loves Nature in her gentle aspects, who delights in the chequered shade on a summer morning and in a walk on the corn-clad upland at sunset, I say, Come to Weimar. And if you are weary of English unrest, of that society of "Eels in a jar" where each is trying to get his head above the other, the somewhat stupid bien-être[4] of the Weimarians will not be an unwelcome contrast, for a short time, at least. If you care nothing at all about Goethe, Schiller and Herder, why, so much the worse for you – you will miss many interesting thoughts and associations; but still, Weimar has a charm independent of these great names.

First among all its attractions is the Park, which would be remarkably beautiful even among English parks and which has one advantage over them all, namely that it is entirely without a fence. It runs up to the houses and far out into the corn-fields and meadows as if it had a "sweet will"[5] of its own, like a river or a lake, and was not planned and planted by human will. Through it runs the Ilm; not a clear stream it must be confessed, but like all water, as Novalis says, "an eye to the landscape". Before we came to Weimar we had had dreams of boating on the Ilm, and were considerably amused at the difference between that vision of

3 'Jupiter in a frock coat'(*Essays*, p. 292). Goethe was frequently referred to as Jupiter. The allusion here is to the popular image made by the sculptor Rauch.

4 French, 'wellbeing'(*Essays*, p. 293).

5 William Wordsworth, 'Composed upon Westminster Bridge', l. 12.

our own and the reality. A few water fowl are the only navigators of the Ilm, and even they confine themselves to one spot as if they were part of a picture. The real extent of the Park is small but the walks are so ingeniously arranged and the trees are so luxuriant and various that we were weeks before we knew the turnings and windings by heart and could no longer have the sense of novelty. In the warm weather of our first month's stay at Weimar our great delight was the walk which follows the course of the Ilm and is overarched by tall trees with patches of dark moss on their trunks in rich contrast with the transparent green of the delicate leaves through which the golden sunlight played and chequered the path before us. On one side of this walk the rocky ground rises for three or four yards and is clothed with mosses and little rock plants; on the other side there are every now and then openings, breaks in the continuity of shade, which show you a piece of meadow land with fine groups of trees. At every such opening a garden seat is placed under the rock, and many a pleasant chat is associated in my memory with these resting-places. It is along this walk that one comes upon a truncated column with a serpent twined round it devouring cakes placed on the column as offerings – a bit of rude sculpture in stone. The inscription *genio loci*[6] enlightens the learned as to the significance of this symbol, but the people of Weimar unedified by classical allusions have explained the sculpture by a story which is an excellent example of a modern myth. Once on a time, say they, a huge serpent infested the park and evaded all attempts to exterminate him until at last a knowing baker made some appetizing cakes which contained an effectual poison, placed them in the serpent's reach and thus merited a place with Hercules, Theseus and other monster slayers. Weimar, in gratitude, erected this column as a memorial of the baker's feat and its own deliverance. As autumn advanced and the sunshine became precious, we preferred the fine broad walk on the higher grounds of the Park, where the masses of trees are finely disposed, leaving wide spaces of turf which stretch on one side to the Belvedere allée with its avenue of chestnut trees and on the other side to the edge of the little cliffs which I have just mentioned as forming a wall by the walk along the Ilm. Exquisitely beautiful were the graceful forms of the plane trees thrown in golden relief on a background of dark pines! Here we used to turn back and back again in the autumn afternoons, at first bright and warm, then sombre with low-lying purple clouds and chill with winds that sent the leaves raining from the branches.

Dear Park of Weimar! In 1854, two loving, happy human beings spent many a delicious hour in wandering under your shade and in your sunshine, and to one of them at least you will be a "joy for ever"[7] through all the sorrows that are to come.

Our lodgings at Weimar were amusing. The sitting room was something like

6 Latin, 'spirit of the place'.

7 Quoted from the first line of Keats, *Endymion*.

a room cut in a wall, such as you may see at Walmer Castle – low and narrow, with four windows along one side of it. Here is a plan to illustrate my description:

[See the illustration on p. 222]

1 stove
2 sofa
3 door
4 door

Our landlady Frau Münderloh was a Weimarian of the Weimarians – "grandios dumm",[8] as Schöll called her, a tall fat woman between 50 and 60, with a rudimentary nose and mouth looking like accidental inequalities on a large hemisphere of fat. G. said her face was like a Turk's posteriors. "What are the specific characteristics of *Turkish* posteriors?" I said. "Want of physiognomy and general fat." This face was puckered into an unvarying smile while she was talking, and her talk was as monotonous as the sound of a Jew's harp. She made the mistake one day of telling us that people were in the habit of making higher charges to the English, but aware of her blunder, she quickly said "Ich nicht, Herr Lewes; ich mache alles sehr billig".[9] There was evidently a disposition to impose on us – to add a groschen or two where-ever there was any pretext, decent or indecent. The landlady's husband was called the "süsser Münderloh"[10] by way of distinction from a brother of his who was the reverse of sweet. This Münderloh who was *not* sweet – but who nevertheless dealt in sweets – in other words was a confectioner, was so utter a rogue that any transaction with him was dreaded almost as if he had been the devil himself, and so *clever* a rogue that he always managed to keep on the windy side of the law. Yet had he "so viel Leckerbissen und Süssigkeiten" that people bent on a fine entertainment used to say "Am Ende muss ich zum Münderloh gehen".[11] And so he got custom in spite of general detestation. This is an amusing illustration of the state of trade in Weimar. We were very much amused with the privacy with which people keep their shops in Weimar. Some of them have no kind of *enseigne*[12] – not so much as their names written up. The distribution of commodities, too, is carried forward according to a peculiar Weimarian logic. We bought our lemons at a *Seiler's* or Ropemakers, and should not have felt ourselves very extravagant if we had inquired for sewing silk at a stationer's: a clever tradesman or artificer is as free from competition as Esculapius or Vulcan in the days of old Olympus.

But to return to our lodgings and their human appendages. Our servant *Lora*

8 German, 'enormously stupid'.

9 German, 'Not me, Mr Lewes; I make everything very cheap.'

10 German, 'sweet Münderloh'.

11 German, 'So many delicacies and candies' and, 'In the end, I must go to Münderloh'. Münderloh is called 'Rabenhorst' in 'Three Months in Weimar'.

12 French, 'sign-board'.

4

by classical allusions have explained the sculpture by a story, which is an excellent example of a modern myth. Once on a time, say they, a huge serpent infested the park & evaded all attempts to exterminate him until at last a knowing baker made some appetizing cakes which contained an effectual poison, placed them in the serpent's reach & thus won him a place with Hercules, Theseus & other monster slayers. Weimar, in gratitude, erected this column as a memorial of the baker's feat & its own deliverance. As autumn advanced & the sunshine became precious, we preferred the fine-broad walk on the higher grounds of the Park, where the masses of trees are finely disposed, leaving wide spaces of turf which stretch on one side to the Belvedere allée with its avenue of chestnut trees & on the other side to the edge of the little cliffs which I have just mentioned as forming a wall by the walk along the Ilm. Exquisitely beautiful were the graceful forms of the plane trees thrown in golden relief on a background of dark pines! Here we used to turn back & back again in the Autumn afternoons, at first bright & warm, then sombre with low-lying purple clouds & chill with winds that sent the leaves raining from the branches. Dear Park of Weimar! In 1854, two loving, happy human beings spent many a delicious hour in wandering under your shade & in your sunshine, & to one of them at least you will be a "joy for ever" through all the sorrows that are to come.

Our lodgings at Weimar were amusing. The sitting room was something like a room cut in a wall, such as you may see at Walmer Castle – low & narrow, with four windows along one side of it. Here is a plan to illustrate my description:

1 Stove
2 Sofa
3 door
4 door

Our landlady Frau Münderloh was a Weimarian of the Weimarians "grandios Dummer", as Schöll called her. A tall fat woman between 50 & 60, with a rudimentary nose & mouth looking like accidental inequalities on a large hemisphere of fat. G. said her face was like a Turk's posterior. "What are the specific characteristics of Turkish posteriors?" I said. "Want of physiognomy & general fat." This face was puckered into an unvarying smile while she was talking & her talk was as monotonous as the sound of a Jew's harp. She made the mistake one day of telling us that people

4. 'Our lodgings at Weimar were amusing. The sitting room was something like a room cut in a wall, such as you may see at Walmer Castle – low and narrow, with four windows along one side of it'.

(short for Leonora) was an inexhaustible joke to us. A little goitrous woman, capless of course, first cousin to Thackeray's "inhabitant of the Rhine country" in his "Kickleburys". The sounds and motions of this tame animal were quite peculiar. The "gesegnete Mahlzeit", "schlafen sie wohl", "Guten Tag"[13] etc. were uttered in a minor key and introduced by a little inarticulate sound. One day we had been eating lemons and when Lora came in we gave her the peel to carry away: "Sie wollen nicht das?" she said with wide eyes of admiring surprize. "Schöne Danke".[14] The puckering of her face at the sight of a gold piece which she was asked to carry to her mistress in payment of our bill was something to be remembered, and her merriment over a supposed joke was still better.

We used to dine at the Erb-prinz for 10 groschen each, and a very good dinner we generally had. The Germans excel us in the variety of their *Mehl-speise*[15] and vegetables and they are bolder and more imaginative in their combinations of sauces, fruits and vegetables with animal food. But their meat bears about the same relation to ours as cat and horseflesh do to theirs. A melancholy sight is a flock of Weimarian sheep, followed or led by their shepherd. They are as dingy as London sheep and far more skinny. Some one who dined with us said the sight of the sheep had set him against mutton, and he resolutely refused it whenever it was brought to table, which however it very rarely was; and I think them very infelicitous in their mode of dressing animal food. Their hares for example would not be recognizable as hares to a blind Englishman, and they seem to think roast meat as great an extravagance as we think Essence of ham. But the variety of dishes they afford to give one at 10 groschen a head is something marvellous. Still, I suppose the living at tables d'hôte gives one a very incorrect idea of the mode in which the people live at home. I fancy raw ham and sausage are the basis of the national food with a copious superstratum of Blaukraut, Sauerkraut and black bread. Sausage seems to the German what potatoes were to the Irish – the sine quâ non of bodily sustenance. Goethe asks the Frau von Stein to send him "so eine Wurst"[16] when he wants to have a makeshift dinner away from home, and in his letters to Kestner he talks about having been ergötzt with *Blaukraut* and *Leberwurst*.[17] But I forget the Kuchen[18] which plays an equally important part in German dietetics. The Kuchen one commonly sees at Weimar as an accompaniment to coffee at places of resort such as Belvedere, in the refreshment room at the theatre etc, is nothing more or less than a piece of paste spread over a tin with plums, cherries, apple, etc stuck all over it.

13 German, literally, 'blessed mealtime' (the German equivalent of French 'bon appetit'); 'sleep well'; and 'good day'.

14 German, 'Don't you want that?'; and 'Thank you very much'.

15 German, 'pudding made with flour'.

16 German, 'just such a sausage'.

17 German, 'delighted with blue cabbage and liver sausage'.

18 German, 'cake'.

A favourite resort of ours, as of all the inhabitants of Weimar, was Belvedere, one of the Duke's summer residences about 2 miles from Weimar. A chaussée bordered by noble chestnut trees leads to the entrance of the grounds which are open to all the world as much as to the Duke himself. Close to the palace and its subsidiary buildings there is an inn for the accommodation of the good people who come to take dinner or any other meal by way of holiday making. A sort of pavilion stands on a spot commanding a delightful view of Weimar and its valley, and here the Weimarians constantly come on summer evenings to smoke their cigar and drink a cup of coffee. In one wing of the palace there is a saloon which was quite new to me in its mode of decoration, and I always went to the open door to enjoy a sight of it when we went to Belvedere. Ivy was trained at regular distances up the walls and all round the edge of the ceiling so as to form pilasters and a cornice; ivy again trained on trellis-work formed a blind to the window which looked towards the entrance court and beautiful ferns arranged in tasteful baskets were placed here and there against the walls. The furniture was of light canework. The contrast of the dark green leaves, with their beautiful forms, and the pure white of the walls was very gratifying to my eyes. Another pretty and unique thing at Belvedere was the *Natur-Theater*, constructed with living trees, trimmed into walls and side scenes. But our inexhaustible delight was the grounds which are laid out with a taste worthy of a first rate landscape gardener. The tall and graceful limes, plane trees, weeping birches etc. the little basins of water here and there with fountains playing in the middle of them and a fringe of broad leaved plants or other tasteful bordering, the long avenue that runs across the grounds, the gradual descent towards the river and the hill clothed with firs and pines on the opposite side affording a fine mass of dark green to contrast with the various and light foliage of the groups which ornament the grounds – all this we went again and again to enjoy from the time when all was bright green until the Virginian creepers which festooned the silver stems of the birches were bright scarlet and the touch of Autumn had turned almost all the green to gold. At one spot where there was a semicircular seat placed against an artificial rock, there were 3 large glass globes of different colours placed at the back of the seat and a fourth on a pillar in front of it. It is wonderful to see how beautifully the scenery round is painted in these globes. Each is like a pre-Raphaelite picture with every little detail of gravelly walk, mossy banks and delicate-leaved interlacing boughs in perfect miniature.

It is pleasant to see how these good, bovine people of Weimar enjoy life in their quiet fashion. Unlike our English people they take pleasure into their calculations and seem regularly to set aside part of their time to recreation. Every day something is to be done besides business and housewifery: the women take their knitting and their children to the Erholung, or walk out with their husbands to Belvedere, or in some other direction where a cup of coffee is to be had. The Erholung, by the way, is a pretty garden with shady walks, abundant seats, an orchestra, a ball-room and place for refreshments. It was founded or laid out at least by Musæus who used to be seen walking towards it in a morning with his ladder in one hand and his coffee pot in the other. Goethe's little poem: Die Lustigen von Weimar, just indicates the round of amusements in this simple little capital.

Donnerstag nach Belvedere,
Freitag geht's nach Jena fort:
Denn das ist, bei meiner Ehre,
Doch ein allerliebster Ort!
Samstag ist's, worauf wir zielen,
Sonntag rutscht man auf das Land;
Zwäzen, Burgau, Schneidemühlen
Sind uns alle wohlbekannt.

Montag reizet uns die Bühne;
Dienstag schleicht dann auch herbei,
Doch er bringt zu stiller Sühne
Ein Rapuschchen frank und frei.
Mittwoch fehlt es nicht an Rührung:
Denn es gibt ein gutes Stück;
Donnerstag lenkt die Verführung
Uns nach Belveder' zurück.

Und es schlingt ununterbrochen
Immer sich der Freudenkreis
Durch die zweiundfunfzig Wochen,
Wenn's man's recht zu führen weiss.
Spiel und Tanz, Gespräch, Theater,
Sie erfrischen unser Blut;
Lasst den Wienern ihren Prater;
Weimar, Jena, da ist's gut![19]

When we arrived in Weimar almost every one was away – "at the Baths" of course – except the bourgeois. As birds nidify in the Spring, so Germans wash themselves in the Summer; their "Waschungstrieb"[20] only acts at a particular season of the year, during all the rest a decanter and a sugar basin are an ample toilette-service for them. For a few days we rested quietly without delivering any letters of introduction, and amused ourselves with little explorations. At Ober-Weimar a little village lying about half a mile from the town we found a wooden theatre called the "Tivoli Theatre", and were very glad of this mild excitement under the rather dull aspect of things during our first week here. It was pleasant enough on

19 In 'The Pleasures of Weimar' the virtues of the various activities to be enjoyed throughout the week in Weimar and nearby Jena are extolled over the attractions of the famous pleasureground, the Prater in Vienna. GE's errors of transcription have been corrected.

20 German, 'urge to wash'.

a warm summer evening to sit on a bank shaded by trees and get a lesson in understanding German dialogue by listening to these strolling players. This little theatre, a temporary wooden structure, was supplied with very smart scenes which were rolled up at the sides, in order to economize space. One evening we saw a very respectable actor in "Der arme Poet".

The first person G. called upon was Adolf Schöll, the editor of the Briefe an die Frau von Stein, to whom Strauss had given him a letter of introduction. He called on us the next day and went with us to the Schloss to show us the *Dichter Zimmer* – a suite of rooms dedicated to Goethe, Schiller and Wieland. In each room there is a bust of the poet who is its presiding genius, and the walls of the Goethe and Schiller rooms are decorated with Frescoes representing scenes from their works. The Wieland room is decorated with arabesques only. The idea of these rooms is a very pretty one, but the frescoes are badly executed. I was delighted with Schöll; he is a bright-looking, well made man, with his head finely set on his shoulders, very little like a German; we discovered after we had known him some time that he is an Austrian, and so has more southern blood in his veins than the heavy Thuringians. His manners are hearty and cordial, and his conversation really instructive; his ideas are so thoroughly shaped and so admirably expressed. His wife whom we saw some days afterwards is a pleasing goodnatured little woman who seems to adore her husband. They have a pleasant home in the Schiller Strasse and to crown all four fine children; the two youngest fit for a picture. Altogether they are a good specimen of a happy German family, enjoying life without pretension. The Sauppes are an excellent *pendant* to the Schölls. Sauppe is also a Gelehrter, Director of the Gymnasium,[21] and editor of a series of classics which are being brought out, and he is evidently thought a great deal of in Weimar. In appearance however he is as much as possible like a shoemaker. We went with the Schölls and Sauppes to Tiefurt and saw the queer little Schloss, which used to be Amalia's residence, and has since been a repertorium for poor Carl Friedrich's childish collections. The walls of every room are crowded with engravings, and the tables with rococo wares. There is a suite of rooms which are so small that the largest of them does not take up so much space as a good dining table, and each of these tiny rooms is crowded with prints, old china, and all sorts of knick-knacks. We saw a picture illustrating "Das neueste von Plundersweilern" and Sauppe read us the poem.

Tiefurt was a favourite resort of ours, for the walk to it is a very pleasant one and the Tiefurt park is a little paradise. The Ilm is seen here to the best advantage; it is clearer than at Weimar, and winds about gracefully among fine trees. One of the banks is a high, steep declivity which shows the trees in all their perfection. In Autumn when the yellow and scarlet were at their brightest, these banks were fairy-like in their beauty. It was here that Goethe and his court friends got up the performance of "Die Fischerin" by torch-light.

21 German, 'scholar, principal of the grammar school'.

About ten days after our arrival we made an excursion to Ettersburg, one of the Duke's summer residences, interesting to us beforehand as the scene of private theatricals and *sprees* in the Goethe-days. We carried provisions with us and Keats's poems. The morning was one of the brightest and hottest that August ever bestowed and it required some resolution to trudge along the shadeless chaussée which formed the first two or three miles of our way. One compensating pleasure was the sight of the beautiful mountain ashes in full berry which, alternately with cherry trees, border the road for a considerable distance. I felt a child's love for the bunches of coral standing out against the blue sky. We talked cheerily as usual, and at last rested from our broiling walk on the borders of a glorious pine wood – a wood so extensive that the trees in the distance form a complete wall with their trunks, and so give one a twilight which is very welcome on a hot summer's day. The ground under the trees is completely covered with soft moss so that one hears no sound of footsteps. The effect is grand and solemn. Presently we passed out of the pine wood into one of limes, beeches and other trees of light foliage through which the sunlight played like a living thing. G. made this place echo with his imitation of Kean's Othello for my amusement. At length, after a rest in the wood, we came into the open park in front of the Schloss which is finely placed on an eminence commanding a magnificent view of the far-reaching woods. Pückler Muskau has been of service here by recommending openings to be made in the woods in the taste of the English Parks. The Schloss is a house of very moderate size and no pretension of any kind. Two flights of steps lead up to the door and the balustrades are ornamented with beautiful creepers. A tiny sort of piazza under these steps is ornamented with creepers too, and has pretty earthenware vases filled with plants hanging from the ceiling. We felt how much beauty might be procured at small expense in looking at these things. The offices which surround the court yard have creepers neatly trained up them in the fashion of pilasters and cornices. A beautiful walk through a beech-wood took us to the Mooshütte where we rested on the rustic bench near the door and took our luncheon. Before this Mooshütte stands the beech on which Goethe and his friends cut their names and from which Goethe denounced Woldemar. We could recognize some of the initials. The tree has been shattered by lightning and is protected by a piece of sheet-lead. We were very jolly over our luncheon and right glad of the small bottle of wine which we had felt it rather a corvée[22] to carry. We rested an hour on the grass under the shade of the beeches and then set off again, while the sun was still burning, on our way home. But we rested again and slept when we got among the trees, then took another stage, and sat down on the grass to read Keats. I read aloud St Agnes' Eve, and at another resting place, part of Hyperion. The solemn pine forest looked still grander than in the morning, and we richly

22 French, 'burden'.

enjoyed it in spite of our weariness. About half past five, hot, aching and adust, we entered Weimar and found a glass of cold water from a pump by the roadside delicious as nectar.

With Ettersburg I shall always associate Arthur Helps, for he was with us the second and last time we saw it. He came to Weimar quite unexpectedly on the 29th August and the next evening we all three drove to Ettersburg. He said the country just round Weimar reminded him of Spain, only that Spain was much browner and had boulders scattered about. This led him to talk of his Spanish travels, and he told us some delightful stories in a delightful way. At one inn, he was considerably embarrassed in eating his dinner by the presence of a handsome woman who sat directly opposite to him resting on her elbows and fixing her dark eyes on him with a fearful intensity of interest. This woman was the cook, anxious to know that her dishes were acceptable to the stranger. Under this terrible surveillance he did not dare to omit a single dish, though sorely longing to do so. He gave us an amusing description of a fat vulgar Englishman who some how or other had got to Madrid not knowing a word of Spanish. One morning Helps on coming down to breakfast or dinner found this man seated in much rage at the misunderstood attentions of the waiters who with their usual vivacity were labouring to ascertain what would be agreeable to him. He burst out in answer to Helps's enquiries into invectives against "these apes, who were making fun of him". Helps said he felt convinced he was a creditor who had come to Spain in search of his debtor. The waiters in this inn were affectionately assiduous. His room was high up in the house, and to encourage him under the labour of mounting the many flights of steps the waiters used to accompany him, and pat him on the back! – On returning we said goodbye to Helps who was on his way to Dresden.

Another delightful place to which we often walked was Bercka, a little village, with baths and a Kur-Haus seated in a lovely valley about six miles from Weimar. The first time G. went I was obliged to stay at home and work, and when he came back he merely said that the place and the walk to it were pretty, and brought me a bunch of berries from the mountain ash as a proof that he had thought of me by the way. He wished to *ménager*[23] a surprize for me by the moderation of his praise and he succeeded, for I was enchanted with the first sight of this little paradise and half inclined to be angry with G. for having been able to restrain the expression of his admiration. The hanging woods, the soft colouring and graceful lines of the upland, the village roofs and spire all of a reddish violet but which harmonized beautifully with the foliage, the shady walks by the side of a wood-covered hill, the little avenue of stately poplars in agreeable contrast with the other trees, the winding stream and the bright green meadows through which it flowed made an enchanting scene. I took a Russian bath – that is to say a vapour bath suc-

23 French, 'prepare'.

ceeded by a shower bath – for the first time, and when our bathing business was done we dined *al fresco* under an awning at the Kur-Haus. We had fresh delight in the road on our way home, from the beauty of the evening tints – the violet horizon against the rich yellow and brown of the fields. We used not to despise the nice plums that were to be plucked on the way after we had reached Gelmeroda, but we were undeceived at last in our idea that we might take the fruit by the roadside as if it were the golden age; we were liable to a *straf-geld*[24] of 10 groschen for this indulgence. One of our visits to Bercka is individualized in my memory by our having read Goethe's "Vier Jahreszeiten", and having seen a lovely rainbow springing from the ploughed ground. This was the day after our return from Ilmenau. We set off in a high wind which was very perturbing to G. It softened a little as we went on, but was still violent enough when we were in sight of Bercka, to blow G's hat off. He ran in pursuit of it and so entirely lost the sense of annoyance in that of the comic, that he began to run with squared legs and arms, making a perfect Töpffer sketch of himself. When we set out home a shower came on to which we were indebted for the said rainbow. We had neither of us before seen a rainbow thus springing from the ground, and we eagerly watched it till it faded away.

When I had finished an article which obliged me to keep at home, our first expedition was to Jena. We had secured our places, or rather spoken for them, the day before and went in a confident leisurely way to the Post at 4, the time of starting, but were considerably nonplussed to find that all the places were taken! However this turned out to be a piece of good fortune, for we had a Bei-Wagen all to ourselves. The first [sight] of the valley of the Saal in which Jena stands was very striking to us – the bold and rocky hills are in strong contrast with the modest elevations round Weimar; but the town itself looked thoroughly dismal and ugly as we walked from our Wagen in search of the *Sonne*. This inn stands in a rather large square which is entered by narrow streets, and is only a little less dismal than those streets themselves. Some one has said that Jena seems to lie in a grave, and there is some truth in the simile. Our inn was not very attractive either, but we got some tolerable bedrooms, and then set out in search of a concert which the waiter told us was to be given a little way out of the town. We found nothing but a wooden structure in which men were smoking and drinking beer, so we had nothing but a pleasant walk along a chaussée bordered with chestnut trees for our pains. The evening was cold, and having nothing to amuse us we went to bed about 8 o'clock under our mountains of down which were very acceptable. The next morning was fine and we set off on an exploring walk. First we were bent on finding the *Tanne* where Goethe used to live on his visits to Jena. A person of whom we inquired the way thither made himself our guide and on asking to be shown Goethe's apartment we were ushered into some delightful rooms with a

24 German, 'fine'.

lovely prospect from them, now inhabited by a niece of Neander's and her husband Dr Widmann. They have the three rooms we saw – a large salon, a small one and a charming study – together with a bedroom which we did not see for 100 thalers per year!

Leaving the Tanne we took our way to the prettiest of the neighbouring hills, which has a green conical summit and is girdled with a pine wood. The walk was glorious. There are nice gravelly paths winding among the pines, and one enjoys at once the sight of these noble trees and the distant view of the valley and town. When we were a little way up the hill we sat down to look and listen. Not a sound was to be heard, except a tune played by some band of wind instruments. The sun shone brightly on hill and winding chaussée on purple roof and rich foliage. When we reached the top of the hill and passed over to the opposite side we found a new sight of beauty – another valley in which stood a little village closely nestled in luxuriant trees. Brown, soft-outlined hills sweep down towards this valley and pretty roads wind along it. We sat and watched this quiet scene, and heard the cocks crowing in the village – a sound which in bright sunshine is as lazy as at early dawn it is importunately industrious. On the top of this hill I found a curious parasitic plant with silvery petals narrow and thin as wire. On returning to our inn we found that Otto Schmidt, like all the rest of the Professors was away, it being the "Ferien",[25] so we began to wonder what we should do with ourselves in the evening, as the days were too short and my legs too weak to admit of more walking. We dreaded the cold and the necessity of going to bed again at 8 o'clock. So we determined to go home the same afternoon and took our places in a diligence which happened to start from our inn at 4 o'clock. We fortunately enough got two of three front places which were endurable, though rather uneasy to the back and exposed to the sun which was in our faces almost all the way. Our companion was a youth apparently of the apprentice calibre. When G. expressed his admiration of the country round Jena, our youth asked him if England were as pretty. No, said G. it is quite different. "Ja, alles ist *abgeschmackt*, nicht wahr?"[26] I was enchanted with the road, which I had not been able to see so well in the close vehicle which brought us to Jena. As we got nearer Weimar and the way became less varied we had another kind of beauty – that of the evening sky, which was fleckered with rosy clouds. We drove through the Webicht by twilight and were glad to find ourselves comfortably at home again with our books about us instead of being shivering at the Sonne with nothing to do. I forgot to write that when we stopped at a half way house, one of our fellow travellers, a man who had dined with us at the *Sonne* and whom we had pronounced to be an *épicier* who looked incomplete without his apron, approached G. who was standing near the horses and said: Parlez-vous Français, monsieur? "Oui, monsieur". Vous allez à Weimar,

25 German, 'holidays'.
26 German, 'Yes, it's all tasteless, isn't it?'

monsieur. "Oui monsieur. J'y ai demeuré depuis six semaines". "*Est-ce que cela vous a plait?*"[27] etc. etc. I enjoyed this dialogue immensely, and we afterward referred to our ambitious grocer who was anxious to shew his knowledge of French. What was our surprize, when on seeing him come to dine at the Erbprinz I asked Mr. Marshall who he was and he told me that he was an employé of the government named Ludecus, the son of the Ludecus, who wrote a contemptible book about it.

G. said we were wrong about our épicier. "No, I said *Weimar* is wrong".

Our greatest expedition from Weimar was to Ilmenau, in which we felt an interest on Goethe's account, apart from the reported beauty of the country. Our journey thither was so far from agreeable in the jolting Postwagen, the state of our stomachs perhaps being a little in fault, that we began when we reached Arnstadt almost to repent our undertaking, and indeed it cost us a heavy tax of headache and sickness which sent us crawling to bed soon after our arrival at the inn. But we quite revoked our grumbling when we had seen something of Ilmenau. The first morning we were feeble and so merely took a quiet walk through the nearest pine wood, from whence we strolled into the meadows and seated ourselves close to a clear rushing stream – our old friend the Ilm, I suppose. G. found a green caterpillar and played the Majendie with it. When it was cut in two the forepart began to devour the hind part. I made a little paper box that we might carry it home and observe the phenomenon; but nothing came of it, for the head did not seem to flourish on the tail, and soon became inanimate. The next day we set out with a determination to find the Gabel-Bach and Kickel-hahn (Goethe's residence) without the incumbrance of a guide. Our walk was glorious along a road bordered by lofty pines. At last we reached a fine spot on the summit of a hill, where a house was being built. We had some suspicion that this might be the Gabelbach, but in our uncertainty still went on through the drizzling rain which now came on, admiring the grand openings here and there which showed pine clad hills rising above each other like wave above wave. At last we met a waggon, and on asking the driver where the Gabel-bach was he told us we had already passed it – that it was near the said spot on the summit of the hill. So we turned back, and found near the unfinished house, the man who inhabits the simple wooden house which used to be Carl August's Hunting box. He sent a man on with us to shew us the way to the Kickel-hahn, which we at last reached – I with weary legs. There is a magnificent view of hills from this spot, but Goethe's tiny wooden house is now closely shut in by fir-trees, and nothing can be seen from the windows. His room, which forms the upper floor of the house is about 10 or 12 feet square. It is now quite empty, but there is an interesting memorial of his

27 French, 'Do you speak French, monsieur.' 'Yes, monsieur'. 'Are you going to Weimar, monsieur'. 'Yes monsieur. I have lived there for six weeks'. 'And do you like it?'

presence in these wonderful lines written by his own hand near the window frame:

Ueber allen Gipfeln
Ist Ruh,
In allen Wipfeln
Spürest du
Kaum einen Hauch;
Die Vögelein schweigen im Walde.
Warte nur, balde
Ruhest du auch.[28]

We walked on from the Gabel-bach, with a theory of finding Elgersburg and dining there, but we soon felt convinced that we should lose ourselves instead of finding anything and so made it our only object to get back to Ilmenau as directly as possible. A perilous descent down what seemed a road rather for a leaping mountain stream than for simple plodding mortals gave us a good deal of jolting and laughing, but we at last reached some even ground and followed a road which to our surprize brought us to the point from which we had set out on our morning expedition to the Gabel-bach. We enjoyed our dinner all the more for this rough exercise, and were rested enough to set out again by 5 o'clock. In walking out towards the valley one sees a great ugly building with an inscription purporting that it was built by a certain dignitary of Ilmenau for the benefit of those townspeople who liked to enjoy "geselligkeit" and "Freundliche Natur".[29] We went in and found an atmosphere of beer and tobacco and men playing at bowls – the unique mode in which the Germans enjoy "freundliche Natur". We walked on and on through the woods, making our way along forsaken paths over-grown with boughs, till we came within sight of Elgersburg. A merry walk! We went on to Elgersburg, but saw neither Kur-Haus nor Gast-Hof,[30] as we had dreamed we should. It is an ugly village scattered on the hill-side, and we soon turned back. G. told me a capital story of John Kemble jun. and his wife, beginning it under a wooden shed where we sat looking at Elgersburg, and finishing it as we turned back. Curious association of places and facts so widely apart! The next morning G.'s head was bad, so we formed no great projects but walked out towards Elgersburg and followed the high-road till we came to Stützerbach. Here an intelligent carpenter of whom we inquired the road to the Gabel-bach sent his old father with us as a guide, a very fortunate incident, for it procured us the sight of the finest beech-wood I ever saw. The pine-woods here are sublime – one would peo-

28 '*Wanders Nachtlied*': 'Over all the mountain peaks is quiet; in the treetops you trace scarcely a breath; the little birds are silent in the woods. Wait now, soon you will rest also.'

29 German, 'sociability'; and 'benevolent Nature'.

30 German, 'spa' and 'inn'.

ple them with hoary sages; the beech woods are graceful, smiling, mildly joyous – one sees busy Hamadryads in them playing with pet squirrels. On reaching home we took our warm baths as usual; for though we had visited the baths in the valley, and G. had promised himself a magnificent *douche* and me a cold sitz-bad, our resolutions came to nothing. On the Sunday morning (we had come to Ilmenau on the Wednesday) we sent on our bag by the Postwagen and set out bravely in spite of a high wind to walk to Arnstadt. A cold, boisterous wind it was, but as the day advanced, it abated and we had a lovely walk. At Arnstadt we dined, and I must record my first sight of a boar's head at table, magnificently garnished with green branches, lemons etc. Arnstadt too is rather an attractive place, with a large Kur-Saal and hydropathic establishments. It has not the bracing air of Ilmenau which one breathes with the same sort of conscious pleasure as if one were taking draughts of a refreshing beverage on a hot day. From Arnstadt we took the coupé of the Post-wagen to Neu-Dietendorf. Here we had to wait some time for the train, and G. beguiled the time by telling me of the fiasco he made with a lecture on Othello at Hackney. Our companions in the railway-carriage were a happy looking couple with their baby. Trivial details these! but every incident is precious in the remembrance of hours made bright by the sunshine of love. We got to our lodgings about six and enjoyed some of Frau Münderloh's good coffee.

About the middle of September, the theatre opened and we went to hear Ernani. Liszt looked splendid as he conducted the opera – the grand outline of his face and floating hair were seen to advantage as they were thrown into dark relief by the stage lamps. The Weimar Theatre is very pretty and commodious, and the Duke seems not to grudge expense in order to maintain a good company of artists both for the opera and drama. We went to see the "Journalisten" and were very much struck with the excellence of the ensemble, the moderation of the acting, and the perception shown in the costume. Genast delighted us with his marvellous acting of an old, burly wine-merchant, come out to enjoy life with his wife and family. It was characteristic of our good friend Mr. Wilson that when I told him how delighted we had been with Genast's acting (which he also saw), he replied: "Ah – although he said *To-ast*." Another evening we saw the "Verwunschene Prinz" a German version of a French version of Christopher Sly – Hettstedt, the Sly of the piece was very good. An absurd little farce followed – "Gute Nacht, Herr Fischer" – which gave us an opportunity of seeing a bit of excellent acting by Franck, a man who had previously appeared to us very stupid.

We were so fortunate as to have all three of Wagner's most celebrated operas while we were at Weimar. G. however had not patience to sit out more than two acts of Lohengrin, and indeed I too was weary. The declamation appeared to me monotonous, and situations in themselves trivial or disagreeable were dwelt on fatiguingly. Without feeling competent to pass a judgment on this opera as music, one may venture to say that it fails in one grand requisite of art, based on an unchangeable element in human nature – the need for contrast. With the

Fliegender Holländer I was delighted – the poem and the music were alike charming. The Tannhaüser too created in me a great desire to hear it again. Many of the situations and much of the music struck me as remarkably fine. And I appreciated these operas all the better retrospectively, when we saw "Der Freischutz", which I had never before heard and seen on the stage. The effect of the delicious music with which one is so familiar was completely spoiled by the absence of recitative and the terrible *lapsus* from melody to ordinary speech. The bacchanalian song seemed simply ridiculous sung at a little pot-house table at a party of *two*, one of whom was sunk in melancholy! The childishness with which Zamiel and all the other horrors were conceived was incredible, and the absurdity reached a *ne plus ultra* when Caspar climbed the tree apparently with the sole purpose of being shot. Herr Milde and his wife, the basso and soprano, are excellent singers. He is a very handsome man – according to good Mr. Wilson's opinion, something like Byron, only "*handsomer than Byron*". The only other opera we heard at Weimar was Flotow's Marthe, or the "Markt von Richmond" a collection of shreds and patches. The patch oftenest repeated being the Last Rose of Summer. It is lively, however, and is evidently a favourite with the audience. G. had the fidgets that evening and longed to turn out, so we went through the rain and paid four shillings to hear this trash. I told him to console himself by regarding the 4s. as an insurance against Flotow for the future.

A propos of the theatre, we were immensely amused to learn that a fair, small-featured man who somehow always looked to me as if he had just come out of the shell, had come to Weimar to fit himself for a dramatic writer by going behind the scenes! He had as yet written nothing, but was going to work in what he considered a "gründlich"[31] way.

When we passed along the Schillerstrasse, I used to be very much thrilled by the inscription "Hier wohnte Schiller",[32] over the door of his small house. Very interesting it is to see his study, which is happily left in its original state. It is a cheerful room with three windows, two towards the street and one looking on a little garden which divides his house from the neighbouring one. The writing table, of which he notes the purchase in one of his letters, and in one of the drawers of which he used to keep rotten apples, stands near the last-named window. On the opposite side of the room near the stove is his little claveçin with his guitar lying upon it. On the walls are some ugly prints of Italian scenes. The bedstead on which he died has been removed into this room from the small bedroom behind, which is now empty. A little table is placed close to the head of the bed with his drinking glass upon it. Here we saw his skull for the first time, and were amazed at the smallness of the intellectual region. Schiller used to occupy the whole of the second story [sic] which consists of an antechamber, now furnished with casts

31 German, 'fundamental, well-grounded'.

32 German, 'Schiller lived here'.

and prints which are sold in order to remunerate the custodiers of the house, a salon, which is now tricked out with a symbolical cornice, statues, and a carpet worked by the ladies of Weimar, the study which I have described and a little bedroom. There is an intensely interesting sketch of Schiller lying dead, which I saw for the first time in this study; but all pleasure in thinking of Schiller's portraits and bust is now destroyed to me by the conviction of their untruthfulness. Rauch tells us that he had a "miserablere Stirn".[33] Waagen says that Tieck the sculptor told him there was something in Schiller's whole person which reminded him of a *camel*.

Goethe's house is much more important looking, but to English eyes far from being the palatial residence which some German writers think it. The entrance hall is certainly rather imposing, with its statues in niches and broad stair-case. The latter was made after his own design and was an aftershine of Italian tastes. Carl August gave him the house after his return from Italy, and he rejoiced that the interior was still so incomplete that he could model it after his own taste. The "Sammlungen"[34] which the public is allowed to see are perfectly insignificant except as having belonged to him. The pictures are wretched, the casts not much better – indeed I remember nothing which seemed intrinsically worth looking at. The M.S. of his Römische Elegien written by himself in the Italian character is to be seen here, and one likes to look at it better than at most of the other things. G. had obtained permission from Frau von Goethe to see the Studier- and Schlafzimmer[35] which are not open to the public, and here our feelings were deeply moved. We entered first a small room containing drawers and shelves devoted to his mineralogical collections. From there we passed into the study. It is rather a dark room, for there are only two small windows – *German* windows. A plain deal table stands in the middle, and near the chair against this table is a high basket, where, I was afterwards told Goethe used to put his pocket handkerchief. A long sort of writing table and book case united stands against one wall. Here hangs the pin cushion, just as he left it, with visiting cards suspended on threads, and other trifles which greatness and death have made sacred. Against the opposite wall, where you enter the bedroom there is a high writing desk on which stands a little statue of Napoleon in creamy glass. The bedroom is very small. By the side of the bed stands a stuffed arm chair where he used to sit and read while he drank his coffee in a morning. It was not until very late in his life that he adopted this luxury of an arm-chair. In the corner against the window is a tiny washing table with a small white basin on it and a sponge. Beyond this room or rather closet is one where his servant used to sleep. From the other side of the study one enters the library, which is fitted up in a very makeshift fashion, with rough deal shelves

33 German, 'wretched brow'.

34 German, 'collections'.

35 German, 'study' and 'bedroom'.

and bits of paper with philosophy history etc. – written on them to mark the classifications of the books. Among such memorials one breathes deeply and the tears rush to one's eyes.

Equally interesting is the *Garten Haus*, which we used to see almost every day in our walks. Within, it is a not uncomfortable homely sort of cottage; no furniture is left in it, and the family want to sell it. Outside, its aspect became to us like that of a dear friend whose irregular features and rusty clothes have a peculiar charm. It stands on a pleasant slope fronting the west, and there is a charming bit of garden and orchard ground attached to it. Close to this garden hedge runs the road which leads to Ober-Weimar; and on the other side of this road a meadow stretches to the trees which border the Ilm. A bridge nearly opposite the Garten Haus takes one to the Borken-Haus,[36] Carl-August's little retreat, from which he used to telegraph to Goethe. The road to Ober-Weimar was one of our favourite walks especially towards the end of our stay at Weimar when we were glad of all the sunshine we could get. Sometimes we used to turn out of it up a grove of weeping birches into the ploughed fields at the top of the slope on which the Garten Haus and other little villas stand. Here we enjoyed many a lovely sun-set; one, in particular, was marvellously splendid. The whole hemisphere was golden, towards the east tinted with rose colour. From this little height we looked on the plantations of the park in their autumnal colouring, the town with its steep-roofed church, and its Castle tower, coloured a gay green, the line of chestnuts along the Belvedere chaussée and Belvedere itself peeping from its nest of trees.

Another very favourite walk of mine was the *Webicht*, a beautiful wood through which ran excellent carriage roads and grassy footpaths. How richly have I enjoyed skirting this wood and seeing on the other side the sky arching grandly down over the open fields, the evening red flushing the west over the town and the bright stars come out as if to relieve the sun in his watch over mortals. And then the winding road through the Webicht on the side towards Tiefurt with its tall overarching trees, now bending their mossy trunks forward, now standing with stately erectness like lofty pillars; and the charming grassy paths through the heart of the wood, among its silvery barked birches!

The Webicht lies towards Tiefurt, and one side of it is bordered by the road thither. I remember as we were returning from Tiefurt one evening, a beautiful effect of the setting sun-light, pouring itself under the trees and making the road before us almost crimson.

Dear Weimar! we were sorry to say good bye to it, with its pleasant group of friends – the grand fascinating Liszt, the bright, kind Princess, the Marquis de Ferrière with his becoming embonpoint and agreeable chat, the hearty, animated Schöll, good Mr. Wilson and his naïf pupil young Osborne, and last not least the sad and lively, the ambitious and resigned Mr. Marshall.

36 German, 'bark-house'.

We breakfasted twice, by way of farewell, with Liszt and the princess – the first time without any other visitors. The princess Marie showed me a remarkable series of sketches from Dante, while Liszt went to rest and G. talked with the Princess. After this, we all sat down together in the Princess Marie's room, Liszt, the Princess and her daughter on the sofa, G. and I opposite to them, and Miss Anderson a little in the rear. I like to recall this moment, and Liszt's face with its serious expression, as we talked about his coming to London and I asked the Princess if she should come too. The next time we breakfasted with them, the Marquis de Ferrière and young Cornelius were there, and I had a long theological séance with the Princess on the sofa. She parted from us very prettily, with earnest wishes for my happiness in particular. G. was so grateful to her for this that he couldn't help saying "God bless you" to her, and she repeated it, calling after me too "God bless you". The evening before I left Liszt called while G. was away and brought me a paper of bon-bons which the Princess had sent me to refresh us on our journey. The last morning was busy with packing; Schöll came at the last moment and brought me Uhland's poems as a present, with letters of introduction for G. at Berlin, and after a stay of less than five minutes took a thoroughly German farewell, kissing G. again and again on the lips! Laura, our maid, was out of the way, when we left, so we could not give her her 10 groschen which I had laid by for her; but when we were walking quietly on the platform at the station lo! we heard a scream behind us and on looking round saw Laura running towards us with a bouquet in her hand; which she had been in quest of while we were leaving. It was touching to see her funny face wrinkled up into a something meant for a smile as she said her good byes and held out her dirty hand that we might give it a parting shake. The morning had been sombre and bitterly cold from the beginning, and now it began to rain heavily. The train soon came up – we rushed under an umbrella into our carriage and so on the 4th of November, after a stay of just three months, we turned our backs on Weimar

To seek new streets and faces new![37]

Berlin, Nov. 30th 1854.

Ana

One of our pleasantest acquaintances at Weimar was the French ambassador, the Marquis de Ferrière, a very favourable specimen of a Frenchman, but intensely French. His genial face and perfect good humour gave one the same

37 Milton, *Lycidas*, l. 193: 'To morrow to fresh Woods and Pastures new'.

sort of bien-être as a well-stuffed arm-chair and a warm hearthrug. The first time G. met him was at Liszt's and he brought me home a very characteristic observation which had fallen from the Marquis in the course of conversation. Speaking of Yvan's accounts of his travels (the Marquis was first secretary to the Chinese Embassy which Yvan accompanied) he said: "C'était faux d'un bout à l'autre; mais c'était spirituel, paradoxale, amusant – enfin *tout ce qu'il fallait pour un journal.*"[38] Another day he observed that the famous words of Napoleon to his Egyptian army: "Forty centuries look down on you from the summits of these pyramids" were characteristic of the French national feeling as those of Nelson – "England *expects the man to make* his duty!" – were of the English. This is a fair specimen of the correctness with which one generally hears English quoted, and we often reminded ourselves that it was a mirror in which we might see our own German. Another amusing sample of the same kind occurred at an evening party at the Princess's. G. asked a young Hanoverian musician (Schreiber) who happened to be by his side who Fraülein Becker was (an awful old maid generally to be seen at the Altenburg on such occasions). Schreiber replied confidentially: "She is an old vir*gh*in". To return to the pleasant Marquis. He had heard that G. was writing a comedy,[39] but had not of course read it; at the utmost, he had heard something of the plot. On the strength of this, one day when G. was dining with him he said (addressing another guest): Eh bien, savez-vous que Monsieur qui écrit de *si belles pièces* est aussi physiologue profond?[40]

Liszt's conversation is charming. I never met with a person whose manner of telling a story was so piquant. The last evening but one that he called on us, wishing to express his pleasure in G's article about him,[41] he very ingeniously conveyed that expression in a story about Spontini and Berlioz. Spontini visited Paris while Liszt was living there, and haunted the opera – a stiff, self-important personage with high shirt collars, the least attractive individual imaginable. Liszt turned up his own collars and swelled out his person so as to give us a vivid idea of the man. Everyone would have been glad to get out of Spontini's way – indeed elsewhere "on feignait de le croire mort".[42] But at Paris, as he was a member of the Institute it was necessary to recognize his existence. Liszt met him at Erard's more than once. On one of these occasions Listz observed to him that Berlioz was a great admirer of his (Spontini's), whereupon Spontini burst into a

38 French, 'It was untrue from beginning to end, but it was spiritual, paradoxical, amusing – in fact all that was necessary for a newspaper'.

39 *The Fox Who Got the Grapes.*

40 French, 'Well, do you know the gentleman who writes such beautiful pieces is also a profound physiologist?'

41 GHL's 'Vivian en Voyage', *Leader* (23 September 1854), p. 909.

42 French, 'One pretended he was dead'.

terrible invective against Berlioz as a man who, with the like of him, was ruining art etc. Shortly after the "Vestale" was performed and forthwith appeared an enthusiastic article by Berlioz on Spontini's music. The next time Liszt met him of the high collars he said: "You see I was not wrong in what I said about Berlioz's admiration of you". Spontini swelled in his collars and replied: "Monsieur Berlioz a du talent comme critique".[43]

Liszt's replies were always felicitous and characteristic. G. observed one evening that the Germans could not give effect to the Italian opera. "Non", said Liszt, "c'est le chemin de fer imité par Thurn et Taxis."[44]

The Princess, too, is very lively and says many humourous things. G. was finding fault with the end of Lohengrin. She said, "Mais qu'est-ce que Wagner a pu faire? Il ne pouvait dire – elle s'est établie dans la Rue Taitbout, No. 70, et puis elle a fait ce qu'elle a pu; tandis que lui, il s'est très bien arrangé" etc. etc. Another day she said "Il n'y a aucune chaleur du sentiment qui préserve du rheumatisme".[45]

* * *

At Herr von Olfers' G. was discussing with several of the company the relative appreciation of Shakspeare in Germany and England. Graf York praised especially the *Wort-spiel*[46] which he appeared to think the main point in Shakespeare's wit. "For example", he said, "I, nod-noddy! Das ist vortrefflich".[47]

At Fraulein Solmar's General Pfuhl told us the following story as an example of what he called *edle Rache*,[48] which does not spare self, which sacrifices self to revenge. A man of wealth in Rome adopted a poor boy whom he had found in the street. This boy turned out a great villain and having previously entered the church by way of consistency, managed by a series of arts to possess himself of a legal title to his benefactor's property, and finally ordered him to quit his own house, telling him that he was no longer master there. The benefactor entirely possessed by indignant rage, killed the villain on the spot. He was imprisoned, tried for the murder and condemned. When in prison he refused to have a confessor and being asked his reason, he said: "*I wish to go to Hell, for he is there, and I want to follow out my Revenge!*"

Vivier called on us January 23 and was very amusing. He says, Germans take

43 French, 'Monsieur Berlioz has some talent as a critic'.

44 French, 'it is like Thurn and Taxis imitating the railway'.

45 French, 'But what could Wagner do? He could not say – she is settled at 70 Taitbout St, besides she did her best; whereas he is well able to look after himself.' 'There is no warmth of feeling that protects one from rheumatism'.

46 German, 'word play'.

47 German, 'That is splendid'. He refers to *Two Gentlemen of Verona*, 1. 1. 112: 'nod – ay – why, that's "noddy" '; and GE alludes to the anecdote in 'German Wit: Heinrich Heine' (1856).

48 German, 'noble revenge'.

off their hats on all possible pretexts, not for the sake of politeness, but pour être embarrassant.[49] They have wide streets simply to embarrass you by making it impossible to descry a shop or a friend. A German always has *three* gloves – on ne sait pas pourquoi.[50] There is a dog-tax in order to maintain a narrow trottoir[51] in Berlin, and every one who keeps a dog feels authorized to keep the trottoir and move aside for no one – if he has two dogs he drives out of the trottoir the man who has only one. The very dogs begin to be aware of it. If you kick one when he is off the trottoir he will bear it quietly, but *on* the trottoir he resents it vehemently.

He gave us quite a bit of Molière in a description of a mystification at a restaurant. He says to the waiter "Vous voyez ce Monsieur là. C'est le pauvre M. Colignon (Il faut qu'il soit quelqu'un qui prend très peu – une tasse de café ou comme ça – et qui ne dépense pas trop) "Je suis son ami. Il est fou. Je le garde. Combien doit-il payer?" "Un franc". "Voilà". Then Vivier goes out. Presently the so-called Monsieur Colignon asks how much he has to pay, and is driven to exasperation by the reiterated assurance of the waiter: "C'est payé, M. Colignon".[52]

49 French, 'to be embarrassing'.

50 French, 'one doesn't know why'.

51 French, 'footpath, sidewalk'.

52 French, 'You see that gentleman there. That is poor M. Colignon' (it must be someone who orders very little – a cup of coffee or something like that – and who doesn't spend much). 'I am his friend. He is mad. I watch over him. How much does he owe?' 'One franc.' 'Right.' 'It is paid, M. Colignon'.

VI. *Recollections of Berlin 1854–1855*

'Recollections of Berlin' (the composition of which is recorded in GE's diary during her stay in Dover in March 1855), like 'Recollections of Weimar' draws together impressions of the activities of GE and GHL during their months in Berlin. The sprightly opening leads into an account which summarises their activities, displaying a keen interest in reported anecdote. The solid regime of reading, writing and translation so prominent in GE's diary, is hardly in evidence in the 'Recollections', which concentrate rather on the almost equally strenuous program of paying and receiving visits, the social life of salons and cafes, and expeditions to museums and theatres.

German beds come in for special mention at two points in the essay. To explain the phenomenon, we invoke the authority of John Murray's *Handbook for travellers on the Continent*:

> One of the first complaints of an Englishman on arriving in Germany will be directed against the beds. It is therefore as well to make him aware beforehand of the full extent of misery to which he will be subjected on this score. A German bed is made only for one; it may be compared to an open wooden box, often hardly wide enough to turn in, and rarely long enough for any man of moderate stature to lie down in . . . Curtains are almost always wanting. The place of blankets is sometimes supplied by a light puffy feather-bed, which is likely to be kicked off, and forsake in his utmost need the sleeper . . . Mr Coleridge has recorded his abhorrence of a German bed, declaring "he would rather carry his blanket about him, like a wild Indian, than submit to this abominable custom."[1]

Murray saw fit to alert English travellers to this hazard. Cross, however, saw fit to censor GE's references to German beds. The end of the fourth paragraph of 'Recollections of Berlin' reads:

> We were amused to hear that Carlyle said he should think no one could die at Berlin, for in beds *without curtains* what Christian could give up the ghost? **To us, the lack of curtains was the smallest fault of German beds.**

1 *A Handbook for travellers on the Continent: being a Guide to Holland, Belgium, Prussia, Northern Germany, and the Rhine from Holland to Switzerland* (10th edn., revised; London, John Murray, 1854), p. 200.

Cross's motive in omitting the second of these sentences (here indicated in bold) can be conjectured. Comment on German beds recurs in the closing section (again bold type restores Cross's excisions, which are all directed to preserving an image of GE as immune from certain frailties):

> **We soon became ill, and so were even thankful to see the cliffs of Dover.**
>
> English mutton, an English fire **and an English bed** were likely to be appreciated by creatures who had had eight months of Germany with its questionable meat, its stove-heated rooms **and beds warranted not to tuck up**. The taste and quietude of a first-rate English hotel were also in striking contrast with the heavy finery, the noise, and the indiscriminate smoking of German inns.

These suppressed references to German beds provide a nice instance of Cross's censorship – and the extent of the bedtalk in the journals.

Cross quotes fairly substantial sections of this essay, omitting personal detail in general (and suggestive personal detail in particular): Haight makes a handful of passing references to it.

VI. Recollections of Berlin. 1854–1855

There are certain persons without any physiognomy the catalogue of whose features, as: Item, a Roman nose, item, a pair of black eyes etc. gives you the entire contents of their faces. There is no difference of opinion about the looks of such people. All the world is agreed either that they are pretty or ugly. So it is with Berlin. Every one tells you it is an uninteresting modern city, with broad monotonous streets, and when you see it you cannot for the life of you get up an emotion of surprize or make a remark about the place which you have not heard before.

We arrived there on the evening of the 4th of November and drove to Kellner's Hotel de l'Europe in the Tauben-strasse. The next morning was spent in looking for lodgings and by 10 o'clock in the evening we had unpacked and were settled in No. 62 Dorotheenstrasse. The following day was Sunday; the sun shone brightly and we went to walk in the Linden, elbowing our way among the *promeneurs endimanchés*,[1] who looked remarkably smart and handsome after the Thuringians. We had not gone far when we met a nice-looking old gentleman with an order round his neck and a gold headed cane in his hand, who exclaimed on seeing G. "Ist's möglich?"[2] and then bid him heartily welcome. I saw at once it was the Varnhagen of whom I had heard so often. His niece, arrayed in smiles and a pink bonnet, was with him. In the evening G. went to Fräulein Solmar's who received him very kindly, and thus ended our first day of domestication in Berlin.

For the first six weeks G's head would not allow him to sit very long at work, so when the weather permitted we took long walks in the Thiergarten, where the straight and uniform avenues of insignificant trees contrasted very disadvantageously with the charming variety of our beloved park at Weimar. Still we now and then noticed a beautiful wintry effect, especially in the part most remote from the town, where the trees are finer and the arrangement more varied. One walk which skirted the Thiergarten on the right hand side coming from the town we were particularly fond of because it gave us on one side an open view, with water and a boat or two, which touched by the magic of sunshine was pleasant to see. At Berlin it was "a day of small things"[3] with regard to the beautiful and we made much of little.

Our little circle of acquaintances was very agreeable and varied. Varnhagen was a real treasure to G. for his library supplied all the deficiencies of the public one where to ask for books was generally like "sinking buckets into empty

1 French, 'Sunday strollers'.
2 German, 'Is it possible?'.
3 Zechariah 4:10, 'Who hath despised the day of small things?'

wells". He is a man of real culture, kindliness and polish (Germanly speaking) and he has besides that thorough liberalism social, religious and political which sets the mind at ease in conversation and delivers it from the fear of running against some prejudice or coming suddenly on the sunk fence of some miserable limitation. The first morning he called on us he talked of his terrible disappointment in Carlyle, a subject to which he often returned. He evidently felt an antipathy to the Teufelsdröckh, which indeed it was not difficult to understand from the mere *manière d'être*[4] of the two men. They had corresponded for years before they saw each other, and Varnhagen was and is a great admirer of Carlyle's best works, but he was thoroughly repelled by his rough, paradoxical talk and, more justifiably, by the despotic doctrines which it has been his humour to teach of late. We were amused to hear that Carlyle said he should think no one could die at Berlin, for in beds *without curtains* what Christian could give up the ghost? To us, the lack of curtains was the smallest fault of German beds.

We went to two very agreeable parties at Varnhagen's, but when the severe weather came on, shortly after Christmas, he became ill and was confined to his room till within a week before we left, so that G. only saw him in short morning visits. We were in both cases invited to take coffee at 5 o'clock, and the party broke up about 8, so that one might very well go to a dinner party, a coffee party and a tea party, each of three hours' duration, in the same day. The first evening, Varnhagen brought out a number of his beautifully arranged autographs and portraits – Goethe at all ages, Kestner, Charlotte, and the unfortunate Kleist. We saw the letter written by the last, the night before he shot himself in company with Frau Vogel. There was no love affair between them, but they had this in common, that they were thoroughly unhappy; he was poor and hopeless and she was suffering from an incurable disease. One evening they went together to an inn on the way to Potsdam, and before going to rest, wrote on a single sheet of paper letters to their friends communicating their intention. Early in the morning they rose, took some coffee and then went to the border of some water close to the inn, where they shot themselves. Director Wilhelm Schadow, one of the Dusseldorf school of painters, and the author of "Der moderne Vasari" which has since come out, was one of the party – a lively old man, with finely cut features and a well-balanced head. Dr. Vehse also, the author of the History of the German Courts since the Reformation – a dark complexioned man, with an unpleasant expression and mean head. The second party was a rather larger one, and I there met for the first time Professor Stahr who was there with Fanny Lewald. The noise from the mere talk of about a dozen people, and those cultivated and chiefly middle-aged, was amazing. It was such as would be made in England by a set of young men after dinner when the wine had made many rounds. This noise, with the atmos-

4 French, 'attitude'.

phere of a stove-heated room, stretches a party of three hours' length into a long term of durance and endurance.

Varnhagen, when well, is a regular visitor at Fräulein Solmar's who for many years has kept an open salon for her friends every evening but one in the week. Here the three-cornered chair next the sofa was reserved for him except when General Pfuhl was there. This General Pfuhl is a fine specimen of an old soldier who is at the same time a man of instruction and of strong social sympathies. He has been in the service of Russia, has been within a hair's breadth of being frozen to death "and so following". He spoke French admirably, and always had something interesting and characteristic to tell or say. His appreciatory groans always in the right place when G. was reading Shylock, did us both good under the chills of a German audience. Fräulein Solmar is a remarkably accomplished woman, probably between fifty and sixty, but of that agreeable *Wesen* which is so free from anything startling in person or manner and so at home in everything one can talk of, that you think of her simply as a delightful presence, and not as a woman of any particular age. She converses perfectly in French, well in English and well also, as we were told, in Italian. There is not the slightest warmth of manner or expression in her, but always the same even cheerfulness and intelligence – in fact she is the true type of the mistress of the *salon*. During the first half of our stay in Berlin we went about once a week to her house, but bad health and bad weather kept us away during the last six weeks, except on one or two evenings. Baron Sternberg, the novelist, used frequently to glide in when we were there and cast strange cold glances around, talking quietly to Fräulein Assing or some other lady who sat in a distant parallel of latitude. Noisy Dr. Vehse was there once or twice, but we generally found only a small knot of insignificant women, and the chief interest lay in Fräulein Solmar herself, Varnhagen and General Pfuhl. A Monsieur Vautageux whom we alighted on twice when there was almost no one else amused us by his *French* knowingness. He said, he found in the music of Meyerbeer's Huguenots the whole spirit of the period of Charles IX. "Lisez les chroniques" – de Froissart, suggested Mlle. Solmar – "oui, quelque chose comme ça, ou bien de Brantome, ou . . . de Merimée, et vous trouverez que Meyerbeer a parfaitement exprimé tout cela; du moins c'est ce que je trouve, moi".[5]

A still more interesting acquaintance was Professor Gruppe, who has written great books on the Greek Drama and on Philosophy, has been a political writer, is a lyric and epic poet, has invented a beautiful kind of marbled paper for binding books, is an enthusiastic huntsman and withal the most simple kindhearted creature in the world. His little wife who is about 30 years younger than himself seems

5 French, '"Read the chronicles" – of Froissart, suggested Miss Solmar – "yes, something like that or else of Brantôme, or . . . of Mérimée, and you will find that Meyerbeer has expressed all that perfectly; at least that is certainly what I find."'

to adore him, and it is charming to see the group they and their two little children make in their dwelling up endless flights of stairs in the Leipziger Platz. Very pleasant evenings we had there, chatting, or playing whist or listening to readings of Gruppe's poems. We used to find him in a grey cloth schlafrock which I fancy was once a great coat and a brown velvet cap surmounting his thin grey hairs. I never saw a combination at all like that which makes up Gruppe's character. Talent, fertility and versatility that seem to indicate a fervid temperament and yet no scintillation of all this in his talk and manner; on the contrary, he seems slow at apprehending other people's ideas and is of an almost childish naïveté in the value he attaches to poor jokes and other trivialities. Apropros of jokes, we noticed that during the whole seven months of our stay in Germany we never heard one witticism or even one felicitous idea or expression from a German!

Gruppe and his wife were delighted with G.'s tricks at cards which he happily fell upon one evening as a transition from *Pochen* or brag, at which he had alarmed Gruppe by his terrible play – "Das mochte bis an zwölf groschen steigen!"[6] he said. The dear Professor then announced to us that *he* too could perform a trick, and went deliberately through the whole process with the three hats and a bit of sugar, telling us that the other evening it had made a grosser Effekt! We were invited to meet Waagen his wife and daughters and Frau Gruppe's relations, and G. was called upon to perform his tricks again, but a terrible girl, Frau Gruppe's sister, watched him so closely with her great eyes that the *tours de force* were not forcible. Waagen we found a very ugly but a very intelligent and amusing man. He told us several stories about Goethe – that some one had pronounced him "Kein dummer man",[7] and that Goethe had said of – – "I thank the Almighty God that thou hast produced no second edition of this man!"

Gruppe has a delightful library with rare books and books too good to be rare, and we often applied to him for some of them. He lent me Lessing and that is an additional circumstance to remember with pleasure in connection with the Laocoon. He one evening read us a translation by himself of one of the Homeric Hymns – Aphrodite – which is very beautiful and generally we were glad when he took up the book but the last evening we were there poor G. perspired under the terrible infliction of "Zulamied" which Gruppe and his wife evidently gloried in, but which to us had but one quality – that of frightful lengthiness, for fatigue and the hot room had made us incapable of perceiving anything else. Gruppe has an epic in Manuscript – Ferdusi – and he read us specimens of it which pleased us, but we found it impossible to sit out the reading of more than one book by the "Rhetor. Julius Schramm" for whose Vorlesung[8] good little Frau Gruppe brought us tickets. The fable on which this poem is founded is very fine. The Sul-

6 German, 'That would amount to 12 groschen'.
7 German, 'not a stupid man'.
8 German, 'lecture'; in this case by the orator Julius Schramm.

tan had engaged Ferdusi to write a great poem on his exploits and had promised to pay for this 100,000 pieces (gold being understood). Ferdusi had delighted in the thought of this sum which he intended to devote to the benefit of his native city. When the poem was delivered and the sack of money given to Ferdusi he found that the pieces were silver! He burst into a song of scorn against the Sultan and paid the miserable sum to his bath-man for a "Glas Fucha" (Beer).

Another pleasant friend was Eduard Magnus, the portrait painter, an acute intelligent kind-hearted man, with real talent in his art. He was the only German we met with who seemed conscious of his countrymen's deficiencies – who would admit, for example, that they talked loudly, that they were given to "embarras", and that they were not polite. He showed in every possible way a hearty desire to do us service – offered to introduce G. to friends, took great trouble about accompanying him to Graf York's – sent us books, came to chat with us, showed us his portraits, and when we were coming away brought us lithographs of some paintings of his that we might carry away a remembrance of him. He has travelled very extensively and had much intercourse with distinguished people and these means of culture have had some of their best effects on his fine temperament and direct, truthful mind. In the little room where we used to be ushered to wait for him there was a portrait of Thorwaldsen and one of Mendelssohn, both of whom he knew well. I was surprized to find in his atelier the original of the portrait of Jenny Lind with which I was so familiar. He was going to send it, together with Sontag's portrait, to the Exhibition at Paris.

His brother the chemist was also a bright, goodnatured-looking man. We were invited to a large evening party at his house, and found very elegant rooms with a remarkable assemblage of celebrated men – Johannes Müller, Du Bois-Reymond, Rosas, Ehrenberg etc. etc. Some of the women were very pretty and well drest. The supper, brought round on trays, was well appointed and altogether the party was well-managed.

Of a very different cast was Professor Stahr pale, nervous, sickly looking, with scarcely any moral radiation, so to speak. Fanny Lewald, whom he married whilst we were at Berlin, after nine years of waiting, is a Jewish looking woman, of soft voice and friendly manners. She seems to have caught or to have naturally something of the literary egoism which is almost ludicrously prominent in Professor Stahr, but, this apart, she is an agreeable person. The first evening we spent with them we had a long discussion about the Wahlverwandtschaften, with which Stahr found fault on the score of its dénouement. This dénouement, he said, was "unvernünftig".[9] So, I said, were dénouements in real life very frequently: Goethe had given the dénouement all would naturally follow from the characters of the respective actors. The next evening we spent with them was after their marriage, for which they seemed all the happier. They distressed us both by

9 German, 'unreasonable'.

giving us a new idea of the Princess Wittgenstein's relation to Liszt, implying that she was an incubus. We were both glad to be able to doubt the truth of this representation. Stahr has a copy of the charming miniature of Schiller taken when he was about 30 – a miniature in the possession of a certain Madame von Kalb. There are the long *Gänsehals*,[10] the aquiline nose, the blue eyes and auburn hair. It is a most real and striking portrait. I saw also a portrait and bust of Madame d'Agoûlt here – both rather handsome. The first evening Stahr told us some of the grievances which the Prussians have to bear from their government, and amongst the rest the vexatious necessity for a "concession" or license before any, the simplest vocation, can be entered on. He observed, with justice that the English are apt to suppose the German Revolution of '48 was mere restlessness and aping of other nations, when in fact there were real oppressions which the Germans had to bear and which they had borne with a patience that the English would not imitate for a month.

By far the most distinguished man we saw at Berlin and indeed, next to Liszt, in Germany was *Rauch* the sculptor. Schöll had given G. a letter for him and soon after it had been left at his house, he called on us in the evening and at once won our hearts by his beautiful person and the benignant and intelligent charm of his conversation. He is indeed the finest old man I ever saw – more than 76 I believe, but perfectly upright, even stately in his carriage. His features are harmonious, his complexion has a delicate freshness, his silky white hair waves gracefully round his high forehead, and his brown eyes beam with benevolence and intelligence. He is above the common height, and his stature and beauty together ennoble the grey working surtout and cap which he wears in his atelier into a picturesque and distinguished costume. The evening he was with us he talked delightfully of Goethe, dwelling especially on his loveable nature. He described very graphically Goethe's way of introducing subjects, showing plates etc., bringing in the cast of Schiller's skull and talking of it, and other little particulars of interest.

We went one morning to his atelier and found him superintending his pupil's work at a large group representing Moses with his hands held up by Aaron and Hur. It was extremely interesting to me to see Rauch's original little clay model of this group, for I had never seen statuary in that first stage before. The intense expression of entreaty in the face of the Moses was remarkable. But the spirit of this group is so alien to my sympathies that I could feel little pleasure in the idea of its production. On the contrary my heart leaped at the sight of old Kant's quaint figure, of which Rauch is commissioned to produce a colossal statue for Konigsberg. In another atelier where the work is in a different stage we saw a splendid marble monument nearly completed of the late King of Hanover – pitiable that genius and spotless white marble should be thrown away on such

10 German, 'goose neck'.

human trash! Our second visit to Rauch's atelier was paid shortly before we left. The group of Moses, Aaron and Hur was clothed up and the dark-eyed olive-complexioned pupil was at work on a pretty little figure of Hope – a child stepping forward with upturned face, a bunch of flowers in her hand. In the other atelier, we saw a bust of Schleiermacher which with the equestrian statue of Fritz and its pedestal Rauch was going to send to the Paris Exhibition. Schleiermacher's face is very delicately cut and indicates a highly susceptible temperament. The colossal head of Fritz, seen on a level with one's eye, was perfectly startling from its living expression. One can't help fancying that the head is thinking and that the eyes are seeing.

Dessoir, the actor was another pleasant variety in our circle of acquaintances. He created in us a real respect and regard for him not only by his sincere devotion to his art but by the superiority of feeling which shone through all the little details of his conduct and conversation. Of lowly birth and entirely self taught, he is by nature a gentleman. Without a single physical gift as an actor, he succeeds, by force of enthusiasm and conscientious study, in arriving at a representation which commands one's attention and feelings. I was very much pleased by the simplicity with which he one day said: "Shakspeare is mein Gott; Ich habe kein anderen Gott,"[11] and indeed one saw that his art was a religion to him. It was very agreeable to have him as a companion, now and then in our walks, and to have him read or discuss Shakspeare for an hour or two in the evening. He paid us the very pretty attention of getting up a dinner for us at Diets's and inviting Roetscher and Förster to meet us, and he supplied us with tickets for the Theatre, which however was a pleasure we used sparingly. The first time we went was to see *Nathan der Weise* – a real enjoyment, for the elegant theatre was new to us and the scenery was excellent – better than I saw there on any subsequent occasion. Döring performed Nathan, and we thus saw him for the first time to great advantage, for though he drags down this part, as he does all others, the character of Nathan sets limits which he cannot overstep, and though we lose most of its elevation in Döring's acting we get *en revanche*[12] an admirable ease and naturalness. His fine, clear voice and perfect enunciation told excellently in the famous monologue and in the whole scene with Saladin. The other actors were wretched: the toothless Gruer as Saladin and Frau Bost, like a fat cook, as Sittah. Our hearts swelled and the tears came into our eyes as we listened to the noble words of dear Lessing whose great spirit lives immortally in this crowning work of his. The next play we saw was Emilia Galotti, which I cannot admire, in spite of laudatory critics. Dessoir's Marinelli was good, and the Fräulein Viereck looked splendid as the Gräfin Orsini. The figure of old Gruer as the Oberst threw a streak of the ludicrous into any recollection of this terrible tragedy. Dessoir was anxious for us to

11 German, 'Shakespeare is my God; I have no other God'.
12 French, 'in compensation'.

see his Othello but we could give it little admiration as a whole, though certain points were good. Döring's Iago was very bad; especially in the great temptation scene where it ought to have been best. But the worst specimen of his acting that we saw was his Shylock, which was perfectly disgusting. It was not even true to any wrong conception of the character, but was a vacillation from one set of mistakes to another. I was very glad to see Dessoir's Richard, both because his representation was a good one and because I had never seen the play before. The queens Elizabeth and Margaret, always disagreeable to my imagination as Shakspeare represents them, were not made more fascinating by being associated with the fat Frau Werner and the haggard Krelinger.

The latter we saw for the first time in the *Fechter von Ravenna*, as Thusnelda, when her long tirades about Deutschland declaimed without any passion made her intensely wearisome. However, she was once a very beautiful "Erscheinung"[13] as Dessoir tells us, and has had adventures too. Her first husband, named Stich, was an actor – a rather feeble personage. She had an amour with Graf Blucher, the nephew of the hero, and one evening her husband came home and found her with this lover. High words followed and at length the Graf stabbed Stich, who after the lapse of about a year died – it was supposed from the injury thus received. The young Graf was imprisoned, but the old King would not allow Frau Stich to be dismissed from the theatre and accordingly she appeared again on the stage. But she was received with revilings and the filthiest missiles, was carried off the stage fainting two or three times and at length came and knelt before the audience entreating them to forgive her, until at length they were pacified. She married a second husband and has had a large family, and now so completely is that episode forgotten that criticism of her acting is met, as Fanny Lewald told me, by the plea: "But there is not a better Hausmutter in Berlin than the Krelinger! I would rather have a servant from her than from any one". Frau Hoppé an actress, who takes the principal female parts, is her daughter, but has not inherited her beauty or her fine voice. She was G's especial detestation, and certainly she is of that unfortunate stamp of women who try hard to be piquante and coquettish and are perfectly harmless in spite of themselves. French pieces and French parts are generally unendurable in a German version, but Frau Hoppé as Margaret of Navarre was a superlative instance of this, and she was well matched by Dessoir as Charles V and Hendricks as Francis I. The last piece we saw at the Theatre was "Das Glas Wasser", a version of "Un Verre d'eau", which was better got up than most of such pieces at Berlin. Dessoir's Bolingbroke was excellent, and we saw the Krelinger and the Hoppé to advantage as The Duchess of Marlborough and Queen Anne.

Our first visit to the Opera was to see Masaniello, in which Formes the younger, was the tenor, and his wife the Fenella. It was prettily put on the stage

13 German, 'vision'.

and the orchestra is excellent, but the singing was poor. Our great anxiety was to see and hear Johanna Wagner, so we took tickets for the Orpheus, which Mlle Solmar told us she thought her best part. We were thoroughly delighted both with her and the music. The caricatures of the Furies, the ballet girls and the butcher-like Greek shades in Elysium, the ugly screaming Eurydice and the droll appearance of Tuczek as Amor in which she looked like a shop girl who had donned a masquerade dress impromptu without changing her head-dress – all these absurdities were rather an amusement than a drawback to our pleasure; for the Orpheus was perfect in himself and looked like a noble horse among mules and donkeys. We heard Fidelio also, in which Frau Cöster acquitted herself very well. Wonderful is that prison scene with the recognition – Ich – Du! Our last operatic treat was the Iphigenia in Aulis – Cöster again as the Iphigenia.

We went to only one Concert, for which Vivier was kind enough to send us tickets. It was given by him and Roger, assisted by Arabella Goddard and Johanna Wagner. Roger's singing of the Erl-König was a treat not to be forgotten. He gave the full effect to Schubert's beautiful and dramatic music, and his way of falling from melody into awestruck speech in the final words, "*war todt*",[14] abides with one. I never felt so thoroughly the beauty of that divine ballad before. The King was present in all his toothlessness and blinkingness, and the new Princess from Anhalt Dessau, young and delicate looking, was there too. Arabella Goddard played the Harmonious Blacksmith charmingly, and the Wagner sang badly two ineffective German songs and Halevy's duet the *Reine de Chypre* with Roger.

The first work of art really worth looking at that one sees at Berlin are the Rosse-bändiger[15] in front of the Palace. They are by a sculptor named Cotes who made horses his especial study, and certainly to us they eclipsed the famous Colossi of Monte Cavallo, casts of which are in the New Museum.

The collection of pictures at the Old Museum has three gems which remain in the imagination – Titian's daughter, Correggio's Jupiter and Io, and his head of Christ on the handkerchief, the Schweisstuch as the Germans call it. I was pleased also to recognize among the pictures the one by Jan Steen which Goethe describes in the Wahlverwandtschaften as the model of a tableau-vivant presented by Luciane and her friends. It is the daughter being reproved by her father, while the mother is emptying her wine glass. Waagen is Director of this museum and under his direction the arrangement of the pictures has been made historical so that the collection though not rich is instructive. The *Kuppelsaal*[16] hung with tapestries from Raphael's cartoons and surrounded with antique statuary is very effective. The statues best worth looking at here are a Jupiter, an Apollo and two reposing Fauns. In the long Saal called the Kaiser saal there is not

14 German, 'was dead'.
15 German, 'horse-tamers'.
16 German, 'dome-shaped room'.

much of interest. A Torso strikes the eye as a chef-d'oeuvre amongst inferior productions, and it is interesting to see the statue of Napoleon, the worker of so much humiliation to Prussia, placed opposite that of Julius Caesar. In another Saal, we were delighted with a Hebe of Canova's, which stands amongst a medley of unattractive things. It is the first of three statues wrought after the same model.

The New Museum is on a magnificent scale and is still far from complete. The *Treppenhaus* or Grand Entrance Hall with its white marble pillars, with its casts of the colossal Dioscuri of Monte Cavallo, with its grand staircase crowned by a marble temple after the model of the Pandroseion in the Erectheum and with its elaborate frescoes painted by Kaulbach, is nobly conceived and when finished will make a splendid ensemble. One of the completed frescoes is the Deutsche Sage, which however gratified us more thoroughly in the colourless cartoon than in the fresco. On looking at it one thinks at once of Michael Angelo's sublime Sybils. The massive figure with one arm upraised and the other resting on her lap, is seated on huge druidic stones; her long grey hair crowned with ivy is tied loosely below her chin; the spirit of the Northern Mythology – with its sense of mystery, its sternness, its terrors and its pathos – looks out from her eyes; two ravens, the good and evil, are whispering their secrets in her ears; at her feet lie, among tufts of fern, a gigantic skull, a golden crown, and fragments of arms and utensils. This figure belongs to one of the subordinate cycles in the series of frescoes. The chief cycle, consisting of 6 great allegorical-historical compositions is intended to represent the historical development of Culture. Three of these compositions are completed and represent: 1. The Destruction of the Tower of Babel: 2. Homer and the Greeks: and 3. The Destruction of Jerusalem. They are the result of much thought and talent, but they leave one entirely cold as all elaborate allegorical compositions must do. In a room in another part of the building we saw several of Kaulbach's cartoons – Architecture, Sculpture and History, with that of the Sage, and a portion of the frieze, where he gives play to his humanistic genius and appears to be representing the course of history in fantastic infantine and animal groups.

From the Treppenhaus we entered the Griechischer Saal, devoted to the divine sculptures of the Parthenon and the Eginetan sculptures. The frescoes on the walls represent Greek scenery and temples; the frieze of the Parthenon is ranged along the walls and on screens which advance crosswise into the room; and the sculptures of the pediments are placed on a sort of long, common pedestals, running along the middle of the Saal. Part of the Eginetan Sculptures are placed on a pedestal of this kind, but the most perfectly preserved group representing the struggle for the body of Achilles (or Patroclus) is arranged against the wall facing the entrance so as to represent its appearance in the pediment of a temple. This was our favourite room. Here we came again and again to feed our eyes and minds with the unspeakable beauty of those works which, all mutilated as they are, exercise a spell over one that no other sculpture commands. The Ilissus, the Theseus, the two female figures, which deprived of heads and arms completely express – the one, eager attention, the other contemplative repose. The backs of a male and female figure, the latter with her lovely arm round the neck of her companion – these were our favourites, and made everything else seem mean or lifeless in comparison.

A little antechamber in which there is a seat where one may rest one's limbs and close one's eyes, satiated with beauty, contains the Laocoon, and beyond this is the Apollo Saal, named of course from *the* Apollo – the *Kallinikos*. In the middle of this Saal is the stupendous group called the Farnesischer Stier, the original of which is in Naples. The figure of Dirke, whom the two sons of Antiope are going to fasten to the horns of a wild ox, struck me as pathetic and beautiful, but on the whole the group excites no emotion. The subject seems too elaborate for sculpture. The Diana of Versailles, also, is in this Saal. Next comes the Kuppel Saal where we used to sit down and watch the Sleeping Faun and could fancy we heard him snore. He eclipsed everything else in this Saal, though there is a fine group of Bacchus supported by two Satyrs, the Pallas of Velletri, Menelaus supporting the body of Patroclus, and others of which I have no distinct image left. The glorious Jupiter and a Medusa, high up on brackets, used to attract my eyes away from the Faun. The original of the Medusa is in Cologne, where it was found. Next comes the Niobe room, second in interest only to the one in which are the Parthenon sculptures. How grieved I shall be if the image of that mother in anguish sheltering her youngest child from the inevitable dart, becomes vague in my imagination! Next to the mother, the son who is looking up in defiance of the arbitrary power which has already struck his brother close by him with death is the finest. The Romischer Saal detained us chiefly before two Venus torsos and a marvellous figure of a Faun lying on his back and snapping his fingers. The latter was found in Herculaneum. Less massive and powerful than the Sleeping Faun, it is full of life, and remains with one as a clearly defined form among so much that is blurred and vague. In this Saal, too, I saw for the first time the group of Ildefonso – Hypnos and Thanatos. The Saal for Modern sculpture is but scantily furnished at present. There are the glorious gates "fit to be the gates of Paradise", Canova's lion, and another, awake, opposite to him, Michael Angelo's Day and Night, and some other groups which have been effaced in my memory by other objects.

One morning, by means of Herr von Olfers, we got admission into the Hall of Northern Antiquities, which is at present not open to the public. Our object was to look at the frescoes, which represent subjects from the Northern Mythology. They were, most of them, very bad; but the figure of Balder, in his sunny beauty, and the departed souls entering Helheim, at the Entrance of which sits Modgodur, the hater of the Gods, were impressive. From hence we went to the Ægyptisches Museum which occupies the rest of the ground floor. I was particularly delighted with the *Atrium* which represents part of the Temple of Karnak. The frescoes on the walls place one in the midst of Egyptian scenery and architecture. The view of the mysterious "Pair" against morning sunlight, and that of Philæ are exquisitely beautiful. Two colossal statues, one of Sesurtasen I, 2000 B.C. and the other of Sesostris, 1400 B.C. are placed side by side here and are a very interesting example of advance in art. The Sesostris is intensely *human* in its expression compared with the other, and the sculpture of the body is remarkably fine. The Historical Saal has its walls painted after the coloured reliefs on the interior walls of Egyptian temples. In a glass case amongst other small curiosities G. discovered a little mummied monster, an acquaintance of his through Geoffroy St. Hilaire. Many of the sculptures in this room have the strongly Jewish type. I had heard much of the Egyptian collection at Berlin as a very rich one, and so it may be for those who are initiated into the arcana of Egyptian lore, but for the common eye there is nothing to compare with the stupendous relics in the British Museum.

One of our greatest art-pleasures at Berlin was a visit to the Raczinsky Gallery – a small but very choice collection of pictures, chiefly by modern artists. Here is a cartoon of Kaulbach's great Hunnenschlacht, which is to form one of the six great frescoes in the Treppenhaus of the New Museum, and by the side of it is a copy of his Deutsche Sage. The Hunnen Schlacht is certainly a wonderful composition, but there seemed to be something wanting in order to give one the idea of the combatants in the air being airy forms and not solid flesh and blood. Near these fine things of Kaulbach's were two perfectly odious pictures by Cornelius, Christ in Hades, and Religion, I think, or some other allegorical female figure with children. The spirit, the conception and the technique of these pictures are all bad, and amazed me after having seen his cartoons for the Royal Mausoleum, which are certainly grandiose in conception and fine in drawing though rather lifeless. On the same wall with these hung a picture by Overbeck – the marriage of Joseph and Mary – with the festoons and canopy and violin players and all the barbarisms of the Pre Raphaelite period, but great beauty in the faces. Under this picture was one by a Viennese artist also shewing a great amount of misapplied power. Jesus sits in a chariot drawn by a bullock and a lion (I think), Popes in their robes pushing along the wheels, and a saintly female figure, the Virgin I suppose, sitting opposite him. It was refreshing to turn from this to the truth and nature of Hildebrand's "Sons of Edward IV", and of Bendeman's charming sunny landscape with the "Shepherd and his lass" looking calmly into the distance, his arm round her waist and his chin on her shoulder. There is a group of Italian peasants seated against St. Peter's by Paul de la Roche, in which a boy seems to be breathing. His round bronze limbs stretching beyond his rough jerkin of sheepskin have the solidity and careless repose of life, and the face startles one – it seems so ready to begin and speak Italian. The whole picture is very remarkable. Below it hangs one by Leopold Robert – a group of field labourers returning joyously home in the golden evening light – which G. admired very much. To me it was too theatrical. "The Two Leonoras" by Sohn has merit; the Princess is well conceived – there is a tender, noble melancholy in her face – and the picture is admirably painted. There are some portraits of interest in the collection – amongst them those of Cornelius, Kaulbach and W. Schadow.

Consul Wagner's collection in the Bruderstrasse appears to have been made by a banking Mæcenas of little discrimination or preference for one style rather than another. But it has at least the merit of being a collection of entirely modern pictures. On the whole it produces much the same effect as a walk through our own Exhibition[17] – the majority of the pictures being what one would rather not look at. The only things that arrested us were a group of fishermen one of whom is recounting to a fisherman's wife the story of her husband's wreck, by *Jordan*, a landscape by Lessing, a slave merchant and his human wares by Horace Vernet, an infant Christ by Hübner, St Catherine being carried by angels to her grave on Mount Sinai, by Mücke and some clever Wilkie-like pictures by Hasenclever.

The Ravené collection is very small, but it is choice. The pictures are hung sparingly in elegant rooms – small, after the German fashion. They are almost all landscapes, and many of these snow-scenes. The names of the artists are not given. G. was suffering while we were there, so we did no more than cast a glance around and came away.

A very interesting visit to us was one which our friend Magnus suggested, to Dr. Parthey's, in the house occupied by Nicolai. We went for the sake of seeing Kaulbach's illustrations of Shakspeare, but we had the additional pleasure of looking at old Nicolai's portrait, a sketch by Thorwaldsen of Dante and Virgil descending into the Inferno, an engraving of Albert Dürer's, and a lovely engraving of the Triumph of Galatea. The old gentleman who owns these and a great many more delightful things received us very politely and seemed to be pleased with the interest Kaulbach's pictures excited. He had only one original of these by him – Macbeth girding on his armour and talking to the Doctor – and an engraving of the meeting of Macbeth and Banquo with the witches.

They were very happy months we spent at Berlin, in spite of the bitter cold which came on in January and lasted almost till we left. How we used to rejoice in the idea of our warm room and coffee as we battled our way from dinner against the wind or snow! Then came the delightful, long evenings in which we read Shakspeare, Goethe, Heine and Macaulay, with German Pfefferkuchen and Semmels[18] at the end, to complete the "Noctes cœneque deûm".[19]

Our neighbour, Graf Bernstorff, was one of our amusements. He was a "sucking Graf" as G. said, studying at the University. The noises he made were so extraordinary that we thought he could scarcely be *compos*, but Frau Holzeyer, our

17 The Royal Academy Exhibition held annually.
18 German, 'gingerbread and muffins'.
19 Latin, 'nights and feasts of the gods'.

landlady, assured us he was very *vernünftig*.[20] Probably the ranting which he occasionally heard in our room when Dessoir paid us a visit, excited equal wonderment in him about us. Little Frau Holzeyer was a terrible example of German energy and vivacity – certainly a rare commodity. To make a remark to her was to pull out a spigot from a vessel brimfull. In all things, except humbug, she was a contrast to our Weimar Landlady, Frau Münderloh.

We used often to turn out for a little walk in the evening, when it was not too cold, to refresh ourselves by a little pure air as a change from the stove-heated room. Our favourite walk was along the Linden on the broad road between the trees. We used to pace to old Fritz's monument which loomed up dark and mysterious against the sky. Once or twice we went along the gas-lighted walk towards Kroll's. One evening, in our last week, we went on to the bridge leading to the Wilhelm-Stadt and there by moon and gas-light saw the only bit of picturesqueness Berlin afforded us. The outline of the Schloss towards the water is very varied, and a light in one of the windows near the top of a tower was a happy accident. The row of houses on the other side of the water was shrouded in indistinctness and no ugly object marred the scene. The next day under the light of the sun, it was perfectly prosaic.

I have forgotten to mention Kroll's, where we went on the second Sunday of our stay. It is a splendid kind of Casino, with theatre and concert and ballroom, a saloon where you can take coffee in the midst of mirrors and tastefully arranged plants, and other apartments with all the appliances for dining smoking etc. We heard some respectable instrumental music there, and saw some farce acting, as well as a large assemblage of the Berlin bourgeoisie.

Our table d'hôte at the Hotel de l'Europe was so slow in its progress from one course to another and there was so little encouragement to talk to our neighbours that we used to take our books by way of beguiling the time. Lessing's Hamburgische Briefe, which I am not likely to take up again, will thus remain associated in my memory with my place at the table d'hôte. The company here as almost every where else in Berlin, was sprinkled with officers. Indeed the swords of officers threaten one's legs at every turn in the streets, and one sighs to think how these "unproductive" consumers of *Wurst* with all their blue and scarlet broadcloth are maintained out of the pockets of the community. Many of the officers and privates are startlingly tall, indeed some of them would match, I should think, with the longest of Friedrich Wilhelm's "lange Kerle".[21]

It was a bitterly cold, sleety morning – the 11th of March – when we set out from Berlin, leaving behind us, alas! G's rug, which should have kept his feet warm on the journey. Our travelling companions to Cologne were fat Madame Roger, her little daughter and her dog, and a Queen's messenger, a very agreeable

20 German, 'rational'.
21 German, 'long lads'.

man, who afterwards persuaded another of the same vocation to join us for the sake of warmth. This poor man's teeth were chattering with cold though he was wrapped in fur, and we, all furless as we were, pitied him and were thankful that at least we were not feverish and ill as he evidently was. We saw the immortal old town of Wolfenbüttel at a distance as we rolled along; beyond this there was nothing of interest in our first day's journey, and the only incident was the condemnation of poor Madame Roger's dog to the coupé, apart from its mistress with her warm cloaks. She remonstrated in vain with a brutal German official and it was amusing to hear him say to her *in German*: *"Wenn Sie können nicht Deutsch verstehen"*.[22] Eh bien! prenez-le – ah! quel Satan de pays![23] was her final word, as she held out the shivering little beast.

We had had visionary projects of going on to Calais without rest, but soon found that it would be folly to attempt this. So we stayed at the Hotel de Mayence at Cologne and the next morning walked out to look at the Cathedral again. Melancholy as ever in its impression upon me! From Cologne to Brussels, we had some rather interesting companions in two French artists who were on their way from Russia. Strange beings they looked to us at first in their dirty linen, Russian caps and other queer equipments, but in this as in so many other cases I found that a first impression was an extremely mistaken one, for instead of being, as I imagined, common, uncultivated men they were highly intelligent. They told us a characteristic fact about the buildings in St. Petersburg – namely, that they are only solid and splendid where they are inevitably near the eye; everywhere else they are trumpery. They also told us of the trouble they had to see the Dresden gallery, and the wretched way in which it is managed. At Brussels, we went to the Hotel de Saxe, a disagreeable place, against which we are insured for the future. As we took our supper we had the pleasure of looking at Berlioz' fine head and face, he being employed in the same way on the other side of the table. The next morning we had to turn out of bed at 1/2 past 5 to get to the station in time for the train to Calais.

Amusing it was to recognize the old horn always out of tune, which had made us laugh at every station on our journey through Belgium in the Summer. We reached Calais at 1/2 past 2 and after a cup of tea were soon on board and on our way across the Straits. The view of Calais was picturesque with its church tower rising from an irregular mass of houses, of varied browns. We soon became ill, and so were even thankful to see the cliffs of Dover.

English mutton, an English fire and an English bed were likely to be appreciated by creatures who had had eight months of Germany with its questionable meat, its stove-heated rooms and beds warranted not to tuck up. The taste and quietude of a first-rate English hotel were also in striking contrast with the heavy

22 German, 'If you cannot understand German'.
23 French, 'Oh well! take him – ah, what a devil of a country!'

finery, the noise, and the indiscriminate smoking of German inns. But after all, Germany is no bad place to live in, and the Germans, to counterbalance their want of taste and politeness, are at least free from the bigotry and exclusiveness of their more refined cousins. I even long to be amongst them again – to see Dresden, and Munich and Nürnberg and the Rhine country. May the day soon come!

Dover. March 27 1855.

VII. *Recollections of Ilfracombe 1856*

This delightful essay was written at a time of peculiar intensity for GE. It is dated 'Tenby, 22 July 1856', and as she recalls in 'How I came to write fiction', it was there that the title 'The Sad Fortunes of the Reverend Amos Barton' came to her as she lay dozing, though it was not until her return to Richmond that she began to write the story, responding to GHL's adjurations that she should realise her longheld 'vague dream . . . that some time or other I might write a novel'. Although she expressed this initiation in terms which hint at visionary possession, or at least gesture towards a Romantic notion of the creative power of the unconscious, the fact is that she was a busy journalist, thoroughly professional in meeting deadlines, and well practised in the craft of prose composition. When the time came, her disciplined working practices were applied to her new activity. 'Recollections of Ilfracombe' was written as she gathered herself for the decisive move to fiction.

GE's account of their time at Ilfracombe has an infectious exuberance and a ripeness that is not simply an invention of the reader looking for the novelist in embryo. It modulates its narrative register, from the detailed responses to their journey, through the Ruskinesque descriptions, notable for a particular interest in the effects of light on landscape and a general consciousness of painterly values (she speaks of the composition of foreground, and refers to the lanes as 'a "Hunt" picture', and the cockle women of the closing paragraph as 'a fine subject for a painter'), to the humorous narrative of their botanising and the splendidly controlled report of their encounter with the pig, and the dramatic vignette of the cockle women.

The familiar pattern in which the 'Recollections' provide fuller detail and more developed anecdote than the corresponding diary section is again apparent. Their seaside expedition occupied three months altogether (8 May–9 August), though the essay does not cover the full period, ending with their departure from Ilfracombe for Tenby on 26 June. While the journey was undertaken on account of GHL's current interests, the description of Tenby in Murray's *Handbook for Travellers in South Wales* (1860) suggests that other considerations may have been relevant for this pair who suffered constantly from ill health and money worries (as the comments on the cost of lodgings and prohibitive sixpenny walks indicate): 'Tenby is a cheap and pleasant place of residence, particularly to those who take pleasure in scenery, geology, or natural history. The lover of marine fauna will find ample occupation by the sea-shore, for Tenby has been made famous by Mr Gosse for the number and beauty of its actinae and zoophytes.'[1] Moreover, GE perhaps retained happy memories of her earlier visit there in 1843 with the Brays and Hennells.

The zeal for 'occupation by the sea-shore' arose from GHL's developing interest in science, which had been given impetus by his work on Goethe as a man of science. With his inimitable capacity for recognising emergent intellectual trends, GHL takes up what he called marine zoology (GHL Journal, 7 January 1857). His journal – the extant portion of which begins with an entry dated Tenby, 24 July 1856 – gives very considerable detail of his observations of marine specimens (and includes some encounters – with a Mormon preacher, for example – which GE does not mention). These studies soon resulted in the production of the first of his *Sea-Side Studies*, despatched to *Blackwood's* on 19 July and published in the August number. GE's enthusiastic participation in GHL's extension of his scientific knowledge beyond mere booklearning is apparent in her own account, and her pleasure in acquiring a whole new vocabulary is evident. GHL's account is a splendid complement to her 'Recollections':

> We are a lady and two men. The lady, except that she carries a landing-net, and has taken the precaution of putting on things which 'won't spoil,' has nothing out of the ordinary in her costume. We are thus arrayed: a wide-awake hat; an old coat, with manifold pockets in unexpected places, over which is slung a leathern case, containing hammer, chisel, oyster-knife, and paper-knife; trousers warranted not to spoil; *over* the trousers are drawn huge worsted stockings, over which again are drawn huge leathern boots . . . Never mind the inelegance: handsome is as handsome does!
>
> In this costume we wooed the mermaids.[2]

1 *Handbook for Travellers in Central Italy* (London, John Murray, 1860), pp. 31–2.

2 G. H. Lewes, *Sea-Side Studies* (Edinburgh, Blackwood, 1858), p. 17. GHL's letters to Blackwood show his developing plans for further expeditions and publications (e.g. *The Letters of George Henry Lewes*, ed. William Baker, 2 vols. (University of Victoria, English Literary Studies Monograph Series 64, 1995), vol. 1, pp. 245–61, notably his entirely warranted claim that 'there is a vast stock of material in my journal', pp. 247–8).

GE's involvement was not only that of a paddler:

> quick female eyes have discerned, and nimble fingers have delicately secured, one of the loveliest of sea-charmers – an *Eolis,* of about three-quarters of an inch in length, tapering into the most graceful of tails . . . The tide may now drive in as fast as it will, we shall go home rich.[3]

'Recollections of Ilfracombe' is not only complemented by *Sea-Side Studies.* Some sections of this essay correspond closely to *Sea-Side Studies* (as Haight pointed out[4]): did GE supply GHL with copy for his *Blackwood's* piece from her journals? Such lending corresponds to her assistance with translations and tabulations during his preparation of the Goethe book, and is a rare (if not unique) instance in which their collaboration can be documented. The sections of GE's text replicated in GHL's are the paragraph dealing with the promenade around the Capstone, and the two long paragraphs on inland walks.[5]

Cross prints an abbreviated version of these 'Recollections', omitting (for example) the pig; Haight prints the whole essay in *Letters*.

3 Lewes, *Sea-Side Studies*, p. 25.

4 Gordon S. Haight, *George Eliot* (Oxford University Press, 1968), p. 96.

5 Lewes, *Sea-Side Studies*, pp. 30–1, 73–9.

VII. Recollections of Ilfracombe, 1856

It was a cold unfriendly day – the 8th of May on which we set out for Ilfracombe, with our hamper of tall glass jars, which we meant for our sea-side Vivarium. We had to get down at Windsor, and were not sorry that the interval was long enough to let us walk round the Castle, which I had never seen before, except from a distance. The famous "slopes," the avenues in the Park and the distant landscape looked very lovely in the fresh and delicate greens of Spring, and the Castle is surely the most delightful royal residence in the world. We took our places from Windsor all the way to Exeter, having bravely made up our minds to do the greatest part of our journey in one day. At Bristol where we had to wait three hours, the misery of my terrible headache was mitigated by the interest we felt in seeing the grand old church of St. Mary Redcliffe, forever associated with the memory of Chatterton –

> "It stands the maestrie of a human hand
> The pride of Bristowe and the western land."[1]

For the rest, Bristol looked dismal enough to us: a compound of dingy streets, bad smells and dreary waiting at a dirty Railway Station. At last the time came for the train to set off, and after a short journey we reached Exeter Station where we were delighted to find that we could get beds, and so save the drive into the town. The next morning before the hour of starting for Barnstaple, we had time for a stroll in the sunshine as far as the town. The country round looked lovely. A fine hilly road, bordered by tall trees led us towards the higher part of the town, which commenced, like a cathedral town, with a row of Gothic almshouses on one side and park like grounds, probably belonging to the episcopal residence, on the other. Our object was to get to the Cathedral; and after inquiring our way for a little while along clean, cheerful looking streets, we found a narrow, flagged side-street which led us into the pleasant square, shaded by tall trees and surrounded by quaintish houses, where stands the fine old temple with its two great square towers. The façade is extremely elaborate and the arch of the doorway especially beautiful; but the rest of the exterior is heavy, and even the façade is spoiled by the gable being so low as to hide part of the rosace window and give the whole roof the appearance of having been cut down from below. However, the two towers, though rather heavy in shape, are very exquisite in the grace and *mod-*

1 From one of Thomas Chatterton's Rowley poems 'On the Same' (i.e. 'Onn Oure Ladies Chyrche'), misquoted here, but quoted correctly ('Thou seest this maestrie') in 'Belles Lettres', *Westminster Review*, 66 (1856), pp. 267–9.

eration of their ornamental detail. As we passed the door it was ajar and we peeped in across the locked gate which shut out free entrance. The interior seemed very fine but our glimpse was interrupted by the approach of the hard, dry looking woman that alternates as key-keeper with the oily sexton in English cathedrals. "Can we see the Cathedral?" I said. "Yes, I can *show* you the Cathedral." We declined to be "shown" and walked on, taking a few more glances at the pleasant streets. One interesting object we passed on our way was a very old bit of building apparently Saxon, which appeared to be used as a Police Station. Back again to the Railway in the sunshine, with the birds singing about the hedges. The journey to Barnstaple lay through a charming country; gently sloping hills, roads winding by the side of hanging woods, little streams, and here and there patches of grey houses.

At Barnstaple we said good bye to the Railway and took to the good old fashioned stage coach. A great fuss, of course, in getting all the luggage on the top, and all the people settled inside and out. I foolishly chose to go inside, being headachy, and had for my companions, a pale, thin, affected lady, and a reddish, stout, affected lady. G. had a pleasanter journey outside, and won golden opinions from the thin lady's husband and daughter, whose name turned out to be Webster. I was not sorry when our coach rattled and swung up the hilly street of Ilfracombe and stopped at the door of the "Clarence Hotel". Our next task was to find lodgings, and we went forthwith to look for Mrs. Williams of Northfield, whom Gosse recommends in his "Devonshire Coast". The reasons for his recommendation were not very patent to us when we saw the shabby ill-furnished parlour and bedroom, so we determined to go a little farther and fare better, if possible. At this spot called Northfield, the beauty of Ilfracombe burst upon us, though we had as yet no glimpse of the sea and no idea – at least *I* had none – in which direction it lay. On our left were gracefully sloping green hills, on our right the clustering houses, and beyond, hills with bold, rocky sides. Walking on a few yards to the right, we came to a pretty house with a verandah, surrounded by a nice garden, with a carriage road up to the door. A notice at the gate told us it was Runnymede Villa and moreover that it was "To Let", but we thought it was far too smart and expensive a dwelling for us. However there could be no harm in asking, so we knocked at the door, and were shown by a pleasant looking young woman into a drawing-room, where we remained to admire and long while she went to ask her mother the rent. The mother came, and we found to our great satisfaction that we could have this large double drawing room for a guinea a week during May and a guinea and a half in June. Before we had decided, another knock came at the door – it was our travelling companion Mr. Webster, who had also been attracted by the pretty outside of the house. The end was, that we took the drawing room with the bedroom and dressing room above, and the Websters – that is, the wife and daughter, for the husband was to be always away on business except in short, fly away visits – took the dining room on the other side.

Having deposited our luggage, and ordered our *thé dinatoire* we set out in search of the sea, and were directed to the "Tunnels" – three long passages cut in the rock. We passed through them all and came upon the most striking bit of coast I had ever beheld – steep, precipitous rocks behind and on each side of us, and before us sharply cut fragments of dark rock jutting out of the sea for some distance beyond the land, for the tide was now approaching its height. We were in raptures with this first look, but could only stay long enough to pick up a few bits of coralline, which, novices as we were, we supposed to be polypes.

It was cheering the next morning to get up with a head rather less aching, and to walk up and down the little garden after breakfast in the bright sunshine. I had a great deal of work before me – the writing of an article on Riehl's books, which I had not half read, as well as the article on *belles lettres* – but my head was still dizzy and it seemed impossible to sit down to writing at once in these new scenes, so we determined to spend the day in explorations.

There can hardly be an uglier town – an uglier cluster of human nests lying in the midst of beautiful hills, than Ilfracombe. The colour of the houses is the palest dingiest grey, and the lines are all rectangular and mean. Overtopping the whole town in ugliness as well as height are two "Terraces", which make two factory-like lines of building on the slope of the green hill. From our windows we had a view of the higher part of the town, and generally it looked uninteresting enough; but what is it that light cannot transfigure into beauty? One evening, after a shower, as the sun was setting over the sea behind us, some peculiar arrangement of clouds threw a delicious evening light on the irregular cluster of houses and merged the ugliness of their forms in an exquisite flood of colour – as a stupid person is made glorious by a noble deed. A perfect rainbow arched over the picture.

Walking on from our gate towards Wildersmouth – a little opening in the hills which allows one to wet one's feet in the sea without descending a precipice or groping through a tunnel – we got a view of the lower part of the town, and turning up a pleasant foot-path to our right we were led on past a dissenting chapel, and then past a new church which is being built, into the streets that lead immediately to the quay, where we see the physical-geographical reason why Ilfracombe was built here and nowhere else. Returning from the quay we entered the promenade round the Capstone, which has been made at great expense since Ilfracombe became a place for visitors. From this end of the Capstone we have an admirable bit for a picture. In the background rises old Hillsborough jutting out far into the sea, rugged and rocky as it fronts the waves, green and accessible landward; in front of this stands Lantern Hill, a picturesque mass of green and grey surmounted by an old bit of building that looks as if it were the habitation of some mollusc that had secreted its shell from the material of the rock; and quite in the foreground, contrasting finely in colour with the rest are some lower perpendicular rocks, of dark brown tints patched here and there with vivid green. In hilly districts, where houses and clusters of houses look so tiny against the huge limbs of Mother Earth one cannot help thinking of man as a parasitic animal – an epizoon making his abode on the skin of the planetary organism. In a flat country a house or a town looks imposing – there is nothing to rival it in height, and we may imagine the earth a mere pedestal for us. But when one sees a house stuck on the side of a great hill, and still more a number of houses looking like a few barnacles clustered on the side of a great rock, we begin to think of the strong family likeness between ourselves and all other building, burrowing house-appropriating and shell secreting animals. The difference between a man with his house and a mollusc with its shell lies in the number of steps or phenomena interposed between the fact of individual existence and the completion of the building. Whatever other advantages we may have over molluscs and insects in our habitations, it is clear that their architecture has the advantage of ours in beauty – at least considered as the architecture of the species. Look at man in the light of a shell-fish and it must be admitted that his shell is generally ugly, and it is only after a great many more "steps or phenomena" that he secretes here and there a wonderful shell in the shape of a temple or a palace.

But it is time to walk on round the Capstone and return home by Wildersmouth. On clear days, I could see the Welsh coast with the smoke of its towns very distinctly, and a good way southward the outline of Lundy Island. Mounting the Capstone we had the best view of the whole town – the Quay, the High Street, and the old Church standing high up on the hill and looking very handsome with its three-gabled end. Our narrow path from Wildersmouth to Runnymede Villa led us by the side of a miniature river, the Wilder, which of course empties itself at Wildersmouth into the sea. It was always a fresh pleasure to me to look at this clear little stream, fringed with Veronica and Stellaria.

About five o'clock, the tide being then low, we went out on our first zoophyte hunt. The littoral zone at Ilfracombe is nothing but huge boulders and jutting rocks of granwacke or clay slate, which when not made slippery by sea-weed are not very difficult to scramble over. It is characteristic enough of the wide difference there is between having eyes and seeing, that in this region of Sea-anemones, where the Mesembryanthemum especially is as "plenty as blackberries", we climbed about for two hours without seeing *one* Anemone, and went in again with scarcely anything but a few stones and weeds to put into our deep well-like jars which we had taken the trouble to carry in a hamper from London, and which we had afterwards the satisfaction of discovering to be quite unfit for our purpose. On our next hunt, however, after we had been out some time, G. exclaimed "I see an anemone!" and we were immensely excited by the discovery of this little red Mesembryanthemum, which we afterwards disdained to gather as much as if it had been a nettle. It was a crescendo of delight when we found a "Strawberry", and a *fortissimo* when I for the first time saw the pale fawn coloured tentacles of an Anthea Cereus viciously waving like little serpents, in a low tide-pool. But not a polype for a long, long while could even G. detect after all his reading; so necessary is it for the eye to be educated by objects as well as ideas. When we put our anemones into our glass wells, they floated topsy-turvy in the water and looked utterly uncomfortable, and I was constantly called upon to turn up my sleeve and plunge in my arm up to the elbow to set things right. But after a few days, G. adventurously made a call on the Curate Mr. Tugwell, of whom we had heard as a collector of anemones and he returned to me not only with the announcement that Mr. Tugwell was a very "nice little fellow", and with three treasures – an *Eolis pellucida*, a *Doris Billomellata*, and an *Aplysia*, the first of each genus I had ever seen – but also with new light as to glass jars. So we determined to dismiss our deep wells, and buy some moderately sized jars with shoulders to them. We had before this found out that yellow pie-dishes were the best artificial habitat for Actiniæ.

It was a considerable stretch to my knowledge of animal forms to pay a visit to Hele's shop, which lies in a quiet pleasant little nook at the back of the dissenting chapel opposite Wildersmouth. Hele gets his bread now by collecting marine animals and sending them to Lloyd in London, and he has a sweet-faced intelligent daughter who goes out with him collecting and manages the stock on hand. The first time we went there, they had a fine show of the Actinia Crassicornis and A. Gemmacea, some Holothuriæ (the first I had ever seen) and the green Anthea Cereus, which was new to me. But I had a still greater addition to my knowledge when G. went to Mort Stone with Mr. Tugwell and Mr. Broderie and brought home several varieties of Polyps, which I had gathered a very imperfect conception of from books – Tubularian, Plumularian and Sertularian – exquisite little Eolides, and some compound Ascidians. Indeed, every day I gleaned some little bit of naturalistic experience, either through G's calling on me to look through the microscope or from hunting on the rocks; and this in spite of my preoccupation with my article, which I worked at considerably *à contre-cœur*,[2] despairing of its ever being worth anything. When at last, by the 17th of June both my articles were dispatched, I felt delightfully at liberty and determined to pay some attention to sea-weeds which I had never seen in such beauty as at Ilfracombe. For hitherto I had been chiefly on chalky and sandy shores where there were no rock-pools to show off the lovely colours and forms of the Algæ. There are tide-pools to be seen almost at every other step on the littoral zone at Ilfracombe, and I shall never forget their appearance when we first arrived there. The *Corallina Officinalis* was then in its greatest perfection, and with its purple pink fronds threw into relief the dark olive fronds of the Laminariæ on one side and the vivid green of the Ulva and Enteromorpha on the other. After we had been there a few weeks the Corallina was faded and I noticed the Mesogloia vermicularis and the M. virescens, which look very lovely in the water from the white cilia which make the most del-

2 French, 'reluctantly'.

icate fringe to their yellow-brown whip like fronds, and some of the commoner Polysiphoniæ. But I had not yet learned to look for the rarer Rhodospermiæ under the olive and green weeds at the surface. These tide-pools made me quite in love with sea-weeds, in spite of the disagreeable importunity with which they are made to ask us from shop-windows – "Call us not weeds",[3] so I took up Landsborough's book and tried to get a little more light on their structure and history.

Our zoological expeditions alternated with delicious inland walks. I think the country looked its best when we arrived. It was just that moment in Spring when the trees are in full leaf, but still keep their delicate varieties of colouring and that *transparency* which belongs only to this season. And the furze was in all its golden glory! I never saw it in such abundance as here; over some hills the air is laden with its scent, and the gorgeous masses of blossom perpetually invited me to gather them as the largest possible specimens. It was almost like the fading away of the evening red when the furze blossoms died off from the hills, and the only contrast left was that of the marly soil with the green crops and woods. The primroses were the contemporaries of the furze and sprinkled the sides of the hills with their pale stars almost as plentifully as daisies or buttercups elsewhere. Perhaps the most enchanting of all our walks was that to Lee, because we had the double beauties of rocky coast and wooded inland hill. Lee is a tiny hamlet which has lodged itself, like a little colony of *Aurora Actiniæ*, in the nick between two ranges of hills, where the sea runs in and makes a miniature bay. From the hills we have to pass over in reaching it, there is an exquisite view on looking back towards Ilfracombe: first the green slopes forming the inland aspect of the Tors, which always reminded me of some noble animal that has reared itself on its fore-legs to look at something, powerfully arresting its attention – as if the land had lifted itself up in amazed contemplation of the glorious sea; then Ilfracombe, at the meeting of many hills, with the graceful green Capstone Hill surmounted by its Flagstaff, and beyond it Hillsborough with its crag of rich, violet-veiled brown, standing like a rugged grand old warrior being played with by that capricious beauty the sea; while in the farther distance the sombre *Hangman* lifts its round, blackened shoulder, softened too with a violet veil, but of a different tone from that of Hillsborough. Another picture of a smaller kind was a single crag sloping in a very obtuse angle toward the sea and sheltering a little sandy bay where the gulls are fond of resting. We saw it once in the bright *Sunday* evening light, when there was a nice platform of sand for the gulls, and the colour of the cliff was a *blue* violet. Turning again towards Lee and pursuing our walk, we come at last in sight of the dip or valley in which the hamlet lies. The wooded hills that slope down towards it on the farther side were not yet of a monotonous summer green when we first saw them, and their sister hills were glowing with furze

3 'Call us not weeds – we are flow'rs of the sea' in E. L. Aveline, *The Mother's Fables in Verse* (1812), p. 157.

blossoms. Down and down we go until we get into the narrow road or lane that winds through the valley. Here we see an ornamental cottage or two, as well as genuine cottages, and close by the side of the road a tiny Gothic chapel where our nice Mr. Tugwell preaches every Sunday. But the great charm of this road, as of all Devonshire lanes, is the springs that you detect gushing in shady recesses covered with liverwort, with here and there waving tufts of fern and other broad leaved plants that love obscurity and moisture. Springs are sacred places still for those who love and reverence Nature. The first time we went to Lee we thought of varying our walk by returning through Slade, but we somehow lost our way and found ourselves after a long journey at a parting of the road where we were in utter uncertainty which way to turn for Ilfracombe. There was no fingerpost, no men near enough to shout to, so we could only adopt Corporal Nym's philosophy – say "things must be as they may", and prove the existence of free will by making a choice without a motive. At last we came in sight of a lone farm-house, and I waited at the gate while G. went to inquire. After considerable knocking a woman put her head reluctantly out of an upper window and after some parleying conveyed the half comforting, half distracting information that we were on the right way for Ilfracombe, but were still *tu mile* away from it. It requires some desperate courage to make these interrogatory visits to lone farm-houses, for you are likely to get a prompt but not categorical answer to your questions from a great dog who protects the premises in the absence of the males.

Our next long walk was to Chambercombe – a name apparently belonging to some woods and a solitary farm-house, for we could see nothing else except fields. G. found out this walk one day and then took me there one lovely, sunshiny day. The chief beauties of the walk began when we arrived at a gate leading into a farm yard which forms a sort of ganglion to two lanes branching from it. Close to this gate there is a spring which is a perfect miniature of some Swiss "Falls". It spreads itself like a crystal fan on successive ledges of the hedge-bank until it reaches a much broader ledge where it forms a little lake on a bed of brown pebbles; then down it goes again till it reaches the level of the road and runs along as a tiny river. What a picture this farm yard remains in my memory! The cows staring at us with formidable timidity, such as I have sometimes seen in a human being who frightens others while he is frightened himself; and the cow-man who pointed out our way to us through the next gate. Just beyond this gate there was a little widening in the lane – several gateways occurring together and here the wild verdure and flowers of the hedgerow and the roadside seemed to take the opportunity of becoming more luxuriant than usual. A few rough trunks lying against the tufts of fern and a quiet donkey made the bit perfect as a foreground, and close behind it rose a steep hill half orchard and half grass. The first time we took this walk the primroses were still abundant, but they were beginning to be eclipsed by the other flowers of the hedgerow. As we advanced along this lane chatting happily and gathering flowers we could see before us the overlapping hills covered by the Chambercombe woods. At length we came to a spot where a brook runs across the lane and a little wooden bridge is provided for foot-passengers. A rough hurdle is fixed up where the brook gushes from the field into the lane over brown stones that the water polishes into agate; against the little bridge there is a tree, and all round its roots by the side of the brook there are tufts of varied leafage. Over the bridge and through a little gate and you approach another farm yard – if it is large enough for so dignified a name. There is a small shabby house, with broken windows mended with rags, called the Haunted House, and from the yard there suddenly rises a rough hill clothed with trees and brushwood. A great awkward puppy which came flopping after us was always an incident at this yard as we passed it. On and on, looking at the fields and woods, until we came to a shady spot which tempted us to sit down. G. smoked a cigar and we looked at the sunlight living like a spirit among the branches of the hanging woods – looked too at a caterpillar which happened to be spending its transitional life, happily knowing nothing of transitions, on the bush beside us. Then we walked on towards the wood and threaded our way under its low branches, listening to the birds and the dash and ripple of water, until we came to the water itself – a streamlet running between the hills, and winding its way among the trees while the sunlight made its way between the leaves and flashed on the braided ripples. Here and everywhere about Ilfracombe the base of the trees and the banks of the lanes are made peculiarly lovely by a delicate trefoil. As we came home again the sea stretching beyond the massive hills towards the horizon looked all the finer to us because we had been turning our backs upon it, and contemplating another sort of beauty.

Of other walks by and bye, when I have said something of our evenings, and other Ilfracombe experience. We seemed to make less of our evenings here than we have ever done elsewhere. We used often to be tired with our hunting or walking and we were reading books which did not make us take them up very eagerly – Gosse's "Rambles on the Devonshire Coast", for example; Trench's Calderon; and other volumes taken up in a desultory way. One bit of reading we had there, however, which interested me deeply. It was Masson's "Life of Chatterton", which happily linked itself with the impressions I had received from the sight of the old church at Bristol. An hour of the evening light used often to slip away in attention to our animals. This helped to make our reading time scanty; and another *distraction* was an occasional visit to Mrs. and Miss Webster – a visit always made agreeable by music. I enjoyed playing to them, because G. seemed to like it as well as they.

On the 29th of May, of course, Ilfracombe set itself to work to rejoice by royal command, at the ratification of the Peace, and we expected to be considerably amused by the spectacle of the Ilfracombe festivities. Pretty, bright little Mrs. Ashwell, our hostess's daughter, helped her brother to make a grand maypole of coloured streamers floating among boughs of laburnum, which was hoisted on the roof of the house, and at 4 o'clock, she told us, she was to go and help make tea which was to be given in the High Street to the working people. So at 4 o'clock, we walked to the High Street, which seemed a chaos of people and tables. Here and there tea was really going on: pretty children were seated with their mug in one hand and their piece of cake in the other, and near them we saw Mrs. Ashwell looking red hot in a primrose-coloured bonnet. Passing along the High Street we met a cavalcade mounting the hill, which, I suppose was intended to symbolize the allied armies – four or five men in miscellaneous uniforms mounted on Rosinantes. After a turn or two on the Capstone we came back again to the High Street to see the festivities in a more advanced stage. The melancholy foot-races of the boys suggested the idea that they were conducted on the principle of the donkey races – the slowest boy winning. At all events in Ilfracombe "the race is not to the swift".[4] In the evening there were some feeble fire-works on the Capstone, and, what was better, bonfires on Hillsborough and the highest of the Tors. It was fine to see these bonfires flashing upwards and then gradually dying out, and made one think of the times when such fires were lighted as signals to arm – the symbol of a common cause and a common feeling.

Another bit of primitive provincial life which used to amuse us were the announcements of the Town crier. On one occasion, for example, he came to inform us, with supererogatory aspirates, that "*H*ironsides, the American Wonder", would start from the London Inn, and walk so many miles in so many minutes, carrying tremendous weights during the last mile. A graver announcement was the fact of two burglaries having been committed, and we never heard that the offenders had been discovered during our stay.

Mr Tugwell's acquaintance was a real acquisition to us, not only because he was a companion and helper in zoological pursuits, but because to know him was to know of another sweet nature in the world. It is always good to know, if only in passing, a charming human being – it refreshes one like flowers, and woods and clear brooks. One Sunday evening we walked up to his pretty house to carry back some proofs of his, and he induced us to go in and have coffee with him. He played on his Harmonium and we chatted pleasantly. The last evening of our stay at Ilfracombe he came to see us in Mrs. Webster's drawing room, and we had music until nearly 11 o'clock. A pleasant recollection!

We only twice took the walk beyond Watermouth towards Berry Narbor. The road lies through what are called the "Meadows", which look like a magnificent park. A stream fringed with wild flowers and willows runs along the valley, two or three yards from the side of the road. This stream is clear as crystal, and about every twenty yards it falls over a little artificial precipice of stones. The long grass was waving in all the glory of June before the mower has come to make it suffer a "love-change" from beauties into sweet odours; and the slopes on each side of us

4 Ecclesiastes 9.11.

were crowned or clothed with fine trees. Little Gyp, Mrs. Webster's dog, whom we had made our pet, was our companion in this walk, exciting, as usual a sensation among the sheep and lambs with his small person, and giving us strong hints to move on when we rested a little too long for his taste. The last time we went through these meadows was on our last day at Ilfracombe. Such sunlight and such deep peace on the hills and by the stream! Coming back we rested on a gate under the trees, and a blind man came up to rest also. He told us in his slow way what a fine "healthy spot" this was – yes a very healthy spot – a healthy spot. And then we went on our way and saw his face no more.

More frequently we walked only as far as Watermouth – and this was a grand walk – over the edges of tall cliffs, revealing to us one inlet after another, each differing in its shades of colour. The limit of our walk was usually somewhere near a handsome castellated house belonging to Mr. Basset, and standing near the little arm of the sea which I suppose is properly "Watermouth", so that he has two very different kinds of beauty from his windows – the sea and the bold rocks, and the charming valley of meadows, with their rippling stream.

One more favourite walk I must record. It was along the Braunton road for a little way; then we turned up a lane which led us by the cemetery and here just where a clear brook (where is there *not* a clear brook in Devonshire?) the lane brought us to a gateway leading into a wood. And now we could either take a steep road leading up the hill among the trees until we came out where this same road formed a belt below the furze covered summit of the hill; or we could go right on along the lane that skirted the wood until we came to another gateway leading into another wood, which clothed another hill. Skirting this second wood we had a ravine below us on our right hand, and could hear the music of the brook at the bottom. The sides of this ravine were feathered with the light, graceful boughs of the ash occasionally thrown into relief by the darker oak. On and on, till we came to a turn on our left, and mounted a very steep road where the wood ceased and we had on one side a wall starred with the delicate pink flowers of a lovely rock plant and on the other some picturesque broken ground. From the breezy field at the top we had a fine view, and G. took advantage of the freedom from the criticism of neighbouring ears to have a lusty shout.

One day we carried out our project of approaching the ravine from the Braunton road, and attempting to walk along it close by the stream. Just about the spot where this ravine begins there is a cottage which seems to be a tributary to a rather important looking farm-house standing near. As we approached this cottage, we were descried by a black pig, probably of an amiable and sociable disposition. But as unfortunately our initiation in porcine physiognomy was not deep enough to allow of any decisive inferences, we felt it an equivocal pleasure to perceive that piggie had made up his mind to join us in our walk without the formality of an introduction. So G. put himself in my rear and made intimations to piggie that his society was not desired, and though very slow to take a hint, he at last turned back and we entered the path by the stream among the brushwood, not without some anxiety on my part lest our self elected companion should return. Presently a grunt assured us that he was on our traces; G. resorted in vain to hishes, and, at last, instigated as he says, by me, threw a stone and hit piggie on the chop. This was final. He trotted away, squealing, as fast as his legs would carry him; but my imagination had become so fully possessed with fierce pigs and the malignity of their bite, that I had no more peace of mind until we were fairly outside the gate that took us out of piggie's haunts. G.'s peace of mind was disturbed for another reason: he was remorseful that he had bruised the cheek of a probably affectionate beast, and the sense of this crime hung about him for several days. I satisfied my conscience by thinking of the addition to the pig's *savoir vivre* that might be expected from the blow; he would in future wait to be introduced.

I have talked of the Ilfracombe lanes without describing them, for to describe them one ought to know the names of all the lovely wild flowers that cluster on their banks. Almost every yard of these banks is a "Hunt" picture – a delicious crowding of mosses and delicate trefoil, and wild strawberries, and ferns great and small. But the crowning beauty of the lanes is the springs, that gush out in little recesses by the side of the road – recesses glossy with liver-wort and feathery with fern. Sometimes you have the spring when it has grown into a brook, either rushing down a miniature cataract by the lane side, or flowing gently, as a "braided streamlet" across your path. I never before longed so much to know the names of things as during this visit to Ilfracombe. The desire is part of the tendency that is now constantly growing in me to escape from all vagueness and inaccuracy into the daylight of distinct, vivid ideas. The mere fact of naming an object tends to give definiteness to our conception of it – we have then a sign which at once calls up in our minds the distinctive qualities which mark out for us that particular object from all others.

We ascended the Tors only twice; for a tax of 3d. per head was demanded on this luxury, and we could not afford a sixpenny walk very frequently. On both occasions Mr. Webster was with us – on the second, Mr. Tugwell and Alice Webster, so that I associate the walk rather with conversation than with scenery. Yet the view from the Tors is perhaps the very finest to be had at Ilfracombe. Bay behind bay fringed with foam, and promontory behind promontory each with its peculiar shades of purple light – the sweep of the Welsh Coast faintly visible in the distance, and the endless expanse of sea flecked with ships stretching on our left.

One evening we went down to the shore through the Tunnels to see the sunset. Standing in the "Ladies' Cove" we had before us the sharp fragments of rock jutting out of the waves and standing black against the orange and crimson sky. How lovely to look into that brilliant distance and see the ship on the horizon seeming to sail away from the cold and dim world behind it right into the golden glory! I have always that sort of feeling when I look at sunset; it always seems to me that there, in the west, lies a land of light and warmth and love.

On the 26th of June it was that we said good bye to Ilfracombe and started by the steamer at 9 o'clock for Swansea, where we had to wait three hours before going on by railway to Narberth Road, on our way to Tenby. Swansea looked dismal and smelt detestably, but we had one sight there quite worth the annoyance of waiting. It was the sight of two "Cockle women", who would make a fine subject for a painter. One of them was the grandest woman I ever saw – six feet high, carrying herself like a Greek Warrior, and treading the earth with unconscious majesty. They wore large woollen shawls of a rich brown, doubled lengthwise, with the end thrown back again over the left shoulder so as to fall behind in graceful folds. The grander of the two carried a great pitcher in her hand, and wore a quaint little bonnet set upright on her head. Her face was weather beaten and wizened, but her eyes were bright and piercing and the lines of her face, with its high cheek-bones strong and characteristic. The other carried her pitcher on her head, and was also a fine old woman, but less majestic in her port than her companion. The guard at the railway told us that one of the porters had been insolent the other day to a cockle woman, and that she immediately pitched him off the platform into the road below!

Tenby, July 22 1856

VIII. *Recollections of the Scilly Isles and Jersey 1857*

This pair of 'Recollections' runs parallel to GE's diary for the period from 15 March 1857 when they left home, to their return to Richmond on 25 July. They were in the Scilly Isles from 26 March to 11 May, and in Jersey from 15 May to 24 July. The expedition recounted here, like that in 'Recollections of Ilfracombe', was undertaken in the interests of GHL's seaside studies. As early as October 1856 he wrote to Blackwood about 'a slowly cherished scheme of mine to pass the spring months of next year at the Scilly Isles – ground unvisited, almost, by travellers, and quite *unwritten* about; ground obviously rich in zoology, and likely to furnish material which the world at large as well as naturalists will be glad to have'.[1] GE's phraseology suggests that GHL's 'slowly cherished scheme' had become something of an obsession ('a fixed idea'), but he wrote it up in *Sea-Side Studies* in a sprightly vein: 'March was already come, the equinoctial gales were near, and the Isles of Scilly beckoned like syrens from their dangerous shores.'[2]

GE dates the beginning of her 'Recollections of the Scilly Isles' 28 June, the day following that on which she notes in her diary 'Finished the second Part of "Janet's Repentance".' As usual, these 'Recollections' amplify the diary account, offering greater detail, particularly in the form of anecdote and natural description. In addition, GE implies in her account of their journey to the Scilly Isles that she does not propose to repeat material from the diary, but rather to complement it in her essay. There are other complementary texts: letters of both GE and GHL, together with his journals, and of course *Sea-Side Studies* (which does not borrow from these 'Recollections').

This pair of essays follows the pattern of earlier ones, with fine natural descriptions, accounts of sorties along the coast and inland, and a keen but sometimes whimsical interest in the local people and their doings. There are lists of reading as eclectic and erudite as ever: particularly notable are the readings of two recently published works about a woman artist, Gaskell's *Life of Charlotte Bronte* and E. B. Browning's *Aurora*

1 *The Letters of George Henry Lewes*, ed. William Baker, 2 vols. (University of Victoria, English Literary Studies Monograph Series 64, 1995), vol. 1, p. 250.

2 G. H. Lewes, *Sea-Side Studies* (Edinburgh, Blackwood, 1858), p. 180.

Leigh ('for the second time'), and the run on Jane Austen: in addition to the novels GE mentions, GHL noted in his journal on 5 June 'After lunch we took *Sense and Sensibility* with us and lying down in the shade behind the castle read it aloud.' Little of GE's pleasure in their botanising comes through in these essays, though it does emerge elsewhere, for instance in such letters as that to Sara Hennell on 5 June 1857.[3]

This was a troubled time for GE, though the 'Recollections' give only oblique hints of her distress. She records with feeling the illness of her sister Chrissey and two nieces, and the death of one of them, but does not refer to the correspondence mentioned in the diary with Holbeche, the Evans family lawyer, who interrogates her about her relationship with Lewes on her brother's behalf: a source of distress to compound her other ailments. GHL had family news of a kind, too, recording in his journal for 28 May 'Letter from Agnes announcing another girl' (Mildred Lewes, last child of Agnes and Thornton Hunt, born 21 May).

Both GE and GHL found Jersey something of a relief after the more austere Scilly Isles, though GHL had other reasons for responding to Jersey:

> Nothing could be more charming than the welcome smiled by the rich meadow-lands and orchards there. After the bold picturesque solitudes of Scilly, it seemed like once more entering civilised nature . . . there is no such spot [as Jersey] in England for marine zoology. Besides all these charms, it had other charms in my eyes. Memory consecrated the ground. Eight-and-twenty years ago I was at school here.[4]

Haight, *Letters*, publishes both 'Recollections' complete; Cross prints selections.

3 *The George Eliot Letters*, ed. Gordon S. Haight, 9 vols. (New Haven, Yale University Press, 1954–78), vol. 2, p. 341.

4 Lewes, *Sea-Side Studies*, pp. 268, 270; cf. *Letters of GHL*, vol. 1, p. 265.

VIII. Recollections of the Scilly Isles and Jersey 1857

Recollections of the Scilly Isles, 1857

It is now the 28th of June, and it seems a long, long while since we said goodbye to kind-looking Charlotte at the Richmond Station on Sunday evening, the 15th of March. G. had a fixed idea that it would be supremely delightful to be at the Scilly Isles at the Spring Equinox, and so we set off in all the certain uncertainty of March weather. A comfortable night at the Paddington Railway Hotel and a bright morning, made an auspicious beginning of our journey, and it was still fine when we reached Plymouth, so that we could walk out on the Hoe, and get a view. But Mount Edgecumbe was leafless then, and the distances were clad in smoky haze. The Globe Hotel, where we put up, was very comfortable, but I was suffering from headache and general malaise, and was unable to enjoy any thing. In the morning we walked out to buy a basket for zoophyte hunting and learned that the excitement we saw in the town was owing to the expectation of Mr. Spurgeon, who was going to preach for the benefit of an indebted Chapel. At 10 or half past, we mounted the coach that was to convey us to Truro and had a cold but not unpleasant journey. I have described our companions in my journal, as well as our week's sojourn at Penzance while we waited for the weather, and our first glimpse of the Scilly Isles as we ascended sick and weary from our berths in the Ariadne. Captain Tregarthen recommended us to take lodgings at the Post Office, kept by Mrs. Scadden, a very nice woman, so to the Post Office we went, and were very well pleased with the rooms, which were clean and well-sized. We had not formed a very brilliant conception of Scilly lodgings, so that there was not much room for disappointment. A little damsel about twelve, came in to attend to the fire, and turning with a smile to me, said, Please, my name's Joyce if you want any thing. Joyce, however was not our usual attendant, but a nice-mannered girl of eighteen. Poor little Joyce was an orphan and had been taken into service from the Union by our landlady Mrs Scadden, whom we liked very well for the first day or two, when we discovered no other qualities than blandness and honesty, which do not always go together. A nearer acquaintance made it evident that there were great resources of stupidity in her, which, with the difficulty of getting meat at Scilly, made the victualling department a matter of considerable anxiety. After one desperate effort at luxury – sending for a loin of mutton, which turned out to be all fat, and a couple of fowls, which were of patriarchal toughness, from Penzance – we resigned ourselves to the monotony of beef and fried polack, the only flesh easily procurable. Partly from the food perhaps, partly from the weather and climate, we were not well at Scilly, and I had a further cause for physical depression in the deep trouble and anxiety I was in on Chrissey's account. We had not been at St. Mary's a fortnight, I think, when the news came of her illness and little Fanny's death – sweet little fair Fanny – and the sad struggle of feeling I had for weeks between the wish to be with her and the impossibility of going to her without renouncing other duties more important, made the time pass painfully in spite of the constant love and mental occupation that filled the days. This will always make the remembrance of Scilly half painful, though the sight of its unique scenery is really an acquisition.

I had never before seen a granite coast, and on the southern side of the island of St. Mary's one sees such a coast in its most striking and characteristic forms. Rectangular crevices, the edges of which have been rounded by weather give many of the granite masses a resemblance to bales of wool or cotton heaped on each other; another characteristic form is the mushroom shaped mass often lying poised on the summits of more cubical boulders or fragments; another is the immense flat platform stretching out like a pier into the sea; another the oval basins formed by the action of the rain water on the summits of the rocks and boulders. The colouring of the rocks was very various and beautiful; sometimes a delicate greyish green from the shaggy byssus which clothes it, chiefly high up from the water; then a light warm brown; then black; occasionally of a rich yellow; and here and there purplish. Below the rocks on the coast are almost everywhere heaps of white boulders, sometimes remarkably perfect ovals, and looking like huge eggs of some monstrous bird. Hardly any weed was to be seen on the granite, except here and there in a rock pool green with young ulva; and no barnacles incrust the rock, no black muscles, scarcely any limpets. The waves that beat on this coast are clear as crystal, and we used to delight in watching them rear themselves like the horses of a mighty sea god as they approached the rocks on which they were broken into eddies of milky foam. The most striking points of the coast were Peninis, a grand promontory where the granite is broken into many separate piles; the Pulpit Rock; Porthelik, a bay where there are huge boulders scattered about the sands, so that at low water, it looks like a giants' playground; the giant's castle; and a jutting wall of rock coloured of the richest yellow ochre tint, towards the Eastern end of the island – of which I could not learn the name. Along a great part of this southern coast, there stretch heathy or furzy downs, over which I used to enjoy rambling immensely; – there is a sense of freedom on those unenclosed grounds that one never has in a railed Park, however extensive.

Then, on the north side of the island, above Sandy Bar; what a view we used to get of the opposite islands and reefs, with their delicious violet and yellow tints – the tall ship or two anchored in the Sound changing their aspect like living things – and when the wind was at all high the white foam prancing round the reefs and rising in fountain-like curves above the screen of rocks. Sandy Bar was one of our frequent objects in our walks – a long stretch of fine pale sand where the large roots of the *laminaria* were thrown up in abundance. It was here we found our first comatula, which looked small and insignificant when we first set eyes on it clutching the root of the laminaria, but expanded like a red and white fern when we put it into the bottle.

Many a wet and dirty walk we had along the lanes, for the weather was often wet and almost always blustering. Now and then however, we had a clear sky and a calm sea, and on such days it was delicious to look up after the larks that were singing above us, or to look out on the island and reef-studded sea. I never enjoyed the lark before, as I enjoyed it at Scilly – never felt the full beauty of Shelley's poem on it before. On wet days the most convenient walk was the Garrison hill, which was in its highest beauty when we arrived. It is covered with splendid furze, with here and there an opening where you see a little rabbit trotting from bush to bush, or a deer making haste to get out of your sight. The hill is a good height and from its highest part, one gets a curious view of St. Agnes with its light-house and its far-stretching chain of reefs. Four pyramidal reefs at the extremity of the chain have been named by the imaginative Scillonians, the Great and Little Smith, and the Haycocks! On the other side lies Trescaid with its sister islands enclosing the sound, for ever changing in the loveliness of their aspect, with the changing sky and sea.

A spot we became very fond of towards the close of our stay was Carne Lea, where between two fine jutting piles of granite there was a soft down gay with the pretty pink flowers of the thrift, which on this island carpets the ground like greensward. Here we used to sit and lie in the bright afternoons, watching the silver sunlight on the waves – bright silver, not golden – it is the morning and evening sunlight that is golden.

A week or two after our arrival we made the acquaintance of Mr. Moyle, the surgeon, who became a delightful friend to us, always ready to help with the contents of his surgery or anything else at his command. We liked to have him come and smoke a cigar in the evening, and look in now and then for a little lesson in microscopy, but we were quite determined for a long while to have no other acquaintances at Scilly. At length, however, he persuaded us to see our next door neighbours the Buckstones, and we dined with them once – a fine old Father, deaf and paralytic, but still intelligent, a silly, ill-bred woman without the slightest presentiment of anything in existence superior to herself, and a stupid, goodnatured, unaffected husband. The husband took us one day to see the new lighthouse being prepared for erection on one of the outer reefs near St. Agnes – the Bishop's Rock, I think. Every morsel of the structure is prepared and fitted before it is carried to the spot, and the light house is thus temporarily built up and taken to pieces again.

The little indications of the social life at Scilly, that we were able to pick up were very amusing. I was repeatedly told, in order to make me aware who Mr. Hall was, that he married a Miss Lemon. The people at St. Mary's imagine that the lawyers and doctors at Penzance are a sort of European characters that every one knows.

We heard a great deal about Mr. Quill, an Irishman, the controller of the customs, and one day that we called on the Buckstones, Mr Buckstone said two or three times at intervals, "I wish you knew Quill!" At last, on our farewell call, we saw the distinguished Quill, with his hair plaistered down, his charming smile, and his trowsers with a broad stripe down each leg. Mr Buckstone amused us by his contempt for curs – 'O, I wouldn't have a cur – there's nothing to look at in a cur.'

Our readings aloud were Cromwell's Letters, Aurora Leigh (for the 2nd time), Life of Charlotte Bronte, Maury's Physical Geography of the Sea, Twelfth Night and Macbeth, Northanger Abbey and Persuasion. I read the Œdipus Tyrannus and the Œdipus Coloneus, De Quincey's Glories of Stage Coach Travelling and Revolt of the Tartars, and the greater part of Shelley's Poems.

We left St. Mary's on the 11th of May about 2 o'clock in the windless after-noon; but after a while a little breeze sprang up, and the good little sailing yacht Ariadne, carried us into Mount's Bay, Penzance about 10 o'clock at night. We went to Dingley's, a quiet comfortable family hotel, and remained there all the next day, enjoying very much our walk through the Penzance lanes and fields, "fed full of noises"[1] by streams not "invisible" but beautifully visible in their clearness as they leaped or rippled over the brown stones. The next morning we went on the top of the omnibus to Falmouth, and after resting and lunching walked through the town to the castle, from which we had a fine view of the pretty harbour. The evening passed by pleasantly reading *Emma*, and early the next morning we set off by the 'Sir F. Drake' to Plymouth. The fog was so dense, that the vessel was stopped repeatedly in order to ascertain how far we were from the shore; but at length it cleared away, and we got into Plymouth Harbour safely under a broiling sun. After dining and resting on shore we returned on board the same vessel at 5 o'clock, and after a night of misery in my berth, I came on deck yellow and frowsy to look at the shores of Jersey. We went to Jeune's Hotel in Royal Square, and were very comfortable there. A walk to St. Aubin's in search of lodgings filled up the time till dinner, but we determined not to decide on our residence till we had seen and considered more, so we remained at the hotel that night and in the morning set out by omnibus to Gorey, which G. thought would be more likely to suit his zoological purposes than St. Aubin's, where there are no fishermen. Gorey proved to be just what we wanted and to Gorey we came, with our traps filling one fly inside and outside, on Saturday evening, the 16th of May.

Recollections of Jersey. 1857

It was a beautiful moment when we came to our lodgings at Gorey. The orchards were all in blossom – and this is an island of orchards. They cover the slopes; they

1 Elizabeth Barrett Browning, *Aurora Leigh* (1856), Book 1, l. 1086, 'Fed full of noises by invisible streams'.

stretch before you in shady, grassy, indefinite extent through every other gateway by the roadside; they flourish in some spots almost close to the sea. What a contrast to the Scilly Isles! There you stand on the hills like a sparrow on the house-top; here you are like the same sparrow when he is hopping about on the branches with green above him, green below, and green all round. Gorey stands on Grouville Bay, where the grand old castle of Mont Orgueil stands and keeps guard on a fine rocky promontory overlooking the little harbour, dotted with fishing craft. The other "limb" of the bay is formed by the St. Clement Reefs which stretch their desultory length far out into the sea, one of them forming the site of a martello tower. Similar towns are placed at intervals almost all round the bay. There is an immense belt of sand laid bare at low water, but it is so uneven and consequently wet, that except towards St. Clement's reefs, one can get no nice walking on the beach. As some compensation, there is a charming piece of common or down, where you can have the quietest easiest walking, with a carpet of minute wild flowers that are not hindered from flourishing by the sandy rain of the coast. I delighted extremely in the brownish green softness of this undulating common, here and there varied with a patch of bright green fern – all the prettier for two little homesteads set down upon it with their garden fence and sheltering trees. It was pretty in all lights, but especially the evening light to look round at the castle and harbour, the village, and the scattered dwellings peeping out from among trees on the hill. The castle is built of stone which has a beautiful pinkish grey tint, and the bright green ivy hangs oblique curtains on its turreted walls, making it look like a natural continuation or outgrowth of the rocky and grassy height on which it stands. Then the eye wanders on to the right and takes in the church standing halfway down the hill, which is clothed with a plantation and shelters the little village with its cloud of blue smoke; still to the right, and the village breaks off, leaving nothing but meadows in front of the slope that shuts out the setting sun and only lets you see a hint of the golden glory that is reflected in the pink eastern clouds.

The first lovely walk we found inland was the Queen's Farm Valley, where a broad strip of meadow and pasture lies between two high slopes covered with woods and ferny wilderness. Pursuing the road to the right as we entered the valley from Gorey, we first ascended a little and saw the grassy flat, with a water-mill, a little pool, a farm-house, and farther on a pasture with tethered cows lying below us; then we began to descend always by the wood side, with the birds singing and the sunlight shimmering in the boughs above us, the curious fresh green *Euphorbia* inviting our attention on the bank close by us, until we came quite to the depth of the valley, and winding our way along a narrow path with a clear musical brook running between banks fringed with long grasses and fern, stopping to pat the mild cows tethered with a view to those long grasses, we reached at last a *perfect* pond – on one side overhung by the outermost bows of the hanging wood, on another bordered by a meadow with its tall grasses, on another by the narrow footpath edged with young oaks. A current ran through the pond, making a river between the tiny forests of white blossoms that covered almost all the rest of the surface. When we first saw this valley it was in the loveliest spring-time: the woods were a delicious mixture of red and tender green and purple. We have watched it losing that spring beauty, passing into the green and flowery luxuriance of June, and now into the more monotonous summer tint of July.

When the blossoms fell away from the orchards my next delight was to look at the grasses mingled with the red sorrel; then came the white umbelliferous plants making a border or inner frame for them along the hedgerows and streams. Another pretty thing here is the luxuriance of the yellow iris that covers large pieces of moist ground with its broad blades. Every where there are tethered cows, looking at you with meek faces – mild eyed, sleek fawn-coloured creatures, with delicate downy udders.

Another favourite walk of ours was round by Mont Orgueil along the coast. Here we had the green or rocky slope on one side of us and on the other the calm sea stretching to the coast of France, visible on all but the murkiest days. But the murky days were not many during our stay, and our evening walks round the coast usually showed us a peaceful, scarcely rippled sea, plashing gently on the purple pebbles of the little scalloped bays. There were two such bays within the boundary of our sea-side walk in that direction, and one of them was a perpetual wonder to us in the luxuriant verdure of meadows and orchards and forest trees that sloped down to the very shore. No distressed look about the trees, as if they were ever driven harshly back by the wintry winds – it was like an inland slope suddenly carried to the coast.

As for the inland walks, they are inexhaustible. The island is one labyrinth of delicious roads and lanes, leading you by the most charming nooks of houses with shady grounds and shrubberies – delightful farm homesteads – and trim villas.

It was a sweet, peaceful life we led here – good creatures, the Amys, our host and hostess, with their nice boy and girl and the little white kid, the family pet. No disagreeable sounds to be heard in the house, no unpleasant qualities to hinder one from feeling perfect love to these simple people. – We have had long rambles and long readings. But our choice of literature has been rather circumscribed in this out of the way place. The Life of George Stephenson has been a real profit and pleasure. I have read Draper's Physiology aloud, for grave evening hours, and such books as Currer Bell's 'Professor', Mde. d'Auney's Mariage en Provence and Miss Ferrier's "Marriage" for lighter food. The last, however, we found ourselves unable to finish, notwithstanding Miss Ferrier's high reputation. I have been getting a smattering of botany from Miss Catlow and from Dr. Thomson's little book on Wild Flowers, which have created at least a longing for something more complete on the subject.

Our only carriage expedition here has been to Bouley Bay, one delicious evening when the sea was glassy smooth. The coast there is an agreeable contrast to that on the Gorey side of the island – tall hills with curving slopes, and perpendicular indentations making dark shadows on the soft green. We came back by Rozel Bay, also pretty.

An amusing episode for us in our quiet life was the Gorey Races which happened on the 15th and 16th of July. We strolled about the ground and saw a little of Jersey human nature between the races – men at the gambling tables, and the crowd round a company of mountebanks.

On the 24th we left this green island – a sweet spot in our memories, while our memories last.

IX. *The Making of George Eliot 1857–1859*

'How I came to write Fiction' and 'History of Adam Bede'

Cara Bray wrote to her sister Sara Hennell on 25 September 1846 Miss Evans 'looks very brilliant just now. We fancy she must be writing her novel'.[1] If Mary Ann Evans, who had published anonymously her translation of Strauss's *Life of Jesus* in June 1846, was writing fiction in September, she did not then confide in her friends, any more than she did when *Scenes of Clerical Life* began its anonymous serial appearance in 1857. By that time the nomenclature of 'Miss Evans' was thoroughly fraught.

Several times during 1857 GE was edgily concerned with names and forms of address. She carefully phrased her belated announcement to her brother Isaac of her union with GHL: 'You will be surprized, I dare say, but I hope not sorry, to learn that I have changed my name, and have someone to take care of me in the world'.[2] Her intention is to declare her *de facto* status as Mrs Lewes, concealing the other name change she had made in her choice of the pseudonym, George Eliot. In September, she wrote to her friend Bessie Parkes, 'you must please not call me *Miss Evans* again' (*Letters*, vol. 2, p. 384: later, 5 July 1859, she emphasised 'My *name* is Marian Evans *Lewes*', vol. 3, p. 111). In these instances, her sensitivity to the stigma attaching to her unsanctioned relationship with GHL is plain. Marian Evans Lewes was already concealing sexual transgression, and sought additional protection in an authorial signature. Consciousness of the need to avoid scandal is patent in GHL's protestations when the secret of the identity of George Eliot is out:

> It makes me angry to think that people should say that the secret has been kept because there was any *fear* of the effect of the author's name. You may tell it openly to all who care to hear it that the object of anonymity was to get the book judged on its own merits, and not prejudged as the work of

1 *George Eliot's Life as related in her letters and journals, arranged and edited by her husband J. W. Cross*, vol. 1, p. 149. It was perhaps 'Poetry and Prose from the Notebook of an Eccentric', published in the *Coventry Herald* on 4 December 1846, that occupied her.

2 26 May 1857, *The George Eliot Letters*, ed. Gordon S. Haight, 9 vols. (New Haven, Yale University Press, 1954–78), vol. 2, p. 331.

> a woman, or of a particular woman. ([30 June 1859], *Letters*, vol. 3, p. 106)

The conventional explanation for a woman's choosing a male pen-name, that the concealment of her gender enables her to compete on even terms in the literary marketplace, has peculiar potency in this case.

Already when she confessed to her brother and rebuked her friend, Marian Evans Lewes had chosen the name under which she planned to publish fiction. The only account of her choice of that particular name comes from John Cross: 'my wife told me the reason she fixed on this name was that George was Mr Lewes's Christian name, and Eliot was a good mouth-filling, easily-pronounced word' (Cross, vol. 1, pp. 430–1). Lewes's surname needed to be used for her conjugal name, but her connection with him is coded in her pen name as well by the use of his Christian name. Speculation that 'Eliot' was a play on 'to L. I owe it' seems to date from Blanche Colton Williams's biography of 1936. Any writer's decision to adopt a pseudonym, Philippe Lejeune argues, has clear implications:

> The pseudonym is the name of an *author.* It is not exactly a false name, but a pen name, a second name, exactly like the one a religious assumes upon taking orders. . . . Literary pseudonyms are in general neither mysteries nor hoaxes. The second name is as authentic as the first; it simply signals this second birth which is the published writing.[3]

The stress here on the sense of commitment to a vocation in taking a pen name is certainly exemplified in the case of GE, as – eventually – is the authenticity of the second name. For a time, though, the pseudonym 'George Eliot' was patently a mystery and apparently a hoax.

Having previously in correspondence with the publishing house of William Blackwood styled herself 'The Author of Amos Barton', she wrote on 4 February 1857:

3 Phillipe Lejeune, *On Autobiography*, ed. Paul John Eakin, trans. Katherine Leary (Minneapolis, University of Minnesota Press, 1989), p. 12. In quoting Lejeune here, we recognise that his arguments (in his 1975 '*Le pacte autobiographique*') are contentious interventions in the debate in which Roland Barthes's 'The death of the author' (1977) and Michel Foucault's 'What is an author?' (1969) are the best-known statements. A fuller discussion of the theoretical issues would engage with deconstructionist work on authorial signature, particularly that of Jacques Derrida, *Of Grammatology*, trans. Gayatri Chakravorty Spivak (Baltimore, Johns Hopkins University Press, 1976), and Peggy Kamuf, *Signature Pieces: On the Institution of Authorship* (Ithaca, Cornell University Press, 1988).

> Whatever may be the success of my stories, I shall be resolute in preserving my incognito, having observed that a *nom de plume* secures all the advantages without the disagreeables of reputation. Perhaps, therefore, it will be well to give you my prospective name, as a tub to throw to the whale in case of curious inquiries, and accordingly I subscribe myself, best and most sympathizing of editors,
>
> Yours very truly,
>
> George Eliot.
>
> (*Letters*, vol. 2, p. 292)

'The Sad Fortunes of the Reverend Amos Barton', the first of the *Scenes of Clerical Life*, began anonymous publication in *Blackwood's Edinburgh Magazine* in January 1857, and the series ran to November 1857. GE's first fiction coincided with her farewell to journalism: she was responsible for about one-quarter of the January 1857 issue of the *Westminster Review* ('Worldliness and Other-worldliness: the Poet Young', the last of her major essays, together with the 'Belles Lettres' and 'History, Biography, Voyages, and Travels' sections). At this time she wrote to Charles Bray – a little mendaciously – 'You needn't observe any secrecy about *articles* of mine. It is an advantage (pecuniarily) to me that I should be known as the writer of the articles in the *Westminster.*' (*Letters*, vol. 2, p. 287) Not until 28 February 1858 did Marian Evans Lewes reveal herself to her publishers as 'George Eliot', and not until the middle of 1859, and then under pressure, was the erstwhile secret of her authorship admitted to her friends.

The journals strikingly document the rite of passage which Rosemarie Bodenheimer sums up by saying 'simply that George Eliot was a woman who found her authority in writing'.[4] At this point she distances her account of her writing identity, the persona of 'George Eliot' under which her fiction went into the world, from her daily record of activity. This section of the journals appears at the same end of the 1854–1861

4 Rosemarie Bodenheimer, *The Real Life of Mary Ann Evans: George Eliot Her Letters and Fiction* (Ithaca and London, Cornell University Press, 1994), p. xvi. Bodenheimer illuminatingly discusses adoption and relinquishment of the pseudonym in Chapter 5, 'The Outing of George Eliot'. See also Alexis Easley, 'Authorship, Gender and Identity: George Eliot in the 1850s', *Women's Writing*, 3 (1996), pp. 143–60; Catherine A. Judd, 'Male Pseudonyms and Female Authority in Victorian England' in *Literature in the Marketplace: Nineteenth-Century British Publishing and Reading Practices*, ed. John O. Jordan and Robert L. Patten (Cambridge University Press, 1995), pp. 250–68; and Alexander Welsh, *George Eliot and Blackmail* (Cambridge, MA, Harvard University Press, 1985), pp. 113–31.

Diary as the 'Recollections' of Weimar and Berlin, and the three English 'Recollections', and immediately follows the last of these, 'Recollections of Jersey, 1857'. It is made up of two brief essays, 'How I came to write Fiction' and 'History of Adam Bede', intercalated with two runs of dated diary entries. The integrity of the sequence that begins with 'How I came to write Fiction' and continues through to the entry for 27 May 1859 has not previously been recognised. Our contention is that it is about the making of GE.

'How I came to write Fiction' is dated 'Dec. 6. 57', and is followed by an entry for 8 December reporting Blackwood's intention to publish an additional 250 copies of *Scenes of Clerical Life* with appropriate additional payment. At the other (diary) end, GE notes on 6 December their current reading (a characteristically rich mix: Agamemnon, Harriet Martineau and Macaulay), and again on 8 December (the Christmas number of *Household Words*). The entries at the diary or front end continue on to 9 May 1859, after which entry there is a rule, and the comment 'My Journal is continued at the opposite end, by mistake, as a continuation of the History of Adam Bede.' That is, for almost a year and a half, there are parallel texts in the two ends of the book, which were being used concurrently.

Our proposition is that GE went to the 'Recollections' end to set down memoranda about her public persona: that this section of the diary keeps separate from the person whose doings are jotted in the diary, the writing identity known already to Blackwood at the end of 1857 as 'George Eliot', and to be more widely known with the publication of *Scenes of Clerical Life* by George Eliot in two volumes on 5 January 1858 (the serial appeared anonymously rather than pseudonymously). The diary from 22 September 1856 when she began 'Amos Barton' has chronicled the composition and serial publication of her stories, but here is the point at which *Scenes* is to go out in a more substantial form. 'How I came to write Fiction' inaugurates documentation of the making of George Eliot, the novelist, consisting of her formalised accounts in the two essays of the experience and processes of decision in writing her first two works of fiction, and brief dated notes on publication arrangements and readers' responses both to *Scenes* and *Adam Bede*. These responses include among other transcribed tributes Dickens's extraordinary (or disingenuous?) letter of 18 January 1858, thanking George Eliot for sending him a copy of *Scenes*, and observing that 'If they originated with no woman, I believe that no man ever before had the art of making himself mentally so like a woman since the world began.' Bodenheimer shrewdly notes: 'The story of how a long-cherished dream is finally realized depends, in this account, on the validating responses of her audiences' (p. 126).

The sequence of entries to do with the sales and reception of *Scenes*, including Dickens's famous letter, continues to 3 April 1858, when we find 'I lay aside this record today – not to take it up again till we return from Germany in the Autumn.' That expedition – 14 April – 27 October 1858 – is the subject of a separate journal. Entries resume with more about the fortunes of *Scenes*, and then, with publication of her next work set down for 1 February 1859, she writes 'History of Adam Bede' dated 'Nov. 30. 1858.' Subsequent entries are all specific to *Adam Bede*, though some such as that for 12 February 1859 are very similar to entries at the other end. The sequence runs through to 1 June – 'At p. 85 of my new novel.' And here the diary 'is continued by mistake', and becomes again the journal of Marian Lewes – not, as it has been so far, George Eliot's journal. It continues so to 19 June 1861, when she signs off from this book (which is now full: the entry for 19 June 1861 is on the verso of that for 9 May 1859 in which she acknowledges her error).

The coincidence of dates is compelling, for this 'mistake' occurred in June 1859, right at the time when, reluctantly, Marian Evans Lewes was 'coming out' as George Eliot. The admission was forced by public controversy over the identity of George Eliot. Conjecture which pointed to the author of *Scenes of Clerical Life* as a native of Warwickshire began quite soon (together, if one heeds the dark hints of Blackwood's Langford, with accurate conjecture in some quarters as to just which native it might be: *Letters*, vol. 2, p. 298). Such speculation intensified with the publication of *Adam Bede*, the great success of which is chronicled in detail.[5] But the pleasure of success was spoiled by the painful experience of various people's laying claim to the authorship, notably one Joseph Liggins, son of a baker at Attleborough in the vicinity of Coventry. This matter, all but invisible in the journal, is highly visible in correspondence: there were reports of Liggins's claims early in April, gathering momentum as support for

5 Lejeune proposes that 'Perhaps one is an author only with his second book, when the proper name inscribed on the cover becomes the "common factor" of at least two different texts and thus gives the idea of the person who cannot be reduced to any of his texts in particular, and who, capable of producing others, surpasses them all' (*On Autobiography*, p. 11). This speculation resonates interestingly in GE's case.

him rallied, letters of denial in *The Times*, continued claims with new champions for Liggins, repeated denials, the emergence of the prototype for Amos Barton in June, and finally a swell of gossip which caused the secret to be yielded up. The Brays and Sara Hennell were told when they visited on 20 June, though urged '*Don't* say you know the authorship' (*Letters*, vol. 3, p. 91). Some readers knew intuitively: Barbara Bodichon in Algiers for one. She wrote in late April that 'one long extract' in a review 'instantly made me internally exclaim that is written by Marian Evans, there is her great big head and heart and her wise wide views' (p. 56). And Sara Hennell, once in the know, reported on 26 June: 'Mr. Evans of Griff has been heard to say, after reading Adam Bede – "No one but his Sister could write the book"' (vol. 2, p. 98).

In one light, the Liggins affair is ludicrous. But the Leweses' reactions to it betray their profound fear of scandal about the identity of 'George Eliot'. When GE wrote to Cara Bray in 1856, 'I can't tell you how happy I am in this double life',[6] she was referring to the harmony of her relationship with GHL: the double life she began under the two assumed names of George Eliot and Mrs Lewes was not so secure. Her secret could hardly have survived indefinitely, and it was well out by the time *The Mill on the Floss* was published on 4 April 1860. Despite the apprehensions both of the Blackwoods and the Leweses, sales did not suffer. The identity of George Eliot, a successful author, could be acknowledged.

Haight publishes 'How I came to write Fiction' and 'History of Adam Bede' complete; Cross publishes the former substantially and the latter complete. Each uses some of the additional memoranda, but neither sees the way in which these essays and memoranda have a particular integrity.

6 Kathleen Adams, '"Dear Cara": a newly discovered letter', *George Eliot Review*, 27 (1996), p. 37.

IX. The making of George Eliot 1857–1859

How I came to write Fiction

September 1856 made a new era in my life, for it was then I began to write Fiction. It had always been a vague dream of mine that some time or other I might write a novel, and my shadowy conception of what the novel was to be, varied, of course, from one epoch of my life to another. But I never went farther towards the actual writing of the novel than an introductory chapter describing a Staffordshire village and the life of the neighbouring farm houses, and as the years passed on I lost any hope that I should ever be able to write a novel, just as I desponded about everything else in my future life. I always thought I was deficient in dramatic power, both of construction and dialogue, but I felt I should be at my ease in the descriptive parts of a novel. My "introductory chapter" was pure description though there were good materials in it for dramatic presentation. It happened to be among the papers I had with me in Germany and one evening at Berlin, something led me to read it to George. He was struck with it as a bit of concrete description, and it suggested to him the possibility of my being able to write a novel, though he distrusted, indeed disbelieved in, my possession of any dramatic power. Still, he began to think that I might as well try, some time, what I could do in fiction, and by and bye when we came back to England and I had greater success than he had ever expected in other kinds of writing, his impression that it was worth while to see how far my mental power would go towards the production of a novel, was strengthened. He began to say very positively, "You must try and write a story", and when we were at Tenby he urged me to begin at once. I deferred it, however, after my usual fashion, with work that does not present itself as an absolute duty. But one morning as I was lying in bed, thinking what should be the subject of my first story, my thoughts merged themselves into a dreamy doze, and I imagined myself writing a story of which the title was – "The Sad Fortunes of the Reverend Amos Barton". I was soon wide awake again, and told G. He said, "O what a capital title!" and from that time I had settled in my mind that this should be my first story. George used to say, "It may be a failure – it may be that you are unable to write fiction. Or perhaps, it may be just good enough to warrant your trying again". Again, "You may write a chef-d'œuvre at once – there's no telling". But his prevalent impression was that though I could hardly write a *poor* novel, my effort would want the highest quality of fiction – dramatic presentation. He used to say, "You have wit, description and philosophy – those go a good way towards the production of a novel. It is worth while for you to try the experiment."

We determined that if my story turned out good enough, we would send it to

Blackwood, but G. thought the more probable result was, that I should have to lay it aside and try again.

But when we returned to Richmond I had to write my article on Silly Novels and my review of Contemporary Literature for the Westminister; so that I did not begin my story till September 22. After I had begun it, as we were walking in the Park, I mentioned to G. that I had thought of the plan of writing a series of stories containing sketches drawn from my own observation of the Clergy, and calling them "Scenes from Clerical Life" opening with "Amos Barton". He at once accepted the notion as a good one – fresh and striking; and about a week afterwards when I read him the early part of 'Amos', he had no longer any doubt about my ability to carry out the plan. The scene at Cross Farm, he said, satisfied him that I had the very element he had been doubtful about – it was clear I could write good dialogue. There still remained the question whether I could command any pathos, and that was to be decided by the mode in which I treated Milly's death. One night G. went to town on purpose to leave me a quiet evening for writing it. I wrote the chapter from the news brought by the shepherd to Mrs. Hackit, to the moment when Amos is dragged from the bedside and I read it to G. when he came home. We both cried over it, and then he came up to me and kissed me, saying "I think your pathos is better than your fun".

So when the story was finished G. sent it to Blackwood, who wrote in reply, that he thought the "Clerical reminiscences would do", congratulated the author on being "worthy the honours of print and pay", but would like to see more of the series before he undertook to print. However, when G. wrote that the author was discouraged by this editorial caution, Blackwood disclaimed any distrust and agreed to print the story at once. The first part appeared in the January No. 1857. Before the appearance of the Magazine – on sending me the proof, Blackwood already expressed himself with much greater warmth of admiration, and when the first Part had appeared, he sent me a charming letter, with a cheque for fifty guineas, and a proposal about republication of the series. When the story was concluded, he wrote me word how Albert Smith had sent him a letter saying he had never read anything that affected him more than Milly's death, and, added Blackwood, "the men at the club seem to have mingled their tears and their tumblers together. It will be curious if you should be a member and be hearing your own praises!" There was clearly no suspicion that I was a woman. It is interesting, as an indication of the value there is in such conjectural criticism generally, to remember that when G. read the first Part of "Amos" to a party at Helps's, they were all sure I was a clergyman – a Cambridge man. Agnes thought I was the father of a family – was sure I was a man who had seen a great deal of society etc. etc. Blackwood seemed curious about the author, and when I signed my letter "George Eliot" hunted up some old letters from Eliot Warburton's brother, to compare the handwritings, though, he said, "Amos seems to me not in the least like what that good artillery man would write". Several pleasant bits of admiration came about that time:- a letter from the Rev. Mr. Swaine, saying that "Amos", in its charming tenderness, reminded him of the "Vicar of Wakefield", is the only one I remember just now. The adverse critics mentioned by Blackwood were Colonel Hamley and Prof. Aytoun. Professor Aytoun came round afterwards, said he had been quite mistaken in his estimate of the powers of the author of "Amos Barton", and expressed great admiration of Mr. Gilfil's Love Story – or rather at the conclusion of it. Colonel Hamley said I was "a man of science, but not a practised writer". Blackwood was eager for the second story, and much delighted with the two first parts of "Mr Gilfil's Love Story", which I sent him together. I wrote the fourth part at Scilly – the epilogue, sitting on the Fortification Hill, one sunshiny morning. Blackwood himself wrote in entire admiration of it, and in the same letter told us that Thackeray "thought highly of the series". When we were at Jersey, he was in London, and wrote from thence that he heard nothing but approval of "Mr Gilfil's Love Story". Lord Stanley, among other people, had spoken to him about the "Clerical Scenes" at Bulwer's, and was astonished to find Blackwood in the dark as to the author.

I began Janet's Repentance at Scilly and sent off the first Part from Jersey, G. declaring it to be admirable, almost better than the other stories. But to my disappointment, Blackwood did not like it so well, seemed to misunderstand the characters, and be doubtful about the treatment of clerical matters. I wrote at once to beg him to give up printing the story if he felt uncomfortable about it, and he immediately sent a very anxious, cordial letter, saying the thought of putting a stop to the series "gave him quite a turn" – "he didn't meet with George Eliots every day" – and so on.

One of the pleasantest little incidents at Jersey was a letter from Archer Gurney to the unknown author of Mr. Gilfil's Love Story, expressing simply but warmly his admiration of the truth and originality he found in the Clerical Scenes. Dear G. came upstairs to me with the letter in his hands, his face bright with gladness, saying, "Her fame's beginning already!"

I had meant to carry on the series beyond Janet's Repentance, and especially I longed to tell the story of the Clerical Tutor, but my annoyance at Blackwood's want of sympathy in the first two parts of Janet (although he came round to admiration at the third part) determined me to close the series and republish them in two volumes.

The first volume is printed, and the advertisements greet our eyes every week, but we are still wondering how the public will behave to my first book.

Dec. 6. 57.

Dec. 8 [1857]. A letter from Blackwood today tells us that Major Blackwood during his brother's absence in England, having some reasons, not specified, for being more hopeful about the 'Clerical Scenes', resolved to publish 1000 instead of 750, and in consequence of this Blackwood proposes to pay me an additional

£60 when 750 shall have been sold off. He reports that an elderly clergyman has written to him to say that "Janet's Repentance" is exquisite – another vote to register along with that of Mrs Nutt's rector, who "cried over the story like a child."

Jan. 2 [1858]. George has returned this evening from a week's visit at Vernon Hill. On coming upstairs he said, "I have some very pretty news for you – something in my pocket!" I was at a loss to conjecture, and thought confusedly of possible opinions from admiring readers, when he drew the "Times" from his pocket;- today's number containing a review of the "Scenes of Clerical Life." He had happened to ask a gentleman in the railway carriage coming up to London to allow him a look at the "Times", and felt quite agitated and tremulous when his eyes alighted on the review. Finding he had time to go into town before the train started, he bought a copy there. It is a highly favourable notice, and as far as it goes, appreciatory.

When G. went into town he called at Nutt's, and Mrs. Nutt said to him "I think you don't know our curate. *He* says the author of Clerical Scenes is a High Churchman; for though Mr. Tryan is said to be Low Church, his *feelings* and *actions* are those of a High Churchman". (The Curate himself being, of course, High C.) There were some pleasant scraps of admiration also gathered for me at Vernon Hill. Doyle happening to mention the treatment of children in the stories, *Helps* said, "O, he is a great writer!"

I wonder how I shall feel about these little details ten years hence, if I am *alive*. At present I value them as grounds for hoping that my writing may succeed and so give value to my life – as indications that I can touch the hearts of my fellow men, and so sprinkle some precious grain as the result of the long years in which I have been inert and suffering. But at present fear and trembling still predominate over hope.

Jan. 5. Today the "Clerical Scenes" came in their two volume dress, looking very handsome.

Friday. 8. News of the subscription. 580, with a probable addition of 25 for Longmans. Mudie has taken 350. When we used to talk of the probable subscription G. always said, "I dare say it will be 250!" (The final number subscribed for was 650.)

I ordered copies to be sent to the following persons: Froude, Dickens, Thackeray, Tennyson, Ruskin, Faraday, "The author of Companions of my Solitude", Albert Smith, Mrs. Carlyle.

On the 20th of January I received the following letter from Dickens.

> Tavistock House, London
> Monday 18th January /58
> My dear Sir
>
> I have been so strongly affected by the two first tales in the book you have had the kindness to send me through Messrs.

Blackwood, that I hope you will excuse my writing to you to express my admiration of their extraordinary merit. The exquisite truth and delicacy, both of the humour and the pathos of those stories, I have never seen the like of; and they have impressed me in a manner that I should find it very difficult to describe to you, if I had the impertinence to try.

In addressing these few words of thankfulness to the creator of The Sad Fortunes of the Rev. Amos Barton and the sad love-story of Mr. Gilfil, I am (I presume) bound to adopt the name that it pleases that excellent writer to assume. I can suggest no better one; but I should have been strongly disposed, if I had been left to my own devices, to address the said writer as a woman. I have observed what seem to me such womanly touches in those moving fictions, that the assurance on the title-page is insufficient to satisfy me even now. If they originated with no woman, I believe that no man ever before had the art of making himself mentally so like a woman since the world began.

You will not suppose that I have any vulgar wish to fathom your secret. I mention the point as one of great interest to me – not of mere curiosity. If it should ever suit your convenience and inclination to show me the face of the man or woman who has written so charmingly, it will be a very memorable occasion to me. If otherwise, I shall always hold that impalpable personage in loving attachment and respect, and shall yield myself up to all future utterances from the same source with a perfect confidence in their making me wiser and better.

Your obliged and faithful Servant and admirer
Charles Dickens.

George Eliot Esq.

On the 21st came the following letter from Froude

Northdown House, Bideford
Jan 17
Dear Sir

I do not know when I have experienced a more pleasant surprise, than when on opening a book parcel two mornings ago, I found it to contain "Scenes of Clerical Life" "from the Author". I do not often see Blackwood, but in accidental glances I had made acquaintance with "Janet's Repentance", and had found there something extremely different from general Magazine stories. When I read the advertisement of the republication, I intended fully, at my leisure to look at the companions of the story which had so much struck me, and now I find myself sought out by the person whose workmanship I had admired, for the special present of it.

You would not, I imagine, care much for flattering speeches; and to go into detail about the book would carry me further than at present there is occasion to go. I can only thank you most sincerely for the delight which it has given me, and both I myself and my wife trust that the acquaintance which we seem to have made with you through your writings may improve into something more tangible. I do not know whether I am addressing a young man or an old, a clergyman or a layman. Perhaps if you answer this note you may give us some information about yourself. But at any rate, should business or pleasure bring you into this part of the world, pray believe that you will find a warm welcome if you will accept our hospitality.

Once more with my best thanks,
Believe me
faithfully yours
J. A. Froude

Sat. 23rd. There appeared a well-written and enthusiastic article on the book in "The Statesman". We hear there was a poor article in the Globe – of feebly written praise – the previous week, but beyond this we have not yet heard of any notices from the Press.

January 26th, came a very pleasant letter from Mrs. Carlyle, thanking the author of Clerical Scenes for the present of his book, praising it very highly, and saying that her husband had promised to read it when released from his mountain of history.

30th. Received a letter from Faraday, thanking me very gracefully for the present of the 'Scenes'. Blackwood mentions in enclosing this letter, that Simpkin and Marshall have sent for 12 additional copies – the first sign of a move since the subscription. The other night we looked into the Life of Charlotte Bronte to see how long it was before 'Jane Eyre' came into demand at the libraries, and we found that it was not until six weeks after publication. It is just three weeks now since I heard news of the subscription for *my* book.

Feb. 4. Yesterday brought the discouraging news that though the book is much talked of, it moves very slowly.

Feb. 16. Today G. went into the city and saw Langford, for the sake of getting the latest news about our two books – his Sea-Studies having been well launched about a fortnight or ten days ago with a subscription of 800. He brought home good news. The Clerical Scenes are moving off at a moderate but steady pace. Langford remarked that while the press had been uniformly favourable, not one *critical* notice had appeared. G. went to Parker's in the evening, and gathered a little gossip on the subject. Savage, author of the "Falcon Family" and now editor of the Examiner, said he was reading the C.S. – had read some of them already in Blackwood, but was now reading the volume; G. Eliot was "a writer of great merit". A barrister named Smythe said he had seen "the bishop" reading them the other day. As a set-off against this, Mrs. Schlesinger "couldn't bear the book". She is a regular novel reader; but hers is the first unfavourable opinion we have heard.

On Sunday, the 28th, Mr. John Blackwood called on us, having come to London for a few days only. He talked a good deal about the "Clerical Scenes" and George Eliot, and at last asked, "Well, am I to see George Eliot this time?" G. said, "Do you wish to see him?" "As he likes – I wish it to be quite spontaneous". I left the room, and G. following me a moment, I told him he might reveal me. Blackwood was kind, came back when he found he was too late for the train, and said he would come to Richmond again. He came on the following Friday, and chatted very pleasantly – told us Thackeray spoke highly of the "Scenes" and said *they were not written by a woman*. Mrs. Blackwood is *sure* they are not written by a woman – Mrs. Oliphant, the novelist, too is confident on the same side. I gave Blackwood the MS. of my new novel to the end of the second scene in the wood. He opened it, read the first page, and smiling, said "This will do". We walked with him to Kew, and had a good deal of talk. Found, among other things that he had lived two years in Italy when he was a youth, and that he admires Miss Austen.

April 3. Since I wrote those last notes, several encouraging fragments of news about the 'Scenes' have come to my ears – especially that Mrs. Owen Jones and her husband – two very different people – are equally enthusiastic about the book. But both have detected the woman.

I lay aside this record today – not to take it up again till we return from Germany in the Autumn.

While we were in Germany several interesting bits of news about the Clerical Scenes came to us. Blackwood saw Mr. Newdegate at Epsom, and that good Conservative expressed admiration of the capital stories which, he said, "are all about my place and county." But he added, that they were written with so much delicacy and in so admirable a spirit, that no one could be offended.

Emile Forgues wrote an article on them in the Revue des deux Mondes, and in consequence of that a review of them was inserted in the Saturday and a subsequent article commenting on Forgues' notice that my stories showed the evil effects of a married clergy!

In August the sale of the book was revived – a remarkable circumstance in the case of a guinea novel – and 29 copies were sold. On September 10, and on the 29th of October when G. saw Langford he heard that there was still a gradual, dropping sale.

In the October No. of the National Review, James Martineau placed the book at the head of his article on Professional Religion, and wrote a paragraph on it, "in gratitude for pleasant hours spent over them", an acknowledgement which Mr. Trollope also shares for his Barchester Towers. James Martineau thinks "Mr. Eliot's strength lies in depicting female character."

In September, I received a second letter from Froude interesting enough to copy, lest the original should be lost:

> Taplow House, Bideford
> Sep. 26
> Sir,
>
> A shadow holds out a hand to me – I try to take it and it fades away. Who are you? I do not ask from curiosity. You send me your book. I tell you how much it has affected me and I express my hope that the George Eliot who has touched me so keenly may allow me to know in him something more than the writer of the volumes on my table. You send me no answer.
>
> Keep yourself to yourself if you please – but I should value your acquaintance beyond that of most men if I was so happy as to possess it.
>
> Yours
>
> J. A. Froude

History of "Adam Bede"

The germ of "Adam Bede" was an anecdote told me by my Methodist Aunt Samuel (the wife of my Father's younger brother): an anecdote from her own experience. We were sitting together one afternoon during her visit to me at Griffe [sic], probably in 1839 or 40, when it occurred to her to tell me how she had visited a condemned criminal, a very ignorant girl who had murdered her child and refused to confess – how she had stayed with her, praying, through the night and how the poor creature at last broke out into tears and confessed her crime. My Aunt afterwards went with her in the cart to the place of execution, and she described to me the great respect with which this ministry of hers was regarded by the official people about the gaol. The story, told by my aunt with great feeling, affected me deeply, and I never lost the impression of that afternoon and our talk together; but I believe I never mentioned it through all the intervening years, till something prompted me to tell it [to] George in December 1856, when I had begun to write the "Scenes of Clerical Life". He remarked that the scene in the prison would make a fine element in a story, and I afterwards began to think of blending this and some other recollections of my aunt in one story with some points in my father's early life and character. The problem of construction that remained was to make the unhappy girl one of the chief *dramatis personæ* and connect her with the hero. At first I thought of making the story one of the series of "Scenes", but afterwards, when several motives had induced me to close these with "Janet's Repentance", I determined on making what we always called in our conversations "My Aunt's Story", the subject of a long novel: which I accordingly began to write on the 22nd of October 1857.

The character of Dinah grew out of my recollections of my aunt, but Dinah is not at all like my aunt, who was a very small, black-eyed woman, and (as I was told, for I never heard her preach) very vehement in her style of preaching. She had left off preaching when I knew her, being, probably, sixty years old, and in delicate health; and she had become, as my father told me, much more gentle and subdued than she had been in the days of her active ministry and bodily strength, when she could not rest without exhorting and remonstrating in season and out of season. I was very fond of her, and enjoyed the few weeks of her stay with me greatly. She was loving and kind to me, and I could talk to her about my inward life, which was closely shut up from those usually round me. I saw her only twice again, for much shorter periods: once at her own home at Wirksworth in Derbyshire, and once at my Father's last residence, Foleshill.

The character of Adam, and one or two incidents connected with him were suggested by my Father's early life: but Adam is not my father, any more than Dinah is my aunt. Indeed, there is not a single *portrait* in "Adam Bede": only the suggestions of experience wrought up into new combinations. When I began to write it, the only elements I had determined on besides the character of Dinah were the character of Adam, his relation to Arthur Donnithorne and their mutual relation to Hetty, i.e. to the girl who commits child-murder: the scene in the prison being of course the climax towards which I worked. Everything else grew out of the characters and their mutual relations. Dinah's ultimate relation to Adam was suggested by George, when I had read to him the first part of the first volume: he was so delighted with the presentation of Dinah and so convinced that the readers' interest would centre in her, that he wanted her to be the principal figure at the last. I accepted the idea at once, and from the end of the third chapter worked with it constantly in view.

The first volume was written at Richmond and given to Blackwood in March. He expressed great admiration of its freshness and vividness, but seemed to hesitate about putting it in the Magazine, which was the form of publication he, as well as myself, had previously contemplated. He still *wished* to have it for the Magazine, but desired to know the course of the story; at *present*, he saw nothing to prevent its reception in Maga, but he would like to see more. I am uncertain whether his doubts rested solely on Hetty's relation to Arthur, or whether they were also directed towards the treatment of Methodism and the Church. I refused to tell my story beforehand, on the ground that I would not have it judged apart from my *treatment*, which alone determines the moral quality of art: and ultimately I proposed that the notion of publication in Maga should be given up, and that the novel should be published in three volumes, at Christmas, if possible. He assented.

I began the second volume in the second week of my stay at Munich, about the middle of April. While we were at Munich George expressed his fear that Adam's part was too passive throughout the drama, and that it was important for him to be brought into more direct collision with Arthur. This doubt haunted me, and out of it grew the scene in the Wood between Arthur and Adam: the fight came to me as a *necessity* one night at the Munich Opera when I was listening to *William Tell*. Work was slow and interrupted at Munich, and when we left I had only written to the beginning of the dance on the Birthday Feast: but at Dresden, I wrote uninterruptedly and with great enjoyment in the long quiet mornings, and there I nearly finished the second volume – all, I think, but the last chapter, which I wrote here in the old room at Richmond in the first week of September, and then sent the M.S. off to Blackwood. The opening of the third volume – Hetty's journeys – was, I think written more rapidly than the rest of the book, and was left without the slightest alteration of the first draught. Throughout the book, I have altered little, and the only cases, I think, in which George suggested more than a verbal alteration, when I read the M.S. aloud to him, were the first scene at the Farm and the scene in the Wood between Arthur and Adam, both of which he recommended me to "space out" a little, which I did.

When, on October 29 I had written to the end of the love scene at the Farm between Adam and Dinah, I sent the M.S. to Blackwood, since the remainder of the third volume could not affect the judgment passed on what had gone before. He wrote back in warm admiration, and offered me, on the part of the firm, £800 for four years' copyright. I accepted the offer. The last words of the third volume were written and dispatched on their way to Edinburgh November the 16th, and now on this last day of the same month I have written this slight history of my book. I love it very much and am deeply thankful to have written it, whatever the public may say to it – a result which is still in darkness, for I have at present had only four sheets of the proof. The book would have been published at Christmas, or rather, early in December, but that Bulwer's "What will he do with it?" was to be published by Blackwoods at that time, and it was thought that this novel might interfere with mine.

8 Park Shot, Richmond. Nov. 30. 1858.

Feb. 6 [1859]. Yesterday a letter came from Blackwood telling me the result of the subscription for "Adam Bede", which was published on the 1st: 730 copies, Mudie having taken 500 on the publishers' terms, i.e. ten per cent on the sale price. At first he had stood out for a larger deduction, and would only take 50, but at last he came round. In this letter Blackwood told me the first *ab extra* opinion of the book, which happened to be precisely what I most desired. A cabinet-maker (brother to B's managing clerk) had read the sheets and declared that the writer must have been "brought up to the business", or at least had listened to the workmen in their workshops.

12. Pleasant news from Edinburgh – that Adam Bede was making just the impression Blackwood had anticipated. First agreeable token – a packet from Dr. John Brown containing "Rab and his Friends".

24. Another pleasant packet from Edinburgh, containing a letter from Mrs. Carlyle, one from Dr. John Brown, and the news that Mr. Caird is a warm admirer; thinks me, however too hard on Hetty!

26. Laudatory reviews in the Athenæum, Saturday, and Literary Gazette. The Saturday criticism is characteristic: Dinah is not mentioned!

The other day I received the following letter, which I copy because I have sent the original away.

> To the Author of Adam Bede.
> Chester Road, Sunderland.
> Dear Sir
>
> I got the other day a hasty read of your "Scenes of Clerical Life", and since that a glance at your "Adam Bede", and was delighted more than I can express; but being a poor man, and having enough to do to make "ends meet", I am unable to get a read of your inimitable books.
>
> Forgive, dear Sir, my boldness in asking you to give us a cheap edition. You would confer on us a great boon. I can get plenty of trash for a few pence, but I am sick of it. I felt so different when I shut your books, even though it was but a kind of "hop, skip and jump read".
>
> I feel so strongly on this matter that I am determined to risk being thought rude and officious and write to you.
>
> Many of my working brethren feel as I do, and I express their wish as well as my own.
>
> Again asking your forgiveness for intruding myself upon you,
>
> I remain, with profoundest respect
> Yours etc.
> E. Hall.

Mar. 8. Letter from Blackwood this morning, saying that the "Bedesman has turned the corner and is coming in a winner". Mudie has sent for 200 additional copies (making 700), and Mr. Langford says the West End libraries keep sending for more.

Mar. 14. Major Blackwood writes to say "Mudie has just made up his number of Adam Bede to 1000. Simpkins have sold their subscribed number and have had 12 today. Everyone is talking of the book".

16. Blackwood writes to say I am a "popular author as well as a great author". They printed 2090 of Adam Bede, and have disposed of more than 1800, so that they are thinking about a second edition. A very feeling letter from Froude this morning. I happened this morning to be reading the XXXth Ode, Book III of Horace. "Non omnis moriar".[1]

24. Mr. Herbert Spencer brought us word that "Adam Bede" had been quoted by Mr. Charles Buxton in the House of Commons – 'As the farmer's wife says in *Adam Bede*, "It wants to be hatched over again and hatched different".'

26. George went into town today and brought me home a budget of good news that compensated for the pain I had felt in the coldness of an old friend. Mr. Langford says that Mudie thinks he must have another hundred or two of Adam – has read the book himself and is delighted with it. Charles Reade says it is "the finest thing since Shakspeare" – placed his finger on Lisbeth's account of her coming home with her husband from their marriage – praises enthusiastically the style – the way in which the author handles the Saxon language. Shirley Brooks also delighted – John Murray says there has never been such a book. Mr Langford says there must be a second edition in 3 vols. and they will print 500: whether Mudie takes more or not they will have sold all by the end of a month. Lucas delighted with the book and will review it in the Times at the first opportunity. "My soul doth magnify".

April 17. I have left off recording the history of Adam Bede, and the pleasant letters and words that come to me – the success has been so triumphantly beyond anything I had dreamed of, that it would be tiresome to put down particulars. Four hundred of the Second Edition (of 750) sold in the first week, and 21 besides ordered when there was not a copy left in the London house. This morning Hachette has sent to ask my terms for the liberty of translation into French. There was a review in the Times last week which will naturally give a new stimulus to the sale, and yesterday I sent a letter to the Times denying that "Mr Liggins" is the author, as the world and Mr. Anders had settled it. But I must trust to the letters I have received and preserved for giving me the history of the book, if I should live long enough to forget details.

Shall I ever write another book as true as "Adam Bede"? The *weight* of the future presses on me and makes itself felt even more than the deep satisfaction of the past and present.
Sunday Morning. Ap. 17. 59

April 29. Today Blackwood sent me a letter from Bulwer, which I copy, because I have to send back the original, and I like to keep in mind the generous praise of one author for another.

1 Latin, 'I will not die completely': Horace is boasting of his literary achievement.

Malvern, Ap. 24. 59
My dear Sir

I ought long since to have thanked you for Adam Bede. But I never had a moment to look at it, till arriving here, and ordered by the Doctors to abstain from all "work."

I owe the author much gratitude for some very pleasing hours. The Book indeed is worthy of great admiration. There are touches of beauty in the conception of human character that are exquisite – and much wit and much poetry embedded in the "Dialect", which nevertheless the author overuses.

The style is remarkably good whenever it is English and not provincial – racy, original and nervous.

I congratulate you on having found an author of such promise, and published one of the very ablest works of fiction I have read for years.

Yrs. truly

E.B.L.

I am better than I was, but thoroughly done up.

May 6. Today came a letter from Barbara, full of joy in my success, in the certainty that Adam Bede was mine though she had not read more than extracts in Reviews. This is the first delight in the book as *mine*, over and above the fact that the book is good. I am not sure that anyone besides Barbara will feel that sort of delight.

7. A letter from Major Blackwood says that the *third* edition (of 500) is already reduced to 100 in the first week of issue.

19. A letter from Blackwood in which he proposes to give me another £400 at the end of the year, making in all £1200, as an acknowledgment of Adam Bede's success.

May 27. Blackwood came to dine with us, on his arrival in London, and we had much talk. The day or two before, he had sent me a letter from Prof. Aytoun, saying that he had neglected his work to read the first volume of "Adam Bede", and actually sent the two other volumes out of the house to save himself from temptation. B. brought with him a correspondence he has had with various people about Liggins, beginning with Mr Bracebridge, who will have it that Liggins is the author of Adam Bede in spite of all denials.

Money received for Adam Bede

	£.	s. d.
Copyright for 4 years according to agreement	800.	0.0
Additional in acknowledgement of success	400.	0.0
American Edition	30.	0.0
From Tauchnitz for German reprint	50.	0.0

Additional for "Adam" in consequence of success	400. 0.0
From Duncker of Berlin for German Translation	25. 0.0
	1705. 0.0
Other monies in 1859	
The Lifted Veil	37.10.0
Clerical Scenes 2d. Edition	150. 0.0
do " do "	50. 0.0
	237. 0.0
Total	1942. 0.0

X. *Germany 1858*

In her diary for 3 April 1858, GE announced, 'I pack up this journal now, since it is not empty enough to be companion [sic] on my second visit to Germany, whither we set out next Wednesday, the 7th.' The next entry in her diary, dated simply 'October', notes their arrival back in London on 2 September and summarises their itinerary, with the comment 'Such record as I made of our time in Germany is contained in another book.' With characteristic economy, GE used this same book again in 1860 for 'Recollections of Italy'.

This 'record ... of our time in Germany' is in two parts: the first, largely in diary form and evidently written on the move, deals with their journey to and stay in Munich (7 April – 7 July); the second is an essay, 'Recollections of our journey from Munich to Dresden', dated 'Richmond, October 27, 1858'. Neither section gives any indication that the principal purpose of their journey was to enable GHL (now celebrated as the author of the *Life of Goethe*, as he reports in his journal) to consult various scientific authorities in his preparation of *The Physiology of Common Life* (published in monthly parts by Blackwood in 1859, and in two volumes 1859–60). However they met not only distinguished scientists, but figures in the literary and artistic communities as well, including the leading figures (Bodenstedt, Geibel, Heyse, Lingg, Meyr) of the *Münchener Dichterkreis*, a group of poets who cultivated neo-classical ideals of beauty, and the English artist Frederic Burton, resident in Munich since 1851, who was to join GE and GHL on their Italian journey of 1864, and to paint GE.

While GE participated in GHL's science, her journal reveals her commitment to developing her theories of art and to writing fiction. Her observations on art and architecture, from the roofs of Nürnberg to the massive sculpture Bavaria in Munich and especially in the 'Madonna' room of the Dresden gallery, make up a major part of this journal. Both Munich and Dresden had great art collections, due to the energetic patronage of King Ludwig I of Bavaria in the early part of the century in Munich, and of Augustine the Strong and his son Augustine III in Dresden in the eighteenth century, who set out to build collections to rival those in Paris. GE's reactions to the galleries and studios they frequented are more sophisticated than her remarks in earlier journals, though still substantially narrative readings of the images she sees, and some of them were amplified in her letters (like that to Sara Hennell, completed on 13 May, which includes robust criticism of aspects of Bavarian society and of the pretentiousness of much modern German art).[1] But there is a relationship also between her reflections on the artworks she was seeing and her fiction. Her interest in Flemish and Dutch painters like Teniers and Gerard Dow informs the famous passage on realism in chapter 17 of *Adam Bede*. (It should be borne in mind also that during this time GE and GHL were reading and discussing a good deal of contemporary German writing, in preparation for GHL's article 'Realism in Art: Recent German Fiction', published later in the year.)

GE had embarked on *Adam Bede* on 22 October 1857, and her progress on this work is reported in a matter-of-fact way during their time in Munich, while in her retrospective account of Dresden she contentedly noted 'Here I wrote the latter half of the second volume of Adam Bede, in the long mornings that our early hours – rising at six o'clock – secured us.' For the most part, however, the journal is given over to GE's responses to the places they saw, and to her account of their social activities. GE and GHL were much busier with visits, paid and received, and with outings to theatre and galleries, when abroad: it is hard to escape the conclusion that GE felt less inhibition about going into society than in England.

The journal also has a number of the vignettes that are so appealing in GE's travel journals: the people in the Catholic Church in Nürnberg, the family with whom they shelter from a storm in Munich, the Italian sentinel in Salzburg. Babies and children seem particularly fascinating to GE at this time, in her life experiences, in the art she was absorbing, and in the novel she was writing: poignant reactions in a woman rising forty, living with a man she cannot marry. Her habit of discussing artistic creativity in the language of biological reproduction, frequently noted, is nowhere better discussed than in Bodenheimer, chapter 7, 'George Eliot's Stepsons'.

There are strong natural descriptions especially of the journey from Munich to Dresden, for which they preferred the picturesque to the direct route, travelling south through the Alps to Salzburg, thence to Vienna, and Prague. Here as in some of the descriptions in Munich, GE's exaltation of Nature over Art is evident. Throughout this journal, not only in the

1 *The George Eliot Letters*, ed. Gordon S. Haight, 9 vols. (New Haven, Yale University Press, 1954–78), vol. 2, pp. 452–6.

natural world, her responsiveness to place is demonstrated. GHL speculated 'Who knows but some day we may have a Nürnberg novel . . . ?' (*Letters*, vol. 2, p. 449), but of the towns and cities they visited it turned out to be Vienna and Prague which provided fictional locales, for the novella *The Lifted Veil* (first published as 'The Lifted Veil' in *Blackwood's* in July 1859). In August 1859, GE wrote self-analytically to Barbara Bodichon, 'there are many strata to be worked through before I can begin to use *artistically* any material I may gather in the present.' (*Letters*, vol. 3, p. 129)

GHL's journal interestingly corroborates and counterpoints GE's, including details of their exchequer (the satisfactory rent in Luitspoldstrasse he translates to ten shillings a week, and calculates their dinner at the Bayerisches Hof to have cost one shilling and threepence; in Dresden he laments that payment of one shilling for entry to the gallery is required on Mondays and Wednesdays). Naturally he includes much material relevant to his science, but he reports also GE's loss of a ring at Lille (entry of 14 April), news of the sales of *Scenes of Clerical Life* and *Sea-Side Studies* (28 May), a discussion with Liebig about Dickens's separation from his wife (14 June), and 'A Night of Bugs!' in Vienna (13 July).

Cross, typically, omits personal responses such as GE's reactions to the people she sees in the Catholic Church. Haight (*Letters*) quotes only a few phrases and sentences.

X. Germany

Munich, April 14th 1858

On Wednesday evening, April 7 we set off on our journey to Munich, and now we are comfortably settled in our lodgings, where we hope to remain three months, at least, I sit down in my first leisure moments to write a few recollections of our journey, or rather of our twenty four hours' stay at Nürnberg; for the rest of our journey was mere endurance of railway and steamboat, in cold and sombre weather, often rainy. I ought to except our way from Frankfurt to Nürnberg, which lay for some distance – until we came to Bamberg – through a beautifully varied country. Our view both of Wurzburg and Bamberg, as we hastily snatched it from our railway carriage, was very striking – great, old buildings crowning heights that rise up boldly from the plain on which stands the main part of the towns. (See Back).

From Bamberg to Nürnberg the way lay through a wide, rich plain, sprinkled with towns. We had left all the hills behind us.

At Bamberg we were joined in our carriage by a pleasant looking elderly couple, who spoke to each other and looked so affectionately, that we said directly "Shall we be so when we are old?" It was very pretty to see them hold each other's gloved hands for a minute, like lovers.

As soon as we had settled ourselves in our inn at Nürnberg – the *Baierische Hof* – we went out to get a general view of the town. Happily it was not raining, though there was no sun to light up the roofs and windows.

How often I had thought I should like to see Nürnberg, and had pictured to myself narrow streets with dark quaint gables! The reality was not at all like my picture, but it was ten times better. No sombre colouring, except the old churches: all was bright and varied, each façade having a different colour – delicate green, or buff, or pink, or lilac – every now and then set off by the neighbourhood of a rich reddish brown. And the roofs always gave warmth of colour with their bright red or rich purple tiles. Every house differed from its neighbour, and had a physiognomy of its own, though a beautiful family likeness ran through them all, as if the burghers of that old city were of one heart and one soul, loving the same delightful outlines and cherishing the same daily habits of simple ease and enjoyment in their balcony windows when the day's work was done.

The balcony window is the secondary charm of the Nürnberg houses – it would be the principal charm of any houses that had not the Nürnberg roofs and gables. It is usually in the centre of the building on the first floor, and is ornamented with carved stone or wood which supports it after the fashion of a bracket. In several of these windows we saw pretty family groups – young fair heads of girls, or of little children, with now and then an older head surmounting them. One can fancy that these windows are the pet places for family joys – that Papa seats himself there when he comes in from the warehouse and the little ones cluster round him in no time. But the glory of the Nürnberg houses is the roofs, which are no blank surface of mere tiling, but are alive with lights and shadows cast by varied and beautiful lines of windows and pinnacles and arched openings. The plainest roof in Nürnberg has its little windows lifting themselves up like eyelids, and almost everywhere one sees the pretty hexagonal tiles. But the better houses have a central open sort of pavilion in the roof with a pinnacle surmounted by a weather-cock. This pavilion has usually a beautifully carved arched opening in front, set off by the dark back ground which is left by the absence of glass. One fancies the old Nürnbergers must have gone up to these pavilions to smoke in the summer and autumn days. There is usually a brood of small windows round this central ornament, often elegantly arched and carved. A wonderful sight it makes to see a series of such roofs, surmounting the tall, delicate coloured houses. They are always high-pitched, of course, and the colour of the tiles was usually of a rich bright red. I think one of the most charming vistas we saw, was the *Adler-gasse*, on the St. Lorenz side of the town. Sometimes instead of the high-pitched roof with its pavilion and windows, there is a richly ornamented gable fronting the street; and still more frequently we get the gables at right angles with the street, at a break in the line of houses.

In this afternoon walk we looked round the grand old churches too – St. Sebald and St. Lorenz – closed according to the Protestant fashion and so, not to be entered without money or trouble. We promised ourselves to enter them by some means on the morrow, but now we were tired, and turned in again for our rest and our meal.

The next morning the sun shone brightly and the streets had the quiet liveliness which one sees in foreign towns on a Sunday – shops closed, but smartly dressed people taking holiday, or bound for the church. Service was to begin at nine and end at eleven, and on our way to the Burg, the first thing after breakfast, we were arrested in front of *St. Sebald's Kirche* by the sound of the organ and voices. So we ventured to turn in, since we saw some other people coming out again, as if exit and entrance were *ad libitum* in spite of Protestantism. It is an exquisite interior, with lofty pointed arches, ornamented at the apex with a sort of zig-zag touched with black – an ornamentation I do not remember to have seen before. The minister was reading a prayer (apparently) in a cold formal voice, and as the air and floor were yet colder, we hurried out again in less than a minute. Outside this church, is the colossal bronze Christ, by Adam Krafft, over the principal entrance.

From the Sebald Kirche we walked on to the Burg which lies on a rise of ground overlooking the whole city, with the plains and far hills beyond. Here we could see the huge moat that surrounds the place, now dry like the other moats in the world. On the summit of the hill stands the tall quaint watch-tower, and in the open space near this tower, we stood, looking at the glorious old town below us, a forest of high-pitched roofs and pinnacles, with a foreground in which we could see here and there a line of façades – all quaint, all with a physiognomy that carried a history. The horizon was hazy, so we could see hardly anything of the distant landscape; but what a view this must be, when the air is clear, and when the few trees sprinkled here and there about the town give some green touches among the red roofs!

Coming back from the Burg, we met a detachment of soldiers, with their band playing, followed by a stream of listening people; and then we reached the marketplace, just at the point where stands "The Beautiful Fountain" – an exquisite bit of florid Gothic which has been restored in perfect conformity with the original. Right before us stood the *Frauen-Kirche*, with its fine and unusual façade – the chief beauty being a central chapel used as the choir, and added by Adam Krafft. It is something of the shape of a mitre, and forms a beautiful gradation of ascent towards the summit of the façade. We heard the organ, and were tempted to enter, for this is the one Catholic Church in Nürnberg. The interior is almost ugly, the arch of the roof low pitched, the walls decorated with coloured statuary in the worst taste. But the delicious sound of the organ and voices drew us farther and farther in among the standing people, and we staid there I don't know how long – till the music ceased. How the music warmed one's heart! I loved the good people about me, even to the soldier who stood with his back to us, giving us a full view of his close cropped head, with its pale yellowish hair standing up in bristles on the crown, as if his hat had acted like a forcing-pot. Then there was a little baby, in a close-fitting cap on its little round head, looking round with bright black eyes as it sucked its bit of bread. Such a funny little complete face – rich brown complexion and miniature roman nose. And then its mother lifted it up, that it might see the rose-decked altar, where the priests were standing.

How music that stirs all one's devout emotions blends everything into harmony – makes one feel part of one whole, which one loves all alike, losing the sense of a separate self. Nothing could be more wretched as art than the painted Saint Veronica opposite me, holding out the sad face on her miraculous handkerchief. Yet it touched me deeply, and the thought of the Man of Sorrows seemed a very close thing – not a faint hearsay.

The music ceased, and the hard prosaic voices began. So we turned out again in search of the *Gänse männchen*,[1] but he is a hibernating statue and only shows himself in the fine seasons. Returning from our unsuccessful quest, we heard a military strain coming from the *Frauen-Kirche* – it was ushering the congregation

1 German, 'little gooseman': a statue by Lawenwolf of a bronze figure of a peasant carrying under his arms two geese spouting water from their mouths.

out into the sunshine. Once more we stopped to look at the Beautiful Fountain, then right on over the bridge to the St. Lorenz side of the town. Here we looked at the outside of the fine old church again, wandered about the beautiful streets and wondered and exclaimed at every turning, until it was time to go in to dinner.

I have forgotten to say that on our way to the Burg, we saw Albert Dürer's statue, by Rauch, and Albert Dürer's house – a striking bit of old building, rich dark brown with a truncated gable and two wooden galleries running along the gable end. My best wishes and thanks to the artists who keep it in repair and use it for their meetings. Besides this, on the St. Sebald's side of the town, we saw the Egydienplatz, where there is a church built in the Italian style, and the Pellersche Haus, also in the Italian style of the Renaissance, only that style is made to keep company with the Nürnberg gable. There is also the Gymnasium with a statue of Melancthon – a very fine one – standing in front with an inscription to him as the founder of the institution. The vistas from the bridges across the muddy Pegnitz which runs through the town are all quaint and picturesque, and it was here that we saw some of the *shabbiest* looking houses – almost the only houses that carried any suggestion of poverty, and even here it was doubtful. The town has an air of cleanliness and well-being, and one longs to call one of those balconied apartments, with their flower pots, clean glass, clean curtains, and transparencies turning their white backs to the street, one's own home. It is pleasant to think there is such a place in the world where many people pass peaceful lives, though we were obliged to turn our backs on it at three o'clock, perhaps never to see it again.

I enjoyed looking at the landscape as we went along the railway. It ran through a well-cultivated plain, studded with villages and small towns – some of the villages charming to see. I remember one particularly where the little church stood perched on a steep rocky eminence that rose quite suddenly from among the little cluster of houses on the level. Sometimes we passed through long fir and pine woods, then we came out on tracts of tilled ground, where the hop poles were standing in tent-like stacks, then on wide-stretching plains, all smooth green and brown. Towards sun-set we passed the Danube, not yet a mighty river. The clouds which had gradually covered the whole sky in the afternoon were now opened in the west, and in the red golden space, made brighter by the dark lines of cumulo-stratus, I saw Venus setting as if in a hurry to follow the sun. She passed one purple line and then another, and at last dipped into the dense cloud below. Then the darkness came on, and I saw no more till we stopped at the Munich Station. Soon we were at the *Baierische Hof*, quietly eating our supper in our own room – a great frescoed comfortless place, with the beds shut off by glass doors. Not so very bad, either, for we had a good sofa to sit on and plenty of tables, but this was the first time on our journey that we had had a carpet-less room and mattresses instead of spring beds. It was Germany *pur et simple*.

The next morning, out we trudged, the first thing, to look for lodgings; but after traversing long streets and seeing no more than two or three advertisements of lodgings to be let none of which suited us, George determined to call on Oldenburg, the publisher, thinking he might help us. He was very good, and took the trouble of conducting us to two *Hôtels garnis*,[2] which he thought might suit us better than private lodgings. But no! They were dear, and not attractive in other ways, so we set off again, peering at the bits of paper stuck at the corners of the streets, trying some of the places advertised, but with no glimmer of a chance that any would do, till at last we begged Mr. Oldenburg not to let us detain him longer – we would do what we could in hunting about by ourselves, and meanwhile he would be good enough to keep his eyes and ears open on our behalf. After much rambling before and after dinner, we found an advertisement of "Zwei *elegant* möbilirte Zimmer".[3] That might do, we thought; for the rooms we had hitherto seen not advertised as *elegant* were so dirty and ill-furnished that we felt we should require a Munich superlative to make a moderate positive. So we made the best of our way to 15 Luitpold Strasse, and to our immense satisfaction found something that looked liked cleanliness and comfort. Sofas and chairs and tables and chests of drawers in abundance, and a great superfluity of glass and china and swiss ornaments. The bargain was soon made – twenty florins per month – and the next day after dinner we were to come and take possession.

So here we came last Tuesday, the 13th, and up to this time, Friday the 16th, we have reason to be content. We have been taking sips of the Glyptothek, and the two Pinacotheks, in the mornings, not having settled to work yet. Last night we went to the opera – Fra Diavolo – at the Hof-Theater. The theatre ugly, the singing bad: still, the orchestra was good and the charming music made itself felt in spite of German throats.

Sunday 11. We went to the Jesuitenkirche for the first time this morning. The effect of the interior is very fine – a roof of great span unsupported by arches and covered with fresco. We lost some of the music by being a little too late, but heard enough to repay us for going – a quire of fresh boys' voices blending with the rolling organ.

There were two confessionals placed opposite each other about half way up the church, and while the sermon was going forward, a priest sitting in each of them, received the confession of one penitent after another – all men or women clad in the dress of the working people. We waited through the sermon, delivered in a monotonous loud tone by rather a hard-looking priest. He stood in the passage between the two rows of benches, and held a book in his hand, to which he referred frequently as if reading passages which he then went on to expound or comment on. But the resonance was too great for us to hear much that he said. We staid to the end, hoping to hear more music, but there was none. The congregation departed in silence.

From the church we went to the Pinacothek, straight into the glorious

2 French, 'lodging-house'.

3 German, 'two elegantly furnished rooms'.

Rubens-Saal. Delighted afresh in the picture of Samson and Delilah, both for the painting and character of the figures. Delilah, a magnificent blond, seated in a chair, with a transparent white shift lightly covering her body and a rich red piece of drapery round her legs, leans forward with one hand resting on her thigh, the other, holding the cunning shears, resting on the chair – a posture which shows to perfection the full round living arms. She turns her head aside to look with sly triumph at Samson, a tawny giant, his legs caught in the red drapery, shorn of his long locks, furious with the consciousness that the Philistines are upon him, and that this time he cannot shake them off. Above the group of malicious faces and grappling arms, a hand holds a flaming torch. Behind Delilah, and grasping her arm leans forward an old woman with hard features full of exultation.

This picture, comparatively small in size, hangs beside the Last Judgment, and in the corresponding space on the other side of the same picture hangs the sublime Crucifixion – Jesus alone hanging dead on the cross, darkness over the whole earth. One can desire nothing in this picture – the grand, sweet calm of the dead face, calm and satisfied amidst all the traces of anguish, the real, livid flesh, the thorough mastery with which the whole form is rendered, and the isolation of the supreme sufferer, make a picture that haunts one like a remembrance of a friend's death-bed.

Monday 12. After reading Anna Mary Howitt's book on Munich, and Overbeck on Greek art, we turned out into the delicious sunshine to walk in the Theresien Wiese, and have our first look at the colossal Bavaria, the greatest work of Schwanthaler. Delightful it was to get away from the houses into this breezy meadow, where we heard the larks singing above us. The sun was still too high in the west for us to look with comfort at the statue except right in front of it, when it eclipsed the sun. And this front view is the only satisfactory one. The outline made by the head and arm on a side view is almost painfully ugly. But in front, looking up to the beautiful calm face, the impression it produces is sublime. I have never seen anything even in ancient sculpture of a more awful beauty than this dark colossal head looking out from a background of pure pale blue sky. We mounted the platform to have a view of her back, and then, walking forward, looked to our right hand and saw – the snow-covered Alps! Sight more to me than all the art in Munich, though I love the Art nevertheless. The great wide-stretching earth and the all-embracing sky – the birth-right of us all – are what I care most to look at, after all. And I feel intensely the new beauty of the sky here. The blue is so exquisitely clear, and the wide streets give one such a broad canopy of sky. I felt more inspirited by our walk to the Theresien-Platz than by any pleasure we have had in Munich. We came back quickly to set out again for the Residenz-Theater, where we were going to see *Lady Tartüffe* in a German dress. A very pretty little theatre it is, ornamented with sculptured wood, all dead white and gold with crimson draperies. The play was very respectably performed, and there was a delicious bit of real comedy in the make up, physiognomy and by-play of the president of the Benevolent Society, by Herr Keller. The Germans are excellent in these quiet bits of humour.

Tuesday 13. We took a droschky to the Maria-Hilf Kirche in the *Au*, and enjoyed this easy way of seeing the streets. The exterior of the church is conspicuous in its beauty, springing up with ease and grace from among the level blocks of houses around it. It is built of brick, the spire, with its sprouting leaf-like ornaments, of stone. The interior is fine and impressive, though the fluted columns are so thick and heavy for so small an area. But the loftiness of their shafts, and the rich colouring of the glass – all the windows are of coloured glass, representing the history of the Virgin and the Saviour – incline one to admire rather than to criticise.

We walked back, taking the *Begräbniss* Platz on our way, that we might see Mrs. Costello's tomb, which George had undertaken to seek out. Dudley and Louisa Costello pay a certain sum yearly to have the grave kept in order, and were anxious to have the testimony of an eye-witness that the sum is not paid in vain. It looks very neat, with a border of violets, now coming into flower. We plucked two, to send to Louisa – then walked on through the cemetery. It affected me strangely, but not unpleasantly – this home of the multitudinous dead (the ancients called dying, going *ad plures*)[4] and I should often walk there if I were alone.

We had meant to go to the Theresien Wiese again, and see the Bavaria by the light of the sinking sun; but we were too early for this, so we went instead to the Hof-garten, where the chesnut-buds are beginning to burst, and drank a *glass* of agreeable coffee – then strolled on to the Englischergarten and looked at the rushing Isar. The light was so delicious as we came back, and the western red at the end of the long vista of the Carlsstrasse was so alluring, that we turned towards that street thinking we would make a little circuit homewards and see the outside of the Basilica. But we saw more than the outside, for one of the doors was open, and we walked in. Very grand it was in the dimness – hardly any colour to be detected by the pale light shed from the line of windows above the bright pillars. We saw a mighty space marked out by long rows of grey columns and a dim arched roof. But we dared not linger lest G. should increase his cold.

Friday 16. On Wednesday, we walked to the Theresien Wiese to look at the Bavaria by sunset, but a shower came on and drove us to take refuge in a pretty house built near the Ruhmeshalle – whereby we were gainers, for we saw a charming family group: a mother, with her three children; the eldest a boy with his book, the second a three-year old maiden, the third a sweet baby girl of a year and a half; two dogs, one a mixture of the setter and pointer, the other, a turnspit; and a relation, or servant, ironing. The baby cried at the sight of G. in beard and spectacles, but kept turning her eyes towards him from her mother's lap, every now and then seeming to have overcome her fears and then bursting out crying anew. At last, she got down and lifted the table-cloth, to peep at his legs, as if to see the monster's nether parts.

Thursday 22. We both had a headache and could not enjoy our walk in the Englischergarten.

4 Latin, 'to the majority'.

Friday 23. Not being well enough to write, we determined to spend our morning at the Glyptothek and Pinacothek. A glorious morning – all sunshine and blue sky. We went to the Glyptothek first, and delighted ourselves anew with the Sleeping Faun, The Satyr and Bacchus, and the Laughing Faun (Fauno colla macchia). Looked at the two young Satyrs reposing with the pipe in their hands – one of them charming in the boyish good humoured beauty of the face, but both wanting finish in the limbs which look almost as if they could be produced by a turning machine. But the conception of this often-repeated figure is charming: it would make a garden seem more peaceful in the sunshine. Looked at the old Silenus too, which is excellent. I delight in these figures, full of droll animation, flinging some nature in its broad freedom in the eyes of small-mouthed, mincing narrowness. We went into the modern Saal also, glancing on our way at the Cornelius frescoes, which seem to me stiff and hideous. An Adonis by Thorwaldsen is very beautiful.

Then to the Pinacothek, where we looked at Albert Dürer's portrait again, and many other pictures among which I admired a group by Jordaens: "A Satyr eating with a peasant shows him that he can blow hot and cold at the same time"; the old grandmother nursing the child, the father with the key in his hand with which he has been amusing baby, looking curiously at the Satyr, the handsome wife still more eager in her curiosity, the quiet cow, the little boy, the dog and cat – all are charmingly conceived.

Saturday 24. As we were reading this afternoon Herr Oldenburg came in, invited us to go to his house on Tuesday and chatted pleasantly for an hour. He talked of Kaulbach, whom he has known very intimately, being the publisher of the *Reineke Fuchs*. The picture of the *Hunnen Schlacht* was the first of Kaulbach's on a great scale. It created a sensation, and the critics began to call it a "Weltgeschichtliches Bild".[5] Since then Kaulbach has been seduced into the complex, wearisome symbolical style, which makes the frescoes at Berlin enormous puzzles.

When we had just returned from our drive in the Englischergarten, returning by the *Sieges*-Thor and glancing into the Ludwigskirche for the first time, Bodenstedt pleasantly surprized us by presenting himself. We had just heard from Oldenburg that he was very ill. Happily he had recovered and was just returned from Berlin. To our great benefit: for he is a charming man, and promises to be a delightful acquaintance for us in this strange town. He chatted pleasantly with us for half an hour, telling us that he is writing a work in five volumes on the Contemporaries of Shakspeare, and indicating the nature of his criticism of the Shakspearian Drama – which is historical and analytical. Presently he proposed that we should adjourn to his house and have tea with him, and so we turned out altogether in the bright moonlight, and enjoyed his pleasant talk until ten o'clock. His wife is not at home, but we were admitted to see the three sleeping children – one a baby about a year and a half old, a lovely

5 German, 'picture of universal history'.

waxen thing. He gave the same account of Kaulbach as we had heard from Oldenburg; spoke of Genelli as superior in genius, though he has not the fortune to be recognized; recited some of Hermann Ling's poetry, and spoke enthusiastically of its merits. There was not a word of detraction about any one – no thing to jar on our impression of him as a refined noble-hearted man.

Sunday 25. We walked in the Englischergarten today and looked at the Munich people in their best clothes. Then came home and began to read aloud Bodenstedt's "Tausend und ein Tag im Morgenland".

Monday 26. In the afternoon Professor Andreas Wagner called, a very kind, unpretending old man. He offered to show us his Petrifacten-Sammlung, and promised to introduce us to Professor Martius and his family: also to mention to Bischoff G.'s wish to see him. In the morning Mr. Burton, the English artist called, an agreeable man, with a little English glazing of shyness.

Tuesday 27. This has been a red-letter day. In the morning, Professor Wagner took us over his Petrifacten-Sammlung, giving us interesting explanations; and before we left him we were joined by Prof. Martius, an animated clever man, who talked admirably, and invited us to his house. Then we went to Kaulbach's studio, talked with him and saw with especial interest the picture he is preparing as a present to the New Museum. In the evening, after walking in the Theresien Wiese, we went to Herr Oldenburg's, and met Liebig, the chemist, Geibel and Heyse, the poets, and Carrière, the author of a work on the Reformation. Liebig is charming – with well cut features, a low quiet voice, and gentle manners. It was touching to see his hands, the nails black from the roots, the skin all grimed.

Heyse is like a painter's poet, ideally beautiful; rather brilliant in his talk, and altogether pleasing. Geibel is a man of rather coarse texture, with a voice like a kettle drum, and a steady determination to deliver his opinions on every subject that turned up. But there was a good deal of ability in his remarks. Carrière is a thin-lipped, petty-faced man, whom one wishes out of the room, like a cold draught.

Wednesday 28. This evening at 7, kind old Professor Wagner came to take us to Martius's, and we spent an interesting evening there. Frau Martius is a charming woman certainly not less than fifty-five, but with a graceful quiet liveliness and intelligence which makes her more interesting than her daughters.

Friday 30. After calling on Frau Oldenburg, and then at Prof. Bodenstedt's where we played with his charming children for ten minutes, we went to the theatre to hear Prince Radziwill's music to the Faust. I admired especially the earlier part, the Easter-morning song of the spirits, the Beggar's Song – and other things, until after the scene in Auerbach's cellar, which is set with much humour and fancy. But the scene between Faust and Margaret is bad – "Meine Ruh' ist hin"[6] quite pitiable, and the "König in Thule" not good. Gretchen's

6 German, 'my peace is at an end'.

second song, in which she implores help of the "Schmerzensreiche"[7] touched me a good deal.

Saturday, May 1. The weather cloudy and rather rainy. In the afternoon Bodenstedt called and we agreed to spend the evening at his house. A delightful evening. Professor Löher, author of "Die Deutscher in America", and another much younger Gelehrte, whose name I did not seize, were there.

Sunday. 2. Still rainy and cold. We went to the Pinacothek and looked at the old pictures in the first and second Saal. There are some very bad and some fine ones by Albert Dürer: of the latter a full-length figure of the Apostle Paul with the head of Mark beside him in a listening attitude is the one that most remains with me. One extremely grotesque by Wohlgemuth, Dürer's master, of Christ risen from the dead and standing something like a propped wooden doll with a frightened expression by the stone grave, the Roman guard (of two men asleep in the fore-ground), and an angel with the air of a school-girl in the middle distance. Others of Wohlgemuth have much more merit. There is a very striking "Adoration of the Magi" by Johannes van Eyck, with much merit in the colouring, perspective and figures. Also "Christ carrying his Cross" by Albert Dürer is striking. "A woman raised from the dead by the imposition of the Cross" is a very elaborate composition by Böhme in which the faces are of first rate excellence. In the evening we went to the Opera and saw the "Nord Stern".

Monday. 3. Pouring with rain the whole day.

Tuesday. 4. Letter from Blackwood today, in which he appears to fall in rather with the idea of separate publication for Adam Bede than of publication in the Magazine. We have read Heyse's Novellen after dinner for the last day or two, after laying aside Bodenstedt's "Tausend und ein Tag im Orient", which has given us much pleasure in its picture of Mirza Schaffige. This evening we have been to the Theresien Wiese and had a glorious view of the Mountains.

Wednesday 5. We have called on Liebig and his wife today, and he gave me one of his silvered glasses as a remembrancer. Then we had a drive beyond the Sieges Thor, and I am now alone going to write while G. is gone with Bodenstedt to a society of literati.

Monday 10. Since Wednesday I have had a wretched cold and cough, and been otherwise ill; but I have had several pleasures nevertheless. On Friday Bodenstedt called with Baron Schack, to take us to Genelli's, the artist, of whose powers B. had spoken to us with enthusiastic admiration. The result to us was nothing but disappointment:- the sketches he showed us seemed to us quite destitute of any striking merit. There were three compositions from Biblical subjects: The banishment from Paradise, The Meeting of Isaac and Rebekah at the Well, and the arrival of Eliphaz with the gifts to Rebekah, who is trying on the bracelet with delight. The rest were mythological; Somnus and the graces,

7 German, 'the deeply afflicted'.

Jupiter holding the infant Hercules to the breast of the sleeping Juno, and a pencil sketch of a large picture – Bacchus manifesting himself as a god on board ship after he has been the object of ridicule and insults to the sailors.

Saturday, the 8th, was a wretched day – snow in the morning, and rain all the rest of the day, so that we only went out to our dinner.

On Sunday we dined with Liebig, and spent the evening at Bodenstedt's, where we met Professor Bluntschli, the jurist, a very intelligent and agreeable man, and Melchior Meyr, a maker of novels and tragedies, otherwise an ineffectual personage.

Monday 10. We went to the Theatre in the evening and saw some wretched pieces; one a disgusting thing taken from the French, turning on a man's passionate inclination towards his Pflegetochter,[8] who turns out to be his own daughter.

Tuesday. 11. We spent the evening at Professor Martius's, and met Geibel.

Wednesday 12. At Prof. von Siebold's – a very agreeable evening. Frau von Siebold sang Schubert's songs charmingly, her husband accompanying her.

Thursday 13. Wrote this morning to Holbeche and Co. and finished my letter to Sara. Then Geibel came and brought me the two volumes of his poems, and stayed chatting for an hour. We spent the evening quietly at home.

Friday 14. After writing we went for an hour to the Pinacothek and looked at some of the Flemish pictures. In the afternoon, we called at Liebig's and he went a long walk with us – the long chain of snowy mountains in the hazy distance. After supper I read Geibel's *Junius Lieder*.

Saturday. Read the 18th chapter of Adam Bede to G. He was much pleased with it. Then we walked in the Englischergarten, and heard the band, and saw the Germans drinking their beer. The park lovely.

Sunday. We were to have gone to Grosshesselohe with the von Siebolds, and went to a Frühstuck[9] with them at 12 as a preliminary. Bodenstedt was there to accompany us. But heavy rain came on, and we spent the time till five o'clock in talking, hearing music, and listening to Bodenstedt's epic on the Destruction of Novgorod. About seven, Liebig came to us, and asked us to spend the evening at his house. We went and found the Prof. von Voelderndorff, Bischoff and his wife, and Carrière and Frau.

Monday. We went out to pay calls, after our reading – G. to Löher and Liebig, I to Frau Erdl. In the evening to the theatre where we heard the "Schauspieldirektor" (Impresario) of Mozart. Charming.

Tuesday. We had a charming drive in the Englischergarten – the blossoms lovely in the orchards.

8 German, 'adopted daughter'.

9 German, 'breakfast'.

Wednesday. Went to the Vorstadt Theater in the Au, and saw "Wurm und Würmer". Schwieger as the Itinerant actor immensely amusing.

Thursday 20. As I had a gathered thumb and a feeble head this morning, we gave up the time to seeing pictures and went to the *Neue Pinacothek*. A "Lady with Fruit, followed by three children", pleased us more than ever. It is by Wickmann. The two interiors of Westminster Abbey by Ainmueller, admirable. Unable to admire Rottmann's Greek landscapes which have a room to themselves. Ditto Kaulbach's "Zerstörung der Jerusalems".

We went for the first time to see the collection of porcelain paintings, and had really a rich treat. Many of them are admirable copies of great pictures. The sweet Madonna and child, Madonna del Tempi in Raphael's early manner; a Holy Family, also in the early manner, with a Madonna the exact type of the St. Catherine; and a Holy Family in the later manner, something like the Madonna della Sedia are all admirably copied. So are two of Andrea del Sarto's – full of tenderness and calm piety.

Wednesday 26. Since I wrote in my journal last there has been very variable weather for the Pfingstfest,[10] which all the Müncheners have looked forward to as their holiday. On Sunday, through the cold wind and white dust we went to the Jesuits' Church to hear the music. It is a fine church in the Renaissance style, the vista terminating with the great altar very fine with all the crowd of human beings covering the floor. Numbers of men! In the evening we went to Bodenstedt's and saw his wife for the first time – a delicate creature, who sang us some charming Bavarian *Volkslieder*.[11] On Monday, we spent the evening at Löher's – Baumgarten, "ein junger Historiker",[12] Oldenburg and the Bodenstedts meeting us.

Delicious Mai-trank, made by putting the fresh 'Waldmeister', a cruciferous plant with a small white flower, something like Lady's Bedstraw, into mild wine, together with sugar, and occasionally other things. Yesterday and today have been drearily rainy and cold. Yesterday we walked under the colonnade at the Hofgarten, looked at Rottmann's frescoes again and went into the Kunstverein.

This evening I have read aloud "Adam Bede" Chap. 20. We have begun Ludwig's "Zwischen Himmel und Erde".

Thursday 27. We called on the von Siebolds today, then walked in the Theresien Wiese and saw the mountains gloriously, came home to dress and spent the evening at Professor Martius's, where Frau Erdl played Beethoven's Andante, and the Moonlight Sonata admirably.

28. We heard from Blackwood this morning. Good news in general, but the sale of our books not progressing at present.

10 German, 'Whitsuntide'.
11 German, 'folk songs'.
12 German, 'a young historian'.

Saturday 29. We had a walk with the Bodenstedts who called and chatted with us for half an hour.

Sunday 30. We heard Wilhelm Tell – a great enjoyment to me.

Monday. At home and to bed early.

Tuesday June 1. To Grosshesselohe with a party – von Siebold and his wife, Prof. Löher, Fräulein von List, Fräulein Thiersch, Frau von Schader and her pretty daughter. It was very pretty to see Von Siebold's delight in nature – the Libellulæ, the Blindworm, the crimson and black Cicadæ, the Orchidæ. The strange whim of Schwanthaler's, the Burg von Schwaneck, was our destination.

Wednesday 2. A splendid thunderstorm with hail, which we saw from under the colonnade of the Hofgarten. Some of the hailstones were as large as cherries.

Thursday 10. For the last week, my work has been rather scanty, owing to bodily ailments. I am at the end of chapter 21 and am this morning going to begin chapter 22. In the interim, our chief pleasure has been a trip to Starnberg by ourselves.

Friday. Went to the Residenz and saw the Reiche Kapelle, and the Odysseus-Saale.

Saturday. In the evening to Nymphenburg, where we drove round the Hirschgarten, and then walked among the magnificent shades of the Garden. I was still suffering from headache, which blunted all impressions.

Sunday 13. This morning at last free from headache and able to write. I am entering on my history of the Birthday[13] with some fear and trembling. This evening we walked between eight and half past nine in the Wiese looking towards Nymphenburg. The light delicious – the west glowing, the faint crescent moon and Venus pale above it; the larks filling the air with their songs which seemed only a little way above the ground.

Thursday 17. This evening G. left me to set out on his journey to Hofwyl.

Friday. Went with the von Siebolds to Nymphenburg, called at Professor Knapp's and saw Liebig's sister, Frau Knapp, a charming gentle-mannered woman with splendid dark eyes.

Tuesday. Tired of loneliness, I went to the Frau von Siebold, chatted with her over tea, and then heard some music.

Wednesday. My kind little friend brought me a lovely bouquet of roses this morning, and invited me to go with them in the evening to the theatre and see the new comedy, the "Drei Candidaten", which I did. A miserably poor affair.

Thursday 24. G. came in the evening at ten o'clock – after I had suffered a great deal in thinking of the possibilities that might prevent him from coming.

13 *Adam Bede*, Book 3, Chapter 22.

Friday 25. This morning I have read to G. all I have written during his absence, and he approves it more than I expected.

Wednesday July 7. This morning we left Munich, setting out in the rain to Rosenheim, by railway. The previous day we dined and sat a few hours with the dear, charming Siebolds, and parted from them with regret – glad to leave Munich, but not to leave the friends who had been so kind to us. For a week before I had been ill – almost a luxury because of the love that tended me. But the general languor and sense of depression produced by Munich air and way of life was no luxury, and I was glad to say a last good bye to the quaint pepper-boxes of the Frauen-Kirche.

Recollections of our Journey from Munich to Dresden

It was raining heavily when we went to the Munich Station to take our places for Rosenheim, and as we were well in advance of the time we had to spend a quarter of an hour in the waiting room. It passed pleasantly enough in talk with von Siebold who had goodnaturedly come to say another Good By, and with the red-cheeked Frau Joly, and with little Frau Baumgarten, who were setting off with their families to the Schlier-See. At the Rosenheim station we got into the longest of omnibuses, which took us to the Gasthof, where we were to dine or lunch, and then mount into the Stell-Wagen which would carry us to Prien on the borders of the Chiem-See. Rosenheim is a considerable and rather quaint-looking town, interrupted by orchards, and characterized in a passing glance by the piazzas that are seen everywhere fronting the shops. It has a grand view of the mountains, still a long way off. The afternoon was cloudy, with intermittent rain, and did not set off the landscape; nevertheless I had much enjoyment in this four or five hours' journey to Prien. The little villages with picturesque wide gables, projecting roofs and wooden galleries – with abundant orchards – with felled trunks of trees and stacks of fir-wood, telling of the near neighbourhood of the forest, were what I liked best in this ride.

We had no sooner entered the steam boat to cross the Chiem See than it began to rain heavily, and I kept below only peeping now and then at the mountains, and the green islands with their monasteries. From the opposite bank of the *See*, we had a grand view of the mountains, all dark purple under the clouded sky. Before us was a point where the nearer mountains opened and allowed us a view of their more distant brethren receding in a fainter and fainter blue – a marsh in the foreground where the wild ducks were flying.

Our drive from this end of the lake to Traunstein was lovely – through fertile cultivated land everywhere married to bits of forest. The green meadow or the golden corn sloped upwards towards pine-woods, or the bushy greeness seemed to run with wild freedom far out into long promontories among the ripening crops. Here and there the country had the aspect of a grand park from the beautiful intermingling of wood and field without any line of fence.

Then came the red sunset and it was dark when we entered Trauenstein, where we had to pass the night. Among our companions in the day's journey had been a long-faced, cloaked, slow and solemn man, whom George called the author of Eugene Aram and I, Don Quixote – he was so given to serious remonstrance with the vices he met on his road. We had been constantly deceived in the length of our stages – on the principle, possibly, of keeping up our spirits. The next morning there was the same tenderness shown about the starting of the Stell-Wagen – at first it was to start at seven then at half past – then, when another Wagen came with its cargo of passengers. This was too much for Don Quixote, and when the stout red faced Wirth[14] had given him still another answer about the time of starting, he began in slow and monotonous indignation: "Warum lügen Sie so? Sie werden machen dass kein Mensch will diesen Weg kommen", etc.[15] whereupon the *Wirth* looked red-faced, stout and unwashed as before without any perceptible expression of face supervening.

At last the horses were put to, and we were happy in the coupé where we had a perfect view of a charming country all the way to Salzburg. The early morning had been damp and cloudy, but by and by the clouds rolled off and as we approached Salzburg the sun was shining. But before then we had gone through the process of having our baggage examined at the boundary. Austrian officials, the pink of politeness, but under the hard necessity of fumbling in our innocent carpet bags, and taking out many of the articles apparently as if their suspicions were strong, but in reality to avoid throwing the things into disorder by turning them over inside the bags. But here was a new evil for Don Quixote. He stood by, having opened his neatly packed box, while our carpet bags were being investigated till his wrath was stirred, and with his dismal look straight before him, like a portrait into which the artist has failed to throw any expression he said to the superintending official at his side: "Man scheint hier sehr feindlich zu sein"[16] – and so on with slow, monotonous remonstrance, to which the Austrians answered with smiling apologies. At Salzburg we betook ourselves to the Goldenes Schiff opposite the Cathedral; rested till dinner and after it, hoping to go out and see the town in the evening. But about four it began to rain heavily and I filled up the time with reading aloud Moleschotte's Kreislauf des Lebens while we waited for the clearing up. At six, we were pleasantly startled by the striking up of

14 German, *der Wirt*, 'host'.

15 German, 'Why do you tell such lies? The result of it will be that no one will travel this way'. (This is Cross's translation; he also silently corrects GE's German: *George Eliot's Life as related in her letters and journals, arranged and edited by her husband J. W. Cross*, 3 vols. (Edinburgh, Blackwood, 1885), vol. 2, p. 48.)

16 German, 'you seem to be very hostile here'.

the chimes, playing a tune of Mozart's. We clung to each other and listened. Meanwhile the rain went on, and we went out at last despairing of its getting better. We wanted to ascend the Mönchsberg, and made our way there after looking into the handsome Italian cathedral, and at the façade of the house where Mozart was born. No sooner were we mounting the steps of the Mönchsberg than the rain came down more heavily. Never mind: we must go on. Precious time, paid for at hotels, must be used to some purpose. So on we went under our umbrellas, and got a very grand view of the mountains for our pains – gloomy purple masses in the foreground, then fainter blue, then pale misty ghosts of mountains closing the distance.

The next morning the weather looked doubtful, and so we gave up going to the Königs See for that day, determining to ramble on the Mönchsberg and enjoy the beauties of Salzburg instead. The morning brightened as the sun ascended and we had a delicious ramble on the Mönchsberg, looking down on the lovely peaceful plain below the grand old Untersberg where the sleeping Kaiser awaits his resurrection in that "good time coming" – der Dinge barrend die einst kommen sollen:[17] watching the white mist floating along the sides of the dark mountains; and wandering under the shadow of the plantation, where the ground was green with luxuriant hawk-weed, as at Nymphenburg near Munich. The outline of the castle and its rock is remarkably fine, and reminded us of Gorey in Jersey. But we had a still finer view of it than that from the Mönchsberg, in the afternoon when we drove out to Aigen, Prince Schwarzenberg's place which is opened to the public. On our way thither we had sight of the Wattmann, the highest mountain in Bavarian Tyrol – emerging from behind the great shoulder of the Untersberg. It was the only mountain within sight that had snow on its summit. Once at Aigen, and descended from our carriage, we had a delicious walk up and up along a road of continual steps by the course of the mountain stream which fell in a series of cascades over great heaps of boulders. Then back again by a roundabout way to our vehicle, and home, enjoying the sight of old Wattmann again, and the grand mass of Salzburg Castle on its sloping rock. To the Mönchsberg again in the evening, and here we encountered a table-d'hôte acquaintance who had been to Berchtesgaden and the Königs See, driven through the salt mine and had altogether a perfect expedition on this day, when we had not had the courage to set off. Never mind! We had enjoyed our day. The evening before as we were resolutely making the tour of the Mönchsberg in the rain, we came on a sentinel whom George asked if we were on the way to the town. G. spoke in German but the Sentinel answered in Italian, and the tones affected me strangely. It was as if the poor fellow, divining that we were foreigners who might probably understand Italian, wished to have a momentary sense of fellow-feeling.

We thought it wisest the next morning to renounce the Königs See and pursue

17 German, 'the things awaited that one day will come'.

our way to Ischl by the Stell-Wagen. We were fortunate enough to secure two places in the coupé, and I enjoyed greatly the quiet outlook from my comfortable corner, on the changing landscape – green valley, and hill, and mountain; here and there a picturesque Tyrolese village, and once or twice a fine lake.

We reached lovely Ischl, I think, about four in the afternoon, took some coffee, and then walked out to look about us. The greatest charm of this charming place is the crystal Traun, surely the purest of streams. Away again early the next morning in the coupé of the Stell-Wagen, through a country more and more beautiful, high woody mountains sloping steeply down to narrow fertile green valleys, the road winding amongst them so as to shew a perpetual variety of graceful outlines where the sloping mountains met in the distance before us. As we approached the Gmunden See, the masses became grander and more rocky, and the valley opened wider. It was Sunday, and when we left the Stell-Wagen we found quite a crowd in Sunday clothes standing round the place of embarkation on the steam-boat that was to take us along the lake.

Gmunden is another pretty place, at the head of the lake, but apart from this one advantage inferior to Ischl. We got on to the slowest of railways here, getting down at the station near the Falls of the Traun, where we dined at the pleasant inn, and fed our eyes on the clear river again hurrying over the rocks. Behind the great fall there is a sort of inner chamber where the water rushes perpetually over a stone altar. We looked at this with a very agreeable Hungarian gentleman, travelling with his wife and daughter to the baths for the sake of his health. At the station, as we waited for the train, it began to rain, and the good-natured-looking woman asked us to take shelter in her little station-house – a single room, not more than eight feet square, where she lived with her husband and two little girls, all the year round. The good couple looked more contented than half the well-lodged people in the world. He used to be a droschky driver, and after that life of uncertain gains which had many days quite penniless and therefore dinnerless, he found his present position quite a pleasant lot.

On to Linz when the train came, gradually losing sight of the Tyrolean mountains and entering the great plain of the Danube. Our voyage the next day in the steam-boat was unfortunate: we had incessant rain, till we had passed all the finest part of the banks. But when we had landed, the sun shone out brilliantly, and so our entrance into Vienna, through the long suburb, with perpetual shops and odd names (*Prschka*, for example, which a German, in our omnibus, thought not at all remarkable for consonants) was quite cheerful. We made our way with our porter and carpet bags through the city and across the bridge to the *Weissen Ross* which was full; so we went on to the Drei Rosen, which received us.

The sunshine was transient: it began to rain again when we went out to look at St. Stephen's, but the delight of seeing that glorious building could not be marred by a little rain. The tower of this church is worth going to Vienna to see. The aspect of the city is that of an inferior Paris; the shops have an elegance that one sees nowhere else in Germany, the streets are clean, the houses tall and stately. The next morning, we had a view of the town from the Belvedere Terrace, St. Stephen's sending its exquisite tower aloft from among an almost level forest of houses and inconspicuous churches. It is a magnificent collection of pictures at the Belvedere, but we were so unfortunate as only to be able to see them once, the gallery being shut up on the Wednesday, and so many pictures have faded from my memory even of those which I had time to distinguish. Titian's Danæ, was one that delighted us: besides this I remember Giorgione's Lucrezia Borgia with the cruel, cruel eyes; the remarkable head of Christ – a proud Italian face in a red garment, I think by Correggio; and two heads by Denner, the most wonderful of all his wonderful heads that I have seen. There is an Ecce Homo by Titian, which is thought highly of, and is splendid in composition and colour, but the Christ is abject, the Pontius Pilate vulgar: amazing that they could have been painted by the same man who conceived and executed the Christo del Moneta! There are huge Veroneses too, splendid and uninteresting.

The Lichtenstein collection we saw twice, and that remains with me much more distinctly – the room full of Rubens's history of Decius, more magnificent even than he usually is in colour; then his glorious Assumption of the Virgin, and opposite to it the portraits of his two boys; the portrait of his lovely wife going to the bath with brown drapery round her; and the fine portraits by Vandyke, especially the pale delicate face of Wallenstein, with blue eyes and pale auburn locks.

Another great pleasure we had at Vienna – next after the sight of St. Stephen's and the pictures – was a visit to Hyrtl, the anatomist, who showed us some of his wonderful preparations showing the vascular and nervous systems in the lungs, liver, kidneys and intestinal canal of various animals. He told us the deeply interesting story of the loss of his fortune in the Viennese revolution of '48. He was compelled by the revolutionists to attend on the wounded for three days running. When at last he came to his home to change his clothes, he found nothing but four bare walls! His fortune, in Government bonds, was burnt along with the house as well as all his precious collection of anatomical preparations etc. He told us that since that great shock his nerves have been so susceptible that he sheds tears at the most trifling events, and has a depression of spirits which often keeps him silent for days. He only received a very slight sum from government in compensation for his loss.

We went one evening to the theatre and saw Laura Schubert in Hans and Anne, which she performed with Fielitz, whom we had seen at the Vorstadt Theater at Munich. It was the Königlichen Theater am Wien, a pretty house about the size of the Lyceum. Another evening we strolled in the Volksgarten; and saw the Theseus killing the Centaur by Canova, which stands in a temple built for its reception. But the garden to be best remembered by us was that at Schönbrunn, a labyrinth of stately avenues with their terminal fountains. We amused ourselves for some time with the menagerie here – the lions especially, who lay in dignified sleepiness till the approach of feeding time made them open eager eyes and pace impatiently about their dens.

We set off from Vienna in the evening, with a family of Wallachians as our companions, one of whom, an elderly man, could speak no German, and began to address G. in Wallachian, as if that were the common language of all the earth. We managed to sleep enough for a night's rest, in spite of intense heat and our cramped positions, and arrived in very good condition at Prague in the fine morning.

Out we went after breakfast that we might see as much as possible of the grand old city in one day, and our morning was occupied chiefly in walking about and getting views of striking exteriors. The most interesting things we saw were the Jewish burial-ground (the alter Friedhof) and the old Synagogue. The Friedhof is unique – with a wild growth of grass and shrubs and trees and a multitude of quaint tombs in all sorts of positions looking like the fragments of a great building, or as if they had been shaken by an earthquake. We saw a lovely dark eyed Jewish child here, which we were glad to kiss in all its dirt. Then came the sombre old synagogue with its smoked groins, and lamp for ever burning. An intelligent Jew was our cicerone and read us some Hebrew out of the precious old book of the Law.

After dinner we took a carriage and went across the wonderful bridge of St. Jean Nepomuck with its avenue of statues, towards the Radschin – an ugly straight-lined building but grand in effect from its magnificent site, on the summit of an eminence crowded with old massive buildings. The view from this eminence is one of the most impressive in the world – perhaps as much from one's associations with Prague as from its visible grandeur and antiquity. The Cathedral close to the Radschin is a melancholy object on the outside – left with unfinished sides like scars. The interior is rich, but sadly confused in its ornamentation, like so many of the grand old churches – hideous altars of bastard style disgracing exquisite Gothic columns. Cruellest of all, in St Stephen's at Vienna! We got our view from a *Damen Stift*[18] (for ladies of family) founded by Maria Theresa, whose blond beauty looked down on us from a striking portrait. Close in front of us sloping downwards was a pleasant orchard; then came the river with its long, long bridge and grand gateway; then the sober-coloured city with its surrounding plain and distant hills.

In the evening we went to the theatre – a shabby ugly building – and heard Spohr's Jessonda.

The next morning early by railway to Dresden, a charming journey, for it took us right through the Saxon Switzerland, with its castellated rocks and firs. At four o'clock we were dining comfortably at the Hotel de Pologne, and the next morning (Sunday) we secured our lodgings – a whole apartment of six rooms all to ourselves for s18/- per week! By nine o'clock we were established in our new

18 German, 'convent'; translated as 'Charitable Institution for Ladies' in Cross, vol. 2, p. 57.

home, where we were to enjoy six weeks' quiet work, undistracted by visitors and visiting. And so we did. We were as happy as princes – are not; George writing at the far corner of the great salon, I at my Schranke[19] in my own private room with closed doors. Here I wrote the latter half of the second volume of Adam Bede, in the long mornings that our early hours – rising at six o'clock – secured us. Three mornings in the week we went to the Picture Gallery from 12 till 1. The first day we went was a Sunday when there is always a crowd in the Madonna Cabinet. I sat down on the sofa opposite the picture for an instant, but a sort of awe, as if I were suddenly in the living presence of some glorious being, made my heart swell too much for me to remain comfortably, and we hurried out of the room. On subsequent mornings we always came in the last minutes of our stay to look at this sublimest picture, and while the others, except the Christo del Moneta and Holbein's Madonna, lost much of their first interest, this became harder and harder to leave. Holbein's Madonna is very exquisite – a divinely gentle golden haired blond, with eyes cast down, in an attitude of unconscious easy grace – the loveliest of all the Madonnas in the Dresden Gallery, except the Sistine. By the side of it is a wonderful portrait by Holbein which I especially enjoyed looking at. It represents nothing more lofty than a plain weighty man of business, a goldsmith; but the eminently fine painting brings out all the weighty calm good sense that lies in a first rate character of that order.

We looked at the Zinsgroschen too every day, and after that at the great painter's Venus, fit for its purity and sacred loveliness to hang in a temple with Madonnas. Palma's Venus which hangs near, was an excellent foil, because it is pretty and pure in itself, but beside the Titian it is common and unmeaning.

Another interesting case of comparison was that between the original Zinsgroschen and a copy by an Italian painter which hangs on the opposite wall of the Cabinet. This is considered a fine copy and would be a fine picture if one had never seen the original; but all the finest effects are gone in the copy.

The four large Correggios hanging together – the *Nacht*, the Madonna with St. Sebastian of the smiling graceful character, with the little cherub riding astride a cloud – the Madonna with St. Hubert – and a third Madonna very grave and sweet painted when he was nineteen – remain with me very vividly. They are full of life – though the life is not of a high order, and I should have surmised without any previous knowledge, that the painter was among the first masters of technique. The Magdalene is sweet in conception, but seems to have less than the usual merit of Correggio's pictures as to painting.

A picture we delighted in extremely was one of Murillo's – St. Rodriguez, fatally wounded, receiving the crown of Martyrdom. The attitude and expression are sublime, and strikingly distinguished from all other pictures of saints I have ever seen. He stands erect in his scarlet and white robes, with face upturned – the

19 German, 'side-board' (GE may be using a travelling desk).

arms held simply downward, but the hands held open in a receptive attitude. The silly cupid-like angel holding the martyr's crown in the corner spoils all.

I did not half satisfy my appetite for the rich collection of Flemish and Dutch pictures here – for Teniers, Ryckaert, Gerard Dow, Terburg, Mieris and the rest. Rembrandt looks great here in his portraits, but I like none of the other pictures by him; the Ganymede is an offence. Guido is superlatively odious in his Christs, in agonized or ecstatic attitudes, much about the level of the accomplished London beggar.

Dear, grand old Rubens does not show to great advantage except in the charming half length Diana returning from hunting, the Love-garden, and the sketch of his Judgment of Paris.

The most popular Murillo, and apparently one of the most popular Madonnas in the gallery, is the simple, sad mother with her child, without the least divinity in it – suggesting a dead or sick father, and imperfect nourishment in a garret. In that light it is touching. A fellow traveller in the Railway to Leipsic told us he had seen this picture in 1848 with nine bullet holes in it! The firing from the hotel of the Stadt Rom bore directly on the picture gallery.

Veronese is imposing in one of the large rooms – the Adoration of the Magi, the Marriage at Cana, the Finding of Moses, etc, making grand masses of colour on the lower part of the walls – but to me he is ignoble as a painter of human beings.

It was a charming life – our six weeks at Dresden. There were the open air concerts at the Grosser Garten and the Bruhl'sche Terrace; the Sommer Theater, where we saw our favourite comic actor Merbitz; the walks into the open country with the grand stretch of sky all round us; the Zouaves with their wondrous make-ups as women; Räder, the humorous comedian at the Link'sche Bad Theater; our quiet afternoons in our pleasant salon – all helping to make an agreeable fringe to the quiet working time.

From Dresden, one showery day, we set off to Leipsic, the first stage on our way home. Here we spent two nights – had a glimpse of the old town with its fine Markt – dined at Brockhaus's – saw the picture gallery, carrying away a lasting delight in Calame's great landscapes, and De Dreux's dogs, which are far better worth seeing than De La Roche's Napoleon at Fontainebleau, considered the glory of the gallery – went with Victor Carus to his museum and saw an Amphioxus, and finally spent the evening at an open-air concert in Carus's company. Early in the morning we set off by railway and travelled night and day till we reached home, on the 2nd of September. On the 7th I sent off the 2nd volume of Adam Bede to Blackwood and tonight, the 27th of October, as I am finishing this fragmentary story of our travels, I am not far off the end of my third volume. "Thus far hath the Lord helped us", as it was said by them of old time.

Richmond, October 27 1858

XI. *Recollections of Italy 1860*

The tour of Italy in 1860 had been long anticipated. In a letter of 5 June 1857, GE wrote to Cara Bray: 'we mean to settle down (after we have once been to Italy) and buy pots and kettles and keep a dog'.[1] She was not disappointed in the experience: writing to Sara Hennell on 2 July 1860 she declared, 'We have had an unspeakably delightful journey – one of those journies that seem to divide one's life in two by the new ideas they suggest and the new veins of interest they open' (*Letters*, vol. 3, p. 311). This is an accurate comment in respect of her writing life, perhaps self-fulfilling prophecy. A reading of 'Recollections of Italy' casts light on the well-recognised division between the early novels, drawn in such large measure from her own family recollections, and the later works. In her relationship with GHL, this journey also marks a shift in the balance of power between them, since GE's reputation and finances are now secure, and from this point hers is to be the dominant career. There is also an imminent change in their domestic arrangements, since Charles Lewes comes home from Hofwyl with them, and they set up house in central London.

This journey establishes a pattern of their taking off for foreign parts immediately a book is finished (in this case, both GE and GHL had completed a major work, respectively *The Mill on the Floss* and *The Physiology of Common Life*). Their relative affluence makes this possible. It is notable that money matters, which had bulked so large in the earlier journals, are in the background of GE's narrative now, though still documented by GHL in his much more prosaic diary record of this tour.

While the journey was avowedly for pleasure, it was the pleasure of improvement rather than pure hedonism they sought, though they did not have the specific motives of research on Goethe or physiology which had taken them to Germany in 1854 and 1858. They set themselves a steady curriculum, which owed a great deal to Ruskin though he is not mentioned in this connection (however, GE copied passages of *The Songs of Venice* in her commonplace book.)[2] The journal is

1 *The George Eliot Letters*, ed. Gordon S. Haight, 9 vols. (New Haven, Yale University Press, 1954–78), vol. 2, p. 339.

2 Joseph Weisenfarth, *George Eliot: A Writer's Notebook, 1854–79, and*

concerned both with natural beauty and with works of art, and GE's responses reveal the influence of Ruskin's conviction that art has the power to translate, not just transcribe, the natural world. They acquired a small library en route, including Liddell's *History of Rome*, 'to repair the breaches in our historical knowledge', Stendhal's *Histoire de la Peinture*, Kugler's *Handbook of Italian Painters*, and Murray on Naples.[3]

This studiousness informs 'Recollections of Italy. 1860' to the extent that even sympathetic readers of the version published by Cross in the *Life* found it inhibiting. The essay was singled out for censure by Lord Acton, for one:

> The Italian journey reveals that weakness of the historic faculty which is a pervading element in her life . . . Italy was little more to her than a vast museum, and Rome, with all the monuments and institutions which link the old world with the new, interested her less than the galleries of Florence. She surveys the grand array of tombs in St Peter's, and remarks nothing but some peasants feeling the teeth of Canova's lion.[4]

These comments are a study in frustration: Acton is filled with admiration of GE's intellectual prowess, worthy of a man, but reads it as compromised by her agnosticism and personal immorality, and her essentially female triviality: 'fortuitous experience' of 'common people in private life' distracts her 'from the heroic subjects, the large questions and proportions of history'.[5] Of all GE's journals, this appears the most deliberately composed, but Acton is unable to read it either on its own generic terms, or as a production of GE the novelist in which she is recasting for herself precisely 'the large questions and proportions of history'.

Henry James was also critical of her 'various journals and notes of her visits to the Continent', which he thought

---

uncollected writings (Charlottesville, University Press of Virginia, 1981), pp. 39–42 and 169. Wiesenfarth conjectures that these notes were made in preparation for the 1860 expedition. An excellent specific discussion of the affinity of GE with Ruskin is G. A. Wittig Davis, 'Ruskin's *Modern Painters* and George Eliot's concept of realism', *English Language Notes*, 18 (1981), pp. 194–201.

3 GHL Journal, 7, 21 and 27 April 1860. The Murray in question is presumably *A Handbook for Travellers in Southern Italy; being a guide for the continental portion of the Kingdom of the Two Sicilies* (3rd edn., 1858).

4 Lord Acton, *Nineteenth Century*, 17 (March 1885), quoted in *George Eliot: Critical Assessments*, ed. Stuart Hutchinson, 4 vols. (Mountfield, Sussex, Helm Information, 1996), vol. 1, p 650.

5 *Ibid.*

> singularly vague in expression on the subject of the general and particular spectacle – the life and manners, the works of art. She enumerates diligently all the pictures and statues she sees, and the way she does so is proof of her active, earnest intellectual habits; but it is rarely apparent that they have, as the phrase is, said much to her, or that what they have said is one of their deeper secrets.[6]

Like Acton, James required something different from what GE provided. Given the material available to him in Cross's *Life*, he is not in a position to realise the extent to which in this journal she exercises her considerable knowledge, for example in considering the attribution of a painting to Leonardo da Vinci (p. 365). Nor does he discern the extent to which this journal works within a particular discourse.

Writing in retrospect, GE constructs her Italian journey as a version of the Grand Tour inflected by English Romanticism. Her account acknowledges the class (aristocratic) and gender (male) implications of the Grand Tour, and is frequently cast in Romantic tropes of dream and transport. Throughout, there is appraisal of the experiences of the travellers against a set of romantic expectations of the classical world, for the most part tacit, which GE finds fulfilled without either reaching heights of romantic epiphany, or confronting Italy as a mystic Other, symbol of the sensuous South.

GE had titled those earlier journal essays written after the events they describe 'Recollections'. For 'Recollections of Italy. 1860', a specifically Wordsworthian inflection of the term may be relevant: 'recollection' as involving more than an act of recalling to mind, rather tending towards a concentration of faculties for intense, even mystical contemplation. Her use of the phrase 'double consciousness' in the opening passage of sententious moralising supports the sense of deliberate activation of memory and related mental processes. She makes clear that what a traveller sees at any given moment may not be fully grasped in that moment, and then proceeds to interpretation of the Alpine crossing as a transcendent experience. There is no declared self-scrutiny such as Goethe avowed in his *Italian Journey* (one of the texts against which GE's essay resonates): 'My purpose in making this wonderful journey is not to delude myself but to discover myself in the objects I see.'[7]

6 Henry James, review of Cross, in *George Eliot: The Critical Heritage*, ed. David R. Carroll (London, Routledge and Kegan Paul, 1971), p. 499.

7 J. W. Goethe, *Italian Journey [1786–1788]*, trans. W. H. Auden and Elizabeth Mayer (1962; Harmondsworth, Penguin, 1970), p. 57.

Goethe of course relished his incognito on his Italian journey: GE was not yet so famous that this was an issue, though in later travels it became so.[8] Though GE does not admit self-discovery as an explicit goal, it is clear how invigorating she found the experience of travel. Among accounts of travel to and residence in Italy which may also have conditioned GE's expectations are those of the second generation English Romantics, notably Shelley and Byron.

The extent to which the journal is written with due regard to genre is clear from the almost complete suppression of reference to current affairs. Beyond the comments on Cavour and the 'widening life' of 'Resuscitated Italy' at Turin, the journal is silent about the extraordinarily volatile Italian political situation in the spring of 1860, when Cavour was engaged in negotiation with France about Piedmont's ceding Savoy and Nice in exchange for French-held duchies in central Italy. By 1861, Cavour had become Prime Minister of an Italy united under the House of Savoy. GE's description of the scene at Turin station in a letter written from Rome is more pointed and engaged than the account in the journals, and continues:

> I feel some stirrings of the insurrectionary spirit myself when I see the red pantaloons at every turn in the streets of Rome. I suppose Mrs Browning could explain to me that this is part of the great idea nourished in the soul of the modern saviour Louis Napoleon, and that for the French to impose a hateful government on the Romans is the only proper sequence to the story of the French Revolution. (*Letters*, vol. 3, p. 288)

Later, she wrote in more – and revealing – detail:

> Tuscany is in the highest political spirits for the moment, and of course Victor Emanuel stares at us at every turn here, with the most loyal exaggeration of moustache and intelligent meaning. But we are selfishly careless about dynasties just now, caring more for the doings of Giotto and Brunelleschi, than for those of Count Cavour. On a

8 During the Spanish journey of 1866–7, GHL wrote 'I never write my name legibly and in full in the hotel books, wishing to preserve the obscurity of nobodies, but at Granada there being only two Frenchmen in the hotel, I wrote my name legibly for the sake of acquaintances or others who might come afterwards. The next day the hotel began to fill with English and Americans. It was whispered round at once who we were, and the attention of the guests was flattering but boring.' (*The Letters of George Henry Lewes*, ed. William Baker, 2 vols. (Victoria, University of Victoria, English Literary Studies Monograph series 64, 1995), vol. 2, p. 118.)

first journey to the greatest centres of art, one must be excused for letting one's public spirit go to sleep a little. (*Letters*, vol. 3, p. 294)

In retrospect, she is conscious of having undertaken a rite of passage. GE and GHL spent some time in Paris and other places en route to Italy. But she made a strategic decision to open the journal with a setpiece. In a letter to John Blackwood she had described 'the passage over the Mont Cenis, in the cramping diligence and traineau . . . with no food except a small loaf' (*Letters*, vol. 3, p. 285). Such privations are ignored as 'Recollections' opens with the dramatic nocturnal scene in the Alps, launching an explicit account of crossing a boundary from the dullness of the mundane into experience of heightened sensibility and romantic dream (she sleeps and wakes several times before dawn). There is textual embodiment of a more strongly characterised narrator than in 'Weimar', as she adopts something of the male-gendered traveller's persona, in part by deployment of her classical learning, in part by the assumption of a male gaze, for instance in the conventional gendering of Nature as female. Consider, for example, the last sentence of the third paragraph: 'The keenness of the air contributed strongly to the sense of novelty: we had left our everyday conventional world quite behind us and were on a visit to Nature in her private home.' Such romantic discourse is not uniformly sustained throughout the essay, but is latent even in the more familiar registers adopted as they proceed towards Rome.

The first challenge to their expectations comes as they make their way to Rome: where 'Not one iota had I seen that corresponded with my preconceptions.' Rome is the test case for the traveller in Italy, as Goethe emphasised. Like GE and GHL, he hurried to be there for a particular religious festival (All Saints, in his case, Easter in theirs), and like them he experienced some initial disappointment – though in reading any of these accounts one should be mindful that disappointment then discovery is itself a traveller's trope.[9] George Eliot's spirits improved on the morning after their arrival, and she soon recounts 'a thrill of awe' as she retrieves the past through experience of its ruined glories. Apprehension of supplanted cultures determines what she sees, whether in the Campo Vaccino or in the Forum, 'our favourite haunt', where vestiges of pedestals are 'utterly confused to all but erudite eyes'. Rome is a text she learns to read, through her knowledge of other texts about it.

9 Goethe, *Italian Journey*, p. 129.

'Let me see what I most delighted in, in Rome', she asks, and gives a lengthy list of 'the traces of Ancient Rome that have left the strongest image of themselves in my mind' – including some picturesque features and a number of views. They took in popular spectacles such as the illumination of St Peter's on Easter Sunday (described by Murray in terms almost as poetic as GE's: 'at the first stroke of the clock [8 p.m.], 900 lamps are lighted so instantaneously that it seems the work of enchantment. The whole process is generally completed before the clock has finished striking the hour, or in about 8 seconds. The lanterns used . . . are iron cups filled with blazing tallow and turpentine').[10]

On a more domestic note, GHL writes of buying cameos (GHL Journal, 18 April 1860), as Dorothea does for Celia – but GE is silent about this activity. Her journal concentrates on the challenge of travel to the exclusion of 'home thoughts'. She makes no mention even of the good news of the sales of *The Mill on the Floss* that reached them in Rome, with better news to come in Florence (including word of the highly favorable review in *The Times: Letters*, vol. 3, pp. 289 and 296). Yet her writing has made their travel possible: by the end of the year, she had earned over £3000 from *The Mill*.

The essayist declares 'How much more I have to write about Rome!' – which, effectively, she reserves for a decade until she writes *Middlemarch*. There are some direct transpositions into *Middlemarch*: Dorothea's disorientation, obviously; the painter Overbeck, whose maroon velvet cap and grey scarf are given to Naumann; GE and GHL's disappointment in the frescoes of Cupid and Psyche in the Farnesina palace, transmuted in Casaubon's obtuse scholarly comments in chapter 20; her pleasure in the Campagna. Perhaps there are similar transpositions into other works also: do the children at play in Genoa (see p. 338) turn up in the opening paragraphs of *Daniel Deronda*? might the experience of the synagogue at Leghorn contribute to the depiction of Judaism in that novel? Beyond such details, more profound reflections germinated over time: questions about scholarship, art, history, and the relativity of knowledge. These issues are inscribed in *Middlemarch* in such details as the misattribution of Raphael's 'Coronation of the Virgin' referred to in Chapter 19. What GE is pointing to in the works of art in the Vatican – the statue of Cleopatra, or

10 John Murray, *A Handbook of Rome and its environs: forming Part II of the handbook for travellers in Central Italy* (5th edn.; London, John Murray, 1858), p. 107.

Ariadne, for example – is not the fixed 'meaning' of a recoverable past, but the continual process of making new meanings.[11] From now on, her fiction was to be explicitly concerned with the presence of the past in the present, with the resonance of Savonarola's Florence in nineteenth-century England, or the interaction in *Middlemarch* of the 1830s and 1870s. The major 'division' for GE before and after the Italian journey of 1860 is evident in her writing life: in the shift from the working out of childhood memories to more studied work on the past in relation to the present, both reading the past in relation to the present, and writing it. The journal gives her account at the time of these issues taking hold: not a new concern for her, but one which now emerges with a new focus and emphasis, to be painfully worked through in the writing of *Romola* and the shorter fictions – *Silas Marner* and 'Brother Jacob' – that intervened between its conception and completion.

Leaving Rome at last they went to Naples, their base for expeditions to a number of places including Pompeii, which moved them deeply. (Apparently they were too soon to see the effects of Giuseppe Fiorelli's assumption of the role of director of excavation, which was much more systematic than under previous directors and included development of a technique for making casts of bodies by pouring cement into the hollows formed in the volcanic ash when the bodies disintegrated – a process which could hardly fail to have interested GE and GHL). At Amalfi, the sight of a macaroni mill and a paper mill varied their pursuit of antiquity. As so often, GE's country childhood makes her responsive to elements in the landscape, such as the 'high cultivation' near Naples. The next place in which they spent any length of time was Florence, where GHL's journal for 21 May records his inspiration that Savonarola 'afforded fine material for an historical romance. Polly at once caught at the idea with enthusiasm' (*Letters*, vol. 3, p. 307) – though George Eliot's journal makes no reference

11 These claims depend on such detailed exegeses as Joseph Wiesenfarth ('*Middlemarch:* The Language of Art', *PMLA*, 97 (1982), pp. 363–77) and Kathleen McCormack ('*Middlemarch:* Dorothea's Husbands in the Vatican Museums', *Victorians Institute Journal*, 20 (1992), pp. 75–91), which show how the whole discourse of art is working in the novel – particularly the capacity of art to interpret and be reinterpreted. Margaret Harris has discussed some of these issues at greater length in 'What George Eliot saw in Europe: the evidence of her journals', *George Eliot in Europe*, ed. John Rignall (Aldershot, Scolar, 1997), pp. 1–16.

to the matter. She was absorbing the ambience, however, as the topography of *Romola* shows.

Then to Siena, Bologna, Padua – and Venice, of which her account is conventionally rhapsodic. There can be no doubt that she was enthralled, but as in Rome her response, conditioned by her textual expectations, lacks the more individual abandon of her account (say) of Weimar. The section on Venice is the clearest evidence of the extent to which 'Recollections of Italy' is an account of GE 'melted into the general life' of the tourist registering prescribed sights and reactions to them. Yet she was not wholly in thrall. She conveys something of the spirit of Anna Jameson, writing about the railway which opened in 1846:

> I hear people talking of the railroad across the Lagune, as if it were to unpoetise Venice, . . . and they call on me to join the outcry, to echo sentimental denunciations, quoted out of Murray's Handbook; but I cannot . . . to me, that tremendous bridge spanning the sea, only adds to the wonderful one wonder more.[12]

The special, protected, set-apart quality of the Italian experience is sustained to the end of the narrative. The significant crossing of the Alps at the beginning of the journal is recalled as the account of the whole experience is concluded and contained, though they are not yet home.

In many respects this journal reads as the fulfilment of expectations which are the outcome of quite conventional (male) assumptions. But GE is rarely accommodated within a genre, and she treats with the assumptions of travel writing in this journal only to repudiate them in later writing. Even in this journal, which so comprehensively shows her stimulation by the exotic aspects of Italy (climatic, topographical, cultural, and antiquarian), she is not seduced by the genre into representing a quest for buried truth or a purer state of being as the goal of her travels. There is a consciousness in the journal of history being constantly remade: in her fiction, especially from *Romola* on, there is an engagement with the layers of previous civilisations and with competing histories (individual and collective). This is a concept of history and historical process which is far from being simply archaeological on the one hand or progressivist on the other.

Cross prints this journal almost complete, intercalated with extracts from letters, providing a number of footnotes

12 Anna Jameson, *Memoirs and Essays* (London, Bentley, 1846), p. 20.

mainly in the Florentine section to identify works of art referred to, at times even correcting GE's attributions. Haight, curiously, quotes it hardly at all. Indeed, in *Letters*, he prints excerpts from Lewes's journals in preference to George Eliot's: the passage about the inspiration for *Romola*, and another about Pompeii, which among other things deplores the impropriety of some frescoes: 'It was curious to see the schoolboy like tendency in these Pompeians, to ornament their bedrooms with pictures of hideous obscenity' (vol. 3, p. 291).

XI. Recollections of Italy. 1860

We have finished our journey to Italy – the journey I had looked forward to for years, rather with the hope of the new elements it would bring to my culture, than with the hope of immediate pleasure. Travelling can hardly be without a continual current of disappointment if the main object is not the enlargement of one's general life, so as to make even weariness and annoyances enter into the sum of benefit. One great deduction to me from the delight of seeing world-famous objects is the frequent double consciousness which tells me that I am not enjoying the actual vision enough, and that when higher enjoyment comes with the reproduction of the scene in my imagination I shall have lost some of the details, which impress me too feebly in the present because the faculties are not wrought up into energetic action.

I have no other journal than the briefest record of what we did each day; so I shall put down my recollections whenever I happen to have leisure and inclination – just for the sake of making clear to myself the impressions I have brought away from our three months' travel.

The first striking moment in our journey was when we arrived, I think about eleven o'clock at night, at the point in the ascent of the Mont Cenis where we were to quit the diligences and take to the sledges. After a hasty drink of hot coffee in the roadside inn, our large party – the inmates of three diligences – turned out into the starlight to await the signal for getting into the sledges. That signal seemed to be considerably on in the future, to be arrived at through much confusion of luggage-lifting, voices, and leading about of mules. The human bustle and confusion made a poetic contrast with the sublime stillness of the starlit heavens spread over the snowy tableland and surrounding heights. The keenness of the air contributed strongly to the sense of novelty: we had left our every-day conventional world quite behind us and were on a visit to Nature in her private home.

Once closely packed in our sledge, congratulating ourselves that, after all, we were no more squeezed than in our diligence, I gave myself up to as many naps as chose to take possession of me, and actually slept without very considerable interruption till we were near the summit of the mighty pass. Already there was a faint hint of the morning in the starlight which showed us the vast sloping snow-fields as we commenced the descent. I got a few glimpses of the pure far-stretching whiteness before the sharpening edge of cold forced us to close the window. Then there was no more to be seen till it was time to get out of the sledge and ascend the diligence once more: not, however, without a preliminary struggle with the wind which fairly blew me down on my slippery standing ground. The rest of our descent showed us fine varied scenes of mountain and ravine till we got down at Suza, where breakfast and the railway came as a desirable variety after our long mountain journey and long fast. One of our companions had been a gigantic French soldier, who had in charge a bag of government money. He was my vis à vis for some time and cramped my poor legs not a little with his precious bag, which he would by no means part from. But he repaid me for that inconvenience by the humourous suggestions of his broad, stupid, good-natured face, and the naiveté of everything he said and did. A dapper little young French officer at my right hand, had suffered from the cold acting on a wretched remnant of teeth: says the good giant to him pointing to his cheek, 'Your face is swelled'. 'Ah, je le sais bien.'[1]

The approach to Turin by the railway gave us a grand view of snowy mountains surrounding the city on three sides. A few hours of rest spent there could leave no very vivid impression. A handsome street, well-broken by architectural details, with a glimpse of snowy mountains at the end of the vista, colonnades on each side, and flags waving their bright colours in sign of political joy – is the image that usually rises before me at the mention of Turin. I fancy the said street is the principal one, but in our walk about the town we saw everywhere a similar character of prosperous well-lodged town-existence – only without the colonnades, and without the balconies and other details which make the principal street picturesque. This is the place that Alfieri lived in through many of his young follies, getting tired of it at last for the Piedmontese pettiness of which it was the centre. And now, eighty years later it is the centre of a widening life which may at last become the life of Resuscitated Italy. At the Railway station as we waited to take our departure for Genoa, we had a sight of the man whose name will always be connected with the story of that widening life – Count Cavour – "imitant son portrait"[2] which we had seen in the shops, with unusual closeness. A man pleasant to look upon; with a smile half kind half caustic; giving you altogether the impression that he thinks of "many matters", but thanks heaven and makes no boast of them. He was there to meet the Prince de Carignan, who was going to Genoa on his way towards Florence by the same train as ourselves. The Prince is a notability with a thick waist bound in by a gold belt, and with a fat face predominated over by a large moustache. *Non ragionam di lui.*[3] The railway journey from Turin was chiefly distinguished by dust, but I slept through the latter half, without prejudice, however, to the satisfaction with which I lay down in a comfortable bedroom in the Hotel Feder.

In Genoa again on a bright, warm Spring morning! I was here eleven years ago, and the image that visit had left in my mind was surprizingly faithful, though

1 French, 'Ah, I am well aware of it'.
2 French, 'imitating his portrait'.
3 Italian, *non ragioniamo di lui*, 'we won't talk about him'.

fragmentary. The outlook from our hotel was nearly the same as before – over a low building with a colonnade, at the masts of the abundant shipping. But there was a striking change in the interior of the Hotel. It was, like the other, a palace adapted to the purposes of an inn; but be-carpeted and be-furnitured with an exaggeration of English fashions.

We lost no time in turning out after breakfast into the morning sunshine. George was enchanted with the aspect of the place, as we drove or walked along the streets. It was his first vision of anything corresponding to his preconception of Italy. After the Adlergasse in Nuremberg, surely no streets can be more impressive than the Strada Nuova and S. Nuovissima at Genoa. In street architecture, I can rise to the highest point of the admiration given to the Palladian style. And here in these chief streets of Genoa, the Palaces have two advantages over those of Florence: they form a series, creating a general impression of grandeur of which each particular palace gets the benefit; and they have the open gateway, showing the cortile within – sometimes containing grand stone staircases. And all this architectural splendour is accompanied with the signs of actual prosperity: Genoa la Superba is not a name of the past, merely.

We ascended the tower of S. Maria di Carignano, to get a panoramic view of the city with its embosoming hills and bay – saw the Cathedral with its banded black and white marble, the churches of the Annunziata and San Ambrogio with their wealth of gilding and rich pink-brown marbles, the Palazzo Rosso with its collection of eminently forgettable pictures, and the pretty gardens of the Palazzo Doria with their flourishing green close against the sea. A drive in the direction of the Campo Santo along the dry pebbly bed of the river, showed us the terraced hills planted with olives, and many picturesque groups of the common people with mules or on carts; – not to mention what gives beauty to every corner of the inhabited world – the groups of children squatting against walls or trotting about by the side of their elders, or grinning together over their play.

We went to the opera in the evening. It was a benefit night for the *basso*, and we had a series of selections – one scene from the Barbiere containing the *Calumnia* – very ill sung, and two acts of Rigoletto, in which the King's part was presented by a fat robust tenor. An incompetent and ugly soprano, who sang "Una Voce", was hissed first and then warmly applauded, perhaps from an alternation of candour and pity. But the grand source of enthusiasm in the house was the ballet, and the premier sujet, a pretty little creature with a *nez retroussé*,[4] so far transcended all the usual signs of admiration, that some males behind us fell into vigorous "*Yahs*".

One of the personages we were pleased to encounter in the streets here was a quack – a Dulcamara –[5] mounted on his carriage and holding forth with much

4 French, 'turned-up nose'.
5 Italian, 'charlatan'.

brio,[6] before proceeding to take out the tooth of a negro already seated in preparation.

We left Genoa on the second evening, unhappily a little too long after sundown, so that we did not get a perfect view of the grand city from the sea. The pale star-light could bring out no colour. We had a prosperous passage, through which I slept with few interruptions till the signal came that we were approaching Leghorn: Leghorn on a brilliant warm morning with five or six hours before us, to fill as agreeably as possible! Of course the first thought was, to go to Pisa, but the train would not start till eleven; so in the meantime we took a drive about the prosperous looking town, and saw the great reservoir, which receives the water brought from the distant mountains: a beautiful and interesting sight – to look into the glassy depth and see columns and groined arches reflected as if in mockery and frustration of one's desire to see the bottom. But in one corner the light fell so as to reveal that reality instead of the beautiful illusion. On our way back we passed the Hebrew synagogue, and were glad of our coachman's suggestion that we should enter, seeing it was the Jews' Sabbath. The congregation was just about to separate, but a few were still occupied in a final private muttering of prayer. Some wore white scarfs in sign of special dignity. Passing round the aisle we saw varied types from the rich merchant to the meagre, bent drudge. The building was not unlike a dissenting chapel – with a gallery on three sides; the chief differences being the absence of the pulpit, and the substitution of the sort of cabinet in which the books of the law are kept, with a reading desk opposite at the distance of three or four yards.

We breakfasted at the same table with a family that amused me by a certain air of provincial, respectable quaintness. Two elderly ladies – sisters – the husband of the sickly one, and the son. We met them several times afterwards and found that they were an Irish family who had been settled in Australia for 20 years, and were come to Europe on account of their son's education and purposed entrance at the bar. The son was a timid slow-spoken youth, with a precocious physique, the father had a certain old fashioned timid air of dignity; the aunt was something like Miss Tox; and the mother had the [page torn] of the one daughter who was pretty and got married and had children, and for these virtues had been made much of in the world, wherefore she now made much of her own ailments.

At Pisa we took a carriage with pleasant quiet Mr. Grant, one of our fellow-passengers, and drove at once to the Cathedral, seeing as we went the well-looking lines of building on each side of the Arno.

A wonderful sight is that first glimpse of the cathedral, with the leaning campanile on one side, and the Baptistery on the other, green turf below and a clear blue sky above! The structure of the Campanile is exquisitely light and graceful – tier above tier of small circular arches supported by delicate round pillars,

6 Italian, 'liveliness'.

narrowing gradually in circumference, but very slightly, so that there is no striking difference of size between the base and summit. The Campanile is all of white marble, but the cathedral has the bands of black and white, softened in effect by the yellowing which time has given to the white. There is a family likeness among all three structures: they all have the delicate little colonnades and circular arches, but the Baptistery has stronger traits of the Gothic style in the pinnacles that crown the encircling colonnade. The interior of the cathedral, also of banded black and white has lofty pointed arches and grand old mosaics in the apsis. A little before the steps of the tribune is the large lamp which is said by its swinging motion to have suggested to Galileo the laws of the pendulum.

In the Baptistery the great object of interest is the pulpit sculptured by Nicolo Pisano in the 13th century. Each side of the hexagon presents a scene from the life of the Saviour. The Nativity is the finest of them all – the figure of the Virgin in a half reclining posture has a mingled grace and grandeur almost equal to anything of the kind in the antique alti-relievi. The other scenes are inferior both in design and in proportion, the heads being all too large for the bodies. The baptismal font and the altar are of exquisite open-work in marble, and were brought from Byzantium: they remind one, in their wonderful delicacy, of Chinese work in ivory. Next to these objects of art, the echo is the thing that inclines one to linger in the Baptistery: it is an aerial fugue of wonderful dying sweetness.

The fourth wonder of Pisa – the Campo Santo – is not visible from the green platform on which the Cathedral stands. One must enter through a door in a high long wall, and then one finds oneself in a large oblong space where the grassy middle is enclosed by a screen of gothic arches or glassless windows admitting the light and the weather into the surrounding corridor which is covered on the opposite side by venerable frescoes – by Giotto, by Orcagna, by Gozzoli – while below there are relics of antique sculpture and tombs of various periods. Here is the Sarcophagus which Nicolo Pisano studied to such memorable result. Giotto's frescoes are almost entirely defaced by the weather; but those of Orcagna and Gozzoli are for the most part in sufficient preservation to be fairly judged. Those of Orcagna are strikingly inferior to his fresco of the Glory of Paradise in Santa Maria Novella at Florence.

After some dusty delay outside the railway station we set off back again to Livorno, and forthwith got on board our steam-boat again – to awake the next morning (being Palm Sunday) at Civita Vecchia. Much waiting before we were allowed to land, and again much waiting for the clumsy process of "visiting" our luggage. I was amused while sitting at the *dogana*,[7] where almost every one was cross and busy, to see a dog making his way quietly out with a bone in his mouth.

Getting into our railway carriage, our vis-à-vis a stout amiable intelligent Livornian, with his wife and son, named Dubreux, exclaimed, "C'en est fini d'un

7 Italian, 'custom-house'.

peuple qui n'est pas capable de changer une bêtise comme ça".[8] George got into pleasant talk with him and his son about Edinburgh and the scientific men there, the son having been there for some time in order to go through a course of practical science. The father was a naturalist – an entomologist I think. It was an interesting journey from Civita Vecchia to Rome: at first a scene of rough hilly character, then a vast plain, frequently marshy, crowded with asphodels, inhabited by buffaloes; here and there a falcon or other slow large winged bird floating and alighting.

At last we came in sight of Rome, but there was nothing imposing to be seen. The chief object was what I afterwards knew to be one of the aqueducts, but which I then in the vagueness of my conceptions guessed to be the ruins of baths. The railway station where we alighted looked remote and countrified: only three omnibuses and one family carriage were waiting, so that we were obliged to take our chance in one of the omnibuses – that is, the chance of finding no place left for us in the hotels. And so it was. Every one wanted to go to the Hotel d'Angleterre, and every one was disappointed. We, at last, by help of some fellow-travellers, got a small room *au troisième*[9] at the Hotel d'Amérique, and as soon as that business was settled we walked out to look at Rome – not without a rather heavy load of disappointment on our minds from the vision we had had of it from the omnibus windows. A weary length of dirty uninteresting streets had brought us within sight of the dome of St. Peter's which was not impressive, seen in a peeping makeshift manner, just rising above the houses; and the Castle of St. Angelo seemed but a shabby likeness of the engravings. Not one iota had I seen that corresponded with my preconceptions.

Our hotel was in the Strada Babuino, which leads directly from the Piazza del Popolo to the Piazza di Spagna. We went to the latter for our first walk, and arriving opposite the high broad flights of stone steps which lead up to the Trinità di Monte, stopped for the first time with a sense that here was something not quite common and ugly. But I think we got hardly any farther, that evening, than the tall column at the end of the piazza which celebrates the final settlement by Pius IX of the Virgin's immaculate conception – O yes, I think we wandered farther among narrow and ugly streets, and came in to our hotel again, still with some dejection at the probable relations our "Rome visited" was to bear to our "Rome unvisited".

Discontented with our little room at an extravagant height of stairs and prices, we found and took lodgings the next day in the Corso, opposite San Carlo, with a well mannered Frenchman named Peureux and his little dark Italian wife – and so felt ourselves settled for a month. By this time we were in better spirits,

8 French, 'It is the end of a people when they are not capable of altering a stupidity like that'.

9 French, 'on the third floor'.

for in the morning we had been to the Capitol (Campidoglio – the modern variant for Capitolium) – had ascended the tower, and had driven to the Coliseum. The scene looking along the Forum to the arch of Titus resembled strongly that mixture of ruined grandeur with modern life which I had always had in my imagination at the mention of Rome. The approach to the Capitol from the opposite side is also impressive; on the right hand the broad steep flight of steps leading up to the Church and monastery of Ara Cœli, placed, some say, on the site of the Arx; in the front a less steep flight of steps à cordon, leading to that lower flatter portion of the hill which was called the *intermontium*, and which now forms a sort of Piazza with the equestrian statue of Marcus Aurelius in the Centre, and on three sides buildings designed or rather modified by Michael Angelo – on the left the Museum, on the right the Museo de' Conservatori, and on the side opposite the steps, the building devoted to public offices Palazzo de' Senatori in the centre of which stands the tower. On each hand at the summit of the steps are the two colossi, less celebrated but hardly less imposing in their calm grandeur, than the Colossi of the Quirinal. They are strangely streaked and disfigured by the blackening weather, but their large-eyed, mild might, gives one a thrill of awe, half like what might have been felt by the men of old who saw the divine twins watering their steeds when they brought the news of victory.

Perhaps the world can hardly offer a more interesting outlook than that from the tower of the Capitol. The eye leaps first to the mountains that bound the Campagna – the Sabine and Alban Hills, and the Solitary Soracte farther on to the left. Then wandering back across the Campagna it searches for the sister hills, hardly distinguishable now as hills. The Palatine is conspicuous enough, marked by the ruins of the Palace of the Cæsars, and rising up beyond the extremity of the Forum. And now, once resting on the Forum, the eye will not readily quit the long area that begins with the Clivus Capitolinus and extends to the Coliseum – an area that was once the very focus of the world. The Campo Vaccino, the site probably of the Comitium, was this first morning covered with carts and animals, mingling a simple form of actual life with those signs of the highly artificial life that had been crowded here in ages gone by:- the three corinthian pillars at the extremity of the Forum said to have belonged to the temple of Jupiter Stator; the grand temple of Antoninus and Faustina; the white arch of Titus: the Basilica of Constantine; the temple built by Adrian with its great broken granite columns scattered around on the green rising ground; the huge arc of the Coliseum; and the Arch of Constantine. The scene of these great relics remained our favourite haunt during our stay at Rome, and one day near the end of it, we entered the enclosure of the Clivus Capitolinus and the excavated space of the Forum. The ruins on the Clivus – the façade of massive columns on the right called the temple of Vespasian; the two corinthian columns, with the letters ESTITVER (from *restituire*)[10] on the entabla-

10 From the Latin verb *restituo*, 'to restore'.

ture, called the temple of Saturn in the centre, and the arch of Septimius Severus on the left – have their rich colour set off by the luxuriant green, clothing the lower masonry which formed the foundations of the crowded buildings on this narrow space, and, as a background to them all, the rough solidity of the ancient wall forming the back of the central building on the Intermontium, and regarded as one of the few remains of republican constructions. On either hand at an obtuse angle from the arch, the ancient road forming the double ascent of the Clivus is seen firm and level with its great blocks of pavement. The arch of Septimius Severus is particularly rich in colour, and the poorly executed bas reliefs of military groups still look out in grotesque completeness of attitude and expression even on the sides exposed to the weather. From the Clivus, a passage underneath the present road leads into the Forum, where immense pinkish granite columns lie on the weather-worn white marble pavement. The column of Phocas with its base no longer "buried", stands at the extreme corner nearest the Clivus, and the three elegant columns of the temple (say some) of Jupiter Stator mark the opposite extremity: between lie traces, utterly confused to all but erudite eyes, of marble steps and of pedestals stripped of their marble.

Let me see what I most delighted in, in Rome. Certainly, this drive from the Clivus to the Coliseum was, from first to last, one of the chief things; but there are many objects and many impressions of various kinds which I can reckon up as of almost equal interest: the Coliseum itself with the view from it; the drive along the Appian Way to the tomb of Cecilia Metella, and the view from thence of the Campagna bridged by the aqueduct; the Baths of Titus, with the remnants of their arabesques, seen by the light of torches, in the now damp and gloomy spaces; the glimpse of the Tarpeian rock, with its growth of cactus and rough herbage; the grand bare arched brickwork of the Palace of the Cæsars rising in huge masses on the Palatine; the theatre of Marcellus bursting suddenly to view from among the crowded mean houses of the modern city, and still more the Temple of Minerva and Temple of Nerva, also set in the crowded city of the present; and the exterior of the Pantheon, if it were not marred by the papal belfries:- these are the traces of Ancient Rome that have left the strongest image of themselves in my mind. I ought not to leave out Trajan's column, and the forum in which it stands; though the severe cold tint of the grey granite columns or fragments of columns gave this forum rather a dreary effect to me. For vastness, there is perhaps nothing more impressive in Rome than the Baths of Caracalla, except the Coliseum; and I remember it was amongst them that I first noticed the lovely effect of the giant fennel luxuriant among the crumbling brick work.

Among the ancient sculptures I think I must place on a level the Apollo, the Dying Gladiator, and the Lateran Antinous: they affected me equally in different ways. After these I delighted in the Venus of the Capitol, and the Kissing children in the same room; the Sophocles, at the Lateran Museum; the Nile; the black laughing Centaur at the Capitol; the laughing Faun; in the Vatican the

Sauroktonos, or boy with the lizard; and the sitting statue called Menander. The Faun of Praxiteles, and the old Faun with the Infant Bacchus I had already seen at Munich; else I should have mentioned them among my first favourites. Perhaps the greatest treat we had at the Vatican was the sight of a few statues, including the Apollo, by torchlight – all the more impressive because it was our first sight of the Vatican. Even the mere hurrying along the vast halls with the fitful torchlight falling on the innumerable statues and busts and bas-reliefs and sarcophagi, would have left a sense of awe at these crowded silent forms which have the solemnity of suddenly arrested life. Wonderfully grand these halls of the Vatican are, and there is but one complaint to be made against the home provided for this richest collection of antiquities: it is, that there is no historical arrangement of them and no catalogue. The system of classification is based on the history of their collection by the different Popes, so that for every other purpose but that of securing to each Pope his share of glory, it is a system of helter-skelter.

Of Christian Rome, St Peter's is of course the supreme wonder. The piazza, with Bernini's colonnades, and the gradual slope upward to the mighty temple, gave me always a sense of having entered some millennial New Jerusalem, where all small and shabby things were unknown. But the exterior of the cathedral itself is even ugly: it causes a constant irritation by its partial concealment of the dome. The first impression from the interior was perhaps at a higher pitch, than any subsequent impression either of its beauty or vastness; but then, on later visits, the lovely marble, which has a tone at once subdued and warm, was half covered with hideous red drapery. There is hardly any detail one cares to dwell on in St. Peter's. It is interesting, for once, to look at the mosaic altar-pieces, some of which render with marvellous success, such famous pictures as the Transfiguration, the Communion of St. Jerome, and the Entombment, or Disentombment of St. Petronilla. And some of the monuments are worth looking at more than once, the chief glory of that kind being Canova's lions. I was pleased one day to watch a group of poor people looking with an admiration that had a half childish terror in it at the sleeping lion, and with a sort of daring air, thrusting their fingers against the teeth of the waking "mane-bearer".

We ascended the dome near the end of our stay, but the cloudy horizon was not friendly to our distant view, and Rome itself is ugly to a bird's eye contemplation. The chief interest of the ascent was the vivid realization it gave of the building's enormous size, and after that, the sight of the inner courts and garden of the Vatican. Our most beautiful view of Rome and the Campagna was one we had much earlier in our stay, before the snow had vanished from the mountains: it was from the terrace of the Villa Pamfili Doria.

Of smaller churches, I remember especially Santa Maria degli Angeli, a church formed by Michael Angelo, by additions to the grand hall in the Baths of Diocletian – the only remaining hall of ancient Rome; and the church of San Clemente, where there is a chapel painted by Masaccio, as well as a perfect specimen of the ancient enclosure near the tribune, called the presbytery, with the *ambones* or pulpits from which the lessons and gospel were read. Santa Maria Maggiore is an exquisitely beautiful basilica, rich in marbles from a pagan temple; and the reconstructed San Paolo fuori le Mura is a wonder of wealth and beauty with its lines of white marble columns – if one could possibly look with pleasure at such a perverted appliance of money and labour as a church built in an unhealthy solitude. After St. Peter's, however, the next great monument of Christian art is the Sistine chapel; but since I care for the chapel solely for the sake of its ceiling, I ought rather to number it among my favourite paintings than among the most memorable buildings. Certainly this ceiling of Michael Angelo's is the most wonderful fresco in the world. After it, come Raphael's School of Athens and Triumph of Galatea, so far as Rome is concerned. Among oil-paintings there, I like best the Madonna di Foligno, for the sake of the cherub who is standing and looking upward; the Perugino also in the Vatican, and the pretty Sassoferrato with the clouds budding angels; at the Barberini palace, Beatrice Cenci, and *Una Schiava* by Titian; at the Sciarra palace, the Joueur de Violon by Raphael, another of Titian's golden-haired women, and a sweet Madonna and child with a bird by Fra Bartolomeo; at the Borghese palace, Domenichino's Chase, the Entombment by Raphael, and The three Ages – a copy of Titian by Sassoferrato.

We should have regretted entirely our efforts to get to Rome during the Holy Week, instead of making Florence our first resting-place, if we had not had the compensation for wearisome empty ceremonies and closed museums, in the wonderful spectacle of the illumination of St. Peter's. That really is a thing so wondrous, so magically beautiful, that one can't find in one's heart to say, it is not worth doing. I remember well the first glimpse we had, as we drove out towards it, of the outline of the dome like a new constellation on the black sky. I thought *that* was the final illumination, and was regretting our tardy arrival from the detour we had to make, when, as our carriage stopped in front of the Cathedral, the great bell sounded and in an instant the grand illumination flashed out and turned the outline of stars into a palace of gold. Venus looked on palely.

One of the finest positions in Rome is the Monte Cavallo (the Quirinal), the site of the Pope's palace, and of the fountain against which are placed the two colossi – the Castor and Pollux, ascribed after a lax method of affiliation to Phidias and Praxiteles. Standing near this fountain, one has a real sense of being on a hill – city and distant ridge stretching below. Close by is the Palazzo Rospigliosi, where we went to see Guido's Aurora.

Another spot where I was struck with the view of modern Rome – (and *that* happened rarely) – was at San Pietro in Vincoli, on the Esquiline, where we went to see Michael Angelo's Moses. Turning round before one enters the church, a palm tree in the high foreground relieves very picturesquely the view of the lower distance. The Moses did not affect me agreeably: both the attitude and the expression of the face seemed to me, in that one visit, to have an exaggeration that strained after effect without reaching it. The failure seemed to me of this kind:- Moses was an angry man trying to frighten the people by his mien, instead of being rapt by his anger and terrible without self-consciousness. To look at the statue of Christ, after the other works of Michael Angelo at Rome was a surprize: in this, the fault seems to incline slightly to the namby-pamby. The Pietà in St. Peter's has real tenderness in it.

The visit to the Farnesina was one of the most interesting among our visits to Roman palaces. It is here that Raphael painted the Triumph of Galatea, and here this wonderful fresco is still bright upon the wall. In the same room is a colossal head drawn by Michael Angelo with a bit of charcoal by way of *carte de visite* one day that he called on Daniele di Volterra, who was painting detestably in this room, and happened to be absent. In the entrance hall preceding the Galatea-room are the frescoes by Raphael representing the story of Cupid and Psyche, but we did not linger long to look at them, as they disappointed us.

We visited only four artists' studios in Rome: Gibson's, the sculptor, Frey's, the landscape painter, Riedel's, *genre* painter, and Overbeck's. Gibson's was entirely disappointing to me so far as his own sculptures are concerned: except that *Cacciatore*, which he sent to the Great Exhibition, I could see nothing but feeble imitation of the antique – no spontaneity and no vigour. Miss Hosmer's Beatrice Cenci is a pleasing and new conception, and her little Puck a bit of humour that one would like to have if one were a grand Seigneur.

Frey is a very meritorious landscape painter – finished in execution and poetic in feeling. His Egyptian scenes – the Simoom, the Pair in the light of Sunset, and the island of Philæ, are memorable pictures; so is the view of Athens with its blue island-studded sea. Riedel interested us greatly with his account of the coincidence between the views of *light* and colours at which he had arrived through his artistic experience, and Goethe's Theory of Colours, with which he became acquainted only after he had thought of putting his own ideas into shape for publication. He says the majority of painters continue their work when the sun shines from the North – they paint with *blue* light.

But it was our visit to Overbeck that we were most pleased not to have missed. The man himself is more interesting than his pictures: a benevolent calm, and quiet conviction breathes from his person and manners. He has a thin, rather high-nosed face, with long gray hair, set off by a maroon velvet cap, and a grey scarf over his shoulders. Some of his cartoons pleased me: One large one, of our Saviour passing from the midst of the throng who were going to cast him from the brow of the hill at Capernaum – one foot resting on a cloud borne up by cherubs; and some smaller round cartoons representing the parable of the Ten Virgins, applying it to the function of the artist.

We drove about a great deal in Rome, but were rather afflicted in our drives by the unending walls that enclose everything like a garden even outside the city gates. First among our charming drives was that to the Villa Pamfili Doria – a place which has the beauties of an English park and gardens, with views such as no English park can show; not to speak of the Columbarium or ancient Roman burying place which has been disinterred in the grounds. The compactest of all burying-places must these Columbaria be: little pigeon-holes, tier above tier, for the small urns containing the ashes of the dead. In this one, traces of peacocks and other figures in fresco, ornamenting the divisions between the rows, are still visible.

We sat down in the sunshine by the side of the water which is made to fall in a cascade in the grounds fronting the house and then spreads out into a considerable breadth of mirror for the plantation on the slope which runs along one side of it. On the opposite side is a broad grassy walk, and here we sat on some blocks of stone, watching the little green lizards. Then we walked on up the slope on the other side, and through a grove of weird ilexes, and across a plantation of tall pines, where we saw the mountains in the far distance. A beautiful spot! We ought to have gone there again.

Another drive was to the Villa Albani, where again the view is grand. The precious sculptures, once there, are all at Munich now, and the most remarkable remnants of the collection are the bas-relief of Antinous, and the Æsop. The Antinous is the least beautiful of all the representations of that sad loveliness that I have seen – be it said, in spite of Winckelmann: attitude and face are strongly Egyptian. In an outside pavilion in the garden, were some interesting examples of Greek masks.

Our journey to Frascati by railway was fortunate. The day was fine, except indeed for the half-hour that we were on the heights of Tusculum, and longed for a clear horizon. But the weather was so generally gloomy during our stay in Rome, that we were "thankful for small mercies" in the way of sunshine. I enjoyed greatly our excursion up the hill on donkey back to the ruins of Tusculum – in spite of our loquacious guide who exasperated George. The sight of the Campagna on one side, and of Mount Algidus with its snow-capped fellows and Mount Albano with Rocco del Papa on its side, and Castel Gandolfo below on the other, was worth the trouble; to say nothing of the little theatre, which is the most perfect example of an ancient theatre I had then seen, in that pre-Pompeian period of my travels. After lunching at Frascati, we strolled out to the Villa Aldobrandini and enjoyed a brighter view of the Campagna in the afternoon sunlight. Then we lingered in a little croft enclosed by plantations and enjoyed this familiar-looking bit of grass with wild flowers perhaps more even than the greatest novelties. There are fine plantations on the hill behind the villa and there we wandered till it was time to go back to the railway. A literally grotesque thing in these plantations is the opening of a grotto in the hill-side, cut in the form of a huge Greek comic mask. It was a lovely walk from the town downward to the railway station – between the olive-clad slopes looking towards the illimitable plain. Our best view of the aqueducts was on this journey, but it was the tantalizing sort of view one gets from a railway carriage.

Our excursion to Tivoli, reserved till nearly the end of our stay, happened on one of those cruel seductive days that smile upon you at five o'clock in the morning to become cold and cloudy at eight and resolutely rainy at ten. And so we ascended the hill through the vast venerable olive-grove, thinking what would be the effect of sunshine among those grey fantastically twisted trunks and boughs; and paddled along the wet streets under umbrellas to look at the Temple of the Sybil and to descend the ravine of the Waterfalls. Yet it was enjoyable; for the rain was not dense enough to shroud the near view of rock and foliage. We looked for the first time at a rock of travertine with its curious petrified vegetable forms, and lower down at a mighty cavern under which the smaller cascade rushes – an awful hollow in the midst of huge rocky masses. But – rain, rain rain! No possibility of seeing the Villa of Hadrian, chief wonder of Tivoli. And so we had our carriage covered up and turned homeward in despair.

This last week of our stay we went for the first time to the Picture gallery of the Capitol, where we saw the famous Guercino – the Entombment of Saint Petronilla – which we had already seen in mosaic at St. Peter's. It is a stupendous piece of painting, about which one's only feeling is that it might as well have been left undone. More interesting is the portrait of Michael Angelo by himself – a deeply melancholy face. And there is also a picture of a Bishop by Gian Bellini which arrested us a long while. After these I remember most distinctly Veronese's Europa, superior to that we afterwards saw at Venice; a delicious mythological Poussin, all light and joy; and a Sebastian by Guido, exceptionally beautiful among the many detestable things of his in this gallery.

The Lateran Museum, also, was a sight we had neglected till this last week, though it turned out to be one of the most memorable. In the Classical Museum are the great Antinous as Bacchus, and the Sophocles; besides a number of other remains of high interest especially in the department of architectural decoration. In the Museum of Christian antiquities, there are, besides sculptures, copies of the frescoes in the Catacombs – invaluable as a record of those perishable remains. If we ever go to Rome again, the Lateran Museum will be one of the first places I shall wish to revisit.

We saw the Catacombs of St. Calixtus on the Appian Way – the long dark passages with great oblong hollows in the rock for the bodies long since crumbled, and the one or two openings out of the passages into a rather wider space, called chapels, but no indication of paintings or other detail, our monkish guide being an old man who spoke with an indistinct grunt that would not have enlightened us if we had asked any questions. In the church through which we entered there is a strangely barbarous reclining statue of St. Sebastian, with arrows sticking all over it!

A spot that touched me deeply was Shelley's grave. The English Cemetery in which he lies is the most attractive burying place I have seen. It lies against the old city walls close to the Porta San Paolo, and the Pyramid of Caius Cestus – one of the quietest spots of old Rome. And there, under the shadow of the old walls on one side and cypresses on the other, lies the "Cor cordium" for ever at rest from the unloving cavillers of this world, whether or not he may have entered on other purifying struggles, in some world unseen by us. The grave of Keats lies far off from Shelley's, unshaded by wall or trees. It is painful to look upon because of the inscription on the stone which seems to make him still speak in bitterness from his grave.

How much more I have to write about Rome! How I should like to linger over every particular object that has left an image in my memory! But here I am only to give a hasty sketch of what we saw and did at each place at which we paused in our three months' life in Italy.

It was on the 29th of April that we left Rome, and on the morning of the 30th we arrived at Naples – under a rainy sky, alas! but not so rainy as to prevent our feeling the beauty of the city and bay and declaring it to surpass all places we had seen before.

The weather cleared up soon after our arrival at the Hôtel des Etrangers, and after a few days it became brilliant, showing us the blue sea, the purple mountains, and bright city, in which we had almost disbelieved as we saw them in the pictures. Hardly anything can be more lovely than Naples seen from Posilipo under a blue sky:- the irregular outline with which the town meets the sea, jutting out in picturesque masses, then lifted up high on a basis of rock, with the grand castle of St. Elmo and the monastery on the central height crowning all the rest; the graceful outline of purple Vesuvius rising beyond the Molo, and the line of deeply indented mountains carrying the eye along to the cape of Sorrento; and last of all Capri sleeping between sea and sky in the distance. Crossing the promontory of Posilipo another wonderful scene presents itself: White Nisida on its island rock; the sweep of bay towards Pozzuoli; beyond that, in fainter colours of farther distance, the cape of Misena, and the peaks of Ischia.

Our first expedition was to Pozzuoli and Misena, on a bright warm day, with a slip-shod Neapolitan driver whom I christened Baboon, and who acted as our charioteer throughout our stay at Naples. Beyond picturesque Pozzuoli, jutting out with precipitous piles of building into the sea, lies Baiæ. Here we halted to look at a great circular temple, where there was a wonderful echo that made whispers circulate and become loud on the opposite side to that on which they were uttered. Here, for our amusement, a young maiden and a little old man danced to the sound of a tamboureen and fife. On our way to Baiæ, we had stopped to see the Lake Avernus, no longer terrible to behold, and the amphitheatre of Cumæ, now grown over with greensward and fringed with garden stuff. From Baiæ we went on to Misena – the Misenum where Pliny was stationed with the fleet, and looked out from the promontory on the lovely isles of Ischia and Procida. On the approach to this promontory lies the *Piscina Mirabilis* – one of the most striking remains of Roman building. It is a great reservoir into which one may now descend dry-shod, and look up at the lofty arches festooned with delicate plants while the sunlight shoots aslant through the openings above.

It was on this drive coming back towards Pozzuoli that we saw the mesembryanthemum in its greatest luxuriance – a star of amethyst with its golden tassel in the centre. The amphitheatre at Pozzuoli is the most interesting in Italy after the Coliseum. The seats are in excellent preservation, and the subterranean structures for water, and for other purposes, probably the introduction of the wild beasts, are unique. The temple of Jupiter Serapis is another remarkable ruin, made more peculiar by the intrusion of the water, which makes the central structure with its great columns an island to be approached by a plank bridge.

In the views from Capo di Monte – the King's summer residence – and from St. Elmo, one enjoys not only the view towards the sea, but the wide green plain sprinkled with houses and in the distance studded with small towns or villages, bounded on the one hand by Vesuvius and shut in in every other direction by the nearer heights close upon Naples or by the sublimer heights of the distant Appennines. We had the view from St. Elmo on a clear breezy afternoon, in company with a Frenchman and his wife, come from Rome with his family after a two years' residence there – worth remembering for the pretty bondage the brusque stern thin father was under to the tiny sickly looking boy.

It was a grand drive up to Capo di Monte, between rich plantations, with glimpses, as we went up, of the city lying in picturesque irregularity below, and as we went down in the other direction views of distant mountain rising above some pretty accident of roof or groups of trees in the foreground. One day we went, from this drive, along the Poggio Reale to the Cemetery – the most ambitious burying place I ever saw, with building after building of elaborate architecture serving as tombs to various *arciconfraternite*[11] as well as to private families, all set in the midst of well kept gardens. The humblest kind of tombs there were long niches for coffins in a wall bordering the carriage road, which are simply built up when the coffin is once in, the inscription being added on this final bit of masonry. The lines of lofty sepulchres suggested to one very vividly the probable appearance of the Appian way when the old Roman tombs were in all their glory.

Our first visit to the Museo Borbonico was devoted to the sculpture, of which there is a precious collection. Of the famous Balbi family found at Herculaneum, the mother, in grand drapery wound round her head and body is the most unforgettable – a really grand woman of fifty with firm mouth and knitted brow, yet not unbenignant. Farther on, in the transverse hall, is a young faun with the infant Bacchus – a different conception altogether from the fine Munich statue, but delicious for humour and geniality. Then there is the Aristides – more real and speaking, and easy in attitude even than the Sophocles at Rome. Opposite is a lovely

11 Italian, 'elite brotherhood', with burial entitlement for members.

Antinous, in no mythological character, but in simple melancholy beauty. In the centre of the deep recess in front of which these statues are placed is the colossal Flora, who holds up her thin dress in too finicking a style for a colossal goddess; and on the floor – to be seen by ascending a platform – is the precious great mosaic representing the Battle of the Issus, found at Pompeii. It is full of spirit, the ordonnance of the figures is very much after the same style as in the ancient bas-reliefs, and the colours are still vivid enough for us to have a just idea of the effect. In the halls on each side of this central one there are various Bacchuses and Apollos, Atlas groaning under the weight of the globe, the Farnese Hercules, the Toro Farnese, and, amongst other things less memorable, a glorious head of Jupiter.

The Bronzes here are even more interesting than the marbles. Among them there is Mercury resting, the sleeping Faun, the little dancing Faun, and the drunken Faun snapping his fingers of which there is a marble copy at Munich, with the two remarkable heads of Plato and Seneca.

But our greatest treat at the Museo Borbonico could only be enjoyed after our visit to Pompeii, where we went unhappily in the company of some Russians whose acquaintance G. had made at the table d'hôte. I hope I shall never forget the solemnity of our first entrance into that silent city and the walk along the street of tombs. After seeing the principal houses, we went, as a proper climax, to the Forum, where amongst the lines of pedestals, and the ruins of temples and tribunal, we could see Vesuvius overlooking us; then to the two theatres; and finally to the amphitheatre.

This visit prepared us to enjoy the collection of *piccoli bronzi*,[12] of paintings and mosaics at the Museo. Several of the paintings have considerable positive merit: I remember particularly a large one of Orestes and Pylades which in composition and general conception might have been a picture of yesterday. But the most impressive collection of remains found at Pompeii and Herculaneum is that of the ornaments, articles of food and domestic utensils: pieces of bread, loaves with the baker's name on them, fruits, corn, various seeds, paste in the vessel imperfectly mixed, linen just wrung in washing, eggs, oil consolidated in a glass bottle, wine mixed with the lava, and a piece of asbestos; gold lace, a lens, a lanthorn with sides of talc, gold ornaments of Etruscan character, patty pans (!), moulds for cakes; ingenious portable cooking apparatus, urn for hot water, portable candelabrum to be raised or lowered at will, bells, dice, theatre-checks – and endless objects that tell of our close kinship with those old Pompeians. In one of the rooms of this collection, there are the Farnese cameos and engraved gems – some of them, especially of the latter, marvellously beautiful, complicated, and exquisitely minute in workmanship. I remember particularly one splendid yellow stone engraved with an elaborate composition of Apollo and his chariot and horses – a masterpiece of delicate form.

12 Italian, 'bronze miniatures'.

The pictures at Naples are worth little: the marriage of St. Catherine, a small picture by Correggio; a Holy Family by Raphael with a singularly fine St. Ann; and Titian's Paul the Third, are the only paintings I have registered very distinctly in all the large collection. The much praised frescoes of the dome in a chapel of the Cathedral, and the oil paintings over the altars, by Domenichino and Spagnoletto produced no effect on me. Worth more than all these are Giotto's frescoes in the choir of the little old church of l'Incoronata though these are not, I think, in Giotto's ripest manner, for they are inferior to his frescoes in the Carmine at Florence – more uniform in the type of face.

We went to a Sunday morning service at the Cathedral, and saw a detachment of silver busts of saints ranged around the tribune; Naples being famous for gold and silver sanctities.

When we had been a week at Naples, we set off in our carriage with Baboon on an expedition to Paestum, arriving the first evening at Salerno – beautiful Salerno, with a bay as lovely, though in a different way as the bay of Naples. It has a larger sweep, grander piles of rocky mountain on the north and north east – then a stretch of low plain, the mountains receding – and finally, on the south, another line of mountain coast extending to the promontory of Licosa.

From Salerno we started early in the morning for Paestum, with no alloy to the pleasure of the journey but the dust which was capable of making a simoom under a high wind. For a long way we passed through a well-cultivated plain, the mountains on our left, and the sea on our right; but farther on came a swampy unenclosed space of great extent, inhabited by buffaloes who lay in groups comfortably wallowing in the muddy water with their grand stupid heads protruding horizontally.

On approaching Paestum, the first thing one catches sight of is the Temple of Vesta, which is not beautiful either for form or colour, so that we began to tremble lest disappointment were to be the harvest of our dusty journey. But the fear was soon displaced by almost rapturous admiration at the sight of the great temple of Neptune – the finest thing, I verily believe, that we had yet seen in Italy. It has all the requisites to make a building impressive: First, *form*. What perfect satisfaction and repose for the eye in the calm repetition of those columns – in the proportions of height and length, of front and sides: the right thing is *found* – it is not being sought after in uneasy labour of detail or exaggeration. Next, *colour*. It is built of travertine, like the other two temples, but while they have remained a cold grey (*for the most part*. In certain spots, the travertine of the larger seems to have begun a process of change), this temple of Neptune has a rich warm pinkish brown that seems to glow and deepen under one's eyes. Lastly, *position*. It stands on the rich plain, covered with long grass and flowers, in sight of the sea on one hand, and the sublime blue mountains on the other. Many plants caress the ruins:- the acanthus is there, and I saw it in green life for the first time; but the majority of the plants on the floor, or bossing the architrave are familiar to me as home flowers – purple mallows, snap-dragons, pink hawkweed, etc. On our way back we saw a herd of buffaloes clustered near a pond, and one of them was rolling himself in the water like a gentleman enjoying his bath.

The next day we went in the morning from Salerno to Amalfi. It is an unspeakably grand drive round the mighty rocks with the sea below; and Amalfi itself surpasses all imagination of a romantic site for a city that once made itself famous in the world. We stupidly neglected seeing the Cathedral; but we saw a macaroni mill and a paper mill from among the many that are turned by the rushing stream which, with its precipitous course down the ravine, creates an immense water-power; and we climbed up endless steps to the Capuchin monastery, to see nothing but a cavern where there are barbarous images, and a small cloister with double gothic arches. Our way back to La Cava gave us a repetition of the grand drive we had had in the morning by the coast, and beyond that an inland drive of much loveliness, through Claude-like scenes of mountain, trees, and meadows, with picturesque accidents of building, such as single round towers on the heights. The valley beyond La Cava in which our hôtel lay is of quite paradisaic beauty: a rich cultivated spot with mountains behind and before – those in front varied by ancient buildings that a painter would have chosen to place there, and one of pyramidal shape, steep as an obelisk, is crowned by a monastery, famous for its library of precious manuscripts and its archives. We arrived too late for everything except to see the shroud of mist gather and gradually envelope the mountains.

In the morning we set off, again in brightest weather, to Sorrento, coasting the opposite side of the promontory to that which we had passed along the day before, and having on our right hand Naples and the distant Posilipo. The coast on this side is less grand than on the Amalfi side; but it is more friendly as a place for residence. The most charming spot on the way to Sorrento, to my thinking, is Vico, which I should even prefer to Sorrento, because there is no town to be traversed before entering the ravine and climbing the mountain in the background. But I will not undervalue Sorrento with its orange groves embalming the air, its glorious sunsets over the sea, setting the grey olives aglow on the hills above us, its walks among the groves and vineyards out to the solitary coast. One day of our stay there we took donkeys and crossed the mountains the opposite side of the promontory and saw the Syren Isles – very palpable unmysterious bits of barren rock now. A great delight to me in all the excursions round about Naples was the high cultivation of the soil, and the sight of the vines trained from elm to elm above some other precious crop carpeting the ground below.

On our way back to Naples, we visited the silent Pompeii again. That place had such a peculiar influence over me that I could not even look towards the point where it lay on the plain below Vesuvius, without a certain thrill.

Amidst much dust we arrived at Naples again on Sunday morning, to start by the steam-boat for Leghorn on the following Tuesday. But before I quit Naples I must remember the grotto of Posilipo, a wonderful monument of ancient labour; Virgil's tomb, which repaid us for a steep ascent only by the view of the city and bay; and a villa on the way to Posilipo with gardens gradually descending to the margin of the sea, where there is a collection of animals both stuffed and alive. It was there we saw the flying fish with their lovely blue fins.

One day and night voyage to Civita Vecchia, and another day and night to Leghorn – wearisome to the flesh that suffers from nausea even on the summer sea! We had another look at dear Pisa under the blue sky, and then on to Florence, which, unlike Rome, looks inviting as one catches sight (from the railway) of its cupolas and towers and its embosoming hills – the greenest of hills, sprinkled everywhere with white villas. We took up our quarters at the *Pension Suisse*, with M. Faisch-Micheli, an agreeable Genevese gentleman, whose acquaintance we made on board the steam-boat. And on the first evening we took with him the most beautiful drive to be had round Florence – the drive to Fiesole. It is in this view that the eye takes in the greatest extent of green billowy hills, besprinkled with white houses looking almost like flocks of sheep: the great silent uninhabited mountains lie chiefly behind; the plain of the Arno stretches far to the right. I think the view from Fiesole the most beautiful of all; but that from San Miniato, where we went the next evening, has an interest of another kind, because here Florence lies much nearer below, and one can distinguish the various buildings more completely. It is the same with Bellosguardo in a still more marked degree. What a relief to the eye and the thought among the huddled roofs of a distant town to see towers and cupolas rising in abundant variety as they do at Florence! There is Brunelleschi's mighty dome, and close by it, with its lovely colours not entirely absorbed by distance, Giotto's incomparable Campanile, beautiful as a jewel; farther on, to the right, is the majestic tower of the Palazzo Vecchio, with the flag waving above it, then the elegant Badia and the Bargello close by; nearer to us, the grand campanile of Santo Spirito, and that of Santa Croce; far away, on the left, the cupola of San Lorenzo, and the tower of Santa Maria Novella; and scattered far and near, other cupolas and campaniles of more insignificant shape and history.

Even apart from its venerable historical glory, the exterior of the Duomo is pleasant to behold, when the wretched unfinished façade is quite hidden. The soaring pinnacles over the doors are exquisite; so are the forms of the windows in the great semi-circle of the apsis; and on the side where Giotto's Campanile is placed especially, the white marble has taken on so rich and deep a yellow that the black bands cease to be felt as a fault. The entire view on this side closed in by Giotto's tower with its delicate pinkish marble, its delicate gothic windows with twisted columns, and its tall lightness carrying the eye upward, in contrast with the mighty breadth of the dome, is a thing not easily to be forgotten. And it was this view that Dante had from his accustomed seat in this Piazza. The Baptistery with its paradisaic gates is close by; but except in these gates, it has no exterior beauty. The interior is almost awful with its great dome covered with gigantic early mosaics – the pale large-eyed Christ, surrounded by images of paradise and perdition. The interior of the Cathedral is comparatively poor and bare; but it has one great beauty – its coloured lanceolate windows. Behind the high altar is a piece of sculpture – the last under Michael Angelo's hand, intended for his own tomb, and left unfinished. It represents Joseph of Arimathea holding the body of Jesus, with Mary his mother on one side and an apparently angelic form on the other. Joseph is a striking and real figure, with a hood over the head.

For external architecture, it is the palaces, the old palaces of the fifteenth century, that one must look at in the streets of Florence. One of the finest was just opposite our hotel: the Palazzo Strozzi, built by Cronaca; perfect in its massiveness, with its iron cressets and rings, as if it had been built only last year. This is the palace that the Pitti was (so tradition falsely pretends) built to outvie, and to have an inner court that would contain it. A wonderful union is that Pitti palace of cyclopean massiveness with stately regularity. Next to the Pitti, I think comes the Palazzo Riccardi – the house of the Medici – for size and splendour. It was here we saw that unique Laurentian library,[13] designed by Michael Angelo: the books ranged on desks in front of seats, so that the appearance of the library resembles that of a chapel with open pews of dark wood. The precious books are all chained to the desk, and here we saw old manuscripts of exquisite neatness, culminating in the Virgil of the 4th century and the Pandects, said to have been recovered from oblivion at Amalfi, but falsely so said, according to those who are more learned than tradition. Here too is a little chapel, covered with remarkable frescoes by Benozzo Gozzoli.

Grander still, in another style, is the Palazzo Vecchio, with its unique cortile, where the pillars are embossed with arabesque and floral tracery, making a contrast in elaborate ornament with the large simplicity of the exterior building. Here there are precious little works in ivory by Benvenuto Cellini, and other small treasures of art and jewellery preserved in cabinets in one of the great upper chambers, which are painted all over with frescoes, and have curious inlaid doors showing buildings or figures in wooden mosaic, such as is often seen in great beauty in the stalls of the churches. The great council chamber is ugly in its ornaments – frescoes and statues in bad taste all round it.

Orcagna's Loggia de' Lanzi is disappointing at the first glance, from its sombre dirty colour; but its beauty grew upon me with longer contemplation. The pillars and groins are very graceful, and chaste in ornamentation. Among the statues that are placed under it there is not one I could admire, unless it were the dead body of Ajax with the Greek soldier supporting it. Cellini's Perseus is fantastic.

13 Cross's pencilled note corrects this 'Slip of memory. The Laurentian Library is at San Lorenzo. This is the Riccardian Library – 30/4/83 J.W.C.'

The Bargello, where we went to see Giotto's frescoes (in lamentable condition) was under repair; but I got glimpses of a wonderful inner court, with heraldic carvings, and stone stairs and gallery.

Most of the Churches in Florence are hideous on the outside – piles of ribbed brick work awaiting a coat of stone or stucco – looking like skinned animals. The most remarkable exception is Santa Maria Novella, which has an elaborate facing of black and white marble. Both this church and San Lorenzo were under repair in the interior, unfortunately for us; but we could enter Santa Maria so far as to see Orcagna's frescoes of Paradise and Hell. The Hell has been repainted, but the Paradiso has not been maltreated in this way; and it is a splendid example of Orcagna's powers – far superior to his frescoes in the Campo Santo at Pisa: some of the female forms on the lowest range are of exquisite grace. The splendid chapel in San Lorenzo, containing the tombs of the Medici, is ugly and heavy with all its precious marbles; and the world-famous statues of Michael Angelo on the tombs in another smaller chapel – the Notte, the Giorno, and the Crepusculo, remained to us as affected and exaggerated in the original as in copies and casts.

The two churches we frequented most in Florence were Santa Croce, and the Carmine. In this last are the great frescoes of Masaccio – chief among them the raising of the dead youth. In the other, are Giotto's frescoes revealed from under the whitewash by which they were long covered, like those in the Bargello. Of these the best are the challenge to pass through the fire in the series representing the history of St. Francis, and the rising of some saint (unknown to me) from his tomb, while Christ extends his arms to receive him above, and wondering venerators look on, on each side. There are large frescoes here of Taddeo Gaddi's also; but they are not good: one sees in him a pupil of Giotto and nothing more. Besides the frescoes Santa Croce has its tombs to attract a repeated visit: the tombs of Michael Angelo, Dante, Alfieri, and Macchiavelli. Even those tombs of the unknown dead under our feet, with their effigies quite worn down to a mere outline were not without their interest. I used to feel my heart swell a little at the sight of the inscription on Dante's tomb: "*Onorate l'altissimo poeta*".[14] In the church of the Trinità also there are valuable frescoes by the excellent Domenico Ghirlandajo, the master of Michael Angelo. They represent the history of St Francis, and happily the best of them is in the best light: it is the death of St. Francis, and is full of natural feeling, with well marked gradations from deepest sorrow to indifferent spectatorship.

The frescoes I cared for most in all Florence were the few of Fra Angelico's that a *donna* was allowed to see in the Convent of San Marco. In the Chapter-house, now used as a guard-room, is a large crucifixion, with the inimitable group of the fainting mother, upheld by St. John and the younger Mary, and clasped round by

14 Italian, 'In honour of the almighty poet'.

the Kneeling Magdalen. The group of adoring, sorrowing Saints on the right hand are admirable for earnest truthfulness of representation. The Christ in this fresco is not good, but there is a deeply impressive original Crucified Christ outside in the Cloisters: St. Dominic is clasping the cross and looking upward at the agonized Saviour, whose real pale, calmly enduring face is quite unlike any other Christ I have seen.

I forgot to mention, at Santa Maria Novella, the chapel which is painted with very remarkable frescoes by Simone Memmi and another artist whose name will not occur to me at this moment.

The best of these frescoes is the one in which the Dominicans are represented by black and white dogs – *Domini Cane*. The human groups have high merit for conception and life-likeness, and they are admirable studies of costume. At this church too, in the sacristy, is the Madonna della Stella, with an altar step, by Fra Angelico – specimens of his minuter painting in oil. The inner part of the frame is surrounded with his lovely angels, with their seraphic joy and flower-garden colouring.

Last of all the churches we visited San Michele, which had been one of the most familiar to us on the outside, with its statues in niches and its elaborate gothic windows designed by the genius of Orcagna. The great wonder of the interior is the shrine of white marble made to receive the miracle-working image, which first caused the consecration of this mundane building, originally a corn-market. Surely this shrine is the most wonderful of all Orcagna's productions: for the beauty of the reliefs he deserves to be placed along with Nicolo Pisano, and for the exquisite gothic design of the whole he is a compeer of Giotto.

For variety of treasures the Uffizi gallery is pre-eminent among all public sights in Florence, but the variety is in some degree a cause of comparative unimpressiveness – pictures and statues being crowded together, and destroying each other's effect. In statuary, it has the great Niobe group; the Venus de' Medici; the Wrestlers; the admirable statue of the Knife-sharpener, supposed to represent the flayer of Marsyas; the Apollino; and the boy taking a thorn out of his foot; with numerous less remarkable antiques. And besides these it has what the Vatican has not – a collection of early Italian sculpture, supreme among which is Giovanni di Bologna's Mercury.

Then, there is a collection of precious drawings; and there is the cabinet of gems, quite alone in its fantastic, elaborate minuteness of workmanship in rarest materials; and there is another cabinet containing ivory sculptures, cameos, intaglios, and a superlatively fine niello, as well as Raffaelle porcelain. The pictures here are multitudinous, and among them there is a generous proportion of utterly bad ones. In the entrance gallery, where the early paintings are, is a great Fra Angelico – a Madonna and child, a triptych, the two side compartments containing very fine figures of saints, and the inner part of the central frame a series of unspeakably lovely angels.

Here I always paused with longing, trying to believe that a copyist there could make an imitation angel good enough to be worth buying.

Among the other paintings that remain with me after my visits to the Uffizzi, are the portrait of Leonardo da Vinci by himself, the portrait of Dante by Filippino Lippi, the Herodias of Luini, Titian's Venus, in the Tribune, Raphael's Madonna and child with the bird, and the portrait falsely called the Fornarina; the two remarkable pictures by Ridolfo Ghirlandajo, and the Salutation by Albertinelli which hangs opposite; the little prince in pink dress, with two recent teeth, in the same room; the small picture of Christ in the garden by Lorenzo Credi, Titian's woman with the golden hair in the Venetian room; Leonardo's Medusa-head; and Michael Angelo's ugly Holy Family:- these at least rise up on a rapid retrospect; others are in the background – for example, Correggio's Madonna adoring the infant Christ, in the Tribune.

For pictures however, the Pitti Palace surpasses the Uffizi. Here the paintings are more choice, and not less numerous. The Madonna della Sedia leaves me, with all its beauty, impressed only by the grave gaze of the infant, but besides this there is another Madonna of Raphael – perhaps the most beautiful of all his earlier ones. It is called the Madonna del gran Duca, and has the sweet grace and gentleness of its sisters without their sheep-like look. Andrea del Sarto is seen here in his highest glory of oil-painting: There are numerous large pictures of his – Assumptions and the like, of great technical merit; but better than all these I remember a holy family with a very fine St. Ann, and the portraits of himself and his fatal auburn-haired wife. Of Fra Bartolomeo, there is a Pietà of memorable expression, a Madonna enthroned with saints, and his great St. Mark. Of Titian, a marriage of St. Catherine of supreme beauty; a Magdalen, failing in expression; and an exquisite portrait of the same woman who is represented as Venus at the Uffizi. There is a remarkable group of portraits by Rubens – himself, his brother and Grotius, and a large landscape by him; a portrait of Veronese's wife, when her beauty was gone, the only picture of Veronese's that I remember here; a remarkable fine sea piece by Salvator Rosa; a striking portrait of Aretino by Titian; a portrait of Vesalius, by Titian; one of Inghirami, by Raphael; a delicious rosy baby – future cardinal – lying on a silken bed; a placid contemplative young woman, with her finger between the leaves of a book, by Leonardo da Vinci; a memorable portrait of Philip II by Titian; a splendid Judith by Bronzino; a portrait of Rembrandt by himself etc. etc.

Andrea del Sarto is seen to advantage at the Pitti Palace, but his chef-d'œuvre is a fresco, unhappily much worn – the Madonna del Sacco in the cloister of the Annunziata.

For early Florentine paintings, the most interesting collection is that of the Accademia. Here we saw a Cimabue which gave us the best idea of his superiority over the painters who went before him: it is a colossal Madonna enthroned; and on the same wall there is a colossal Madonna by Giotto, which is not only a demonstration that he surpassed his master, but that he had a clear vision of the noble in art. A delightful picture – very much restored, I fear – of the Adoration of the Magi made me acquainted with Gentile da Fabriano. The head of Joseph in this picture is masterly in the delicate rendering of the expression; the three Kings are very beautiful in conception; and the attendant group or rather crowd shows a remarkable combination of realism with love of the beautiful and splendid. There is a fine Domenico Ghirlandajo – the adoration of the shepherds; a fine Lippo Lippi; and an Assumption by Perugino which I like well for its cherubs and angels, and for some of the adoring figures below. In the smaller room, there is a lovely Pietà by Fra Angelico, and there is a portrait of Fra Angelico himself by another artist.

One of our drives at Florence which I have not mentioned was that to Galileo's tower, which stands conspicuous on one of the hills close about the town. We ascended it, for the sake of looking out over the plain from the same spot as the great man looked from more than two centuries ago. His portrait is in the Pitti Palace – a grave man with an abbreviated nose, not unlike Mr. Tom Trollope.

One fine day near the end of our stay we made an expedition to Siena – that fine old town built on an abrupt height overlooking a wide, wide plain. We drove about a couple of hours or more, and saw well the exterior of the place – the peculiar piazza or Campo, in the shape of a Scallopshell, with its large old Palazzo *pubblico*, the Porta Sanviene and Porta Romana, the Archbishop's palace and the cemetery. Of the churches we saw only the Cathedral, the Chapel of John the Baptist, and San Domenico. The Cathedral has a highly elaborate Gothic façade, but the details of the upper part are unsatisfactory – a square window in the centre shocks the eye, and the gables are not slim and aspiring enough. The interior is full of interest: there is the unique pavement in a sort of marble niello presenting Raffaelesque designs by Boccafumi, carrying out the example of the older portions which are very quaint in their drawing; there is a picture of high interest in the history of early art – a picture by Guido of Siena, who was rather earlier than Cimabue; fine carved stalls and screens in dark wood; and in an adjoining chapel a series of frescoes by Pinturicchio, to which Raphael is said to have contributed designs and workmanship, and wonderfully illuminated old choir books. The chapel of St. John the Baptist has a remarkable Gothic façade, and a baptismal font inside, with reliefs wrought by Ghiberti and another Florentine artist. To San Domenico we went for the sake of seeing the famous Madonna by Guido da Siena: I think we held it superior to any Cimabue we had seen. There is a considerable collection of the Siennese artists at the Accademia, but the school had no great genius equal to Giotto, to lead it. The Three Graces – an antique to which Canova's modern triad bears a strong resemblance in attitude and style – are also at the Accademia.

An interesting visit we made at Florence was to Michael Angelo's house – Casa Buonarotti – in the Via Ghibellina. This street is striking and characteristic: the houses are all old, with broad eaves, and in some cases with an open upper story so that the roof forms a sort of pavilion supported on pillars. This is a feature one sees in many parts of Florence. Michael Angelo's house is preserved with great care by his descendants – only one could wish their care had not been shown in giving it entirely new furniture. However the rooms are the same as those he occupied, and there are many relics of his presence there – his stick, his sword, and many of his drawings. In one room, there is a very fine Titian of small size – the principal figure a woman fainting.

The Last Supper, a fresco believed to be by Raphael is in a room at the Egyptian Museum. The figure of Peter, of which, apparently, there exist various sketches by Raphael's hand, is memorable.

We left Florence on the evening of the 1st of June, by diligence, travelling all night and until eleven the next morning to get to Bologna. I wish we could have made that journey across the Appennines by daylight; though, in that case, I should have missed certain grand startling effects that came to me in my occasional wakings. Wonderful heighths and depths I saw on each side of us by the fading light of the evening. Then in the middle of the night while the lightning was flashing and the sky was heavy with threatening storm-clouds, I waked to find the six horses resolutely refusing, or unable, to move the diligence; till, at last, two meek oxen were tied to the axle, and their added strength dragged us up the hill. But one of the strangest effects I ever saw was just before dawn, when we seemed to be high up on mighty mountains which fell precipitously and showed us the awful pale horizon far, far below.

The first thing we did at Bologna was to go to the Accademia, where I confirmed myself in my utter dislike of the Bolognese school – the Caraccis and Domenichino *et id genus omne* – [15] and felt some disappointment in Raphael's St. Cecilia. The pictures of Francia here, to which I had looked forward as likely to give me a fuller and higher idea of him, were less pleasing to me than the smaller specimens of him that I had seen in the Dresden and other galleries. He seems to me to be more limited even than Perugino: but he is a faithful, painstaking painter, with a religious spirit. Agostino Carracci's Communion of St. Jerome is a remarkable picture, with real feeling in it – an exception among all the great pieces of canvas that hang beside it. Domenichino's figure of St. Jerome is a direct plagiarism from that of Agostino; but in other points the two pictures are quite diverse.

The following morning we took a carriage and were diligent in visiting the churches. San Petronio has the melancholy distinction of an exquisite Gothic façade which is carried up only a little way above the arches of the door ways: the sculptures on these arches are of wonderful beauty. The interior is of lofty, airy, simple gothic, and it contains some curious old paintings in the various side-

15 Latin, 'and all of that kind'.

chapels; preeminent among which are the great frescoes by the so-called Buffamalco. The paradise is distinguished in my memory, by the fact that the blessed are ranged in seats like the benches of a church or chapel. At Santa Cecilia, now used as a barrack or guard room, there are two frescoes by Francia – the marriage and burial of St. Cecilia – characteristic but miserably injured. At the great church of San Domenico the object of chief interest is the tomb of the said saint, by the ever-to-be-honoured Nicolo Pisano. I believe this tomb was his first great work; and very remarkable it is; but there is nothing on it equal to the Nativity on the pulpit at Pisa. On this tomb stands a lovely angel, by Michael Angelo. It is small in size, holding a small candlestick, and is a work of his youth: it shows clearly enough how the feeling for grace and beauty were strong in him, only not strong enough to wrestle with his love of the grandiose and powerful.

The ugly, painful leaning towers of Bologna made me desire not to look at them a second time; but there are fine bits of massive palatial building here and there in the colonnaded streets. We trod the court of the once famous university, where the arms of the various scholars ornament the walls above and below an interior gallery. This building is now, as far as I could understand, a communal school, and the university is transported to another part of the town.

We left Bologna in the afternoon, rested at Ferrara for the night, and passed the Euganean mountains on our left hand as we approached Padua in the middle of the next day.

After dinner, and rest from our dusty journeying, we took a carriage and went out to see the town – desiring most of all to see Giotto's chapel. We paused first, however at the great church of San Antonio, which is remarkable both externally and internally. There are two side chapels opposite each other which are quite unique for contrasted effect. On the one hand is a chapel of oblong form, covered entirely with white marble relievi, golden lamps hanging from the roof; while opposite is a chapel of the same form covered with frescoes by Avanzi, the artist who seems to have been the link of genius between Giotto and Masaccio. Close by, in a separate building, is the Capella di San Giorgio, also covered with Avanzi's frescoes; and here one may study him more completely, because the light is better than in the church. He has quite a Veronese power of combining his human groups with splendid architecture.

The Arena Chapel stands apart, and is approached at present through a pretty garden. Here one is uninterruptedly with Giotto: the whole Chapel was designed and painted by himself alone, and it is said that while he was at work on it, Dante lodged with him at Padua. The nave of the chapel is in tolerably good preservation but the apsis has suffered severely from damp. It is in this apsis, that the lovely Madonna with the infant at her breast is painted in a niche, now quite hidden by some altar piece or woodwork which one has to push by in order to see this tenderest bit of Giotto's painting. This chapel must have been a blessed vision when it was fresh from Giotto's hand: the blue vaulted roof; the exquisite bands of which he was so fond, representing inlaid marble, uniting roof and walls and forming the divisions between the various frescoes which cover the upper part of the wall – the glory of Paradise at one end, and the histories of Mary and Jesus on the two sides; and the subdued effect of the series of monochromes representing the virtues and vices below.

There is a piazza with a plantation and circular public walk, with wildly affected statues of small and great notorieties, which remains with one as a peculiarity of Padua: in general the town is merely old and shabbily Italian, without anything very specific in its aspect.

From Padua to Venice!

It was about ten o'clock on a moonlight night – the 4th of June – that we found ourselves apparently on a railway in the midst of the sea: we were on the bridge across the Lagoon. Soon we were in a gondola on the Grand Canal, looking out at the moonlit buildings and water. What stillness! What beauty! Looking out from the high window of our hotel on the Grand Canal, I felt that it was a pity to go to bed: Venice was more beautiful than romances had feigned.

And that was the impression that remained and even deepened during our stay of eight days. That quiet, which seems the deeper because one hears the delicious dip of the oar (when not disturbed by clamorous church bells), leaves the eye in full liberty and strength to take in the exhaustless loveliness of colour and form.

We were in our gondola by nine o'clock the next morning, and of course the first point we sought was the piazza di San Marco. I am glad to find Ruskin calling the Palace of the Doges one of the two most perfect buildings in the world: its only defects to my feeling are the feebleness or triviality of the frieze or cornice and the want of length in the gothic windows with which the upper wall is pierced. This spot is a focus of architectural wonders; but the palace is the crown of them all. The double tier of columns and arches with the rich sombreness of their finely outlined shadows contrast satisfactorily with the warmth and light and more continuous surface of the upper part. Even landing on the piazzetta one has a sense, not only of being in an entirely novel scene, but one where the ideas of a foreign race have poured themselves in without yet mingling indistinguishably with the preexistent Italian life. But this is felt yet more strongly when one has passed along the piazzetta and arrived in front of San Marco, with its low arches and domes and minarets. But perhaps the most striking point to take one's stand upon is just in front of the white marble guard house flanking the great tower – the guard house with Sansovino's iron gates before it: on the left is San Marco with the two square pillars from St. Jean d'Acre standing as isolated trophies; on the right the piazzetta extends between the doge's palace and the Palazzo Reale to the tall columns from Constantinople; and in front is the elaborate gateway leading to the white marble Scala de' Giganti, in the court yard of the doge's palace. Passing through this gateway and up this staircase we entered the gallery which surrounds the court on three sides, and looked down at the fine sculptured vase-like wells below. Then into the great Sala, surrounded with the portraits of the doges; the largest oil-painting here, or perhaps anywhere else, is the Gloria del Paradiso, by Tintoretto, now dark and unlovely. But on the ceiling is a great Paul Veronese – the Apotheosis of Venice – which looks as fresh as if it were painted yesterday, and is a miracle of colour and composition; a picture full of glory and joy of an earthly fleshly kind, but without any touch of coarseness or vulgarity. Below the radiant Venice on her clouds, is a balcony filled with upward-looking spectators; and below this gallery is a group of human figures with horses. Next to this Apotheosis I admire, another coronation of Venice on the ceiling of another Sala; where Venice is sitting enthroned above the globe with her lovely face in half shadow – a creature born with an imperial attitude. There are other Tintorettos, Veroneses and Palmas in the great halls of this palace but they left me quite indifferent, and have become vague in my memory. From the splendours of the palace we crossed the bridge of Sighs to the Prisons and saw the horrible dark damp cells that would make the saddest life in the free light and air seem bright and desirable.

The interior of St. Mark's is full of interest, but not of beauty: it is dark and heavy, and ill suited to the Catholic worship, from the massive piers that obstruct the view everywhere, and shut out the sight of ceremony and procession, as we witnessed at our leisure on the day of the great procession of Corpus Christi. But every where there are relics of gone-by art to be studied, from mosaics of the Greeks to mosaics of later artists than the Zuccati; old marble statues embrowned like a meerschaum pipe; amazing sculptures in wood; Sansovino-doors, ambitious to rival Ghiberti's; transparent alabaster columns; an ancient Madonna, hung with jewels, transported from St. Sophia in Constantinople; and everywhere the venerable pavement, once beautiful with its starry patterns in rich marble, now deadened and sunk to uneveness like the mud floor of a cabin. Then outside, on the archway of the principal door, there are sculptures of a variety that makes one renounce the study of them in despair at the shortness of one's time – blended fruits and foliage and human groups and animal forms of all kinds.

On our first morning we ascended the great tower and looked around on the island city and the distant mountains, and the distant Adriatic. And on the same day we went to see the Pisani palaces – one of the grand old palaces that are going to decay. An Italian artist who resides in one part of this palace interested us by his frank manners and the glimpse we had of his domesticity, with his pretty wife and children. After this we saw the Church of San Sebastiano, where Paul Veronese is buried, with his own paintings around mingling their colour with the light that falls on his tombstone. There is one remarkably fine painting of his here:- it represents, I think, some saints going to martyrdom, but apart from that explanation, is a composition full of vigorous spirited figures, in which the central ones are two young men leaving some splendid dwelling on the steps of which stands the mother, pleading and remonstrating – a marvellous figure of an old woman with a bare neck.

But supreme among the pictures at Venice is the death of Peter the Martyr, now happily removed from its original position as an altar-piece and placed in a good light in the Sacristy of San Giovanni e Paolo (or San Zanipolo, as the Venetians conveniently abbreviate it). In this picture, as in that of the tribute money at Dresden, Titian seems to have surpassed himself, and to have reached as high a point in expression as in colour. In the same sacristy there was a crucifixion by Tintoret, and a remarkable Madonna with Saints by Giovanni Bellini; but we were unable to look long away from the Titian to these, although we paid it five visits during our stay. It is near this church that the famous equestrian statue stands, by Verocchio.

Santa Maria della Salute, built as an ex voto by the Republic on the cessation of the plague is one of the most conspicuous churches in Venice; lifting its white Cupolas close on the Grand Canal where it widens out towards the Giudecca. Here there are various Tintorettos, but the only one which is not blackened so as to be unintelligible is the *Cena*, which is represented as a bustling supper-party, with attendants and side board accessories in thoroughly dutch fashion! The great scene of Tintoretto's genius is held to be the Scuola di San Rocco, of which he had the painting entirely to himself – with his pupils; and here one must admire the vigour and freshness of his conceptions, though I saw nothing that delighted me in expression, and much that was preposterous and ugly. The Crucifixion here is certainly a grand work, to which he seems to have given his best powers, and among the smaller designs in the two larger halls, there were several of thorough originality, for example, the Annunciation, where Mary is seated in a poor house, with a carpenter's shop adjoining, the Nativity in the upper story of a stable, of which a section is made so as to show the beasts below, and the Flight into Egypt, with a very charming (European) landscape. In this same building of San Rocco, there are some exquisite iron gates, a present from Florence, and some singularly painstaking wood-carving, representing, in one compartment of wainscoat, above the seats that surround the upper hall, a book-case filled with old books, an inkstand and pen set in front of one shelf, *à s'y méprendre*.[16]

But of all Tintoretto's paintings the best preserved and perhaps the most complete in execution is the Miracle of St. Mark, at the Accademia. We saw it the oftener because we were attracted to the Accademia again and again by Titian's Assumption which we placed next to Peter the Martyr among the pictures at Venice. For a thoroughly rapt expression I never saw anything equal to the Virgin in this picture; and the expression is the more remarkable because it is not

16 French, 'in imitation'.

assisted by the usual devices to express spiritual ecstasy, such as delicacy of feature and temperament, or pale meagreness. Then what cherubs and angelic heads bathed in light! The lower part of the picture has no interest – the attitudes are theatrical; and the Almighty above is as unbeseeming as painted Almighties usually are; but the middle group falls short only of the Sistine Madonna.

Among the Venetian painters Gian Bellini shines with a mild serious light that gives one an affectionate respect towards him. In the Church of the Scalzi, there is an exquisite Madonna by him – probably his chef-d'œuvre – comparable to Raphael's for sweetness.

And Palma Vecchio too must be held in grateful reverence for his Santa Barbara, standing in calm grand beauty above an altar in the church of Santa Maria Formosa. It is an almost unique presentation of a hero-woman, standing in calm preparation for martyrdom, without the slightest air of pietism, yet with the expression of a mind filled with serious conviction.

We made the journey to Chioggia, but with small pleasure on account of my illness which continued all day. Otherwise that long floating over the waters with the forts and mountains looking as if they were suspended in the air, would have been very enjoyable. Of all dreamy delights that of floating in a gondola along the canals and out on the Lagoon is surely the greatest. We were out one night on the lagoon when the sun was setting and the wide waters were flushed with the reddened light: I should have liked it to last for hours; it is the sort of scene in which I could most readily forget my own existence and feel melted into the general life.

Another charm of evening-time, was to walk up and down the Piazza of S. Marco, as the stars were brightening, and look at the grand dim buildings, and the flocks of pigeons flitting about them, or to walk on to the Bridge of La Paglia and look along the dark canal that runs under the Bridge of Sighs – its blackness lit up by a gas light here and there, and the plash of the oar of blackest gondola slowly advancing.

One of our latest visits was to the Palazzo Manfrini, where there are still the remains of a magnificent collection of pictures – remains still on sale. The young proprietor was walking about transacting business in the rooms as we passed through them – a handsome, refined looking man. The chief treasure left – the Entombment by Titian – is perhaps a superior duplicate of the one in the Louvre. After this, we went to a private house (once the home of Bianca Capello) to see a picture which the joint proprietors are anxious to prove to be a Leonardo da Vinci. It is a remarkable – an unforgettable picture. The subject is the supper at Emmaus, and the Christ with open almost tearful eyes, with loving sadness, spread over the regular beauty of his features is a master-piece. This head is *not* like the Leonardo sketch at Milan, and the rest of the picture impressed me strongly with the idea that it is of German, not Italian origin. Again, the head is not like that of Leonardo's Christ in the National Gallery: it is far finer, to my thinking.

Farewell, lovely Venice, and away to Verona, across the green plains of Lombardy, which can hardly look tempting to an eye still filled with the dreamy beauty it has left behind. Yet I liked our short stay at Verona extremely. The amphitheatre had the disadvantage of coming after the Coliseum and the Pozzuoli amphitheatre and would bear comparison with neither; but the Church of San Zenone was equal in interest to almost any of the churches we had seen in Italy. It is a beautiful specimen of Lombard architecture, undisguised by any modern barbarisms in the interior, and on the walls – now that they have been freed from their coat of whitewash, there are early frescoes of high historical value – some of them, apparently of the Giotto school showing a remarkable striving after human expression. More than this, there is in one case an underlayer of yet older frescoes partly laid bare, and showing the lower part of figures in mummy like degradation of drawing, while above these are the upper portion of the later figures in striking juxtaposition with the dead art from which they had sprung with the vitality of a hidden germ. There is a very fine crypt to the church, where the fragments of some ancient [statue][17] are built in wrong way upwards. This was the only church we entered at Verona, for we contented ourselves with a general view of the town, driving about to get coups d'œil of the fine old walls, the river, the bridges, and surrounding hills, and mounting up to a high terrace for the sake of a bird's eye view: this, with a passing sight of the famous tombs of the Scaligers was all gathered in our four or five hours at Verona.

Heavy rain came on our way to Milan, putting an end to the brilliant weather we had enjoyed ever since our arrival at Naples. The line of road lies through a luxuriant country, and I remember, the picturesque appearance of Bergamo, half of it on the level, half of it lifted up on the green hill.

In this second visit of mine to Milan, my greatest pleasures were the Brera gallery and the Ambrosian library, neither of which had I seen before. The Cathedral no longer satisfied my eye in its exterior; and though the interior has very grand effects there are still disturbing elements.

At the Ambrosian library, we saw MSS. surpassing in interest any even of those we had seen in the Laurentian library at Florence – illuminated books sacred and secular – a little Koran rolled up something after the fashion of a measuring tape – private letters of Tasso, Galileo, Lucrezia Borgia etc. and a book full of Leonardo da Vinci's engineering designs. Then upstairs in the picture gallery we saw a delicious Holy Family by Luini, of marvellous perfection in its execution – the cartoon for Raphael's School of Athens, and a precious collection of drawings by

17 There is a gap in GE's text at this point: Cross supplies 'statue' (*George Eliot's Life as related in her letters and journals, arranged and edited by her husband J. W. Cross,* 3 vols. (Edinburgh, Blackwood, 1885), vol. 2, p. 247).

Leonardo da Vinci and Michael Angelo. Among Leonardo's are amazingly grotesque faces, full of humour: among Michael Angelo's is the sketch of the unfortunate Biagio who figures with asses' ears in the lower corner of the Last Judgment.

At the Brera, among a host of pictures to which I was indifferent, there were several things that delighted me: some of Luini's frescoes, especially the burial or transportation of the body of St. Catherine by angels, some single figures of young cherubs, and Joseph and Mary going to their marriage; the drawing in pastel by Leonardo, of the Christ's head, supposed to be a study for the *Cena*; the Luini – Madonna among trellises – an exquisite oil-painting; Gentile Bellini's picture of St. Mark preaching at Alexandria; and the Spozalizio, by Raphael.

At the church of St. Maurizio Maggiore, we saw Luini's power tested by an abundant opportunity: the walls are almost covered with frescoes by him, but the only remarkable felicity he has is in his female figures, which are eminently graceful. He has not power enough for a composition of any high character.

We visited, too the interesting old church of San Ambrogio, with its court surrounded by cloisters, its old sculptured pulpit, chair of St. Ambrose and illuminated choir books; and we drove to look at the line of old Roman Columns which are almost the solitary remnant of antiquity left in this ancient city – ancient at least in its name and site.

We left Milan for Como on a fine Sunday morning, and arrived at beautiful Bellagio by steamer in the evening. Here we spent a delicious day – going to the Villa Sommariva in the morning, and in the evening to the Serbelloni gardens, from the heights of which we saw the mountain peaks reddened with the last rays of the sun. The next day we reached lovely Chiavenna at the foot of the Splugen pass, and spent the evening in company with a glorious mountain torrent, mountain peaks, huge boulders, with rippling miniature torrents and lovely wild flowers[18] among them, and grassy heights with rich Spanish chestnuts shadowing them. Then, the next morning we set off by post and climbed the almost perpendicular heights of the pass, chiefly in heavy rain that would hardly let us discern the patches of snow when we reached the tableland of the summit. About five o'clock we reached grassy Splugen, and felt that we had left Italy behind us. Already our driver had been German for the last long post, and now we had come to an hotel where host and waiters were German. Swiss houses of rich dark wood, outside staircases and broad eaves, stood on the steep green and flowery slope that led up to the waterfall, and the hotel and other buildings of masonry were thoroughly German in their aspect. In the evening we enjoyed a walk between the mountains whose lower sides down to the torrent beds were set

18 Cross transcribes 'lovely wild flowers' as 'lovely young flowers' (*Ibid*., p. 250.)

with tall dark pines. But the climax of grand, nay terrible scenery came the next day, as we traversed the Via Mala.

After this, came open green valleys with dotted white churches and homesteads. We were in Switzerland, and the mighty wall of the Valteline Alps shut us out from Italy, on the 21st of June.

XII. *Italy 1864*

The plan for this journey developed out of a visit from the artist Frederic Burton, whom GE and GHL had met in Munich in 1858, and later dubbed 'the maestro'. Lewes records in his journal an evening during which Burton 'Talked of going to Venice, and when he departed he left in our bosoms the desire to go there also and in his company.' (23 April 1864) The desire was rapidly translated into action: the party set off on 4 May 1864, returning to London on 20 June. GE's journal entries are terse, and Burton's presence is not always explicitly mentioned: indeed, towards the end of the trip she neglects to mention that he stayed in Venice when she and Lewes moved on, meeting up with them again in Milan. However his influence is implicit in the detailed listing she provides of the buildings, paintings and other works of art they study. GHL's journal on this trip is much fuller than GE's, including more descriptive comment on both the cultural and material aspects of their travels. He also enunciates their particular object:

> We are paying special attention to the works of the early Venetian painters which on our former visit we had scarcely time to notice. The splendour of Titian and Veronese carries away the attention . . . Titian still seems to us *the* supreme painter; but Cina [sic] da Conegliano, Carpaccio, Gian Bellini, & the Vivarini are so intensely moving that we cannot *enjoy* Veronese's worldly sensual magnificence after them.[1]

They had two nights in Paris en route to Italy, taking the opportunity on one of them to go to the opera. Their recreation later on this tour was not always so highbrow. Many of the performances they saw were farces or similar: the Teatro Malibran in Venice for instance was noted for circus acts like rope-dancing and sword-swallowing. It is usually Lewes who provides comment on such performances. Similarly, though both journals mention their securing the coupé of the diligence to cross the Alps (Murray notes that this privilege incurs a small extra charge),[2] GE does not say as GHL does that they

1 *The Letters of George Henry Lewes*, ed. William Baker, 2 vols (Victoria, University of Victoria, English Literary Studies Monograph Series 64, 1995), vol. 2, p. 64.

2 John Murray, *Handbook for Travellers in Northern Italy. Comprising*

then proceeded by train from Turin to Milan: 'Went second class and found it perfectly comfortable with the advantage of having Italians instead of English as companions.' (GHL Journal, 8 May 1864) His satisfaction in their economical mode of travelling is ubiquitous. Where GE summarily notes on 13 May 'Left the Hotel Barbesi and established ourselves in our old quarters at the Hotel de la Ville', Lewes gives an account of the negotiation with the disagreeable landlord at the Barbesi, and of the highly satisfactory arrangement at the Hotel de la Ville: '9 frs *each* per diem, for lodging, lighting, service, breakfast and dinner with wine' (GHL Journal, 13 May).

GHL had been somewhat disappointed by Italy in 1860. On this tour, however, he enthuses constantly, both in his journal and letters, about Italy in general and Venice in particular. His scientific interests were not entirely dormant: after concluding the accommodation arrangements in Venice, he reports 'walked to the Rialto through the fishmarket, – picturesque figures – young cuttlefish exciting my desires.' (GHL Journal, 13 May) Though GE in this journal does not dilate on her experience, her pleasure was none the less deep, as her account of their journey to D'Albert-Durade shows:

> Venice and her art seemed more beautiful to us than the images our memory had retained. We entered the more thoroughly into the art from having a friend with us who is like yourself, a brother of the brush, and having never been in Italy before felt an ardour of curiosity and enjoyment that was an added stimulus to his companions.[3]

GHL dwells more on creature comfort than GE. In her journal, she rarely mentions washing, as he routinely does when they arrive at a new destination, nor does she allude much to what they have to eat – a lack GHL supplies: on 17 May 'At dinner we had dogfish, . . . which on our coasts is regarded as offal and never eaten, [but] surpasses in delicacy combined with flavour any fish I can think of.' He frequently refers to their enjoying ices, and to the men having cigars. At this time he is shamelessly taken up with shopping: on 11 May in Milan 'Left Polly in the Gallery with Burton as I had had enough of sightseeing. Rambled; bought some capital kid gloves at 1 fr 25 c a pair – a shilling a pair!' and later – more intriguing – 'Bought a

---

Piedmont, Liguria, Lombardy, Venetia, Parma, Modena, and Romagna (8th edn.; London, Murray, 1860), p. 13.

3 *The George Eliot Letters*, ed. Gordon S. Haight, 9 vols (New Haven, Yale University Press, 1954–78), vol. 4, p. 158.

couple of black lace veils for 30 fr.' The alethoscope (a kind of stereoscope) is a major purchase, coming to 56 francs with carriage and photographs (about £3 10s.), and on the way home in Lucerne 'Bought a fine wolfskin' (14 June). The vignettes of everyday life that elsewhere punctuate GE's journal are not evident here: it is Lewes who is rhapsodic about the crossing of the Alps, describes their travelling companions, fleshes out the visit to the home of the gondolier Antonio, and notes on 21 May 'While Burton went into another church we remained in the gondola and watched a man loading a barge with cabbages – on the bank a "holy family" in real life'. It is he also who notes down his study of guidebooks and travel literature: on arrival in Padua, he reads Kugler, and on several occasions mentions Murray as their travelling companion. But they were not intimidated by Murray's judgements: 'Walked to the *palazzo Papafava*, on the faith of Murray and the landlord', Lewes notes (30 May): 'hardly worth the pains', GE sums up. Just as GHL was the more copious journaliser on this trip, he also appears to have been the more conscientious correspondent. His letters to his family in London are lively and amusing, with a tendency to be fussily demanding in reminders to Charles of errands and commissions that in later years becomes more marked, and already is indicative of the extent to which he took upon himself day-to-day arrangements for the household.

Though both of them were poorly at times on this trip, as the Journal testifies GE kept up a fierce pace. At one point GHL refers to her as 'the best man of the three' (*Letters of GHL*, vol. 2, p. 62). Their itinerary covered some new ground, both places such as Brescia where they had not been, or sights not taken in during their previous visits in 1860. While the Italian political situation post-unification is not dwelt on, GE and GHL were well aware of it, observing various military personnel and especially the Austrian occupation of Venice. Shortly before their departure they had gone to see Garibaldi at the Crystal Palace, but despite her 'real reverence' for Mazzini, GE declined to contribute to a fund for him (*Letters*, vol. 4, p. 200).

Parts of this journal appear to have been written in pencil, and later overwritten in ink. In some places, it seems that the pencilled text may have been different from the inked version, but it is impossible to recover more than a few words. The last entries printed here (following '20. Home.') are from the other end of the notebook, preceding 'Normandy and Britanny'.

None of this material has been published previously. In the *Life*, Cross uses only the entries from Diary 1861–1877, recording their departure and return, for this journey, and in the *Letters* and the biography, Haight makes no explicit use of this material either in text or footnotes.

XII. Italy 1864

May 4. Started from the Charing Cross station at 7 1/2 a.m. Reached Paris at 6. Hotel du Helder.

5. Saw La Sainte Chapelle and Notre Dame. Drove in the Bois de Boulogne. In the evening, to the Theatre Lyrique to hear *Faust*.

6. Friday. To the Louvre. Fine Andrea Mantegna, with adoring Knight (Gonzaga) in full armour. Two fine Morettos – St. Louis, the finest. Started at 8 o'clock p.m. on our journey to St. Michel.

7. Arrived at St. Michel 1 1/2. Set off about an hour after in the coupé of the diligence on our ascent of the Mont Cenis. Effect of light on white horse and harness. Arrived at Susa 10 1/2 – waited till 1 1/2.

8. Sunday. Arrived at Turin at 3 1/2 Hotel Liguria. Went to bed and after a good rest went to the picture gallery. A great great Veronese – the Washing of Christ's feet: the Stuart children, by Vandyk: Holy Family, by Andrea Mantegna. Had a bath. On our walk saw a very grand looking woman performing feats of strength. Went to the Teatro Prossini and heard L'Elisire d'Amore.

9 May. Monday. Started for Milan. Beautiful Novarese nurse-maid: a Sicilian deputy and a Neapolitan, amiable and politically hopeful. At the Grand Bretagna. Went to the Brera as soon as possible. Saw the Luini frescoes: Joseph leading Mary to the marriage; Holy Family, with landscape: Flying angel, in fragment: grand Madonna, with Santa Barbara and a male saint, a fine angeletto playing the lute below: two little kneeling angels: the burial of Saint Catherine. Ancona, by Giovanni d'Allemagna and Antonio da Murano. Great Crivellis, one the Madonna enthroned alone, another enthroned with Saints beside her: Exquisite Cima da Conegliano.

10 May. Tuesday. Ambrosian Library manuscripts. Supremely beautiful fresco by Luini – *Rex gloriæ spinis coronatur*.[1] This is in the former dispensatory of the Hospital, which the building originally was. Above, we saw the collection of drawings, and some exquisite Luinis and Leonardos. Holy Family by Luini after Leonardo's design, with a beautiful St Anne. Delicate female portrait on panel, and majestic chalk head by Leonardo. After dinner to the open air theatre *'della Commenda*. Saw La Rivincita, heroine a handsome woman and good actress, Adelaide Donzelli.

11 May. Wednesday. Walked to the Colonne di San Lorenzo, then to San Ambrogio. Exquisite bit of quaint sculpture under the pulpit, representing Love: male and female figures clasping hands. To San Maurizio to see the Luini

1 Latin, 'The king of glory is crowned with thorns'.

frescoes. To see the Cenacolo. In the evening again to the Teatro della Commenda – saw the Donzelli act remarkably an old woman with the palsy.

12. Thursday. To the Brera again for a last look. Saw the first time a gorgeous Coronation of the Virgin by Crivelli. Started at 12.25 for Venice. Glorious views of Bergamo, Lago di Garda and Verona. At Venice by 10 1/2. Hotel Barbesi.

13. Friday. Left the Hotel Barbesi and established ourselves in our old quarters at the Hotel de la Ville. Walked to the Rialto. Then to St. Mark's. Grand old mosaic of Christ on the right hand under the central archway.

14. Saturday. To the Ducal Palace. Saw the Veroneses. Went over the Bridge of Sighs down into the Pozzi. Fine dark cicerone, holding the light – deep red berretta. Floated down the Grand Canal to see the Ca d'oro and the Fondaco de' Turchi, Church of the Carmini: beautiful adoration of the Shepherds with Tobias and his angel, exquisite landscape behind, by Cima da Conegliano. At the Frari, saw the Madonna by Gian Bellini, little angel piping, and another playing the lute below.

15. Sunday. *Whit*sunday. Went to hear mass at St. Mark's. Then to the Accademia, where we confined ourselves to the two first rooms. The Assumption and the Miracle of St. Mark occupied us chiefly in the 2nd: in the first I noticed especially a Madonna in blue in the Ancona by Bartolomeo Vivarini, and a grand madonna and child with saints and angels – a large picture by Giovanni and Antonio da Murano.

16. Monday. To San Rocco. Greatly impressed by Tintoretto's originality and power of conception. The Christ before Pilate – and his figure in white garments unforgettable. In the Great Crucifixion, the foremost woman lying in the listlessness of absorbing Grief a marvellous bit of expression. To the Accademia: John the Baptist by Cima da Conegliano. On the Giudecca in the Gondola. At night, along the Grand Canal.

17. Tuesday. To San Zanipolo. Statue of Coleoni. Coronation of the Virgin attributed to Carpaccio. Time chiefly taken up by Titian's Peter the Martyr. To the Arsenal: Great Greek lions: Model of the Bucintoro: model of old Venetian galley: great banner taken from the Turks at Lepanto. To Santa Maria Formosa to see Santa Barbara, and saw for the first time a Madonna by Vivarini, stretching out her robe to cover saints below.

18. Wednesday. San Giorgio dei Schiavoni to see Carpaccio's series of St. Jerome and St. George – also St. Trifonius slaying the Basilisk. To the Accademia. Saw with Mr. Burton, Titian's "Presentation"; a magnificent large picture by Carpaccio – the infant Christ presented to Simeon: Bordone's Fisherman presenting the ring of the Doge; the most interesting Bonifacio I ever saw, the rich man at table with his courtesans, and Carpaccio's series of St. Ursula. In the evening went in a train of gondolas to hear the Austrian band play in a gondola lit by paper lanterns – all in honor of the Austrian general Benedeck. Then out on the Giudecca by moonlight.

19. Thursday. Went to San Giovanni in Bragora but could not see the pictures because service was going on. Went to San Zaccaria and saw a grand Gian Bellini, with a St. Jerome reading especially fine in its calm abstraction. The other saints are Catherine, Agatha and St. Peter. In a side chapel there is an Antonio da Murano – an ancona of which the central figure is a sweet Giottesque Madonna. Over the door there is an old ancona with a fine archangel. To the Accademia. Dwelt on two Bellinis. One with downcast eyes, Magdalen on one side, and St. Catherine on the other. The other an open-eyed madonna, the flesh greyer than usual – fine manly saints standing with sculpturesque quietude on each side. St. Thomas putting his finger into the wound in Christ's side, by Cima da Conegliano: supremely beautiful sky and landscape. Fine adoration of the Magi by Bonifazio. Fine portrait of the Senator Sovrango by Titian. After dinner to the *Teatro Malibran*.

20. Friday. To the Frari again. Madonna with the Pesaro family by Titian, two Vivarinis, and Gian Bellini's exquisite Madonna. Dead doges in their stone sleep. Beautiful wood carving and inlaying. Then to our gondolier Antonio's dwelling to see his wife and children. Turned into the church of S. Pantaleone and saw an interesting Antonio Vivarini – coronation of the Virgin – children under the throne in a naked multitude, evangelists below – rows of saints on each side, and above, rows of angels. To the Accademia. In the Contarini collection, another lovely Madonna by Bellini, a Bissolo – Christ (dead) supported by two angels. Bought photographs. Had a Giro in the gondola in the evening, Prof. Thomas accompanying us. Lovely moonlight.

21. Saturday. Went to Murano. Saw the glass works. Then to the church of San Pietro Martine, where there is a grand Gian Bellini, with a fine portrait of a doge kneeling; a probable Basaiti, Madonna on the cloud above, and semicircle of Saints below. A fine large Vivarini, and 4 angels by him, one of them perfectly lovely, with the hands crossed on the breast, walking on the uppermost clouds. Then to the fine old San Donato, where we delighted in the exterior of the apse, and in the single figure of the Madonna on the golden interior. Pavement as splendid as St. Mark's. Filled with scaffolding in tardy promise of restoration.

22. Sunday. To Saint Mark's. Went on to the external gallery and saw the horses etc. Then into the Baptistery, where we dwelt on the old mosaics. G. had headache, so we walked to the Giardini pubblici, and then rowed back from the Piazzetta to our hotel. After a moment's pause there, Antonio rowed us to the Palazzo Cicogna.

23. Monday. To San Giovanni in Bragora, where we saw some fine Vivarinis – an ancona with St. Andrew in the centre, St. George and St. Jerome at the sides, another with a rather fine Madonna and a risen Christ by Luigi Vivarini. Then, a supremely fine Cima da Conegliano – the Baptism of Christ. To San Francesco della Vigna where we saw nothing worth memory except a fine Madonna and Child by Nigroponte. To San Giovanni e Paolo where we looked again at the Coronation of the Virgin attributed to Carpaccio, and at Peter the Martyr.

24. Tuesday. To San Lazzaro, and the Accademia.

25. Wednesday. To San Salvatore to see Gian Bellini's Christ at Emmaus. To San Giovanni Crisostomo to see the pictures of San Girolano, St Cristoforo, and Sant'Agostino by Gian Bellini, and San Crisostomo reading with a fine group of women, by Sebastiano del Piombo and Giorgione. To the Abbazia, where we saw Tobias and the angel, with two saints by Cima da Conegliano, and a characteristic sketch of a Last Supper by Paolo Veronese.

26. Thursday. *Corpus Christi*. Saw the procession in the church and Piazza.

27. A very wet day. Went to S. Vitale to see a picture by Carpaccio in a wretched light, San Vitale on horseback. Then home because of the rain. Afterwards to the Accademia where we staid till after 3. Then home to pack. Staid at home in the evening.

28. Saturday. To San G. Crisostomo again. Then to the Scalzi to see Bellini's Madonna there. Then to the Redentore where we found three Bellinis – two of them important. Then to Ponti's where we bought an alethoscope. At 7 we set off for the Railway to Padua, but as it did not start till 8.10 the maestro and I had a giro in the Gondola, and saw the sun set behind the Alps. Arrived at Padua at 1/2 past 9 and went to bed.

29. Sunday. Went to see the Chapel of the Eremitani painted by Andrea Mantegna. Mantegna's frescoes are the finest things of his we have seen but are sadly injured. The architectural background to the death of San Cristoforo is eminently beautiful, and so are some figures in the opposite frescoes of St. James's Life. To the Arena Chapel. Giotto's frescoes finer than we had remembered them to be. To the Botanical Gardens, the oldest in Europe: we sat there a little while in the sunshine. After dinner a lovely drive through the country within sight of the Euganean hills. At 9 o'clock to the theatre.

30. Monday. To San Giorgio to see D'Avanzi's frescoes. The Crucifixion and the death of St. Catherine very fine. To the Scuola del Santo, where there is nothing worth seeing. Then into the church of San Antonio, where we sat some time, and looked again at the frescoes in the chapel of San Felice. To the Palazzo Pappafava; hardly worth the pains. To the theatre again in the evening.

31. Tuesday. Set off for Verona at 1/4 past 10. Arrived at 2 at the Albergo delle due Torri, dined at 4. Went out at 1/2 past 7 to see the town. Turned into S. Anastasia and the Duomo, sat in the Piazza dei Signori to hear the Austrian band and look at the buildings. Then walked to the tombs of the Scaligers and the Piazza dell'Erbe, and finally to the Piazza Brà where we walked round the amphitheatre.

1 June. Wednesday. Went into S. Anastasia again. Then to the Duomo, where we looked at Titian's Assumption. Then to take a bath. Rain drove us to the hotel a little while. When it ceased, we went to the picture gallery. Saw some interesting old paintings, with the symbols of the Passion, forming in one case a border, in

the other two compartments in which they seemed to float on a sea. Several fine pictures by Libri. Looked at the outside of S. Fermo, and bought some photographs.

2 June. Thursday. To the Castel Vecchio and San Zanone. Gigantic Byzantine figure opposite the San Cristoforo. Exquisite colour of the exterior. To San Fermo, where we saw the interior, then home to rest.

3. Friday. Station 10–5 to Brescia. Peschiera and Desenzano – views of Lago di Garda. Duomo Vecchio. Assumption by Moretto. Giorgione's Holy Family. Crypt: old Frescoes. San Giovanni Evangelista: Moretto's Madonna and Saints: altarpiece by Giovanni Bellini – three Maries. Moretto's Elijah and Manna and Romanino's Spozalizio. To San Francesco. St. Margaret, Jerome and Francis. Sposalizio, by Francesco da Prato da Carnagio. Glowing altarpiece: Madonna and saints by Romanino. San Nazaro and Celso: altarpiece by Titian, Resurrection of Christ in the Centre – Christ an extravagant figure: landscape – sunrise and one gazing figure in shadow, fine. Moretto: Coronation of the Virgin by Moretto: Virgin sweet; Christ not good; St. Joseph fine; archangel Michael very beautiful but feeble. Walk in the evening on the ramparts. Fine evening sky.

4. Saturday. Walk along the ramparts. San Clemente: Moretto: Madonna enthroned canopy of trellis and flowers, cherubs peeping through. Saint Clement in the centre below. Heads and hands, as usual, rather affected. Saint Ursula with a banner in each hand, surrounded by her virgins. Sta. Afra: Titian's Woman taken in adultery. Transfiguration by Tintoretto as an altar-piece; fine in conception. Santa Maria delle Grazie: Pietro Rosa's Santa Barbara anticipating immediate death. Moretto's Nativity, almost in the dark. St Sebastian, St Martin and St. Roch, affected – also Saint Anthony of Padua with his lilies. To the Museo Patrio: entrance of broken columns with an overgrowth of green. Winged Victory and miscellaneous antiquities. Museo Civico, or Galleria Tosi: Raphael's Pietà, Lotto's adoration of the Shepherds a charming portrait picture the angels with blue wings – their hands resting on the shoulders of the shepherds: the Child lying on its back caressing the lamb's nose. A lovely annunciation by Moretto, a half length picture. Two portraits by Moroni one of them remarkable. Several Francias. Some modern pictures worth notice especially two by Hayez – one, the meeting of Jacob and Esau, the other the flight of the Greeks, and one by Podesti – the old subject of Tasso reading his poem aloud. – Started at 4 o'clock for Padua.[2] A delicious journey. Looking at the mountains all the way.

5. Sunday. Went to San Giorgio in Palazzo to see a great oil painting by Luini – the Deposition from the Cross. Went to the Duomo and heard a sermon on the Devotion to the Sacred Heart of Jesus. Then to see the military procession to commemorate the fifth anniversary of Italian freedom. Went a second time to

2 Slip of the pen, they are heading to Milan.

S. Giorgio to see the Luini. In the evening waited in doors till the Maestro came. Then went out with him to see the illuminations and stayed out till 1/2 past 12.

6. Monday. Went again to S. Giorgio in Palazzo. Then to San Maurizio to see the Luini frescoes again; then to the Palazzo Litta. Saw a Madonna and child by Leonardo; exquisite attitude of the child sucking at the breast and looking up; rapture in the mother's face. Frescoes by Luini: adoration of the Shepherds, and adoration of the Magi. Curius Dentatus declining to eat off gold plate, and a head of the Saviour. To Santa Maria della Passione to see another larger and much praised Deposition by Luini. Disappointed in it. In the same church is a scourging by some pupil of Leonardo's and a Last Supper by Gaudenzio Ferrari. In the evening went to the Teatro Re and heard Lucrezia Borgia.

7. Tuesday. To the Brera. Went into one of the large rooms for the first time, where there is a sublime picture by Marco d'Ogionno of the Archangel Michael overcoming Satan – the other two archangels on each hand. The martyrdom of St. Catherine by Gaudenzio Ferrari. A fine Assumption by Borgognone, with delicious little trumpeting cherubs. An Annunciation said to be "da Luini" – exquisite in design. To the Ambrosian Library to see the Crowning with thorns again – *Caput regis gloriæ spinis coronatur*.[3] After dinner went to the Teatro della Commenda and saw La Figlia Unica.

8. Wednesday. To the Ambrosian Library to see the woodcuts and drawings: then to the Brera. In the evening drove out to see the Arco della Pace. Then as we were lounging in the Corso, we entered a church apparently dedicated to San Carlo – a new Rotunda – where a wedding was going on.

9. Thursday. To Como. Looked at the beautiful façade of the Cathedral; then entered to look at the pictures by Luini. Two in distemper, one in oil. Also one (not good) by Gaudenzio Ferrari. Then to San Fedele: exterior singular and very old – dating from the tenth century. Then to San Abbondio, a wonderful old Church built on the site of a still earlier church, which again was built on the site of a pagan temple. A handsome young Jesuit, Director of the Seminary to which the Church belongs was our Cicerone. After dinner we went up the Lake to Cadenabbia, rain the whole way. In the evening we walked on the terrace and saw vivid sheet lightning and the fireflies hovering over the lake.

10. Friday. Walked along the side of the Lake, the Sommariva way. Then in a boat to Menaggio. From whence we had a delicious drive to Porlezza, at the head of Lake Lugano. An hour of Steam boat took us to Lugano by 3 o'clock. Went to the Church near the Hotel du Parc to see Luini's frescoes. The great fresco representing the history of the Passion – the Last Supper, and the Madonna with the infant Jesus and John. In the evening a delightful walk along the lake.

11. Saturday. To San Lorenzo on the hill. Then to see the Luini again. At 5 o'clock started in a carriage for Bellinzona – a magnificent drive of 4 hours.

3 Latin, 'The head of the king of glory is crowned with thorns'.

12. Sunday. From Bellinzona to Airolo, dining at Faido.

13. Monday. Started at 8 on our passage over the mountain. Lunched at Hospenthal. At Fluellen by 5, and Lucerne at 1/2 past 7. Rambled out in the evening.

14. Tuesday. To see Thorwaldsen's Lion. Then to see the show of Alpine animals. To the hill Gibraltar to see the view of the mountains. In the evening to the Drei Linden.

15. Rainy. Started at 5 for Bâle.

16. Thursday. From Bâle to Paris.

20. Home.

Notes for Italy. *Rome*
Church of Santa Prassede, built 817 – Mosaic with an army of Martyrs.

Milan
Santa Eustazio (Lombard)
9th century
San Gottardo, 1336

XIII. *Normandy and Brittany 1865*

The first half of 1865 was a period of exceptional activity even for GE and GHL. GE had started work on *The Spanish Gypsy* in September 1864, but made such slow progress that stern measures were needed: '*George has taken my drama away from me*' she reported in her diary (entry for 19, 20, 21 February 1865). Before the end of March, however, *Felix Holt the Radical* was under way. Progress with this work too was painfully slow, and in her diary entry for 23 July she declared 'I am going doggedly to work at my novel, seeing what determination can do in the face of despair.' Lewes having severed his connection with the *Cornhill* in October 1864, accepted the editorship of the new *Fortnightly Review* in March 1865, not without misgivings on the part of his consort who none the less contributed two articles to the first number, published on 15 May (these were 'The Influence of Rationalism', a review of W. E. H. Lecky's *History of the Rise and Influence of the Spirit of Rationalism in Europe*, and 'The Grammar of Ornament', a review of their friend Owen Jones's book of that name).

Since the pair had 'been fixed in London through the season – Mr. Lewes doing a miraculous amount of work, though with health frequently disturbed',[1] it is not surprising to find GE announcing on 1 August 1865 that 'We have almost made up our minds to start some time in this month for a run in Normandy and Brittany.' (*Letters*, vol. 4, p. 199) Decision followed promptly: on 3 August she wrote to Barbara Bodichon: 'It is settled now that we are to go for a month's holiday in Normandy and Brittany starting next Thursday. So I am reading Villemarqué and setting my mind towards Celtic legends, that I may people the land with great shadows when there are no solid Bretons in sight' (vol. 8, p. 349). At this stage she was reading Villemarqué's *Contes populaires des Anciens Bretons* (1842), from which she took notes on Celtic literature including Welsh and Breton poetry.[2] On the journey she took up another of his works, *La Légende Celtique et la Poesie des Cloitres* (1864), but judged it 'a poor book' (25 August).

1 *The George Eliot Letters*, 9 vols. (New Haven, Yale University Press, 1954–78), vol. 4, p. 197.

2 *George Eliot: A Writer's Notebook, 1854–1879*, ed. Joseph Wiesenfarth (Charlottesville, University Press of Virginia, 1981), pp. 128–9, 215–6.

The relatively impromptu nature of this tour had its cost, as she reported to Sara Hennell on her return: 'Our traveling in Brittany was a good deal marred and obstructed by the Emperor's fête which sent all the world on our track towards Cherbourg and Brest. But the Norman churches, the great cathedrals at Le Mans, Tours, and Chartres with their marvellous painted glass were worth much scrambling to see' (*Letters*, vol. 4, p. 202: the fête involved the English fleet's being entertained at Cherbourg and Brest from 15 August, with reciprocal entertainment for the French fleet at Portsmouth on 29 August). The inconvenience is mentioned in the journal for 13 August, but is not prominent in the day-to-day account of their tour.

On this occasion she used a separate notebook for the journey: the next diary entry is for 7 September, the day of their return home. In her accustomed manner, she used the other end of a notebook which had already done service for the trip to Italy the previous year. Where that Italian journal gives a staccato record of where they went and what they saw, this account of travels through new terrain in Normandy and Brittany has more of the enlivening salient detail of earlier journals. GE had no need of recourse to Celtic legend to 'people the land'.

Their friend Richard Congreve offered advice on their itinerary (*Letters*, vol. 4, 201), which took them from Boulogne westward along the coast to Dieppe, then inland to Rouen, northwest towards the coast to Caen, from where they moved westward by stages as far as St Malo. They then turned south to Rennes, on to the southwest to Auray and Carnac on the coast (where the Celtic megaliths, surely the reason for going to Carnac at all, do not rate a mention), south again to Nantes before turning eastwards to Tours, Le Mans, Chartres and Paris (where they had been as recently as January), then back to London via Rouen, Dieppe and Boulogne. This was a solid schedule, involving some early starts and long days of travelling, though on many days the distances involved were not great. The pleasures of the tour came from scenery and architecture rather than works of art (compare the catalogues of paintings in 'Italy 1864'), though the travellers were generally conscientious in visiting the chief sights of each place.

On this tour, as on other occasions, the Leweses travelled with the relevant Murray handbook. In this case, GE quoted extensively (and with a reasonable degree of accuracy) from Murray's *Handbook for Travellers in France* (in its ninth edition in 1864) in the account of the church of St Ouen at Rouen, following it quite closely also in the account of Rouen Cathedral. Mostly she omitted the occasional phrase or substituted one word for another; now and again she improved Murray, who notes that the south portal of St Ouen is called *des Marmouzets* 'from the figures of the animals carved on it':[3] compare GE's 'from the little baboon-like demons who are oozing out below the arch of the doorway'. Again GE's entries on Caen, especially in the description of the grotesque carvings in the church of St Pierre, and in the long quotations about the funeral of William the Conqueror, drew directly on Murray[4] – though there are wonderful snatches here of personal observation (the old woman in the flower market, the workmen in blue blouses).

They had been to Paris for ten days in January 1865, 'going to the theatre or opera nearly every night, and seeing sights all day long' (*Letters*, vol. 4, p. 176). On this occasion they stayed on the rue St Honoré, in a hotel described by Murray as 'good, and charges moderate'.[5] Despite GE's indisposition, they sampled a good range of Parisian possibilities, including a melodrama at the Gaïeté as well as the opera, favourite paintings at the Louvre and new works by contemporary French artists at the Luxembourg. In addition they had outdoor pleasures, driving in the Bois de Boulogne and enjoying an unplanned afternoon in the grounds of the imperial palace at St Cloud. Returning via Rouen, they revisited some places and took in new sights such as the Musée des Antiquités, before turning home by easy stages.

This journal has never been published, except for two sentences of GE's comments on the glass in Chartres Cathedral quoted by Haight (*Letters*, vol. 4, p. 202n). In the biography, Haight characteristically observes of the journey: 'Lewes took her away on 10 August for a month'.[6] Cross reports this particular expedition by quoting GE's diary entry for 7 September 1865, which summarises the itinerary.

3 John Murray, *Handbook for Travellers in France* (9th ed.; London, John Murray, 1864), p. 39.

4 *Ibid.*, pp. 73 and 42.

5 John Murray, *A Handbook for Visitors to Paris* (London, John Murray, 1864), p. 28.

6 Gordon S. Haight, *George Eliot* (Oxford University Press, 1968), p. 382.

XIII. Journey to Normandy in 1865

1 Bayeux and St. Lô
2 Vire
3 Avranches
4 Dinon
Rennes
Morlaix
Vannes
Quimper

Aug. 10. 1865. At 20 minutes past 9 on this not too bright but fine morning we started from home on our expedition to Normandy and Brittany. Happily we were in good time at the Charing Cross Station, for all London seemed to be bent in our direction. We had an excellent passage, to Boulogne, where we dined; then to Noyelles by train. Here we had to wait nearly an hour, the train to St. Valéry not arriving til $^1/_4$ to 8. We were rather dismayed to find that we must stay at St. Valéry all night. However, we were tolerably comfortable.

11th. We had a very agreeable journey by diligence from St. Valéry to Dieppe, being fortunate enough to get the coupé. The country was flat and monotonous, but cheerful with cornfields, pastures and green crops, with here and there a group of houses, and the sea in the distance, disclosing itself at some opening in the coast. At Eu, we stayed nearly an hour and walked into the gardens of the Château. They are neglected now, and the walks are grass-grown, but we had a pleasant stroll along the avenues of elm and larch. The Chateau is not imposing but has the quaint picturesqueness which belongs to all the genuine French buildings with their steep roofs and eyelids. The people are rather coarse and German or English-looking. At Dieppe we had time to see the church of St. Jacques; the tower and façade are handsome; the choir very good. From Dieppe to Rouen the journey by railway was delightful, especially the latter part from Monville, where the valley looks as if it realized the paradox of a happy region of cotton factories.

We arrived rather late at Rouen and had some disagreeables in getting into the Hotel de France, but at last we were settled comfortably enough and slept peacefully.

12th. We were out early to see the churches which close at 12. In the façade of the Cathedral one tower – the *Tour de Beurre* so called because paid for with the fines for eating butter in Lent – has a round summit; the other has a steep tiled roof of the French wedge-shaped fashion. In the interior there is some magnificent painted glass, especially in the choir aisles: it is of the 13th century. Here lies or lay the heart of Richard Cœur de Lion. It is deposited in the Sacristy at present and is wrapt in a sort of green taffeta enclosed in a leaden case. His body was buried at Fontevrault. St. Maclou has a beautiful exterior in the flamboyant style; one tower towards which the buttresses seem all to converge.

But the great glory of the old town is the church of St. Ouen. "The first stone was laid in 1318 by Abbot Jean Roussel, the choir, the chapels and nearly all the transept were completed in 21 years, and the nave and towers finished by the end of the 15th (14th?) century." Above the cross rises the central tower, 260 feet high. The South Portal is called *des Marmouzets* from the little baboon-like demons who are oozing out below the arch of the doorway etc. Over the door in bas-relief is the Assumption (and below it the death) of the Virgin. The church is 443 feet long and 106½ high. High gallery round the triforium, in nave, choir and transept. The clerestory is very large, and the windows seem to absorb all the solid wall, the roof being maintained in its place by the pillars and buttresses alone. It is beautiful to see the whole interior inverted in the *bénitier*[1] of black and white marble. The windows are here and there glorious with remnants of painted glass – a range of large figures running round the windows of the choir, looking life size from below.

"The master mason under and by whom this church was reared is buried in St. Agnes' chapel. His name was Alexander Berneval, and according to tradition, he murdered his apprentice through envy, because the youth had surpassed in the execution of the rose window in the North transept (into the tracery of which the pentalpha is introduced) that which his master had constructed in the South transept. Though the mason paid the penalty of his crime, the monks, out of gratitude for his skill, interred his body within the church." We saw the tombstone, or rather stones, which are now removed to the chapel of St. Joseph and are placed perpendicularly. The enchased figures supposed to be those of the above-named mason and his pupil, are in the style of drawing of the late 15th century. One is old, one in the prime of life. Both have compasses in their hands, and the elder holds in his left the design for his own rose window in the South. The younger holds, not the design for the pentalpha window, but apparently the plan of a church. (See History of St. Ouen) But by the side of these two figures, on another stone, is a much older piece of work – an enchased figure of an architect holding some instrument before him, and surmounted by elaborate gothic fretwork also enchased: the drawing of this figure is of the 13th century, I should think, or early in the 14th.

The material used in building St. Ouen is a limestone containing flints, which have been often patiently cut through in the delicate carving and tracery. (St. Ouen was bishop of Rouen and died 678).

We went up to the inner and outer gallery. From the inner we had a fine view of the interior, with the lights sending dashes of colour across the shafts and mouldings; and we could see the remains of the frescoed angels in the spandrils of the arches in the choir as well as the remains of gilding on the mouldings. From the outer gallery we had a splendid view of the town, with the old houses immediately surrounding the church. On the South the winding Seine where it

1 French, translated by Murray as 'holy-water basin'.

is finely bridged by some stone arches and divided by woody islets. Above it rises the Mont Ste. Catherine. On the North the tower in which Joan of Arc was imprisoned is discernible below the Mont des Malades. To the right is another eminence called the Bois de Guillaume. A very fine old wooden house is in the rue de la Savonnerie near a grotesque fountain.

13th. Sunday. Caen. We made the most unfortunate choice of coming hither by steamer, as far as Honfleur, and thence by rail. Both steamer and railway train were crowded with passengers going to the Cherbourg fêtes. However we reached Caen at six, got our dinner and went to bed, worn out by our fatiguing and uncomfortable day.

14th. Monday. We walked first to St. Pierre, the church with the supremely beautiful tower and spire. In the flower market, which was in the space at the east end, an old woman came up to give her sympathy as we stood admiring the church. It is curious that on one capital alone of the interior the whim of some artist has carved grotesque subjects – Lancelot passing the sea on his sword, Aristotle bestridden and flogged by a woman, a figure riding on an ass etc. – while all the other capitals are in an ordinary style. The great beauty of the tower is chiefly produced by the long lancet windows with the multitudinous lines of their delicate mouldings. Walking along the Rue St. Pierre we saw two very fine old houses, of which the wood work was elaborately carved. One female figure in good preservation was really graceful. Our way took us by St. Sauveur, which has a tower imitated from that of St. Pierre. A tree-lined broad road took us to St. Etienne, the church of the Abbaye aux Hommes founded by William the Conqueror. (A group of workmen in blue blouses of all shades, looked picturesque at a corner of the avenue of poplars on our way). The church remains as it was built in the 11th century as far as the transept: the choir is of later date and pointed. The effect of the West towers is very grand, and the colour, a fine greenish grey softened by a minute lichen. There is no painted glass. Here William the Conqueror was buried. – "Tortured by the wound he had received at the cruel sack and burning of Mantes, he repaired to the retired monastery of St. Gervais (at Rouen) to die. His deathbed was a melancholy example of the vanity of human grandeur. Deserted by his own sons, when the breath was scarce out of his body, and plundered by his servants, his body remained stripped and deserted until the pity and charity of an unknown knight in the neighbourhood provided the funds necessary for the burial; and he himself escorted the body to its last resting place in Caen. The funeral was interrupted, even within the precincts of the church, and before the service was concluded by the cry of a man of low degree who claimed the site of the grave, saying that it occupied the site of his father's house, that he had been illegally ejected from it in order to build the church, and he demanded the restitution of his property. The claim, thus boldly made, in the presence of the dead monarch's son Henry, the chief mourner, being backed by the assent of the town's people, who stood by, was not to be denied or rejected, and the bishop was obliged to pay down on the spot 60 sous for a place of burial for the royal corpse. Even then, it is related, that as the coffin was being lowered, it struck against some obstacle and was broken into pieces, so that the corpse fell out and diffused so horrid a stench that the service was hurried to a close".

Then we went to the Ste. Trinité, the church of the Abbaye aux Dames, founded by Matilda the wife of the Conqueror in 1066. It is undergoing a thorough repair, but with strict adherence to the original style. The facade has a bas relief in which apparently the Trinity is represented as three human forms, surrounded by the emblems of the evangelists. The interior is very beautiful – the Norman style carried out in the choir as well as the nave. The workmen are still busy in the choir which is therefore closed up; but on one side we could see into the transept which appeared to be of a later date than the choir and nave, the main arches being pointed. A beautiful colour was cast on these arches from a window which to us was invisible.

We sat a long while in the church, waiting till the rain had ceased, and listened to the music of the workmen's hammers, with thoughts of many things in our hearts. In the afternoon we walked out again, saw the Tour aux Gens d'armes and the banks of the river grandly fenced with poplars. Prolonging our walk in search of nothing in particular, we came to a church, where we heard delicious chanting and glorious organ thunder. It was the church of St. John the Baptist, and today is the Fête of the Adoration of the Holy Sacrament. After dinner we went to a Café chantant and heard an excellent *basso* – Des Louis.

14 [15]th. We left Caen at 10 by railway and arrived at Bayeux under a grey sky, the rain already falling in sparse drops as we walked from the station towards the town. The Cathedral is visible from the station rising with its two spires and central tower above the masses of poplars and willows. Walking up to the town we saw a meadow with willows, a stream and cows which reminded me of my glimpse at the neighbourhood of Oxford. The cathedral is very fine, the nave nearly in the same style as St. Etienne and the Sainte Trinité at Caen, but more elaborately ornamented: the choir exquisite pointed gothic. We went into the crypt and saw the frescoed angels still fresh from the 14th century. After going back to the station to dine at the restaurant, we returned to the Cathedral, saw the procession and heard the mingled music of organ, cannon and military band; having previously seen the Tapestry, now at the Library. It rained furiously when we got into the train which after long delays brought us to St. Lô, the evening star shining upon us.

15 [16]th. We left our comfortable German-looking bedroom at 1/2 past 5, and soon after 6 set off by malle-poste, travelling rapidly through a wooded, fertile, well cultivated country, extremely like the more smiling parts of England, arriving at Vire by 1/2 past 10. Breakfasted, walked out to see the town, the remains of the old Keep on a precipitous rock, and the winding roads above and below the cloth factories. We were comfortable at our unpretending inn, the Cheval Blanc, and slept well. In the morning rain and sunshine alternated. We had a walk along a fine straight road which showed us the surrounding fruitful and wooded valley. We have seen no old houses – the town is like a Derbyshire

town, all stone and slate. We left Vire for Avranches in a most uncomfortable diligence and I was feeling ill all the way; nevertheless I felt the beauty of the smiling bushy country, and was pleased with the neighbourly politeness of the people to each other. Our second conductor said he had driven along that road 25 years and had never had an accident. The road seems to be as direct as the flight of a bird and may be seen making a broad ribbon across the green country for many miles. It is a succession of ups and downs. As soon as we reached Avranches I went to bed ill.

18. After a good night I was better. The morning was grey and rainy, but cleared off, and we went out to see the points of view, and the town. The country round is lovely – green, bushy, prosperous-looking – and with a bright sun the view must be magnificent; but we had *not* a bright sun. At the extremity of the town we came upon the yard which attracted us by the picturesqueness of a wall and trough and an old shed – also by a bitch with three pups. Presently the matron, a pleasant looking woman, came out and asked us if we should like to go down into the orchard. We accepted the invitation and found a charming orchard on a slope – the horse and cart standing under a tree and two men sitting by a little pond sorting apples. There are no picturesque old bits in the streets, but we saw a couple of head-dresses of old fashion in the market before our hotel windows. When we were caught in the rain on the Esplanade an old English gentleman invited us to enter his house. It is in one of the finest, if there are any equally fine, positions in Avranches, has a nice garden and poultry yard, and a pleasant interior. He pays £16 a year for rent, and with the hire of his furniture, taxes etc. his expenses upon it altogether are not more than £30! After this, we walked on and found the Jardin des Plantes, a delightful spot, where there are avenues and grass and some picturesque grey buildings to the right. But the rain was never weary and at last sent us in.

19. Saturday. We started by the diligence for Dol, at 1/2 past seven, and though the sky was grey, we had a magnificent drive. The country is what Walter Scott calls the scene from Richmond Hill – a sea of verdure. I never saw anything but that Richmond view at all like it for extent of boskiness. Approaching Dol we had a sight of Mont Dol which is a striking bold height rising suddenly from the plain. The town – the first Breton town we have seen – is really old and picturesque. The houses have a physiognomy; almost every one of them in the principal street has the high dormer window in the centre, like the houses of Nuremberg. They are of black granite with white mortar. We entered a church which has been turned into a market. The men in their blue blouses, the corn-sacks and the light entering at the west end made a picture. The Cathedral is of granite (grey not black) and has only one west tower completed; the other is stunted and unfinished. The exterior has a rough majesty. It is in the early pointed style. The finest bit is the liberal southern porch, with an inner double arched doorway contained in a deep receding arch. Pretty walk under the trees with glancing lights, and distant view, round the old fortifications. We left at 3 by railway for St. Malo. The beauty of the country much diminished. At St. Malo

we descended from the omnibus at the Hotel de la Paix; and after a 6 o'clock dinner we walked out on the sands just in time to see the sunset over the water, and the black reefs against the western glory. The outline of the town is wonderfully varied and pretty; the sands, the broadest I ever saw, and uninterrupted by wet patches. After this we walked in the town, entered the Cathedral, walked outside the walls again and finished the evening by going to a theatrical performance in a "barraque" just outside the gates. M. Follet "the English artist" performing gymnastics, M. Schlax, "the man-serpent" really doing wonders in the way of twisting and doubling his body.

20. Delicious walk on the sands – Cathedral and walk again along the pier and the ramparts. Heavy rain in the evening.

21. Monday. A glorious morning walk on the sands. Read Victor Hugo's Petit Roi de Galice. Started at 5 o'clock for Rennes and arrived at the Hotel St. Julien about 8 am.

22. Tuesday. From Rennes to Auray.

23. To Carnac. (Species of fir tree?). Names at Auray: Gubury, Guyonrashi, Seveno. On returning from Carnac we walked out to the Southern end of the town and discovered its beauties.

24. A brilliant morning. We walked by the water, rested in a summer house, and found out the various promenades of Auray. At 2 o'clock, by the train to Nantes which we reached about 7, putting up at the Hotel de France.

25. At Nantes again. The Cathedral is old but not beautiful. The church of St. Nicolas looks like a restoration of an old and very beautiful church. I have read through Villemarqué's Celtic legends of the cloister – a poor book.

26. Set off from Nantes at 7 o'clock in the morning. Arrived at Tours at 11. Saw the Cathedral and ascended the Tower. Entered the church of St. Julien, expecting to find it a *Remise and Ecurie*;[2] but found it completely restored and fitted up for worship. Dined at the Hotel de l'Univers and set off at 5 for Le Mans, which was so full that we were obliged to put up with a poor bedroom in the second rate Hotel de France. Glimpse of Café chantant in the open air.

27. After coffee, set off to the Cathedral. Finely placed on an eminence a little above the large *Place*, near which there are promenades under trees. The Place was covered on one side with a market. Scattered elsewhere about the space were the women in white caps and the men in variously shaded blue blouses.

The Cathedral took me by surprise from its great mass. It is an immense pile. The west end (exterior) a fine bit of Romanesque or Norman with two original monsters worthy almost of Verona. A Druidic stone in one corner, turning from the west end. A fine porch on the South. Entering, the impression of vastness comes first of all. Then the impression of

2 French, 'restoring and cleaning'.

unsurpassable beauty in the choir, which is of exquisite thirteenth century gothic. The Nave is extremely fine Romanesque. The painted glass is splendid in the choir, and in the Lady Chapel there are remains of fresco on the ceiling and walls. We were sorry that our uncomfortable quarters forced us to leave Le Mans which seems altogether a remarkable and interesting place. We arrived at Chartres at 2 o'clock. It is a fête-day and we were fortunate in getting a fine effect both at Le Mans and at Chartres from the presence of a large congregation and the extra services.

At Chartres the organ was sublime, and the voices came in fine alternating chant, assisted by a speaking trombone. The painted glass in this Cathedral is transcendent. For the first time I witnessed the supreme effect of light coming thro' painted glass *exclusively*. The Choir is faulty, and quite offensively degenerates downward into paltry Renaissance stucco work. Beautiful adornment of the Virgin's altar, and lighting of tapers amongst flowers. Steps into a chapel at East End. The exterior of this Cathedral is the most memorable, after the wondrous glass – the great North and South porches and the portals of the West End. After dinner, the Saltimbanques in the Place – walk to the river Eure – fête – old women on the wall – old turreted gate. Doré pictures in the streets. Mass of the Cathedral by starlight – *Place* by starlight.

28. We were so delighted with Chartres that we determined to stay another day. The Gardeners' fête made a special fête for us. We spent the morning till 12 in the Cathedral, where we saw the people with their little children go to kiss some relic – apparently to preserve them from the cholera. There was mass and sublime music. We bought a book about the Cathedral and studied the portals. In the evening we walked out to the old gate again.

29. Started for Paris, where we arrived at 1/2 past 9, a.m. To the Hotel de France et de Bath, where we got a comfortable apartment. It rained and the streets were very dirty, so that the walks to the Post Office and dinner were not agreeable.

30. I was not very well, so we were not enterprising. But we went to Mass at the Russian Church – a great enjoyment to me. The bass voice of the officiating priest alternating with the rapid chant of the choir, the sense of being in a church like those of the Byzantine christians ages ago – the grave pictures of the Saints on their golden background – the opening of the doors disclosing the altar, and the figure of Christ seated with uplifted hands all impressed me deeply.

Then we went to the Palais d'Industrie, but saw nothing very exhilarating. In the evening we walked about the Boulevards.

31. Thursday. I was feeling very poorly, and we did hardly anything but wander and go into the Louvre, where we looked at some of our favourite pictures. In the evening to the Gaïté.

Sep. 1. Drove in the Bois de Boulogne, and went to the Luxembourg where we saw some new pictures. To bed early, not being well.

2. Kept quiet during the day, preparing for the Théâtre Lyrique in the evening. To our great disappointment we had Rigoletto instead of the Flauto Magico.

3 Sunday. On arriving at the station for Rouen, we found there was no train at 1 o'clock on Sundays, so we deposited our luggage and spent our hours till 6 very pleasantly at St. Cloud. In the evening at Rouen we had a beautiful sight of the river by moonlight and gas-light. Pillared city under the water.

4. Spent the day in seeing the Cathedral, the Musée, St. Ouen, and the old streets. Names of the streets – Rue de la Savonnerie, Rue St. Amand, Rue de la Croix de fer.

5. From Rouen to Dieppe.

6. Started at $7^1/_2$ by diligence for Abbeville. Then from Abbeville to Boulogne.

7. From Boulogne home.

Explanatory index

Readers are referred to the Preface, pp.ix–x, for a statement of the rationale of this *Explanatory index.*

Adler, Hermann (1839–1911), Principal of the Jewish Theological College, London (1863); from 1864 Rabbi of the Bayswater Synagogue, and Chief Rabbi 1891–1911 146

Adrienne Lecouvreur, see Scribe

Aeschylus (*fl.* 6 BC), Ancient Greek playwright whose works include the *Oresteia* trilogy comprising *Agamemnon, Choephori,* and *Eumenides*, and *Prometheus* 70, 71, 73, 76, 124, 125

Agamemnon, see Aeschylus

Agnes, *see* Lewes, Agnes

Agoût, Marie Catherine Sophie de Flavigny (Comtesse d'Agoult, pseudonym Daniel Stern, 1805–76), in 1835 left her husband for the musician Liszt with whom she lived until 1839. One of the three children of the liaison, Cosima, became the second wife of the composer Richard Wagner. After the relationship ended completely in 1844, the Comtesse d'Agoult published a number of works including the autobiographical novel *Nélida* (1846) 21, 26, 248

Aidé, Charles Hamilton (1826–1906), novelist 187, 197

Ainmueller, Max-Emmanuel Ainmiller (1807–70), German painter of glass and porcelain 317

Akkadians, *see* Sayce

Albertinelli, Mariotto (1474–1515), Florentine painter 358

Alemagna, Giovanni d' (Giovanni da Murano, d. 1450), Italian artist 373, 374

alethoscope, *see* Ponti

Alfieri, Vittorio, Conte (1749–1803), Italian dramatist whose work centred on struggle against tyranny 337, 356

Alkie, Alexander Cross Hall (1869–1920), son of Elizabeth Dennistoun (née Cross, 1836–69) and William Henry Hall 175

All the Year Round (1859–95), weekly journal edited by Charles Dickens 81

Allbutt, Thomas Clifford (1836–1925), physician to the Leeds General Infirmary, inventor of the clinical thermometer, and possible prototype of Tertius Lydgate in *Middlemarch*, met GHL at a meeting of the British Medical Association in Oxford in July 1868 133, 148, 158, 163, 164, 169

Allen, Ellen Lewen, governess, introduced to GE by Barbara Bodichon 106, 107

Allen, Grant (1848–99), following an ill-fated academic career, became an author, notorious for his New Woman novel *The Woman Who Did* (1895), though initially he published scientific works such as *The Colour Sense: Its Origin and Development. An Essay in Comparative Psychology* (1879) 166, 167

Allingham, William (1824–89), poet, editor of *Fraser's Magazine* (1874–9), and Helen (née Paterson, 1848–1926), artist, married in 1874 198, 200, 202

Alpine animals (Lucerne), 'an excellent collection of Swiss birds and quadrupeds, extremely well mounted' (John Murray, *A Handbook for Travellers in Switzerland, Savoy, and Piedmont* (10th edn, 1863)) 379

Amalia, Grand Duchess, *see* Sachsen-Weimar

Amelia, servant, possibly at Witley 194

Ammirato, Scipione (1531–1601), *Delle famiglie nobili fiorentine* (1615) 106

Ancient Geography, possibly William Smith's *Dictionary of Greek and Roman Geography* (1854–7) 136

Anders, Henry Smith, *see* Liggins, Joseph

Anderson, Janet ('Scotchy', 1816–*c.* 1871) 21, 237

Andrea del Sarto (1486–1531), Florentine artist 317, 358

essays and reviews (*cont.*)
'Life and Opinions of Milton', *Leader*, 6 (1855), p. 750 57
'Life of Goethe', *Leader*, 6 (1855), pp. 1058–61, in which GE praises GHL's methodology 58
'Liszt, Wagner, and Weimar', *Fraser's Magazine*, 52 (1855), pp. 48–62 56, 58, 216n., 217
'Lord Brougham's Literature', *Leader*, 6 (1855), pp. 652–3 56
'Love in the Drama', *Leader*, 6 (1855), pp. 820–1 57
'The Lover's Seat', *Leader*, 7 (1856), pp. 735–6 62, 65
'Margaret Fuller and Mary Wollstonecraft', *Leader*, 6 (1855), pp. 988–9 57, 59, 65
'Menander and the Greek Comedy', *Leader*, 6 (1855), pp. 578–9 56
'Memoirs of the Court of Austria', *Westminster Review*, 63(1855), pp. 303–35 43, 44, 45, 46, 54, 64, 68
'Michelet on the Reformation', *Leader*, 6 (1855), pp. 843–4 57
'Modern Housekeeping', *Pall Mall Gazette*, 1 (1865), p. 880 124
'The Morality of Wilhelm Meister', *Leader*, 6 (1855), p. 703 57
'The Natural History of German Life', *Westminster Review*, 66 (1856), pp. 51–79 59, 60, 61, 63, 65, 264
'Pictures of Life in French Novels', *Saturday Review*, 2 (1856), pp. 69–70 59, 64
'The Poets and Poetry of America', *Leader*, 7 (1856), p. 210 59, 64
'Rachel Gray', *Leader*, 7 (1856) p. 19 58, 64
'Recollections of Heine', *Leader*, 7 (1856), pp. 811–2 63, 65
'Servants' Logic', *Pall Mall Gazette*, 1 (1865), p. 310–1 123
'*The Shaving of Shagpat*', *Leader*, 5 (1856), pp. 15–7 58, 64
'Sight-seeing in Germany and the Tyrol', *Saturday Review*, 2 (1856), pp. 424–5 65
'Silly Novels by Lady Novelists', *Westminster Review*, 66 (1856), pp. 442–61 63, 65, 290
'Story of a Blue-bottle', *Leader*, 7 (1856), pp. 401–2 59, 64
'Thomas Carlyle', *Leader*, 6 (1855), pp. 1034–5 65
'Three Months in Weimar', *Fraser's Magazine*, 51(1855), pp. 699–706 56, 58, 216, 217, 221n.
'A Tragic Story', *Leader*, 7 (1856), p. 691 65
'Translations and Translators', *Leader*, 6 (1855), pp. 1014–5 57
'Westward Ho!', *Leader*, 6 (1855), pp. 474–5 56
'Who Wrote the Waverley Novels?', *Leader*, 7 (1856), pp. 375–6 59, 64
'Woman in France: Madame de Sablé', *Westminster Review*, 62 (1854), pp. 448–73 11, 19, 24
'A Word for the Germans', *Pall Mall Gazette*, 1(1865), p. 201 123
'Worldliness and Other-Worldliness: The Poet Young', *Westminster Review*, 67 (1857), pp. 1–42 59, 62, 64, 65, 96, 158n., 185
fiction
Adam Bede (1859) 4, 70–88 *passim*, 96, 101, 113, 129, 143, 158, 286, 287, 288, 296–304 *passim*, 315–18, 325–6; see *Athenaeum*, *Literary Gazette*, *Saturday Review*
'Brother Jacob' (working titles, 'The Idiot Brother' and 'Mr David Faux, confectioner'), short story first published in *Cornhill* July 1864 86, 96, 109
Daniel Deronda (1876) 11, 91, 92, 96, 145, 146, 147, 148, 176, 196, 197, 332
Felix Holt, the Radical (1866) 10, 91, 92, 96, 124, 125–30 *passim*, 380
Impressions of Theophrastus Such (1879) 165, 167, 174–9 *passim*, 183; *see Times*
'The Lifted Veil', short story first published in *Blackwood's Edinburgh Magazine*, July 1859 77, 96, 302, 305
Middlemarch (1871–2) 6, 91, 92, 96, 134–9 *passim*, 142, 145, 146, 332
'Middlemarch' 96, 137
'Miss Brooke' 96, 141, 142
The Mill on the Floss (1860) 4, 77, 80–8 *passim*, 96, 102, 327, 332
Romola (1862–3) 91, 92, 96, 99–118 *passim*, 124, 125, 138, 146, 183

Humphrey Clinker, *see* Smollett
Hunger and Thirst, *see* Lewes, *essays and reviews*
Hunnenschlacht, *see* Kaulbach
Hunt, Thornton (1810–73), journalist; with GHL, joint founder of *The Leader* 4
Hunt, William Holman (1827–1910), artist and a founder of the Pre-Raphaelite Brotherhood: *Isabella and the Pot of Basil* (1868) 132; the '"Hunt" picture' may be by either William Holman, whose *The Light of the World* (1851–3) GE saw early in 1854 216, or William Henry (1790–1864), noted for his detailed watercolours of birds' nests and flowers whose art Ruskin admired 259, 272
Huth, Mrs and Miss, wife and daughter of Henry Huth (1815–78), banker and bibliophile 143
Huxley, Thomas Henry (1825–95), British scientist 106, 125, 127, 166, 173
Hyrtl, Joseph (1810–94), anatomist, known for his work in comparative anatomy, especially of fishes 323
I promessi sposi, *see* Manzoni
Idiot Brother, *see* Eliot, *fiction*
Ilfracombe 59–61, 67, 259–73
Il Principe, *see* Machiavelli
Iliad, *see* Homer
Immermann, Karl (1796–1840), German poet 70
Imogen, character in Shakespeare's *Cymbeline* 121
International Exhibition, at South Kensington; '1851 was a great industrial exhibition; 1862 is international of all industries and all arts upon a much larger scale' (*Athenaeum*, 3 May 1862) 112
Iphigenia in Tauris, *see* Gluck
Iphigenia, *see* Goethe
Isaacs, Abram Samuel (1851–1920), Professor of Hebrew at New York University 146
Italiänische Reise, *see* Goethe
Jackson, Martha, GE's close friend from schooldays: in about 1850 she married a dentist, Henry Barclay, and emigrated to South Africa 80
Jacobi, Friedrich Heinrich (1743–1819), German philosopher and novelist, whose *Eduard Allwills Briefsammlung* was said to contain an unflattering portrait of Goethe, with whom Jacobi had quarrelled over money and philosophy. Goethe subsequently produced a parody of Jacobi's *Woldemar* (1779) and nailed the original to a tree 227; *Uber die Lehre des Spinoza* (1785), a work on the teachings of Spinoza, based on Spinoza's letters to Moses Mendelssohn 35
Jagermann, Caroline (1777–1848), German actress and singer; mistress of Duke Karl August for 30 years 27
Jameson, Anna Brownell (1794–1860), English writer and feminist; *Sacred and Legendary Art* (1848) 100, 101; *Legends of the Monastic Orders* (1850) 107; 100, 101, 334
Jane Eyre, *see* Brontë, Charlotte
Jeanne d'Arc, perhaps Southey's *Joan of Arc* (1793) 183
Jebb, Richard Claverhouse (1841–1905), Fellow of Trinity College, Cambridge 143, 211
Jeffreys, John Gwyn (1809–85), author of *British Conchology* (1862–9) 124
Jersey 53, 69–70, 274–5, 279–82
Jewish Chronicle, London journal edited by Asher Myers from 1878 158
Jewish question in Germany, possibly pamphlets by Wilhelm Marr (1818–1904), which include the best-selling *Der Siegdes Judenthums über das Germanenthum vom nicht confessionellen Standpunkt aus betrachtet* (1879). He presented the Jewish question as a racial not a religious one, and coined the term *anti-Semitism* 197
Joachim, Joseph (1831–1907), Hungarian violinist and composer 110, 127, 132, 135
Johnston, James Finlay Weir (1796–1855), GHL revises his *Chemistry of Common Life* (2 vols, 1853–5) 72
Jones, Mrs Owen, wife of the architect and designer 295

from 1848 to 1859 5–6, 10, 11, 12, 21, 22, 23, 24, 26, 28, 29, 233, 236, 237, 238, 239, 248. GE read, then translated and abridged, a long article by Liszt on Meyerbeer and Wagner in *Neue Zeitschrift für Musik* for GHL; see Lewes, *essays and reviews*

Liszt, Wagner and Weimar, *see* Eliot, *essays and reviews.*

Literary Gazette (1817–62), founded by publisher Henry Colburn. Its review of *Adam Bede* (26 February 1859) described the novel as 'a very uncommon performance' 76, 299

Litta, Pompeo, Conte (1781–1852), author of *Famiglie Celebri di Italia* (1819) 106

Littré, Maximilien Paul Emile (1801–81), French lexicographer and Positivist leader after Comte's death in 1857 137

Lizzie, Mary Elizabeth Lee, later Huddy, distant cousin of GHL's mother 122

Llorente, Juan Antonio (1756–1823), *History of the Inquisition of Spain* (1817–18) 128

Lloyd in London, W. Alford Lloyd, 19–20 Portland Road, Regent's Park, sold naturalists' equipment: an 1857 price list included 'Actinia mesembryanthemum (four varieties)' for one shilling to one shilling and sixpence 60

Locker, Frederick (later Locker-Lampson), (1821–95), poet and man-of-letters, father of Eleanor Locker who married Lionel Tennyson 189

Lohengrin, *see* Wagner

Löher, Franz von (1818–92), honorary professor of law at Munich, author of works on the law as well as *Geschichte und Zustände der Deutschen in Amerika* (1847) 315, 316, 317, 318

London Library, founded in 1841 largely at the instigation of Carlyle. In 1853 GE could not afford to subscribe; GHL belonged by 1859, and by 1871 was serving on the committee 99, 100, 104, 106, 109

Longfellow, Henry Wadsworth (1807–82), American poet, whose *Song of Hiawatha* GE reviews in 'Belles Lettres' 58; *see* Eliot, *essays and reviews*

Longman, William (1813–77), of the publishing house founded in 1724 124, 292

Los Judios en Espana, perhaps Adolfo de Castro (1832–98), *Historia de los judios en Espana desde los tiempos de sa estable cimiento hasta principios del presente siglo*, translated as *The history of the Jews in Spain, from the time of their settlement in that country till the commencement of the present century* by Edward D. G. M. Kirwan (1851) 130

Lotto, Lorenzo (1480–1556), Venetian painter 377

Louis XVII (1785–95), was acknowledged as King of France by monarchists after the execution of his father, Louis XVI, in 1793. There were many claims that the young king did not in fact die in captivity, and Dessoir's watchmaker was probably one of these pretenders 38

Louvre 78, 89, 204, 373, 389

Lovers' Seat, The, *The Lover's Seat. Kathemérina or Common Things in Relation to Beauty, Virtue and Truth* by Kenelm Henry Digby (1800–80); *see* Eliot, *essays and reviews*

Lowell, James Russell (1819–91), American author of *Under the Willows and Other Poems* (1869), reviewed in 'Disconnected Memories', *Spectator* (23 January 1869), pp. 102–3 135

Lubbock, John (1803–65), author of *Pre-Historic Times as Illustrated by Ancient Remains, and the Manners and Customs of Modern Savages* (1865) 132

Lucas, Samuel (1818–68), editor of *Once a Week* 81, 82, 300

Lucretius, Titus (98 BC–*c.* 55 BC), *De Rerum Natura* 133, 136

Lucrezia Borgia, *see* Donizetti

Lucrezia Floriani, *see* Sand, George

Ludecus, W., author of *Aus Goethes Leben: Wahrheit und keine Dichtung* (1849) 231

Ludwig, Otto (1813–65), German playwright and critic, author of *Zwischen Himmel und Erde* 317; see also Lewes, *essays and reviews*